McGRAW-HILL SERIES IN EDUCATION
HAROLD BENJAMIN, Consulting Editor

Student Teaching

Selected Titles from

McGraw-Hill Series in Education

HAROLD BENJAMIN, *Consulting Editor*

Will his dreams, aspirations, ambitions, and hopes all come true? Perhaps you hold the answer, for it may depend on the quality and the competence of his teachers.[N]

Student Teaching

BY

RALEIGH SCHORLING

Director of Instruction in the University High School
and Supervisor of Student Teaching, School
of Education, University of Michigan

SECOND EDITION
SECOND IMPRESSION

NEW YORK   TORONTO   LONDON

McGRAW-HILL BOOK COMPANY, INC.

1949

STUDENT TEACHING

*This book is dedicated to the
memory of my son Clark*

Preface

The first edition of *Student Teaching* was published in 1940. In the intervening years no other comprehensive guide has appeared in this area of professional education. During this period many things have happened. We have had a second world war. We have learned something about audio-visual aids. We have seen certain devastating social forces operate so as to make it necessary for the classroom teacher to assume a larger role in the total guidance program of the school. We have come to realize that the atomic bomb, although perhaps of no great significance in a world in which disease, ignorance, and meanness—the real enemies of men—remain unshackled, nevertheless has started us on the last lap in "the race between education and catastrophe." Much more has happened in the swift panorama of events.

In professional education there has in recent years been even more emphasis on child growth and development. This has been brought to a sharp focus by the recent report on laboratory experiences by a committee (John G. Flowers, Allen D. Patterson, Florence B. Startemeyer, and Margaret Lindsey) of the American Association of Teachers' Colleges with the cooperation of the executive committee of the Association of Student Teaching.

With regard to student teaching one additional trend needs to be mentioned. It is that there has been a marked shift toward using a textbook for student teachers. Ten years ago there was almost a prejudice against the use of a textbook. Today many supervisors of student teachers are convinced that a textbook when used in the right way is a valuable tool. Indeed, some hold that a coherent and meaningful program is impossible without a guide that keeps a picture of the total job before the student teacher. The program in student teaching that operates without an up-to-date guide is almost certain to leave serious gaps which later cause beginning teachers to be critical—in many cases even resentful—of their preservice laboratory experiences.

These considerations have placed a grave responsibility upon the author to keep this textbook up to date. The present revision represents a serious effort to meet this obligation. The reader will find many pages that the author's student teachers have long enjoyed and found helpful. However, he will also find much that is new. Our profession has made some progress in student teaching during the past decade, but much remains to be done. As evidence the following paragraphs are reprinted from the first preface *unchanged*.

Student teaching always has been and is likely to continue to be the most important phase of the professional education of prospective teachers. But there are many aspects of these preservice experiences as they are commonly found in practice that can be improved. The deficiencies cannot all be listed here, but among those that need urgent attention in many institutions are the following:

1. The concept of student teaching is too limited. We need to think of it as living with pupils in a great variety of situations in which the emphasis is on the effort to get a desirable interplay between individual and environment that contributes to normal growth. Student teaching should be broadened to include experiences with tasks that carry the teacher beyond the classroom; *e.g.*, directing trips and excursions, cooperating in social activities of pupils, supervising playground activities, organizing exhibits, and studying resources of the community available for teaching purposes. In brief, there should be experiences with tasks representing a fair sampling of the things a teacher needs to do in and also outside the classroom.

2. Supervising teachers are overloaded. In addition to the usual teacher contacts, the supervising teacher needs to work cooperatively with various faculty groups, confer with visitors, and answer inquiries concerning curriculum and methods that may involve endless hours of study in the library. Then, too, the staff of a training institution is almost certain to include resourceful and restless individuals who can think of many challenging tasks. The job of the supervising teacher is made especially difficult by the lack of comprehensive and up-to-date textbooks, and by the problem of finding and directing the reading that a prospective teacher should do while undergoing these experiences. It is generally admitted that the load of a supervising teacher is excessive under the best of conditions, but sensible attempts to make the load one that is humanly possible are few in number. Beyond question, supervising teachers as a group are among the ablest and most resourceful to be found in the teaching profession, but they are only human and, lacking materials, the task of keeping abreast with present-day demands is very great.

3. The instructional materials for courses in student teaching are amazingly meager. In contrast to other areas of teacher education and of public education, the scarcity and meagerness of recent instructional materials for student teaching are astonishing. Though student teaching is the crux of teacher education, men possessing analytical discernment and scientific competence have seldom given this

problem their serious effort and undivided attention. Rather they have tended to operate in other fields—administration, philosophy, and psychology of education. We may as well admit that we do not have and never have had in the designing of programs of student teaching a Dewey, a Thorndike, or a Terman.

4. The manuals of the guidance of student teachers are obsolete, fragmentary, and inadequate. Since satisfactory textbooks are not available, it is the common practice for an institution to develop a manual that tries to do two things: (*a*) provide guidance in teaching experiences, and (*b*) acquaint the prospective teacher with local requirements and administrative routine. However, the supervisors are busy persons, and the years pass by very rapidly, with the result that it is practically impossible to keep such a guide up to date. A survey of the many existing manuals provides convincing evidence that the typical guide is wholly inadequate when evaluated in terms of student-teaching needs. It would seem desirable for an institution in which supervisors carry heavy loads to provide only a brief manual of materials covering state requirements and local administrative routine. Such a manual can with very little time and effort be kept up to date.

5. Preservice experiences too often fail to give pedagogical competence. To the greatest extent possible everything that a student teacher does should come to have meaning. His study of philosophy, educational psychology, the curriculum, method, the needs of public education—all these should be integrated into a single pattern of his knowledge and control of pupil growth and development. To be sure, many supervising teachers have a program of integration clearly in mind, but the educational theories fail to carry over into the experiences of the student teacher when both supervising and prospective teachers operate with only an obsolete manual as a guide. In most teacher-education institutions there are very serious gaps between the theories of the supervising teacher and the practices of the student teacher.

The purpose of this volume is to present a program that will help to correct these deficiencies. On most questions that will emerge from the experiences of student teachers this book will provide something that both supervising and student teachers can read and discuss with profit in individual and small group conferences. Both will be stimulated to broaden the concept of student teaching to include all that a teacher does, and direct these experiences toward the total growth of the student teacher as a person, as a classroom practitioner, and as a member of the school family and the community group. They will have recent emphases in education called to their attention; for example, the growth and development of children, the adjustment of personality, the education of the emotions, the need for taking into account all the forces in the education of an individual, the broader concept of the curriculum, the interplay between the school and the community, the psychology of adolescence, and the evolving decision to provide conscious practice in the democratic way of life.

The gap between what institutions are doing with respect to student teaching and what leaders have so long advocated is still very great. It is hoped that a wise use of this book will help in making the needed changes.

Turning now to subsidiary matters, the reader will note a different pattern in the supplementary readings. The earlier book provided a comprehensive list for each chapter. These proved to be disappointing. In the first place the busy student teacher doesn't have much time for reading. In the second place many references, especially magazine articles, become obsolete very fast. Therefore, in this revision we are listing only the books that have inspired teachers for several generations and the best of recent volumes in professional reading for the classroom teacher.

An inportant innovation is the creation of five sound pictures and five filmstrips that are geared to specific objectives of this book. There are two sound pictures on learning to understand children, one on discipline, and two that deal with method and planning. It is assumed that the showing of a picture either at the beginning or at the end of a unit will be followed by a discussion period. At this point some discussion leaders will find the frames of the appropriate filmstrip to be useful in that they direct the attention of students to important matters. It is altogether clear that the new sound pictures will greatly improve a program in student teaching. The filmstrips accompanying this textbook, if skillfully used, will (1) lead to animated discussion, (2) summarize the main objectives of a unit, and (3) greatly increase the applications of the concepts and principles.

The author wishes to express his appreciation to the many persons who have contributed to this volume. These are too numerous to list here, but special recognition is due the members of the staff of the University High School, to the author's colleagues in the School of Education at the University of Michigan, and to persons who have in recent years made especially fine contributions to student teaching; *e.g.*, Leonard O. Andrews, Fritz C. Borgeson, Edith E. Beechel, J. W. Carrington, Esther Dunham, John G. Flowers, Margaret Lindsey, Jane McAllister, Allen D. Patterson, Horace D. Pickens, C. W. Sanford, Florence B. Stratemeyer, and Louise Wilson. Then, too, as was the case in the earlier volume, the author is greatly indebted to the sound scholarship, resourcefulness, and imagination of Howard Batchelder. Without his help and that of Ted Karp of the Caravel Corporation, the sound pictures and filmstrips would not have been so good as they are— indeed they might not have come to exist.

The author also gratefully acknowledges his indebtedness to the officials of certain school systems for providing him with some of the illustrations that appear in this book. Unless otherwise designated, an illustration marked with an (F) was contributed by Dearborn, with an (E) by the Edison Institute of Dearborn, with an (L) by Los Angeles, with an (M) by Milwaukee, with an (N) by the City of New York (those marked (N₁) are from "All the Children"), with an (S) by Santa Barbara, with a (C) by Baltimore, an (H) by Hamtramck, Michigan, with a (B) by Battle Creek, with a (D) by Detroit, with a (G) by Grosse Pointe, Michigan, and with a (Y) by the Lincoln School at Ypsilanti, Michigan. Some of the new materials in this volume were printed in *Swords into Ploughshares*, distributed by the Department of Public Instruction, Lansing, Michigan, or in *Education and Social Trends* (now out of print). I am greatly indebted to Dr. Eugene B. Elliot, Professor Howard Y. McClusky, and the World Book Company for making it possible for me to use these materials in the appropriate spots in this book.

Finally, special acknowledgement is due to users of the earlier edition, who, from time to time, have made suggestions for improving the book. It is to be hoped that such constructive proposals will continue to be made, in order that they may be used in the next revision, some five or six years hence.

RALEIGH SCHORLING

ANN ARBOR, MICH.
April, 1949

Contents

Editor's Introduction

In the introduction to the first edition of this book, the editor spoke of a growing interest in the improvement of teacher education, a vigorous spirit of self-criticism among school people, and a willingness to try any well-considered plan for the betterment of teaching. He recommended the volume as an admirable exemplification of ways in which detailed discussion of professional practice could furnish foundations for improved theories of education.

The years since 1940 have been disturbed and tragic years. They have been years devoted to preparing for a known war, carrying on a clearly understood war, searching for a dimly conceived peace, and fearing a darkly envisioned further conflict. In every important phase of these elemental but confused years, the impacts and strains upon our society have been passed directly to our educational institutions and enterprises. The teachers, their ranks relatively thinning in most of our school areas, have taken these shocks with resiliency and courage. They have become more conscious than before of the crucial importance of the program of professional education.

In bringing the present thoroughly revised edition of this book to the profession, the author has drawn upon his added experience in the direction of student teaching and in the preparation of a pioneer series of audio-visual aids to accompany this text. Above and beyond all these matters of techniques and devices, he has brought an increased warmth and breadth of insight that must come to any scholar who takes full part in the triumphs and the defeats, the joys and the heartaches of his people. The author's title to this characterization is poignantly suggested by his dedication of the volume to a gallant soldier of the United States who will remain forever young.

HAROLD BENJAMIN

UNIVERSITY OF MARYLAND
April, 1949

Top: There are lots of things that an assistant teacher can do to help the regular teacher, especially when an activity like this is under way.[N1] *Center:* This is one of the many situations in which a student teacher can make himself useful from the very beginning.[F] *Bottom:* In a supervised study period you will be doing about the same things that the supervising teacher does—provided you know what to do.[N1]

Chapter I

A Successful Beginning

And what of teaching? Ah, there you have the worst paid and the best rewarded of all the vocations. Dare not to enter it unless you love it. For the vast majority of men and women it has no promise of wealth or fame, but they to whom it is dear for its own sake are among the nobility of mankind. I sing the praise of the Unknown Teacher . . .

Famous educators plan new systems of pedagogy, but it is the Unknown Teacher who delivers and guides the young. He lives in obscurity and contends with hardship. For him no trumpets blare, no chariots wait, no golden decorations are decreed. He keeps the watch along the borders of darkness and leads the attack on the trenches of ignorance and folly. Patient in his duty, he quickens the indolent, encourages the eager, and steadies the unstable. He communicates his own joy in learning and shares with boys and girls the best treasures of his mind. He lights many candles which in later years will shine back to cheer him. This is his reward.

Knowledge may be gained from books; but the love of knowledge is transmitted only by personal contact. No one has deserved better of the Republic than the Unknown Teacher. No one is more worthy to be enrolled in a democratic aristocracy—king of himself and servant of Mankind.

—Henry van Dyke

Conditioning Yourself for Student Teaching

You are now entering into a period of your education as a student teacher. It may be that you are a trifle bewildered by some of the real or imaginary experiences that may confront you. But, while most of these experiences will be new to you, your introduction to teaching has no doubt been planned so as to initiate you gradually and to develop confidence in your work as you proceed.

Since you are confronted with this period of training, what are some of the specific things you can do to get acquainted with the nature of your work as a student teacher? To create favorable conditions for your teaching, the following suggestions are offered for your attention:

1. *Reduce your load other than student teaching to a minimum.* Many student teachers do not give themselves a fair chance. Some

1

attempt to carry an excessive number of hours of college work, whereas others are distracted by social and extracurricular activities. To achieve satisfaction in your student teaching you need to give it first place on your program. In brief, it must always be at the focus of your attention. Your development will be dependent largely on the time, energy, and interest you devote to the task

From the very beginning make yourself useful in classroom management, which means a good deal more than efficient handling of materials, checking of roll, and the like. In this case it meant creating good conditions for work from a situation that was not too easy because of seats nailed to the floor.(M)

ahead of you. Therefore you should take as few hours of formal college courses as possible and try to free your time and energy from the numerous distractions afforded by college or university communities. There may be some worth-while activities, however, that you cannot afford to neglect, for they may directly contribute to a well-rounded personality, which is essential to vital and effective teaching.

✓ 2. *Recognize that the school to which you have been assigned expects a minimum of disturbance caused by your entrance upon the scene.*

The school has a definite, planned program for the year, and it needs to protect its pupils by maintaining a high standard of efficiency. The less confusion and interruption, the more effective will be your work and that of the regular teacher. You have a cooperative relationship with the school, your supervising teacher, and the classes in which you do your student teaching. If your part in the work is to be consistent with the usual conduct of affairs, you will need to add something of value to the life and work of the school to which you have been assigned.

3. *Find out where and when you are due for formal assignments, conferences, and other appointments.* Punctuality and promptness on the part of teachers and pupils are necessary for the functioning of a well-organized school. These important traits will be expected of you when you begin your work as a regular teacher. Therefore, the period of directed teaching is the place to strengthen these habits. In case of unavoidable absence or inability to do the assigned task, notice should be telephoned or sent to the supervising teacher or, if more convenient to you, to the director of student teaching, at the earliest appropriate moment.

4. *Recognize that in the modern secondary school the teacher must control a broad area of subject matter.* There are good reasons for believing that subject matter is far more important in the school of today than it was in grandfather's day. The teacher using modern methods must know more subject matter and know it better. He needs to draw materials from various related fields. He must know it well enough to be able quickly to find significant parts from a vast amount of source material.

The teacher deals with boys and girls who know more than the children of grandfather's day. He needs to deal with parents who are better informed. Furthermore, the different fields of knowledge, as for example science, are making great strides. And even in conservative schools there is a growing demand that the sharp dividing lines between the school subjects shall be made less restrictive so that the pupil may gain a perspective of these fields in relation to the problems of life.

The training school expects you to exhibit a high standard of general culture and to be especially well prepared in the subjects you teach. An increasing number of institutions now administer examinations covering the subject matter to be taught by the student teacher. The student teacher should have a respectable record of achievement in his college courses.

5. *Provide yourself with all instructional materials, such as the textbooks to be used by the class you are to teach.* Obviously you need to be entirely familiar with all the materials used by the students. Assuming that the cost is not excessive you will be expected to provide yourself with all the teaching materials used by the pupils in the classes to which you have been assigned. Even in the early weeks the training teacher will probably call on you for contributions to the activities of the class and, since you have the status of an assistant teacher, it is desirable that your part represent, if not a model, at least a fine quality of workmanship. Be sure that you know the assignments and that you have prepared them faithfully in every detail.

6. *Recognize the specific values you will gain from student teaching.* If you can do constructive, effective, and intelligent work you will undoubtedly enjoy your new experiences. Your future reading on social and educational problems will certainly be more meaningful. In all probability you will come to the end of your student teaching with the feeling that your experiences have been of great value, even if you should never teach.

7. *Begin your work with a determination to conquer weaknesses and to profit by criticism.* Your supervising teacher and your general supervisor have the task of helping you develop into a competent teacher. Their suggestions will be based on your accomplishments and needs, and will be designed to increase your competence as a teacher. Accept their suggestions in a professional spirit by realizing that they are interested primarily in your improvement and growth.

You can begin your work with confidence. There is no reason why your thinking in the early weeks of your student teaching should be weakened and disorganized by the fear of failure. The early tasks are usually so small in amount and involve so little difficulty that it is practically impossible for you to fail to do them. In the beginning, the development and maintenance of confidence on your part are highly important, and for that reason your first assignments will involve only brief periods of time, on tasks to be done at a high level. Your program of student teaching begins with small units of work which increase gradually in difficulty and in amount. Moreover, the load is adjusted to your own powers. Those who are strong and eager to teach will be in the midst of teaching situations within a very short time, whereas those who develop slowly will be given ample time. The old form of teacher education in which one semester was devoted entirely to observation, not always carefully guided, and another term devoted to directed teaching in which the student teacher began his work with a "cold plunge" is passing rapidly.

In some of your college courses you may have been handicapped by being in large groups in which you scarcely had a chance to know your instructor or to be known by him. In this work you have the very great advantage of having individual attention by those who are keenly interested in your success. If you are suited to the teaching profession you may go forward confident that every merit will be quickly observed and appreciated.

8. *Recognize that every activity a teacher undertakes needs to be carefully planned.* You probably accept this suggestion as far as it concerns regular classroom teaching, but you may not see that it is equally important when you undertake the miscellaneous tasks of a teacher, such as supervising a home room, serving as counselor to some class, meeting with a committee of pupils to plan an assembly program, or planning a tea with a committee of parents. In all the tasks of a teacher you will need to think through what you are going to say and do, and you will need to anticipate what others will do, feel, and say in response to a total situation.

9. *Find out what are considered good practices with respect to dress, speech, manner, and pupil-teacher relations.* In later sections of this chapter we shall discuss these matters in some detail. Read those sections several times with great care before you report for duty to your class. Several helpful things can be stated at this point. In the first place, even students who come from good homes need, when they begin teaching, to give careful attention to these items, for sometimes college conditions and customs break down desirable habits, or at least establish standards that may not be acceptable in many communities. For that matter, you may succeed in college in spite of some serious deficiency. Finally, it is not wise to trust your own judgment solely when the opinions of friendly and competent judges among your companions or supervising teachers are available to you.

There is good reason for believing that high-school pupils are becoming more aware of the importance of dress and manners. Certain it is that they are becoming more articulate, for pupils in school after school in various parts of our country have urged that more attention be given to these topics in the curriculum. Basically their suggestions undoubtedly stem from the universal desire of young people to be acceptable to other members of their group. Then, too, it may be that the motion picture and the radio are indirectly teaching higher standards of dress and manners. At any rate, these two supplementary educational agencies have been condemned for so much that it is not amiss to suggest that they may be helping the schools in these respects.

In addition to gaining specific information with regard to dress and social graces, it may be well to keep in mind the general principles embodied in the following quotation:

> Of dress our true aristocrat thinks little. Clean it must be if he can keep it so; and if possible he likes to have it fit the occasion and the work or pastime that engages him . . . Of manners our true aristocrat thinks more. But he saves five dollars by dispensing with a code book of etiquette, and behaves naturally in such a way as to make nobody uncomfortable and to add what he can to the pleasure of the company. To be a bumptious bounder would shame him. To be a social climber would make him sick. To be himself with due regard for others is what he aims at. Of one who behaves thus we say that he has good manners; whether he learned them from his father or worked them out himself makes no difference; he is one of nature's gentlemen.[1]

10. *Make a general survey visit to the school.* We suggest that you do this in the early weeks of student teaching, before your tasks become too heavy. We urge you, after consulting with your supervising teacher, to do wide visting not only in the classes of your major and minor subjects, but in as many activities of the school as time will permit. Try to get a wide sampling of the activities of the whole school. This survey will give you an opportunity to learn something of the school's organization, its philosophy, and its tradition. Moreover, you may never again have as good an opportunity to look at the total offering of a school.

11. *Keep a professional log.* We suggest that you keep a loose-leaf notebook with pages of standard size (8½ by 11 in.) in a sub-

[1] This statement is quoted from Henry van Dyke's well-known address "Democratic Aristocracy," in which he sings the praise of the unknown teacher. The address was reported in the *Journal of the National Education Association*, January, 1927.

stantical cover. The notebook may well include two types of material: (*a*) anything that you do in response to your written assignments, and (*b*) material that you believe will be genuinely useful in your future work as a regular teacher. For (*b*) we have in mind illustrative materials pertinent to your teaching fields, such as pictures, graphs or cartoons, significant articles from the public press,

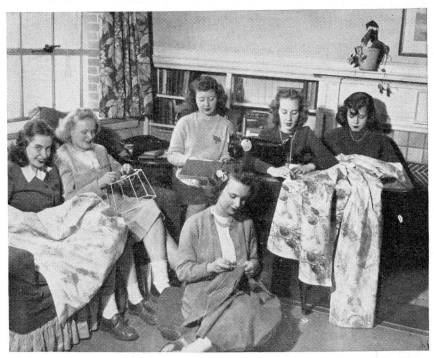

Courses in homemaking have long employed the techniques of the project method. If you teach in another field, drop in on a class like this to see how they get a project under way and how they manage it.[G]

information derived from lectures or assemblies, notes taken during observations, lesson plans, plans for units of work, guide or work sheets, notes taken in individual conferences with the supervising teacher and the supervisor, standardized and informal tests, careful write-ups of all conferences with students, bibliographies, self-appraisals for each lesson taught, descriptions of functional devices gained from either observation or experience, brief discussions of methods used for specific purposes, and a list of basic principles of teaching.

In all probability your supervising teacher will prefer (*a*) that you be extremely critical of what you collect and keep in the professional log; (*b*) that you systematize and perhaps index the materials; (*c*) that you have your professional log with you whenever you are on the job as a student teacher; (*d*) that you submit it to your supervising teacher, up to date in all respects, at least once a month for appraisal and suggestions; and (*e*) that you avoid collecting a mass of miscellaneous and unorganized material.

12. *Be ready, when assigned or encouraged to do the specific things that a student teacher can do in the early days as an assistant teacher, to improve the general efficiency of a class.* It is obvious that your training will entail a great deal of extra work on the part of your supervising teacher. To compensate him and the pupils and to learn by doing, you can make yourself useful in many ways. In order to stimulate your thinking along this line we suggest the following list. Remember that you are not expected to do all of these things, or even very many of them, nor are you to limit yourself to the tasks that are listed here.

(1) Studying carefully the pupils in a class to see which need special attention.

(2) Administering achievement tests to see what remedial treatment should be given to special cases.

(3) Giving assistance to students who have been absent.

(4) Planning a series of lessons.

(5) Collecting supplementary materials.

(6) Constructing examinations.

(7) Marking papers, making inventories of the degree of mastery, etc.

(8) Posting results by means of progress charts which show the advancement made by each pupil.

(9) Teaching independently when strong enough, thus permitting the supervising teacher to visit some of the work of his colleagues in related fields.

(10) Serving as substitute teacher when the regular teacher is ill.

(11) Teaching a group when a class has been divided into several groups so as to permit different projects as individual needs may require. It is, of course, impossible to keep 20 or 30 pupils at the same task because of the obvious differences in ability and interests, and often two or three groups can be formed to advantage. In this case the teacher will find an assistant valuable, for ordinarily there is not enough energy and time to meet the needs of instruction or to provide adequate supervision of study.

(12) Supplying technical information and ability. Even a gifted teacher will meet a variety of work that far exceeds her ability and preparation. Sometimes a project requires special knowledge in science, fine arts, dramatics, music, and the like. The student teacher, coming as he does fresh from subject-matter courses, should be able to make a valuable contribution to classwork.

(13) Assisting in the supervision of extracurricular activities.

(14) Coaching plays and helping with assembly programs and radio forums that are initiated in the home rooms or in the regular courses.

(15) Taking charge of the bulletin board or at least posting from time to time materials contributing to the unit that the class is studying.

13. *Formulate for yourself a list of aims that you will strive to achieve as a student teacher.* This, again, is a task that you must do for yourself. To stimulate your thinking, however, we suggest that you plan your work so that you may become:

The best person possible for you to be: by removing those personal handicaps that impede your growth and improvement. Cultivate good mental health and broad scholarship. Remember that you are getting ready to exercise desirable leadership over youth.

An active participant in the social scene: aware of social and economic trends, realizing the importance of the place and function of the American public school in the preservation and the continued improvement of our democratic institutions. Prepare yourself to discuss intelligently community, state, and national problems, and resolve to have a part in the building of a better America.

A teacher with a personalized philosophy of education: firm in the conviction that nature and nurture must work in harmony. Recognize that the individual grows as a unit and that the teacher must, therefore, create situations that provide a natural development of the whole child. Seek to individualize the work with the ideal that the individual shall be placed in the appropriate environment. Set tasks and standards in terms of the needs and abilities of the individual. Resolve to have no part in assembly-line education.

A critical student of method: by developing skill in setting up desirable and specific aims for each area, arranging subject matter for specific teaching purposes, ever conscious of the importance of motivation, and by selecting methods appropriate to the task. Avoid the blind acceptance of devices and tricks of the trade and hold in mind as your ideal the competent professional worker who solves his pedagogical problems by applying fundamental principles of learning. Fix the habit of analysis and learn to use appraisal techniques in an effort to insure continued growth as a classroom practitioner. Resolve to be a master teacher and to avoid the rut of the routine teaching of classes in which pupils waste endless hours in mental torture and boredom.

A teacher with ideals of sound scholarship: by securing comprehensive knowledge of your teaching field. Acquire the skill to select significant materials from related fields and reorganize these in terms of the specific purposes of a teaching unit. Provide at all times examples of fine quality of workmanship and guide pupils in fixing proper habits of study. Stimulate pupils to sustained application in the search for truth, and be critical of standards employed in evaluating results. Strive to use the hour as a work period with emphasis on laboratory techniques in which pupils are given practice in reflective thinking.

A worthy member of the teaching profession: by taking an active and effective part in the activities, curricular and extracurricular, of the staff of the training school. Learn how to cooperate with other teachers, with parents, supervisors, and administrators. Develop professional attitudes and techniques, and those social traits that are necessary to continued professional growth and development. Help to develop a code of professional ethics and be sure to include in it the Golden Rule as a fundamental guide. Resolve to be a constructive force in the teaching profession.

Some Important Factors That Condition the Success of a Beginning Teacher

There are many desirable traits, personal and social, that a beginning teacher should possess in marked degree. Some of these are so important that you cannot afford to report for duty without careful consideration of them. We have in mind such factors as purpose, personality, appearance, manners, and speech. Keep in mind that first impressions of young people are extremely vivid and that they tend to persist. Since the "kick-off" is so important, some of the important factors are here given a brief treatment which you are expected to read several times before beginning your work with pupils.

A Realistic Examination of Your Purpose. It is probable that many of you will teach only a few years. Some of you may turn to other professions, and others will take up homemaking at an early date. To the future homemakers this may be said: A schoolroom is a sociological laboratory in which you will be given practice in solving problems of human relations. This is very helpful experience for your future responsibilities. In practically every community you will find excellent homemakers whose early training was in the schoolroom. Though we may regret that teaching is more a procession than a profession, we need not be too critical of the person who uses teaching as a steppingstone if he possesses fine native ability and renders efficient service while he teaches. A considerable number of our leaders in government, religion, law, and medicine have taught in their early years, and presumably their pupils had good teachers.

In just a few years you may be the parent of a boy or girl starting off to school. When that day comes you will be desperately concerned about the professional ethics of the teacher to whose care you commit your child. We therefore beg you to examine your purpose and, in all fairness, to live up to the finest traditions of the teaching profession while you are enrolled in its ranks. In all probability there is no more desirable criterion for predicting your success as a teacher than that of purpose.

Other things being equal, the strength of your own purpose may easily be the deciding factor in your success. If you are being shoved into teaching or if you are turning to teaching because you do not see another opportunity, your task and that of those who guide you will be difficult. There are two things that you can now do: (1) examine realistically the disadvantages of teaching, and perhaps decide to turn to something else; (2) consider the advantages of teaching, and in case you do decide to continue, do all that you can to deepen your purpose as a teacher. To this end we urge you to answer candidly the following questions:

1. *Are you willing and able to work relatively long hours?* Teaching is hard work. In fact, the tasks are never done. Even if you manage somehow to avoid carrying home an armful of papers to be evaluated, your mind is likely to be occupied by the necessary planning and reading for the next day. The teacher in the modern school is expected to be well versed in social, economic, and educational trends, to guide numerous extracurricular activities, to carry a heavy load of classroom instruction, to take an active part in the affairs of the community, and, finally, to integrate the personality of the child. We speak today of educating the whole child. As an ideal this is admirable; in practice it means an impossible task for the teacher. Any mother who has attempted to educate each of three or four lively youngsters on a "whole-child" basis is likely to be completely exhausted at evening. Any father who has tried it with one is a wreck by noon. But society has deposited "whole children" in excessive numbers at the teacher's desk. It is now considered that 20, 30, 40, or 50 pupils is a reasonable hourly load for the teacher. To the mediocre teacher these tasks soon become dismal drudgery, and he is lucky if, in addition, he is not driven by worries and devastating fears. But to the person who has a real "call" to teach, all this takes the form of challenging problems which are a delight to solve and for which the days are all too short.

A significant guide to note at this point is your attitude toward books, which still are and will continue to be to a large extent the tools of a teacher. If you do not like reading and study, you are likely to find teaching very irksome.

It is also clear that far too many teachers lack sound health, both physical and mental, for this strenuous job. Have you been absent a good deal from either high school or college because of illness? If so, you should have a very thorough physical checkup before you report for student teaching. Do not hesitate to include in this examination psychiatric services. The mind and body seem to be highly interrelated, and the intelligent person no longer hesitates to obtain guidance from every available source. Teaching is not a career for anyone who does not have an ample reserve of rugged health.

2. *Do you like to work with people?* If you do not enjoy being with young people, their restless energy and immaturity are likely to get on your nerves. To

live through a typical school day in which one deals with perhaps as many as two hundred pupils tends to subject one to nervous fatigue. Besides, there is the work that you have to do with other teachers, the principal, and the parents. The teacher who is a "natural" in dealing with pupils will be stimulated to greater nervous energy and will enjoy these experiences as much as the actor does his audience. Before going further you should ask yourself these questions: Do I know how to win the cooperation of boys and girls? Am I tactful and tolerant?

It should not be too hard for you to establish cooperative pupil-teacher relationships with two youngsters like these.[N]

Can I take suggestions? Studies of failure and success suggest that a goodly fraction of teachers fail because they cannot work with people.

3. *Are you willing to forego the chance to receive a large salary?* You are of course aware that the average salary of school teachers is pitifully low. However, the *average* includes a vast number of teachers with inadequate training and mediocre ability. Many successful teachers receive at least a comfortable living income. The important point here, however, is that very few of our million teachers get high salaries, and none has an income that would be considered large by a successful businessman, lawyer, or doctor. It is normal, of course, for you to expect an income that will support a decent standard of living in the community in which you work, and it is sensible for you not to expect to get much more than

that in teaching. Therefore you must be content with a simple standard as regards creature comforts, and you must look for your real returns to something other than money. "I am come that they might have life and that they might have it more abundantly." Thus the Greatest of all teachers defined the main purpose and reward of teaching.

The real teacher gets his greatest satisfactions by rendering a social service of major importance, by watching boys and girls grow to possibilities that even they themselves do not perhaps expect, and in the joy of doing the daily tasks. Professor George H. Palmer expressed the sentiment of many teachers when he said, "The fact is that Harvard College is paying me for work that I gladly would pay them to allow me to do."

4. *Do you adjust easily to new situations?* The mores of communities differ. If you find employment in a community of less than 10,000 inhabitants you may find that you are judged by standards of conduct that irritate you. In general, parents, either because of provincialism, ignorance, and intolerance, or because they care so much about the welfare of their children, tend to hold teachers for high standards of conduct. It often happens that these standards are higher than parents are willing to live up to themselves. Indeed, it is the exceptional town that will grant the same degree of freedom as regards dress and deportment to a teacher that it does to members of other professions.

5. *Are you tolerant about social, moral, and economic issues?* That is to say, if you found yourself out of harmony with most of the people of the community would you question your own position as objectively as you would that of the community? After all, the community may be right! For example, some communities object to a teacher's smoking, a habit which you may have formed in a highly cultured home. However, it would be difficult even for one who enjoys a good cigar to make a strong enough case for the use of tobacco to justify offending a whole community. But assuming that your position is desirable with respect to some moral, social, or economic issue, are you willing to begin where the community is, to bide your time until you have won a substantial following, and to work tactfully toward more sensible standards? As the great teacher Horace Mann said long ago, "Where anything is growing, one former is worth a thousand reformers." In any case, if you feel that your private life is strictly your own affair and that you cannot be happy while conforming to a good many requirements that may seem picayunish, you may need to turn to some other vocation.

The prospective teacher is entitled to know that there is a brighter side of the picture. In the larger cities any decent and tolerant teacher will find it possible to be a very active member of the community and still enjoy a large measure of personal freedom. In the preceding paragraphs we have by implication at least faced, rather frankly, some of the disadvantages that persons find in teaching. To make the picture more nearly complete we need to turn to the advantages. There are many excellent statements of these in educational literature. The list of suggested readings at the end

of this chapter includes several for future use, for even the gifted
teacher needs to stop from time to time to "recharge his battery."
It will be sufficient at this time for you to read carefully the following sample:

THE REWARDS OF TEACHING[1]

Throughout the ages civilization has ever accorded high honors to teachers.
Witness for example the great esteem shown to such individuals as Confucius,
Socrates, Plato, Aristotle, Jesus, Seneca, Quintilian, St. Augustine, Alcuin, Aquinas,
Abelard, da Feltre, Erasmus, Melanchthon, Loyola, Comenius, Pestalozzi, Cheever,
Lancaster, Mann, Eliot, Mary Lyon, Alice Freeman Palmer, and hosts of others.
Think of the many distinguished names that have made your own alma mater
famous as a center of learning. Recall the esteem in which certain teachers of
your own elementary and secondary schools were held by you—and perhaps are
still being revered in your home communities. Surely the world at large has ever
thought well of its true teachers; it has regarded their work as of the greatest
social significance and their influence upon posterity as almost limitless in range
and persistence.

But teaching is not alone of great worth to society; it yields notable personal
satisfactions to its own individual members. Some of these rewards are intellectual, some emotional, but all are at the same time cultural. Indeed in few
callings or professions in life may the sum total of human recompenses be so
numerous, deep, and varied as in the work of teaching. The farmer takes pride
and joy in his growing crops; the industrialist, in his manufactured products; the
artist, in his created masterpieces; the scientist, in his laboratory discoveries. But
the teacher, unlike all these, works with human materials; his efforts are concerned
with the minds and souls of boys and girls, of youths and maidens. Through his
ministrations endless transformations take place in respect to all human attributes.
Nor do the influences he exerts ever terminate. Like a wave set in motion on
the ocean the impetus to worthily ambitious living, once started in a pupil, continues to affect him to the end of his days. Indeed, it is doubtful that such influences cease there; in all probability they will have already been transmitted to
others and will continue to be so transmitted from generation to generation.

But just what specifically are these alleged great personal rewards of teaching?
Let us list a few.

First, teaching satisfies the almost universal desire to render social service. Self-
preservation and self-gratification no doubt constitute the first laws of life. But
closely allied to these—at least in most normal individuals—is the natural passion
or instinctive desire to be of service to others; to give pleasure and happiness to
associates, to relieve pain and misery, and to aid fellow mortals to realize their
own best potentialities. True, sordid selfishness and brutal callousness stalk
brazenly through every land much of the time. But beside them also go idealism
and altruism, the chief traits that distinguish man from the lower animals. And

---

[1] Quoted by permission of the author, Calvin O. Davis, in *School and Society*, L (Nov. 25,
1939), 691–694.

these traits are largely the products of teaching. Without education there would be no such thing as civilization, but merely raw naturalism. In short, education is the one indispensable element of human civilized existence; and without teachers there would be little if any education. Schools are therefore the world's best insurance policy and society's most profitable investment. Without their contributions free government, the safety of life and property, and in short the very means necessary to the pursuit of happiness would be wanting. Without education all the great professions, such as law, medicine, engineering, journalism, and the like, would be impossible; all modern art and science would be nonexistent; all cultural advances of the civilized world would disappear. Surely, therefore, the very nature and needs of the contemporary world make the teacher an indispensable member of society. Hence the student whose highest ambition is to render social service to his age and generation can find no wider field in which to play his part than that of the profession of teaching.

Second, teaching satisfies the desire for the continuous development of one's mental powers. No one can be an effective instructor of youth who fails to keep abreast of the intellectual life of his times. Teaching is essentially an interpretative process; hence, it demands of its servants a reasonable familiarity with a wide range of human interests and knowledge. A teacher must constantly relate fact to fact, idea to idea, circumstance to circumstance, and motives to motives. Furthermore, this correlation of classroom instructional materials must take place not only within the narrower confines of a particularized subject of study but also within and among subject matter of many sorts and kinds. Indeed it may truly be said that a teacher who knows intimately only one field of knowledge does not really know it. Complete mastery of any division of learning signifies, not only expert knowledge respecting the elements, laws, and principles of that subject when abstracted and isolated, but also an understanding of these constituents in their collective interrelationships with other bodies of knowledge and in their general applications to the world of contemporary affairs. Only a contintually expanding liberal education will permit a teacher to make these necessary interconnections.

Moreover a successful teacher, in our age particularly, cannot restrict his intellectual interests to matters of an academic kind; the science of education itself is today raising challenging professional problems of many sorts. The alert teacher must constantly be grappling with these. They involve questions relating to curriculum reform, the psychological adjustments of pupils, new administrative and supervisory procedures, new methods of teaching and of testing, and scores of similar topics. Surely, teaching provides ample intellectual stimulus for those who can envision its range of possibilities and who possess the ability, ambition, and training necessary to their successful handling of its problems.

Third, teaching satisfies the desire for the prolongation of youthful spirits and vigor. Ponce de Leon spent a fortune in quest of the mythical fountain of perpetual youth. Since his time, thousands have conducted a like fruitless search for the elixir of life. Today on every side crowds dash hither and yon in a restless effort to stay the hand of time and to flaunt the summons of old age. And yet every true teacher knows full well where the source of buoyancy is to be found; it

In the early days, note the groups that work well together. Be sure that your entrance strengthens rather than weakens such cooperating committees.[M]

is hidden in the schoolroom. Like produces like no less surely in the realm of the spirit than in the world of biology. Men and women who mingle understandingly with youth must, of necessity, be affected by their enthusiasms, good cheer, and optimism. Teachers stay young through the very contagion of youth. They may grow older in years but not in interests and attitudes. Truly, if one would stay young in spirit, health, and appearance, he needs but mingle as a teacher with those who possess these qualities—the youth in the schools of the nation.

Fourth, teaching satisfies the desire for the continual development of one's selfhood. Nothing in life is perhaps so sacred to an individual as his own personality. Sensitive to some degree as every person doubtless is respecting his own weaknesses, inhibitions, and handicaps, each nevertheless yearns for opportunities to overcome them and to assume among his fellows positions of trust and honor marked by largeness of scope and bigness of responsibility. Nor can it be denied that there is usually a close correlation between success in life and traits of personality. An enriched, exuberant, and glowing selfhood is both a condition and a concomitant of effective activity in most undertakings in life, whether these be physical or social. But the development of these desired characteristics comes largely through contacts with other individuals of like qualities and from participation in cultural agencies generally. A teacher, therefore, is peculiarly circumstanced to avail himself of these influences. With a unique degree of satisfaction he may expose himself to the uplifting forces of art, music, drama, literature, travel, social intercourse, and like agencies. Daily a teacher is permitted to remake for himself a new world of liberal culture. Like the chambered nautilus he is ever

16

building for himself more stately mansions and is encouraged to furnish each one with equipment superior in quality to the others.

Fifth, teaching satisfies the desire for association with congenial colleagues. Man is distinctly a social animal. He finds contentment usually only when permitted to hold communion with individuals of like tastes, interests, and habits. While every form of group relationship is likely to furnish a quantum of such experiences, teaching affords unique opportunities of the sort. By means of innumerable educational associations, societies, and clubs which the profession of teaching has developed within its ranks, and by means of the daily comminglings with other teachers in faculty meetings and school assemblies and in the halls, on the streets, and in rooming houses, teachers have unusual facilities for making friends and extending friendships. Today there are close to one million public-school teachers in America. They are actuated in their daily lives by high standards of esthetic taste, civic judgment, and moral idealism. To be affiliated with this large army of public-spirited individuals is indeed a rare privilege.

Thus it appears that for individuals with the right hereditary equipment, proper personal qualities, adequate academic and professional training the rewards of teaching are rich, deep, and abiding.

The Best Liked Teacher—The Least Liked Teacher

We can give you one more aid by giving you a picture of the kind of teacher that high-school youngsters like best and the type they like least. Frank Hart[1] asked each of 10,000 high-school seniors to think of the teacher they had liked best and then write the reasons for their choice. He also asked each of them to think of the teacher they had liked least of all and to state the reasons for not liking that teacher. He obtained 3,725 responses to these requests. In commenting on the reasons given, the investigator says, "One can scarcely fail to be profoundly impressed, if not actually amazed, by the keen, searching analysis, the mature critical judgment, the exacting standards, the high purpose, and the idealism of the high-school senior."[2] Using these responses Hart presents a composite picture of the best liked and another of the least liked. In general the traits used to describe the best liked teachers are human qualities—friendly, companionable, cheerful, interested in understanding people, and the like. The judgments of high-school seniors were consistent in that the reasons given most frequently in the list for the best liked teacher take a negative form in the evaluation of

[1] FRANK W. HART. *Teachers and Teaching.* New York: The Macmillan Company, 1934.
[2] *Ibid.*, p. 130.

the least liked teacher.   For example "cheerful, happy, etc.," takes
the form "too cross, crabby, grouchy, etc."

More recently the Quiz Kids radio program gave a scholarship to
the teacher most convincingly described in a pupil's composition
under the title, "The Teacher Who Has Helped Me Most."   About
12,000 letters were received from pupils in grades two to twelve.
The traits mentioned by the pupils in the order of frequency were:

1.   Cooperative, democratic attitude.
2.   Kindliness and consideration for the individual.
3.   Patience.
4.   Wide variety of interests.
5.   General appearance and pleasing manner.
6.   Fairness and impartiality.
7.   Sense of humor.
8.   Good disposition and consistent behavior.
9.   Interest in pupils' problems.
10.   Flexibility.
11.   Use of recognition and praise.
12.   Unusual proficiency in teaching a particular subject.

By way of summary Paul A. Witty[1] says:

The above reactions—typical of the thousands made—show the significance of a
mental hygiene approach in the classroom.   In fact, this emphasis is the outstanding feature of the letters.

These boys and girls appear to be grateful to the school in proportion to the
degree that it offers security, individual success, shared experience, and opportunities for personal and social adjustments.   And these are precisely the factors which
promote good learning.

THE TEACHER PERSONALITY

Given equal amounts of intelligence, command of subject matter,
and classroom techniques, teachers yet will vary widely in the relative success which they achieve in the profession.   One explanation
no doubt lies in the personality.

It is very difficult to define what one means by *personality*.   Even
the definitions by those who have made detailed studies of personality traits do not agree.   The basis of an attractive personality is
often an emphasis on one or more desirable traits.   For practical
purposes we may conceive of it as analogous to a curious piece of
cloth with numerous and varied threads of which there must be

[1] PAUL A. WITTY.   "The Teacher Who Has Helped Me Most," *NEA Journal*, XXXVI
(May, 1947), 386.

enough sufficiently strong and attractive strands to present a substantial and pleasing effect. To an increasing degree officials, when employing new teachers, tend to place emphasis on those qualities which make for a pleasing teaching personality. It is obvious that this is a desirable policy. In everyday adult life it is possible for the most part to avoid dealing very much with people we do not

Learning to establish a desirable pupil-teacher relationship is all important for a student teacher. Don't you agree that it is fine between the two shown here? As you perhaps know, this teacher is administering a well-known test.(M)

like. In school, however, children are forced to look at their teacher day after day. They have no choice!

The important thing about this matter of personality is that it can be improved, since the habits underlying the traits that compose this fabric of personality are acquired. It is never too late to change a repulsive effect to one that is definitely pleasing. The first step, however, is to recognize the specific quality or qualities in your personality that will prevent you from doing your best work, or indeed disqualify you from the teaching profession.

CHECK LIST OF IMPORTANT FACTORS IN THE TEACHER'S PERSONALITY

Directions: Consider each of the ten divisions in this list separately. Read each statement under the major headings carefully and underline any of the qualities or traits which obviously are missing in the personality being rated. Before you proceed to the next division, look back over any of the statements you may have underlined and then place a check mark in the column that expressed your general opinion of the person with respect to the particular aspect of personality being considered.

Suggested standards for traits or qualities	Below average	Fair	Good	Excellent
1. *Emotional Stability and Mental Health.* Free from fears, remorses, humiliations, and worries about trivial things; is disposed to make a realistic inventory of his mental resources; not supersensitive to criticism; has a mind stored with wholesome resources for self-entertainment; not easily irritated; is free from excessive shyness and from temper tantrums and daydreams; meets unexpected situations well; adapts readily to changing situations; exercises self-control; is free from complexes of inferiority and superiority; has control over moods, with no sudden shifts in extremes from ups to downs; can take disappointments in life in full stride.				
2. *Personal Appearance.* Is dressed appropriately for the occasion; is alert and well poised; is well groomed; gives appearance of being self-possessed; exercises good taste in selection of clothes; impresses one as being refined and cultured; color combinations are harmonious; clothes are pressed and clean; looks to be in good health.				
3. *Health and Vitality.* Shows evidence of a "driving force"; is physically and mentally alert; is enthusiastic and cheerful; looks the picture of health; is dynamic; is wide awake to the potential possibilities in every situation; has a happy expression; has reserve energy.				
4. *Honesty, Character, and Integrity.* Shows a good sense of values; can be expected to do the right thing under all conditions; is trustworthy and loyal; admits mistakes; keeps his word; is fair and just in his dealings with others; fulfills obligations; is intellectually honest; maintains high standards of conduct.				
5. *Adaptability.* Accepts gracefully and understands quickly suggestions from others; accepts responsibility for making a positive contribution to a situation; is willing to inconvenience self in helping others; is challenged by new situations; is sympathetic and patient in sharing and understanding the thoughts and difficulties of others; says what must be said with diplomacy and minimum offense; responds readily to necessary routine.				

CHECK LIST OF IMPORTANT FACTORS IN THE TEACHER'S PERSONALITY.—(*Continued*)

Suggested standards for traits or qualities	Below average	Fair	Good	Excel- lent
6. *Cooperation.* Can work with others for attainment of a common end; volunteers services when they are needed; fits in where most needed; welcomes suggestions and tries to improve; places welfare of the group before self; is willing to share in the "extra" tasks; is a constructive worker on a committee.				
7. *Voice and Speech.* Shows refinement and evidence of cultural background; is clear and distinct; has proper degree of inflection; is well modulated, controlled, and adapted to the size of group; has an accepted and natural accent; arrests favorable attention; is easy to understand; words are pronounced correctly; speech is free from distracting and irritating mannerisms or defects.				
8. *Leadership.* Commands respect; is self-confident; shows ability in planning, organization, and execution; can persuade others of a proper course of action; can act in emergencies with decision; uses good judgment; inspires others to do their best; shows mastery of a situation; exercises initiative and originality; has the ability to put into words the inarticulate desires of a group; possesses courage to support sound convictions.				
9. *Resourcefulness.* Is prolific in suggestions for meeting a difficulty; is discerning and quick in selection of the most promising solution; can "see around a corner"; has an abundance of reserve energy upon which to draw; is intuitive in "striking when the iron is hot"; suggests power of mental strength and vigor.				
10. *Sociability.* Reveals knowledge of the rules of etiquette sufficient to avoid embarrassing, offending, or irritating others; is unselfishly interested in "just folks"; is a dynamic human spark; is a stimulating conversationalist with a wide range of interests; has a vicarious point of view; puts others at ease; seeks association with others; is tolerant of the opinions of others, of community life, and in the numerous agencies for social expression; wins and holds his friends; is a good listener; knows when to be playful; creates a comfortable and pleasant atmosphere; sees the humorous element in situations; can jest and frolic at parties and picnics but recaptures his dignity at the appropriate time; is a good sport.				

To aid you in making a careful study of your own personality, a check list of characteristics is provided here. In it you will find those social and personal qualities which have been generally accepted as contributing to teaching success. A sensible person will realize that he does not rate excellent on all the traits. The teaching personality pictured here is an ideal!

The list will reveal shortcomings and give you a picture of your strong points on which you can build. It might be more interesting for you if we used a rating scale on which each of the traits is given a number value. However, we believe that such a device would be fallacious, particularly with regard to teachers, for by the use of such an instrument a personality may be given a fairly high rating and yet include a trait so low that few if any communities would employ that person as a teacher. What you need at this point is a picture of your low and high spots, particularly the traits which you need to improve, and the check list will give you this picture.

You may wish to use the check list in two ways. In the first place, it may be used for self-appraisal. If you use this procedure you should be entirely frank with yourself and constantly face the question: Can I qualify? Self-analysis is indeed valuable, but it must be candid. There seems to be a tendency for most of us to be easy with ourselves, to rationalize to a point where we excuse our own shortcomings.

In the second place, you may wish to ask one or more of your friends or perhaps successful teachers to evaluate your personality from time to time in order to see what improvement has been made. Unfortunately, one usually has great difficulty in discovering that one is low in some desirable trait, and ratings by others who are friendly and competent may help. Insist, however, that they be objective in their ratings and, moreover, be equally objective in your analysis of these judgments.

Personal Appearance

If you are altogether sure of a high rating on the second item in the preceding check list you should proceed to a more detailed analysis of your personal appearance. That this factor is important in determining successful social relations is scarcely debatable. Then, too, the teacher is always a very important part of the child's environment. If the classroom setting is to be appropriate and

AN INVENTORY OF PERSONAL APPEARANCE

Directions: Check each item carefully and place an X in the appropriate column opposite the quality being considered. For example, if your handkerchiefs are always fresh, place an X in the "Yes" column opposite that item. When you have finished, try to determine whether you present an appearance that is pleasing (1) all the time, (2) sometimes, or (3) not at all. Check marks in the two outside columns should serve as reminders or "conscience ticklers" that you still have room for improvement.

Appearance factors	Yes	Some-times	No
Clothing:			
1. Are your clothes always clean, pressed, and free from unpleasant odors?			
2. Do you keep your shoes cleaned, shined, and heels straightened?			
3. Do you attempt to "freshen up" at noon or in the evening?			
4. Are your handkerchiefs always fresh?			
5. Are color combinations in good taste?			
6. Are your clothes becoming to your type and size?			
7. Do you consider quality in clothes when making a selection?			
8. Do you get up early enough to have plenty of time to devote to your personal appearance?			
9. When in doubt about style do you consult a reliable clothier or a current fashion guide?			
10. Do you adapt clothes and appearance to the time, place, occasion, and your age?			
Skin, Hair, and Nails:			
1. Do you avoid all evidence of dandruff?			
2. Do you visit a barbershop or hairdresser frequently enough to keep looking "trim"?			
3. Do you wash your hair frequently enough to keep it soft and healthy?			
4. Are you free from skin eruptions? (The cause of such eruptions may be improper cleansing or diet, but see your physician.)			
5. Do you keep your nails trim and clean?			
Health (Physical):			
1. Is your weight about normal (so that you are neither overweight nor underweight)?			
2. Are you alert, free from a tired and worried appearance?			
3. Are you sensitive about your posture?			
4. Is your breath free from obnoxious odors?			
5. Are your teeth clean and free from cavities?			

attractive we cannot ignore the teacher as a part of the picture. A teacher with careless habits of personal appearance may be very offensive to children, particularly during the close associations of a conference or the supervised study period.

The first impression is of the utmost importance in student teaching as it is in the other social situations. A sense of having done all in your power to be well groomed and clean adds to self-confidence and contributes directly to self-respect, and you must respect yourself before you can expect respect from others. We should like to emphasize that the maintaining of satisfactory standards for student teaching does not involve excessive costs. With regard to personal appearance you need to keep in mind three basic things: (1) cleanliness, (2) the right choice of clothes in the first place, (3) keeping your clothes in order. You should dress for school as you would if you were a receptionist, a lawyer, a doctor, or anyone who needs to meet the general public. Gaudy clothes, loud colors, and lurid make-up probably won't prevent you from being a good teacher, but they will certainly label you as having bad taste.

The main thing to remember when you dress for school is that you are getting ready to go to work—not to a party at the country club. To aid you in making a more detailed study of this factor, in case you believe you need to do so, we have provided in this section desirable standards that you may use as guides.

The Speech Problem

The voice is a very important factor in teaching. If you have no speech defects, this does not mean that you know how to use your voice as a teacher. In the typical classroom few sentences are heard by all students. It may happen time and again in a single hour that not one-half hear what is said. Is it any wonder that achievement is low, that pupils are bored, and that disciplinary problems develop?

Few people seem to be aware of their own speech defects. For this reason you may need to secure several ratings of your voice. The check list that appears here contains in brief form some of the more important aspects of voice and speech.

In recent years many higher institutions have installed equipment, especially wire recording, for making records of one's voice. Such records have proved to be of great value in the diagnosis and remedial treatment of voice and speech defects.

The First Assignment

Obviously your first assignment is to make yourself acceptable to the supervising teacher and the pupils. This will be easy to do with the supervising teacher, for he undoubtedly was selected because of

A Check List for Voice and Speech[1]

There are two ways in which this check list may be useful: (1) you may wish to ask some trained person to evaluate your teaching voice; (2) the results may prove helpful when two or three student teachers rate each other, and later compare notes.

Speech factors	Needs attention	Satisfactory or superior
Quality of Voice: Is his voice		
1. Too high pitched?		
2. Nasal?		
3. Strained?		
4. Breathy?		
5. Varied in pitch?		
6. Clear and distinct?		
7. Rich and colorful?		
8. Adapted to the size of the listening group?		
9. Well controlled and modulated?		
10. Resonant?		
Unpleasant Speech Mannerisms: Does he speak		
1. Too fast?		
2. In a drawling manner?		
3. Lispingly?		
4. Gruffly?		
5. Too slowly?		
6. In an uncertain, halting, or stumbling manner?		
7. With an affected accent?		
General Speech: Does he		
1. Pronounce words correctly?		
2. Enunciate carefully?		
3. Use slang inappropriately or excessively?		
4. Keep calm, free from anger and excitement?		
5. Employ concepts adapted to his audience?		
6. Adapt voice to the occasion?		
7. Use proper inflection?		
8. Show evidence of an adequate vocabulary?		

[1] Only two columns at the right are employed in order to emphasize the items to which the teacher should give remedial attention.

his special interest in the education of teachers. It may help you to get acquainted with your supervising teacher if you provide him with a short story of your life, referring particularly to early and later education, habits, recreation, amusements, purposes in life, initiative, family life, your major and minor subjects, and anything else of importance that you care to mention, including an inexpensive photograph of yourself. You may safely assume that this informal autobiography will not be used with prospective employers.

The part that relates to pupils is another story. In the early days you can easily overplay your hand, or fail by doing too little. No one will be able to tell you how to win your pupils, for each must do this in his own way. Even if we knew what to say, we certainly should not tell you, for this is a very important test of your ability as a teacher and one that you will have to face every time you are assigned to a new class as long as you teach. However, you are entitled to the following hints:

1. Learn the names of pupils promptly.
2. Be interested in the things that interest your pupils, in and out of school.
3. Forget yourself in the interests of your pupils. Try to be of special help to pupils who need it and want it.
4. Be friendly, but maintain a certain reserve; avoid familiarity with pupils.
5. Be sympathetic and understanding, but firm, in your dealings with pupils.
6. Identify yourself with the school; show an interest in all school affairs.

The Professional Worker

When you report for duty you will be taking your first step as a professional worker. We welcome you to the oldest of all learned professions. You will be in the company of a group of which former President Hoover has said,

It is truly remarkable, I think, that so vast an army of people . . . so uniformly meets its obligations, so effectively does its job, so decently behaves itself, as to be almost utterly inconspicuous in a sensation-loving country. It implies a wealth of character, of tact, of patience, of quiet competence, to achieve such a record as that.

As a summary of this chapter we now expect and urge you to keep ever before you the three great challenges to the teaching profession:

The Significance of the Social Service Rendered. Some years ago H. G. Wells said, "Civilization is a race between education and catastrophe." The atomic bomb starts us on the last lap of this race. Admitting that the school is not the only educational agency, it yet remains true that whether or not society will ultimately solve its problems systematically and efficiently or resort to violent and disorderly measures depends on the zeal and efficiency of teachers. Disease, ignorance, and meanness are the real enemies of man. A world free from devastating wars and unnecessary suffering is not likely to be created in conferences of diplomats and ministers. Rather, that is the long-time job of the schoolmaster in every land. But the part that concerns society is only half the story, for the teacher helps the individual to find a more satisfying way of life. In this sense the teacher is perhaps the modern equivalent of the missionary of an earlier day.

The Contagion of Youth. In the motion picture, "Goodbye, Mr. Chips," Katherine says to her lover, the schoolmaster, "Why, I should think you would never grow old in a world where everyone is young." Good teachers respond to the hope and enthusiasm that are the marked attributes of youth. They may grow in years but in no other profession do they have the same opportunities to remain young in enthusiasms. It is not uncommon in large high schools that offer long tenure to find among the oldest teachers one who is in spirit the youngest in the building.

The Stimulation to Personal Growth. Other things being equal, the richer the personality the more effective is the teaching. Recent discussions concerning the revision of the curriculum in teacher-education institutions suggest that a greater emphasis will be placed on selecting and building, first of all, the right kind of person. In all probability prospective teachers as well as teachers in service will be encouraged, and to some extent required, to travel, to have work experiences, and to extend their interests in art, music, the social studies, drama, literature, etc., throughout their teaching careers. This merely means that you can do what you like to do anyway, as a cultured person, and it will all count in teaching.

Suggested Readings[1]

Hart, Frank W.: *Teachers and Teaching.* New York: The Macmillan Company, 1934. Pp. ix + 285.

> This book presents a composite picture of teacher *A*, the best liked teacher, and a composite picture of teacher *Z*, the least liked teacher as constructed from the responses of 10,000 high-school seniors.

Palmer, George Herbert: *The Ideal Teacher.* Boston: Houghton Mifflin Company, 1910. Pp. v + 32.

> This inspired statement by one of America's greatest teachers has stimulated the professional zeal of countless teachers for generations. He lists four characteristics which, in his judgment, every teacher should possess: (*a*) aptitude for vicariousness, (*b*) rich

---

[1] *Note to the Supervising Teacher:* It is assumed that the prospective teacher will read widely in professional literature during his period of internship. It is further assumed that this reading will be almost altogether optional. This list of suggested readings at the end of each chapter exposes the student to a few of the best books that have a bearing on his work, but how many of these he will read should certainly be a matter largely of his own choice.

intellectual wealth, (*c*) the power to invigorate life through learning, and (*d*) a readiness to be forgotten.

PARKER, FRANCIS W.: *Talks on Pedagogics.* New York: The John Day Company, 1937. Pp. xxi + 342.

Col. Parker ranks as one of America's great schoolmen. Though he wrote some of the lectures in this book nearly half a century ago, there are many pages that express modern education at its best. The lectures that comprise the main part of this book were first published in 1891. This edition is a reprint intended to serve as a guide for study groups of modern education.

Teaching as a Man's Job. Homewood, Ill.: Phi Delta Kappa, 1938. Pp. 79.

This book is directed to young men who are considering teaching as a life profession. It was prepared by a committee of Phi Delta Kappa, an honorary professional and fraternal association of men in education.

Toward Better Teaching, A Report of Current Practices. 1949 Yearbook, Association for Supervision and Curriculum Development of the National Education Association, 1949. Pp. xii + 282.

In the opinion of the committee that contributed this volume, better teaching involves the following: (1) fostering security and satisfaction, (2) promoting cooperative learning, (3) helping pupils develop self-direction, (4) fostering creativity, (5) helping pupils develop values, (6) providing opportunities for social action, and (7) helping pupils evaluate learnings. The committee selected and edited descriptions of situations or stories which illustrate procedures in these seven areas submitted by teachers.

WAHLQUIST, JOHN T.: *An Introduction to American Education.* New York: The Ronald Press Company, 1947. Pp. xii + 333.

If you have a little extra time read Chapter 4, entitled "Attributes of the Successful Teacher." This book is characterized by common sense.

WELLS, H. G.: *Joan and Peter.* New York: The Macmillan Company, 1918. Pp. 594.

This book, written more than thirty years ago, predicted in amazing fashion the coming of the chaotic world that threatens to engulf mankind. Although a novel, it is essentially a book on education in which the thesis that a sound education is the only solution for the problems of society is convincingly presented. Needless to say, the author is bitterly critical of the existing schools.

Chapter II

Learning to Understand Pupils

I Taught Them All[1]

I have taught in high school for ten years. During that time I have given assignments, among others, to a murderer, an evangelist, a pugilist, a thief, and an imbecile.

The murderer was a quiet little boy who sat on the front seat and regarded me with pale blue eyes; the evangelist, easily the most popular boy in the school, had the lead in the junior play; the pugilist lounged by the window and let loose at intervals a raucous laugh that startled even the geraniums; the thief was a gay-hearted Lothario with a song on his lips; and the imbecile, a soft-eyed little animal seeking the shadows.

The murderer awaits death in the state penitentiary; the evangelist has lain a year now in the village churchyard; the pugilist lost an eye in a brawl in Hong Kong; the thief, by standing on tiptoe, can see the windows of my room from the county jail; and the once gentle-eyed little moron beats his head against a padded wall in the state asylum.

All of these pupils once sat in my room, sat and looked at me gravely across worn brown desks. I must have been a great help to those pupils—I taught them the rhyming scheme of the Elizabethan sonnet and how to diagram a complex sentence.

Is the Clinical Approach Possible?

John Dewey led the teachers in the schools of an earlier generation to see that education is life. So today we say that education is growth. Our attention is focused not on what a pupil is, but on what he has experienced and on what he may become. A teacher operating with the growth concept interprets the pupil's responses, achievement, and behavior in terms of the history of the organism and the present level of development; he thinks in terms of individual patterns, needs, and social requirements; he takes many factors into account when he uses the phrase the "whole child"; he recognizes that the personality is to no small extent the resultant of strong social forces; he places the emphasis on processes rather than on the product; and finally he strives to become a specialist in human relationships. But growth to be effective must be given direction,

[1] This statement signed N. J. W. appeared in *The Clearing House*, for November, 1937.

29

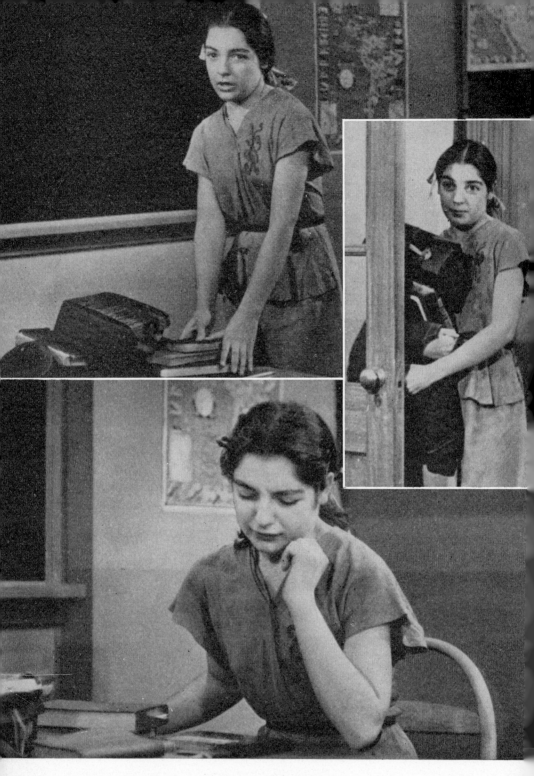

Top: To stand and make a simple report on her recreational interests is torture to Ada. *Center:* Ada, a problem case, reports to her English class. *Bottom:* Ada knows how badly she has failed, and shows how very unhappy she is about it.

and so it has come about that guidance[1] is not only one of the important functions of a teacher but is in fact the essence of all good teaching.

If a teacher knew all that he should about a pupil he would seldom be surprised or disappointed by anything a pupil might say or do. It is generally recognized that one cannot teach another person effectively unless he knows a good deal about him. Now the regrettable fact is that, in general, teachers do not know their pupils very well. One study suggests that only about one-fourth of the teachers know one-fourth of the total number of facts which well-trained workers consider important in order to plan a desirable educational program for youth. In the typical school a teacher should collect, or be provided with, many times as much factual material about pupils as he now finds available for use. Obviously, in the short period you will devote to student teaching you cannot collect all the data that you would like to have concerning each pupil. However, certain experiences will be provided in which you can learn to use important techniques that will surely prove useful in your future work.

Even in the early days of teaching it is important to know how to make a systematic study of the human material in your classes. Unfortunately the failure to keep continuous and accurate records of the pupil's growth and progress is perhaps one of the weakest spots in American education. In most schools few records other than the pupils' names, ages, school subjects, and marks are available to teachers on the opening day of school. Indeed, in a number of well-organized high schools the teacher on the opening day knows nothing of the children who crowd into the classroom other than the names as they appear on class rolls sent from the office. It is probable that an up-to-date hospital develops a more adequate record of a patient in a week's time than the typical school does for a problem pupil who has been enrolled eight years.

If we are eager to have a clinical approach to the problem of adjusting the individual personality or, more practically stated, to the problem of organizing a setting or a curriculum that will develop normal growth of each pupil, we will need to have systematic procedures in pupil accounting. Ideally, the record should be con-

[1] By guidance we mean any help that may be given a person in order to define and improve his scale of values. Its main objective is the conservation of human resources.

tinuous and it should travel ahead of, or at any rate with, the pupil. But since this does not happen in many schools you will need to practice certain techniques that will enable you to make the best of conditions and await the day when adequate school records will travel with the pupil.

Many schools nowadays provide a good deal of data including scores on standardized tests to aid the classroom teacher in understanding children.(M)

AN ILLUSTRATION OF A TECHNIQUE

We turn now to what a resourceful teacher did to solve this problem. Mary Brown was an English teacher in the Middletown High School. It was five o'clock in the afternoon of the opening day and Miss Brown was somewhat tired as she turned away from the seating charts she had completed of the pupils in her five English classes. As she leaned back wearily in her chair, she reviewed her day—five different groups of boys and girls entering and leaving her room—a total of 140 personalities making a confused picture of blurred faces. "My!" she thought, "will I ever remember so many names? But here! What am I thinking of? I won't be teaching merely names. I will be teaching individual personalities. Let's see, I remember now—her name was Ada Adams. She came into my second-period class after the other pupils had taken their seats. Yes, I remember her clearly. As she came into the room she looked at me as though she knew I was going to yell 'Sit down!' at her. Her arms were full of books, and she carried an old metal lunch box. She hurried to a seat at the rear of the room and, most unfortunately for her, attacted the attention of the rest of the class when her lunch box fell to the floor with a great clatter, opening up and spilling its contents. Several of the pupils laughed at her awkwardness but I was able to quiet them quickly. Poor child, her dress was old-fashioned and she looked as if she didn't have a friend in the world. I wonder what her home conditions are like? I'm sure she is unhappy—but look here! It's already five o'clock and I'd better be getting home."

The next day Miss Brown asked the pupils in her second-period English class to talk informally about themselves, their interests and hobbies. The group responded readily and each pupil talked freely about himself—that is, all but Ada. When Ada was called upon she didn't go to the front of the room as the others had done. Instead she rose slowly from her seat, looking apprehensively at Miss Brown and at others in the room. It was obviously an effort for her to say anything at all. Then, leaning on the edge of the table for support, she gave a very brief account of herself. About all she mentioned was her name, her age, her address, and the number of the schools she had attended previously.

While Ada's account of herself revealed none of the usual interests of normal, healthy adolescents, it did seem to reveal that here was a lonely, unhappy soul. Indeed, some of the other pupils seemed to sense Ada's loneliness, for two of the girls—one a daughter of a social worker—went out of their way after class to meet Ada at the door and to invite her to join them for a soda later that afternoon. Ada declined this invitation, however, excusing herself on the ground that she didn't care for sodas.

Miss Brown made a mental note of Ada's behavior that day. Later on her way home she began to develop a plan, not only for knowing more about Ada but also a plan that would provide her with information about the interests, abilities, and personal characteristics of all the pupils in her classes. "What I need," she said to herself, "is more information about my pupils. I need to find out about the type of homes they come from, their mental abilities, their interests, their educational achievements, their physical conditions, and their mental stability. I need to bring all these data together so that I will have a much better picture of the potentialities and

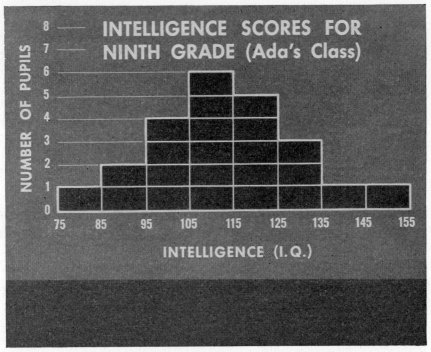

Chart A. Distribution of pupils on intelligence scores (I.Q.).

disabilities of the pupils in my classes. Then, I'll be ready to adjust my teaching to serve the needs of my pupils."

MAKING AN INVENTORY OF THE HUMAN MATERIAL

At this point we need to interrupt the story of Ada to emphasize the fact that Miss Brown was getting a picture, while she was developing a case study of Ada, of the *structure* of her class as a *group*. In the years ahead you are likely to hear a good deal about *group dynamics*. This is a fancy name for a fairly simple concept. The idea is that a class, a community, a nation, and a "one world," like a person, has personality, morale, abilities, potentialities, ideals, ways of working, and the like. One can and should make a study of the human resources in a class.

By the end of the first week, Miss Brown had made a systematic search in the school for data that would help her to become better acquainted with her classes. She consulted the records in the principal's office and found that the California Test of Mental

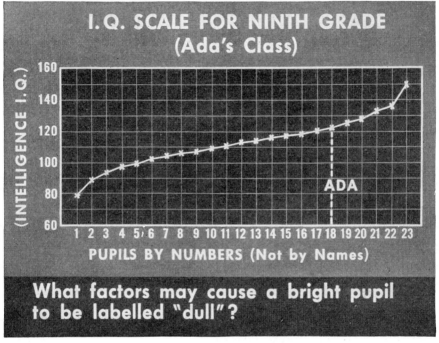

Chart B

Maturity, the Stanford Achievement Test in Spelling, the Iowa Silent Reading Test, and the New Stanford Arithmetic Test had been given pupils in several grades, including the ninth, during the first week of school. Miss Brown borrowed the tests of her own pupils and over the week end compiled the following data based on the scores of pupils in her second-period English class.

Miss Brown made two graphs for each of these measures. The general picture of the intelligence scores is shown by the first graph (Chart *A*). What does the horizontal scale show?—the vertical scale? What is the lowest I.Q.?—the highest?—the range?—the norm (score of the largest group)? Do you think Miss Brown knew

36

Student Teaching

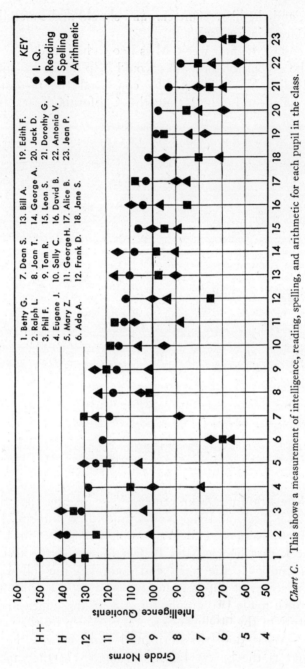

Chart C. This shows a measurement of intelligence, reading, spelling, and arithmetic for each pupil in the class.

whether this was a bright or dull class before she made this chart? What do you think her conclusion was after studying these data?

The second graph (Chart *B*) shows the scores of individual pupils in order from lowest to highest. What is Ada's score? Why does Miss Brown use code numbers?

When Miss Brown had completed the graphs for all the test scores, she transferred the scores to a single chart (Chart *C*). What advantages do you see in this graph?

FOR DISCUSSION

1. How close, do you guess, is the correlation between intelligence and achievement in (*a*) arithmetic, (*b*) reading, (*c*) spelling?

2. How many pupils in this class do you think are retarded in (*a*) reading, (*b*) arithmetic, (*c*) spelling?

3. Mention one thing Miss Brown could do that might help to bring the retarded pupils in reading up to the level where they should be.

4. Explain in terms of your own major and minor teaching areas the specific uses that you could make of the types of data in this chart. What types of standard test data other than those shown in this chart would you like to have about the pupils in your class? Explain the use which you would make of these other types of data.

5. Assuming that Miss Brown did not find any standard test results in the office, what might she have done to obtain all or part of the test data in this chart?

A SOCIOGRAM

To get further light on the *relationships* within the group Miss Brown constructed the chart or sociogram shown here. To get the information needed, she had each pupil write the names of the two pupils that "he got along best with in doing schoolwork." As a newcomer to the school, Miss Brown felt that this information might be significant to her, especially since most of the pupils came from the same neighborhood and had gone to school together from one to eight years.

When she totaled the choices, she obtained the accompanying table. The total number of times chosen—sometimes called *social status score*—is of course an index of a child's popularity. Naturally such an index is more reliable[1] if counts are taken in additional situations, such as the extent to which a pupil is chosen as a companion at luncheon and movie. With the data in the table and the

[1] See WILLARD C. OLSON. "The Improvement of Human Relations in the Classroom," *Childhood Education*, March, 1946.

names turned in by the pupils, Miss Brown constructed the sociogram opposite.

Triangles indicate boys and circles represent girls. The direction of an arrow shows "who chose whom." Thus girl 6 chose girl 17 and girl 10. A rhombus, or double-headed arrow, indicates mutual choice. Thus boy 2 chose boy 14 and boy 14 chose boy 2.

SOCIAL STATUS OF PUPILS

Number of Pupil	Number of Times Chosen
1	1
2	2
3	2
4	1
5	Absent[1]
6	0
7	4
8	2
9	2
10	1
11	0
12	6
13	1
14	7
15	0
16	0
17	4
18	3
19	3
20	Absent[1]
21	Absent[1]
22	1
23	0

[1] Interrelationships with absentees are not shown in the sociogram because their choices were not available.

By this time you will be asking, "What do the concentric circles mean?" This is merely a device for grouping pupils in fourths. Thus the top 25 per cent, those that were chosen most frequently, are placed in the inner circle. The next quarter are placed in the next ring, the third quarter in the third ring, and the lowest quarter, that is to say those chosen fewest times, in the outside ring. Presumably a skillful teacher will keep a watchful eye on the lonesome souls in this outer ring and will be well aware of the fact that there may also be serious problems within the inner circle. By referring to the chart relating to intelligence, you will see that number 6 is Ada. Whom did she choose? How often was she herself chosen as a companion?

It is obviously impossible for a busy teacher to draw a sociogram of every class. However, the procedure is practical for a home-room teacher or for anyone with specific guidance responsibilities to a group that is not too big. In the case of a large group, a socio-

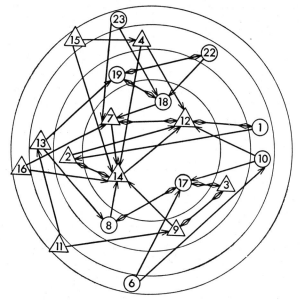

Chart D. Sociogram showing relationships within the group.

gram would become too complicated. Moreover, to one who can visualize statistical data, the diagram is not necessary because the *table* of choices would no doubt enable him to spot the problem cases.

On her way to school Monday morning, Miss Brown met the head of the Department of Physical Education. She learned that the department kept the results of the health examinations that had been given each child in the school. She discovered, too, that these data would be available to her whenever she wanted them. And so Miss Brown consulted these records. She was able to list the fol-lowing information relating to the disabilities in physical health of fifteen out of twenty-three pupils in her second-period English class:

Disabilities in Physical Health

Defective eyesight.................Bill A., David B., Jane S., Mary Z.
Defective hearing..................Eugene J., Alice B.
Diseased tonsils...................Antonia V., Leon S.
Poor dentition.....................Dean S., Eugene J., Ada A., Antonia
                                   V., Edith F., Jack D.
Malnutrition.......................Eugene J., Dorothy G., Ada A.
Goiter.............................Jean P.
Speech defects.....................Antonia V., Phil F., Eugene J.
Poor posture.......................Edith F., David B., Alice B., Ada A.

For Discussion

1. Pick out one of the physical defects listed above and show how it might affect the achievement of a pupil.

2. Which disabilities in this list might escape the attention of teachers for years if records were not available or not used?

3. What special seating arrangements would you make to take care of the first two disabilities in this list?

4. Is this an unusual number of disabilities in physical health in a ninth-grade class of this size?

During the next two weeks Miss Brown made it a point to talk informally with many of her pupils about their interests and hobbies. By combining these data with the information pupils had supplied in their informal talks in class, Miss Brown was able to develop the following table of the special interests of pupils in her second-period English class.

Special Interests of Pupils

Bill A...................Hiking; fishing; skating; reading adventure stories
George A.................Collecting rocks; reading geology books; scouting
Ada A....................Art
Alice B..................Making dolls' clothes; cooking
David B..................Track; fishing; hiking; movies
Sally C..................Reading girls' stories; movies
Jack D...................Making model airplanes; flying kites
Frank D..................Camping; hiking
Phil F...................Scouting; fishing; hunting; western movies; reading
                        adventure stories
Edith F..................Painting; drawing; growing flowers
Betty G..................Reading fiction; roller skating; swimming; tennis;
                        collecting stamps; dancing
Dorothy G................Cooking; keeping house; movies
George H.................Reading science magazines; doing chemistry experi-
                        ments; tennis
Eugene J.................Making things out of wood; whittling, carving
Ralph L..................Camping; scouting; boating; reading outdoor
                        stories; football

In gathering data about children, you can often pick up valuable information when observing children in informal situations; as, for example, the playground, camp, and school excursions.[E]

Jean P. . . . . Dancing; movies; reading fiction
Tom R. . . . . Photography; collecting coins; reading science magazines
Jane S. . . . . Making dresses; cooking; movies
Leon S. . . . . Scouting; camping; basketball; baseball; golf
Dean S. . . . . Making model airplanes; scouting; reading adventure stories
Joan T. . . . . Reading girls' stories; movies
Antonia V. . . . . Movies
Mary Z. . . . . Scouting; swimming; movies

FOR DISCUSSION

1. Why did Miss Brown want this information?
2. Select a unit that you are likely to teach in the weeks ahead and show how you might utilize several of the special interests listed above.

With a little teamwork Miss Brown and two other teachers decided to pool the information they were able to obtain about the same pupils in their classes. To economize further on time and effort, they planned to divide between them the task of visiting the homes of a few pupils who had not been visited in recent semesters and to share their findings with each other. By the end of the second week, Miss Brown with the help of these other teachers was able to build the following table relating to the home conditions of nearly all the pupils in her second-period English class.

Home Conditions

Mother dead, pupil living with father...............Frank D.
Father dead, pupil living with mother...............Edith F.
Both parents dead, pupil living with grandparents.....Sally C.
Parents divorced, pupil living with father............Eugene J.
Parents divorced, pupil living with mother...........Bill A.
Unpleasant home, parents disagree.................Joan T., Leon S.
Unpleasant home, child is subject to parental nagging..Mary Z.
Parents in poor economic condition..................Dorothy G., Antonia V.
Parents overindulgent; child is overprotected........Tom R.
Satisfactory homes; pleasant atmosphere; good
    economic condition............................Betty G., Jean P.,
                                                    Alice B., George H.,
                                                    Ralph L., Phil F.

For Discussion

1. What are the desirable outcomes of visiting the homes of pupils other than a record of information about the homes?

2. What general cautions should be observed in meeting and visiting with parents in their homes?

3. What behavior might be expected of pupils from homes in which parents (*a*) are overprotective? (*b*) quarrel with each other? (*c*) show greater perference for another child? (*d*) keep nagging their children? (*e*) are too strict?

In the meantime Miss Brown was observing her pupils in class, in the lunchroom, and between classes. She kept anecdotal records of what seemed to her to be descriptions of significant behavior and revealing bits of conversation of several of her pupils. She checked the accuracy of her observations with those of other teachers. With these data she was able to compile tentatively the following table relating to the mental health of certain pupils in her second-period English class.

Poor Mental Health

Excessively shy........................Eugene J., Ada A.
Has periods of depression................Antonia V.
Feelings too easily hurt.................Sally C.
Inferiority complex.....................Ada A., Frank D., George H.
Has pronounced tendency to daydream.....Jack D., Dorothy G.
Constantly on the defensive.............Tom R.
Superiority complex....................Joan T.

1. What traits other than the ones listed above indicate poor mental health?
2. Pick out one of the characteristics in this list and describe the pattern of conversation and behavior that would convince you of the presence of that particular trait in a pupil.
3. Are there traits in this list that are more serious than others from a mental hygienist's point of view?
4. What conditions in a classroom may contribute to feelings of inferiority in pupils?

Miss Brown looked over the information she had accumulated and felt highly pleased with the results of her two weeks' effort in making an inventory of her pupils. She had found many sources that were yielding information about the adjustment, abilities, interests, mental and physical health, achievement, and home conditions of her pupils. But there was still much to be done. She wanted to visit the homes of more of her pupils. She planned a written assignment in which pupils would be asked to write about their future plans. There were still sources of data in the school and community to be looked into during the weeks ahead. For example, she wanted to consult two or three of the junior high-school teachers who had taught her pupils. From them she hoped to obtain more information about the personal traits of some pupils. She planned also to see the scoutmaster and the director of the local youth center. From these sources she hoped to supplement her information about the personal traits and social adjustment of her pupils.

Miss Brown's summary of her information about her class as a group showed that she had (1) a chart showing four measures of each pupil; (2) a sociogram; (3) several case studies developed by her fellow teachers in previous years; and (4) brief lists suggesting (*a*) disabilities in physical health, (*b*) special interests, (*c*) problems in home conditions, and (*d*) poor mental health. She was beginning to see the structure of her ninth-grade English class.

THE CASE STUDY

However, there were some special problem cases that had worried her these first two weeks and for which no further data would be available until other teachers of the class turned in their case studies. There was, for example, George Harris, whose excellent written

Top: A conference after school. Mary Brown, the teacher, manages to arrange for a visit to the home. *Center:* Some days later Ada takes part in a committee report. Again the outcome is failure. *Bottom:* Ada's teacher talks to her mother and gains considerable understanding. Learning how to get into all kinds of homes and knowing just what to do is not easy, but some teachers manage to do it.

work was in sharp contrast to his inability to answer a single question correctly in class.   Then, too, she felt that she had not yet come to grips with the case study that in faculty meeting she herself had agreed to do—the case of Ada.   Ada's work in class had not been at all satisfactory.   She obviously needed special attention.   So Miss Brown looked over the data she had already collected about Ada.

The results of Ada's intelligence and achievement tests suggested some puzzling questions.   Miss Brown was bothered by the fact that while Ada's intelligence ranked high in the class as a whole, her achievement in reading, spelling, and arithmetic was far below the average for the group.   Miss Brown looked over the other data she had brought together about Ada.   Ada was not in good shape physically.   She was excessively shy and seemed to be burdened with an inferiority complex.   She did not mix with other pupils.   "Here is a real case of maladjustment," thought Miss Brown, and she was determined to help her.

A day or so later Ada was a member of a group that had the responsibility of reporting to the class on the stories they had read. Ada appeared fidgety and uncomfortable as she sat with the group facing the class.   When it came time for her to report she appeared panic-stricken.   She began, but her voice was hardly audible. Then, suddenly, she choked and broke into tears.   Miss Brown suggested that she go to her seat and rest there while the others in the group continued with their reports.   After class Miss Brown asked Ada to stop by and see her later that afternoon.

Miss Brown's pleasant, informal manner that afternoon led Ada to talk quite freely about herself.   It seems that Ada was ashamed of her poor clothes and this fact accounted for her embarrassment before the class.   Ada talked, too, about the work she had to do in helping her mother around the house.   Finally, at the close of their conference, Miss Brown told Ada that she planned to visit her home the next week as one in a series of visits she was making to the homes of pupils.   They agreed on the hour of the visit.

A VISIT TO THE HOME

Late one afternoon the next week, Miss Brown appeared at Ada's home.   She was met at the door by Ada's mother, a heavy-set woman of about forty, who, like the shabby furnishings in her home, presented an unkempt, run-down appearance. True to Ada's description of her own responsibilities in the home, Miss Brown found Ada taking care of a younger baby sister.

Mrs. Adams took the lead in the conversation that followed and complained bitterly about all her troubles. She complained about her work, her husband, and life in general. Her husband, it seemed, was unable to hold down a job for any length of time. When she tried to make him toe the mark he would disappear for days. An older boy had just joined the Navy. In all the family woe, she pictured herself to Miss Brown as the innocent victim.

But Miss Brown's visit turned out to be far more valuable than she had anticipated. The baby's crying had interrupted the conversation momentarily and at that point Mrs. Adams had directed Ada to see what she could do to quiet the child. As Ada left to take the baby out of the room she brushed by one of the tables and upset a notebook with half a dozen drawings. Miss Brown noticed the drawings and picked them up. They revealed at a glance more than the usual artistic talent of a fifteen-year-old girl and upon inquiry, Miss Brown learned that Ada had drawn them.[1] As her mother put it, "She is always wasting her time on such foolishness." Later, as Miss Brown left the house, she delighted Ada by telling her that she liked her drawings. She mentioned that the art teacher might like to see them, too, and suggested that Ada bring her drawings with her to school the next day.

That evening Miss Brown compiled all the information she had about Ada and this is the picture she was able to develop.

PERSONAL RECORD OF ADA ADAMS

A. Intelligence. Chronological age: 15 years 5 months; mental age: 18 years 8 months; I.Q.: 121.

B. Standard Tests. Achievement tests show her retarded in reading, spelling, and arithmetic. Her grade classification in reading is 6.6, in arithmetic 5.5, and in spelling 6.0.

C. Pupil Load. She is taking English, social studies, general science, mathematics, and art. She has many duties at home; *e.g.*, takes care of her baby sister, washes dishes, makes beds.

[1] We can hear the excessively skeptical say, "Oh! This is Hollywood stuff and wasn't it lucky that Ada could draw!" The fact is that such fortuitous circumstances happen again and again when a *complete* study is made of a pupil. You have to believe that most people have something worth developing or your days of teaching will be drab.

D. General School Record. She is having trouble in English, science, social studies, and in mathematics. She likes art but is developing bad attitudes toward her other subjects.

E. Elementary School Record. Accumulated records in the office reveal very low marks made during the past six years. She was passed on "condition" into grades six, seven, and eight.

F. Physical Condition. Her general physical tone is low. She is underweight, suffers from malnourishment, and her teeth are in bad condition.

G. Attendance. She has been absent and tardy numerous times; *e.g.*, in the eighth grade she was absent a total of 40 days. She has changed schools four times in six years. The first three grades were spent in a one-teacher rural school.

H. Family Background and History. Neither parent completed the grades of the elementary school. Ada has an older brother who dropped out of school in the seventh grade. There is one other girl in the home besides Ada—a nine-months-old baby.

I. Home Conditions. Parents are in poor economic condition. The father is unable to hold down a job. The mother complains that she has too much work to do. The mother is too strict and nags too much at Ada.

J. Reading Interests. Her reading is confined to an occasional "Big-Little" book.

K. School Activities. Belongs to no clubs or other activities. Does not take part in group activities during the lunch hour. Ada seems happier when left alone. She takes part reluctantly in required activities in physical education.

L. Other Interests. Enjoys painting and drawing.

M. Social Relations. Is extremely self-conscious of her poor clothes and general appearance. She has no friends among the other pupils.

N. Special Abilities. Has considerable talent in art.

THE DIAGNOSIS

As Miss Brown looked over the data she had collected about Ada, she thought, "The whole picture is wrong for Ada. The main thing that is wrong is the home, and the parents are the key to that. What the father is like, I don't know; but the mother will certainly be difficult to deal with. More fundamental still is the lack of a sound economic basis for the home. There is no way the school can help in providing the father with a job that will support this family. But even if a job could be found for him the parents would not have the disposition or the training to provide a good home. It may be that Ada's personality can be built up in school so that she will 'break through.' Certainly it has been done for many youngsters, and our school should try."

Reviewing the data again, Miss Brown continued, "It seems to me the key to Ada's improvement may be art. She likes art and has some talent for it. Her work in art must be encouraged. Her other work must in some way be tied in with it. A program built around art may help her develop the confidence and self-respect which she needs. She likes me. Perhaps I can assume a broad guidance program for Ada in which the main goals are to enlist the cooperation of her other teachers and set up friendly relationships with other boys and girls. However, basic to her schoolwork is her disability in reading. We won't get very far with Ada until she learns how to read. To enlarge her reading interest, I must get her interested in reading something. I have to start where she is. Here is what I'll do," she thought, as she developed the following outline of a remedial program: "(1) build a remedial program around art; (2) obtain the cooperation of other teachers; (3) watch for situations in which Ada can be given recognition and praise in class; (4) help her develop friendly relationships with other boys and girls; (5) develop a reading interest around art; (6) encourage her to take art books home from the library; (7) help her get started in building a list of unfamiliar words based on her reading; (8) give practice exercises in locating the main idea of paragraphs; (9) give practice exercises in word recognition; (10) give practice exercises in answering fact questions; above all I must (11) build for confidence; I must not stigmatize her before the group by asking her to read something orally before I know she is ready to read that particular thing."

As Miss Brown looked again at the remedial program she had planned, she said to herself, "Here, I think, is a beginning. Will she come through?—I wonder!"

A Remedial Program

Miss Brown decided that her first task was to enlist the cooperation of Ada's other teachers. The next day she called on them, taking with her Ada's drawings.

Miss Clark, the art teacher, was understanding and cooperative. She suggested an attractive art book that Miss Brown might use for Ada's remedial reading work. Miss Davis, the science teacher, was pleased to learn that Ada could draw. She pointed out that a unit in plant life that the class was studying would give Ada a chance to draw flowers and to label their parts. Miss Davis agreed with Miss Brown that art might be a direct road to a better understanding of science.

Miss Brown was not as successful with Ada's other teachers. Mr. Bradford, who taught social studies, was a bit skeptical. He pointed out that a retarded reader like Ada was at a great disadvantage in the study of civics and government relations because of the amount of reading required. Mr. Henry, Ada's "math" teacher, was even more skeptical. He could see no relationship between art and mathematics. Furthermore, he pointed out that a diagnostic test which he had just given showed Ada to be markedly deficient in basic skills in mathematics. However, Miss Brown felt that her efforts with these teachers, although not completely successful, at least gave Ada a better than even chance in her subjects.

A day or so later during the supervised study period, Miss Brown gave Ada the art book which had been suggested by Miss Clark. She felt if only her reading could be improved her general level of achievement would be raised. Ada took a great interest in the pictures in the book and asked Miss Brown if she could take the book home with her. Although it was a slow, difficult task for her, she read all the stories connected with the pictures. Shortly thereafter she took another art book from the library, and with Miss Brown's help, Ada began building a list of unfamiliar words derived from her reading.

Miss Brown noticed during the weeks that followed that Ada's reading habits were improving. She still had a long way to go, but there was evidence that she was developing somewhat greater speed in reading and in comprehension. Her improvement in reading was reflected in her written work in which she had made some gains in spelling and sentence structure. Miss Brown was convinced that Ada was off to a good start in the remedial program that she had planned for her.

There was much to be desired, however, in Ada's social adjustment. She had made no friends, and it was obvious that she was suffering from a deep feeling of inferiority. Miss Brown continued to look for opportunities that would provide for Ada a feeling of success and of recognition. Such an opportunity came a few days later in connection with the reading the class was doing in Shakespeare's *Twelfth Night*.

Ada had voluntarily made a number of drawings from the characters of *Twelfth Night*. These she placed one morning on Miss Brown's desk before the period started. Here was the opportunity

Miss Brown had been looking for. Later in the period she used
Ada's drawings to illustrate a point she was making in connection
with the characters in the play. The response of the pupils to the
drawings was exactly that which Miss Brown hoped for. They liked
them and wanted to know where they came from. At that point
Miss Brown told the class that they were Ada's work and then she
asked Ada to pass them around so that all might see them.

That was an important day for Ada. At Miss Brown's suggestion, and with the obvious approval of the group, Ada arranged her
drawings on the bulletin board. The pupils regarded Ada with a
new interest after that and, in turn, Ada became a little more responsive to the friendliness of the group.

Shortly thereafter the class decided to present scenes from
Twelfth Night as a class project. Ada was placed on the costume
committee, and the group with which she was working arranged to
meet at the home of one of the other girls to finish their work.
Somehow Ada managed to get her mother's permission to meet with
the other girls.

Miss Brown heard the story later from Ada. It seems that the
girls on the committee had a pleasant afternoon working, stopping
for tea, and keeping up a steady stream of gossip. When it came
time to try on the costumes, one of the girls suggested that Ada's
hair, which had received little care heretofore, could be arranged to
make her look different. The new hairdo was becoming to her.
She looked more grown-up and far more attractive. It was a new
experience for Ada and she was thrilled by it all.

When Ada arrived home, Mrs. Adams was startled at the change
in her appearance. However, softened by her daughter's enthusiasm, she agreed to let her keep her hair as the girls had arranged it.
Then, moved further by a remark that Ada made about the old-
fashioned appearance of her clothes, Mrs. Adams agreed to make
over for her an old woolen skirt and to see what she could do to buy
Ada a sweater such as the other girls wore.

The new hairdo, the sweater, and the skirt did a lot for Ada.
She found herself acceptable to the other pupils, and for the first
time she began to feel the joy of companionship.

Miss Brown checked on Ada's work with her other teachers.
She had produced some excellent drawings in art. Her skill in art
was helping her in science. Her notebook in that subject was one

of the best in the class. Her work in civics reflected her improvement in reading. She was doing passing work in that subject. Mr. Henry, the mathematics teacher, continued to remain somewhat skeptical about Ada's chance for success in his class. However he pointed out that, although she was still weak in fundamental skills, he thought that with continued effort she might make up for her poor start.

Just before the end of the semester the committees made their final reports to the class on the status of the play project. Ada was called upon to report for the costume committee. She had designed the costumes and the girls on the committee insisted that the job of reporting was rightfully hers. Ada had no difficulty in presenting her report, although Miss Brown could not help recalling the panic that had seized her during her first attempts to speak in front of the class.

The day finally arrived that the class was to present scenes from *Twelfth Night*. There were guests from other classes and parents were also present. Ada had invited her mother but did not know whether, with her household duties and her baby, she would be able to come. Seated in the class with other pupils who were not taking part in the play, Ada looked anxiously as each person entered the room. She obviously wanted nothing so much as to have her mother surprise her and actually come. But she was bound to be disappointed.

Miss Brown remained at the rear of the room while the scenes from the play were presented. Standing there she was torn between the performance on the stage and the drama of Ada being enacted before her. With the help Miss Brown had given her, Ada had come a long way. But she still had far to go. There were deeper currents in Ada's life than Miss Brown could touch—currents that sprang from her environment as well as her heredity.

Ada will remain in Miss Brown's class a few more short months. What, then, will happen to her?

For Discussion

1. What remedial program would you suggest if Ada had had no special talent in art?

2. Are you convinced that Ada's teachers next year should glance very early at Ada's record? At the beginning of a new term you may have several pupils like Ada and the school may have a fairly good record for each.

Other Ways of Knowing More about Pupils

There are certain informal procedures that may be very helpful in knowing pupils. An autobiography, if it is a free narrative, is an approach with good possibilities. A second approach is the written composition on various topics; *e.g.*, "Reading That Appeals to Me," "The Movies I Like Best," "Courses I Wish Our School Would Offer," "What a Holiday Means to Me," "What I Should Like to Do if I Had an Automobile," and "What I Should Like to Be Ten Years from Now." A third device is the brief questionnaire, of which two samples[1] are submitted here.

Grade......   Age.......   Sex.....

WHAT I WOULD LIKE TO KNOW

There are very few, *if any*, people in the world who do not wish to know certain things. In school there are many ways suggested to learn things, but you may not have had the opportunity to receive the information you would like. Do not be afraid to write what is really on your mind. You *need not sign* this paper. Just expressing your ideas here may help you.

When you have finished writing, go back and *underline* the thing you would like most of all to know. Would you like to talk to someone about the information you desire? If so, whom would you like to consult, if possible?....................

A fourth approach is a rather detailed questionnaire of interests and needs, a sample of which is provided as Appendix C. We suggest that you look at it now for it may save you time some day. For example, the data collected by this questionnaire would be very helpful to you as a home-room teacher.

Additional approaches of an informal nature are systematic observation of reading and play activities, diaries, and interview blanks. The various approaches for knowing more about pupils as discussed in this section, with the exception, of course, of reading and play activities, should not be used during the period of student teaching. They are printed here for two purposes: (1) to call your attention to some important needs of high-school youngsters and (2) to make these instruments available to you in the future when you have won a substantial place in some school. When you get around to using the questionnaire, think through the detailed steps. Though many teachers have employed this instrument without

[1] Here I am indebted to Howard Y. McClusky and O. I. Frederick.

Grade...... Age....... Sex.......

WHAT ARE YOUR DIFFICULTIES?

If you are one of those persons who never have any serious personal troubles, you may be very fortunate. Most people worry about some things part of the time, and often face difficulties which they do not even care to tell their closest friends. We are asking you along with students in other cities to list your problems. From thousands of such answers it may be possible to find out what kinds of things most often bother high-school students.

Do not be afraid to write fully and freely whatever you wish for you are not to sign your name to this paper. The following questions may help you to think over the things that bother you:

1. What do you worry about, or always keep thinking about?
2. What troubles do you have at home or at school?
3. What are you afraid to discuss with your parents or friends?
4. When do you feel out of place, not knowing what to do or how to act?
5. What makes you unhappy in your everyday life?
6. What keeps you from being the person you would like to be?
7. Why can't you do the things you would like to do?

Things Which Trouble and Worry Me Are:

objections from anyone, tactless teachers sometimes administer questionnaires in such a manner that the experiences are not valuable for pupils and thus subject their schools to annoying criticism.

A Faculty Meeting Discusses Growth[1]

As chairman of the program committee, Alice Adams placed the following memorandum in the teachers' mailboxes:

Your program committee suggests that we discuss the following statements about child growth and development at our next faculty meeting.

1. Optimum intellectual growth (including school achievement) is an interaction between an inner growth potential of the pupil and an educational setting sagaciously directed to personal and social goals.

2. The job of a teacher is to assist the pupil in achieving social goals according to his basic pattern without forcing or deprivation.

3. School is not a good place for a pupil to be if the setting deprives him of such experiences as are essential to his growth pattern.

[1] To the supervising teacher: Don't overlook the very important outline on child growth and development provided as Appendix A. Be sure at this point to look at it with your student teachers. You will also find a paragraph which suggests how a beginning teacher may use the outline.

4. Two valid guides for selecting and managing curriculum experiences are: (*a*) the pupil's tendency to select nurture in terms of his growth needs and (*b*) his abilities to do tasks successfully and with satisfaction.

5. When under wise guidance pupils participate in the planning of school experience, their interests and proposals will seldom be trivial or whimsical.

6. Pupils at different stages of maturation will tend to select and certainly will thrive upon different experiences.

Here are four youngsters, each twelve years old, starting the seventh grade. No, this picture isn't misplaced. We just want you to remember that children have different needs.[L]

7. The work of every grade in the elementary school or in a subject in the high school should provide a variety of experiences at many levels of difficulty without uniform assignments and without uniform standards.

8. Fixed desks in straight rows, and exclusive use of recitation or question-and-answer method tend to foster an authoritarian or teacher-dominated situation; whereas an informal arrangement—face-to-face in a circle or semicircle in which pupils conduct themselves as members of an interactive group—provides practice in cooperative thinking and democratic action.

9. Pupils who have been retarded and failed constitute an excessive number among our truants, our delinquents, and our criminals.

10. Competitive practices and conventional marking schemes are not in harmony with the modern theory of growth patterns.

11. In the lives of many pupils, the gap between the normal growth pattern and the expectation of family and school is the devastating factor that causes frustration, despair, and rebellion.

12. The security of a pupil is undermined if he is subjected to (*a*) rejection by his classmates, (*b*) excessive and unfair criticism by the teacher, (*c*) failure on tasks beyond his ability, and (*d*) faulty classification in school.

A fairly accurate record of the faculty meeting follows:

ALICE ADAMS: I hope you have had time to give careful consideration to the twelve statements relating to growth. Perhaps I should confess that they are notes which I took in a course last summer. I am not sure that I fully understand them. Obviously there are two questions: (1) are they true? and (2) what are the implications for our school?

BILL TAYLOR: The idea is very simple. It is: *let nature take its course*. As a teacher or parent I can't do much good and I can't do much harm.

RUTH BELDING: I wasn't conscious after reading the first one. But I can't believe it is as simple as Bill suggests. If my parents had not gone into action, I probably would now be number 426783 in Jackson prison. I am convinced that teachers have to do something beyond functioning as glorified nursemaids.

TOM SELLERS: The suggestion is that children select nurture from their environment according to their growth needs. I believe my son, aged eleven months, would eat rat poison if we were so foolish as to let it lie in the path of his creeping.

MAY ALDEN: I wish someone would translate this jargon into simple English. I confess I don't get it. However, I do get the general impression that a very poor teacher would easily get by in a school operating with the growth concept. I visited a so-called progressive school last year. It took me 10 minutes to spot the teacher in the confusion, noise, and disorder. A good governess or nurse does not have to be too bright. Perhaps we can solve our teacher shortage by certifying persons who have I.Q.'s as low as 85.

ALICE ADAMS: Oh! I must protest! I didn't get the ideas that I am hearing today in my course on growth. Why it would take a supremely *fine* teacher to operate successfully with the growth concept. First of all, you would have to identify the basic pattern of each pupil. Then you would need to put into the environment of each pupil the particular nurture that his growth needs require. This means an *individual curriculum* for every last youngster in your room. Believe me, that would take a smart teacher and a well-trained teacher. I don't believe there is a person in this faculty that would be sure to identify all the future scientists or artists in his group, and be able to provide the appropriate nurture for each. And yet in an ideal school that is precisely what we ought to be able to do.

MARY BROWN: Alice, I think you are on the right track. My hobby is growing blueberries. Now a blueberry bush will select its nurture according to its growth need. No doubt about it! But you *try* growing a blueberry. You will have to know a blueberry when you see it, and surely you will have to know a lot about its nurture. For example, if your soil isn't sour, you had better go into action fast or your blueberries will soon look very sick. It never occurred to me as I read these statements about growth that a teacher's responsibility would be less or easier.

The task of teaching 25 children would be like growing 25 different varieties of garden plants. Why, I think one would have to be gifted and very skillful to make the growth idea click.

HENRY SOBOLESKI: I like what you are saying, Mary. It seemed to me that the class May described was not taught by a teacher who knew anything about the growth of children. She probably was just "messing around" without a plan. I am convinced that when pupils have a "real-for-sure" part in planning school experiences they can easily be guided so as not to waste time on the trivial. They can be taught to do cooperative thinking in the same way they learn to do lots of other things.

ELLEN QUINN: Ah—but let us be critical of *how* we guide when we teach cooperation. Someone has defined cooperation as "You coo, while I operate."

RUTH DOBSON: I agree. Alice asked us to suggest implications. Well, I think our school is still teacher-dominated. I know our finest students think so too. Nor will we solve our problem by merely ripping out the fixed desks and sitting in a circle.

ROBERT CLARK: That's right. Teaching cooperative thinking, or shall we say planning with pupils, is as hard to learn as teaching decimal fractions in the right way. I confess I am not good at either one.

ALICE ADAMS: I, too, have a long way to go. But I am convinced that we should move in that direction. The last statement hits our school hard. My guess is that about 40 per cent of our pupils feel insecure. The frustration caused by the gap between what they can do well and what we and their parents expect of them is devastating and is probably the cause of most of the undesirable behavior. I am convinced we should try harder to take interests, growth needs, or individual patterns more into account. I believe that a sustained effort in every classroom to provide more practice in cooperative thinking and planning would make this a better school.

No doubt you are confused as you compare the schools in which you have lived with the one that is suggested by the preceding discussion. Such a school would involve small classes, exceedingly fine teachers, and adequate materials. With regard to secondary schools you may not see many fully in accord with the growth concept in your times. The ideal is more applicable in the elementary grades for the reason that many pupils in the high school will want more system, organization, and rigor than is desirable in the earlier grades. Even so the implications of growth and development constitute a challenging ideal for all teachers from the preschool through the graduate division.

WORKING WITHIN THE GROWTH PATTERN

Referring to the growth of a child, Arnold Gesell says: "The total ground plan is beyond your control. It is too complex and mysterious to be altogether entrusted to human hands. So Nature takes over most of the task, and simply invites your assistance." Upon reading this statement you may get a feeling of futility. Perhaps you think that there is nothing you can really do as a teacher or a parent. That is far from true. You don't fly with an automobile, but there is a lot you can do to get maximum efficiency out of your car. For many pupils the gap between what they can do and what the family, the school, and the community expect is not only tragic but a deteriorating factor in the normal growth of personalities. It is futile for parents and teachers to fight the "ground plans." Rather it is wiser and more effective to work within the frame of reference that nature and nurture hand to you. This idea is convincingly stated in the poetic and philosophic quotation from *The Prophet:*[1]

> And a woman who held a babe against her bosom said, Speak to us of Children.
> And he said:
> Your children are not your children.
> They are the sons and daughters of Life's longing for itself.
> They come through you but not from you,
> And though they are with you yet they belong not to you.
> You may give them your love but not your thoughts,
> For they have their own thoughts.
> You may house their bodies but not their souls,
> For their souls dwell in the house of tomorrow, which you cannot visit, not even in your dreams.
> You may strive to be like them, but seek not to make them like you.
> For life goes not backward nor tarries with yesterday.
> You are the bows from which your children as living arrows are sent forth.
> The Archer sees the mark upon the path of the infinite, and He bends you with His might that His arrows may go swift and far.
> Let your bending in the Archer's hand be for gladness;
> For even as He loves the arrow that flies, so He loves also the bow that is stable.

SUMMARY

In this chapter we have (1) presented a vivid case study and (2) focused your attention on certain techniques that are widely used by successful practitioners in classrooms at both elementary-school and the high-school levels. The sound picture, "Learning to Understand Children, Part I—A Diagnostic Approach," has been geared

[1] KAHLIL GIBRAN. *The Prophet*, pp. 21-22, New York: Alfred A. Knopf, Inc., 1923.

to the objectives of this chapter. A second sound picture, "Learning to Understand Children, Part II—A Remedial Program," has been designed with the concepts of this chapter and of the next one in mind.

WRITTEN PROBLEMS

1. Select one pupil in your class who seems to be in need of special attention. Write a brief analysis covering such items as (*a*) classroom performance, (*b*) personality traits, (*c*) special disabilities, and (*d*) desirable factors on which to build. Include specific suggestions for a remedial program. Use a fictitious name for the pupil. Supply your supervising teacher with a copy of your analysis, but avoid the possibility of having notes, carelessly left, fall into the hands of pupils.

2. If possible,[1] secure from your supervising teacher at least one reading score for each pupil enrolled in your class. Construct a chart showing the distribution of scores by grade norms. This should appear in your professional log.[2]

3. If possible,[1] secure the intelligence scores for each pupil enrolled in your class and construct a chart showing the distribution as follows: pupils with I.Q.'s between 70 and 80; 80 and 90; 90 and 100; etc. This should appear in your professional log.

FOR DISCUSSION

1. What range would you expect in a seventh-grade class in reading? in intelligence? in chronological age? in ability to compute?

2. What is the meaning of the phrase "intelligence quotient"? What does it measure? To what extent is the I.Q. a valid basis for predicting school success? What is meant by the phrase "school-dull and life-bright"? What are some of the common errors that teachers make in dealing with information relating to I.Q.'s?

3. To what extent is reading a problem common to the various school subjects?

4. Do you favor telling a pupil his score on an intelligence test?

5. What type of parent is too strict with children, especially with regard to limitations of self-expression?

6. What information about the pupil should the school send the parents?

7. Among the practices that some schools employ to adapt high-school work to the individual differences of pupils are:

(1) Variation in the number of subjects a pupil may take.

(2) All subjects in the general curriculum are elective.

(3) Guiding a pupil into activities that are appropriate for him.

(4) Credit for work done outside of the school, as in music.

(5) Promoting a pupil more frequently than at the end of each semester.

(6) Having small groups undertake projects that supplement the work.

(7) Tutoring of slow or failing students.

(8) Assignments on several levels of difficulty.

(9) Homogeneous grouping.

---

[1] Do not undertake these problems unless the supervising teacher has the data available.

[2] It is of the utmost importance that fictitious names be used when recording scores in the professional log and on charts.

(10) Special classes for pupils who fail to do satisfactory work.

(11) Special classes for gifted pupils.

(12) Systematic study of problem cases.

(13) New units or courses especially adapted to very bright or dull pupils.

If possible, try to visit a high school that probably does a good job in adapting its work to the individual differences of students and report which of the preceding procedures or any other effective ones are employed by that school.

8. Have you seen a teacher who was excessively repelled or unduly attracted by certain pupil personalities? How do you propose to guard against this?

9. If you have seen the motion pictures that are geared to this textbook discuss the following:

(1) Was the initial unkind attitude toward Ada a matter of nature or nurture? Is intolerance taught or inherited? What types of students would invite Ada to join them the first day?

(2) Describe from your experience how a pupil's special interest or ability was used to motivate learning in several subjects.

(3) Evaluate: "All pupils need individual attention."

(4) What part does "a little success" play in your life? the growth of every personality?

(5) Cite from your experience a case of a pupil's growth in confidence.

(6) What place has dramatization in the development of a personality? Are there school subjects that cannot use dramatization?

(7) Summarize the essential steps in making a case study.

(8) What specifically did Miss Brown do in making an inventory of the human material that (a) would be difficult to do in some schools? (b) can be done in any school?

(9) What standardized tests can you name, other than those referred to in this chapter, that might be used in the grades of the junior and senior high school?

(10) What must precede the planning of a remedial program for a maladjusted pupil?

(11) What is the relationship between pupil adjustment and (a) teacher personality? (b) curriculum? (c) teaching methods and techniques? (d) intelligence?

SUGGESTED READINGS

Adolescence. Forty-third Yearbook of the National Society for the Study of Education. Chicago: University of Chicago Press, 1944.

    This yearbook is an extremely good report of recent studies that takes us one step nearer the scientific method in research dealing with child growth and development.

GESELL, ARNOLD, and FRANCES L. ILG: *The Child from Five to Ten.* New York: Harper & Brothers, 1946. Pp. xii + 475.

    This book provides the outcomes and interpretation of basic research in childhood and adolescence. Although it covers the span from five to ten years, it nevertheless throws much light on the teaching problems in secondary education.

Helping Teachers Understand Children. Washington: American Council on Education, 1945. Pp. xv + 468.

This book describes the behavior of children and provides guides for the collection and interpretation of data.   The beginning teacher will find the book hard to read.   Nevertheless if you persist you will find some useful needles in the haystack.   If you haven't much time you might try reading the summaries of the chapters first and then backtrack as sentences tempt you.

How Children Develop.   University School Series, No. 3.   Columbus, Ohio: Ohio State University, 1946.   Pp. 79.

This little pamphlet is a truly workmanlike job in evaluating the scientific literature in child growth and development, in classifying the findings in convenient categories, and in making constructive suggestions for appropriate modifications of school programs.   It is well written and includes some interesting illustrations done by a junior in the University School.   The document is packed with useful and up-to-date information.

KELIHER, ALICE V.:   *Life and Growth.*   New York: Appleton-Century-Crofts, Inc., 1938.   Pp. x + 245.

This is one of the recent outstanding books dealing with personal and social problems of young people.   It should definitely aid the beginning teacher to a better understanding of the human material in the classroom.

OLSON, WILLARD C.:   *Child Development.*   Boston: **D. C.** Heath and Company, 1949.   Pp. xiv + 417.

This book is certainly a "must" for teachers of young people.   The emphasis throughout is on early and middle childhood education; however, growth is continuous, and therefore, the basic principles of development are the concern of teachers of pupils in all age groups.   High-school teachers too need "to understand the many facets and interrelationships of factors in the growth of children."   We urge that you consult the table of contents from time to time and read the parts that have a bearing on your problems in student teaching.   The book is written by one of the outstanding professional educators of our times who is especially strong in the area of child growth and development.

Organizing the Elementary School for Living and Learning.   Association for Supervision and Curriculum Development, 1947 Yearbook.   Washington: National Education Association, 1947.   Pp. 211.

Opposite page 68 you will find the chart entitled "Child Growth and Development, Characteristics and Needs for Ages 5 to 16."   It is a good idea to keep it and to consult it when you study a pupil who is not well adjusted.

RASEY, MARIE I.:   *Toward Maturity.*   New York: Hinds, Hayden and Eldredge, 1947.   Pp. xii + 242.

This is something more than just another educational psychology.   It is educational psychology enlivened by a mass of exciting evidence on growth and development of "real-for-sure" youth strewn along the mental pathway down which the author guides his reader in a sure-footed manner.

Were We Guinea Pigs?   New York: Henry Holt and Company, Inc., 1938.   Pp. ix + 303.

This is a fascinating story written by the 55 members of the first graduating class of the University High School, Columbus, Ohio.

ZACHRY, CAROLINE B.:   *Personality Adjustments for School Children.*   New York: Charles Scribner's Sons, 1929.   Pp. xiii + 306.

The material in this book should prove of material assistance to any classroom teacher involved in elementary case work.   The book is based on actual experiences, is written informally, and offers concrete suggestions for those undertaking the investigation of pupil maladjustment.

TEXT-FILMS

The following McGraw-Hill Text-Film on Teacher Education has been correlated directly with Chaps. II and III. [The running time (min), whether it is silent (si), or sound (sd), and whether it is a motion picture (MP) or filmstrip (FS) are listed with each title throughout the book. All the motion pictures are 16 mm; filmstrips are 35 mm.]

Learning to Understand Children: Part I—A DIAGNOSTIC APPROACH (21min sd MP). A case study of an emotionally and socially maladjusted girl of fifteen. The film records the efforts of her English teacher, Mary Brown, to help her. Techniques for collecting data, such as observation of the child's behavior, study of her previous records, personal interviews, home visits, as well as their proper interpretation in diagnosis, and formulation of a plan for remedial measures are shown in detail. The techniques apply when diagnosing difficulties of many types of problem children.

A silent follow-up filmstrip provides provocative statements and significant questions superimposed over scenes from the motion picture; these frames motivate class discussion in a manner that results in clearer understanding of concepts and principles stemming from a wide variety of applications. The filmstrip is a convenient tool for systematic review and meaningful summary.

Top: Ada is fascinated by a book that touches her special interest. *Center:* With all the data bearing on the problem before her, and with no great confidence, teacher Mary Brown tries to find a solution. *Bottom:* Here she gets her first taste of recognition by her fellow students, and the personality grows.

Chapter III

The Role of the Classroom Teacher in the Total Guidance Program

I shall not make the dreams, the aspirations, the ambitions, the hopes of these strong, rested, restless, curious children all come true. But I shall wake in them new dreams, new visions of Canaans that each by effort may call his own, and arriving there find the joy of labor and success.

> "To better God's work!
> What audacity, and yet
> His will
> And my privilege."
> —THOMAS H. BRIGGS

CUTTING DOWN THE DRASTIC WASTE OF HUMAN RESOURCES

The waste of human materials is tragic. At least half of our people are limited by physical and mental deficiencies. But this figure does not include those in mental institutions, hospitals, and prisons. A shocking fraction of those who now sit in pleasant schoolrooms will some day be inmates of mental institutions. It is estimated that about eight million of our people have mental disorders to some degree. The figure for crime and delinquency is equally disquieting and incidentally this costs society in typical years at least six times as much as we spend for schools. Then, too, about 15 per cent of our adult population are in a mental concentration camp by virtue of the fact that they have not completed the fourth grade of schooling. The total of all these groups is a very high fraction of all our people. What most of them can achieve in the way of an abundant life is pitifully small. Spiritually they are doomed for the rest of their days to live in "scorched earth" areas. For them the phrase "a better world" is empty—though mercifully for many it is without meaning. The picture is truly depressing to all thoughtful persons.

In general it is too late to do much for wasted lives when they have become adults. The experts in all these fields agree that

63

crime, delinquency, mental deterioration, and the like, can be sharply
cut by better schools. The problem apparently calls for something more than merely good classroom instruction—important as
that is to mental health. It requires more personal attention to the
individual human being. Therefore many schools seek to provide
better guidance.

The Unifying Goal

But the guidance movement needs a unifying goal. Guidance
means different things to different persons. It means all things to
some evangelists for the movement in the sense that they take in so
much that guidance has for them come to be synonymous with all of
education.

The *crux of guidance is the conservation of human resources.* In
war years human beings as well as copper, tin, and paper rise sharply
in value. The truth of the matter is that human beings are equally
precious in the common walks of life in peacetimes. Each of us has
just one life to live and certainly it should be as pleasant for us and
as useful to others as possible. As teachers we have, in fact, a dual
responsibility. We need to see to it that the individual pupil
throughout his school days is in a setting conducive to his best development and we need to guide him to a way of life, and if possible, to
a competence so that in adulthood he can be reasonably adjusted as
a person and of some use to his fellowmen. As many an educator
knows, even in our better and larger high schools from 20 per cent to
40 per cent of the pupils enrolled may be badly adjusted and not
making normal progress on the road to a satisfying competency.
Therefore we are convinced that the conservation of human resources
should be the common objective of all guidance activities.

It follows that providing a fine guidance program is the most
important responsibility of a school—especially at the high-school
level. It is obviously futile to teach social studies, algebra, or any
subject in an efficient manner to a youngster if in the end he turns
out to be an unhappy and unadjusted person.

Why People Crack Up

There are many factors in modern life that increase the complexity of our social and personal problems; *e.g.*, the widening gap between our wants and the things we can have to satisfy these wants,

the decrease in the controls exercised by the church and the home, the caprice and fluctuations of economic instability accompanied by a sense of personal insecurity, and the nerve-shattering noises of our machine age. Presumably you realize the devastating effect of these social forces on growing personalities. Nevertheless we will take time out to comment briefly on two: (*a*) the gap between our wants and what we can have and (*b*) our environment of increasing noises.

THE WIDENING GAP

The gap between what we want and what we can have is rapidly widening because we are not able to increase the purchasing power of the masses to keep pace with their wants, which, though already great, are constantly being stimulated by the movies, the radio, the school, and the press. The increased numbers of wants and wishes have made greater demands on the adjustment of the individual. The modern man has desires for clothes, food, travel, shelter, culture, education, etc., which his ancestors never experienced. The wish life of the individual is therefore bombarded with greater intensity and variety of stimuli than man has ever known.

Clearly, the masses in cities at least are going to be very restless as the gap between *wants* and *things* widens. Neither is it to be assumed that this widening gap is altogether a bad thing for society or for the individual. But its existence should be recognized if we are to deal intelligently with the situation.

The vast gap between our wants and our ability to satisfy them is widening, but let us not deceive ourselves that the people are going to be satisfied to return to the simple life of their pioneer fathers. If they were willing to do so, many who are today classified as below the "mere subsistence level" might consider themselves as reveling in the greatest luxury. The poverty line is a psychological one. You are desperately poor if you think you are. Poverty is the inability to buy the things which the standards of the group require.

OUR INCREASING NOISES

Another source of added strain on the modern man and woman is the growing number of mechanical and physical stimuli. Our machine age makes a great noise. The roar of traffic, the drone of the airplane, the blare of the radio, the ring of the telephone, the clatter of the typewriter, the bustle of sheer proximity combine to surround us with an environment of noise which our ancestors never knew in the silence of their rural life. And there is good scientific evidence to demonstrate that the human organism pays a heavy tribute of energy to the great and ever-present tyrant of noise. Thus another level of vitality is drawn off from man's reserve of nervous energy.

Human nature possesses an admirable capacity for adjusting to changing circumstances, but even human nature has its limits of flexibility and endurance. It is becoming more and more clear that if our civilization increases in strain and complexity there must be some effort made to enable people to withstand greater punishment from life. Techniques of constructive diversion, recreation, renewal, facing reality, relaxation, integration of purposes, reduction of conflicts, must be developed and transmitted through our educational system. All of this argument therefore points to the necessity for a type of guidance program that will enable people to develop a realistic and creative ethic for modern life, and for a type of mental-hygiene program that will enable people to live on a higher level of personal vitality and adjustment. Our life of increasing complexity and strain is making a great demand on the individual; the school is forced to aid him to meet this greater challenge of modern existence.

The Enduring Truths about Man

The intricacy of shifting social habits has blurred the line between right and wrong, and where the line is clearly drawn the social conscience has not kept pace with the realities of our complex life. The question of personal and social ethics is no longer a simple matter. Character education and good citizenship are not merely a matter of the inculcation of generally accepted virtues, but a problem of defining what those virtues mean in our complex social and economic life.

What a guidance program intelligently conceived and implemented might achieve is suggested in the following quotation:[1]

All over the world, but most particularly in the countries where civilization is supposed to be most advanced, there are collected in great cities huge masses of

[1] From a syndicated article by Walter Lippmann appearing in the public press under date of Nov. 3, 1938. Article copyrighted by New York Tribune, Inc. Note that this inspired statement was written *before* the Second World War.

people who have lost their roots in the earth beneath them and their knowledge of the fixed stars in the heavens above them. They are crowds that drift with all the winds that blow, and are caught up at last in the great hurricanes.

They are the people who eat but no longer know how their food is grown, who work and no longer see what they help to produce, who hear all the latest news and all the latest opinions but have no philosophy by which they can distinguish the true from the false, the credible from the incredible, the good from the bad.

Is it surprising that as civilization has become more streamlined, democracy has become more unworkable? For these masses without roots, these crowds without convictions, are the spiritual proletariat of the modern age, and the eruption of their volcanic and hysterical energy is the revolution that is shaking the world. They are the chaos in which the new Caesars are born.

No one need delude himself into thinking that there is a quick and easy remedy at hand, or that one will be found until enough men have mustered up the courage to see the malady without flinching. But we can perhaps discern, though dimly as yet, the direction in which we must go.

We can do this by recovering and remembering the enduring truths about man and his relations with other men, and about the government of men, which in the modern age we have been too sophisticated, too restless, too remote from reality and too uneducated to comprehend.

Thus it is always true that if the forces of the law are not indisputably stronger than all other forces, the law will perish. It is always true that a society is dissolving in which the privileges of the few are greater than their services, in which the rights of the many are greater than their duties.

It is always true that men must earn their living in the sweat of their brows, and that there is no streamlined substitute for this perennial necessity.

It is always true that the object of policy within a state must be to protect individuals and natural communities in the property on which and by which they earn their living, and thus to attach them to the state not by commands and doles and slogans but by their immediate and self-respecting interest.

It is always true that the accumulation of property is an evil whether it be in the hands of a plutocracy or of a socialist or fascist state. For it is always true that the arrival of masses without property will in the end destroy a civilization.

It is always true that a society of free men is a society of men with secure and sufficient property. It is always true that individuals cannot be free if their community is not independent. It is always true that independence has to be maintained by the willingness to fight and die for it.

And finally, it is true that men will not have the will to live or the courage to die if they have ceased to believe that they are in communion with things that transcend entirely their personal affairs.

Are these truisms? Or are these truths, enduring truths, that modern men have forgotten, have rejected, and have violated to their own confusion and despair?

It is not the fashion to believe that there are truths, like these, which are indeed fundamental and universal. For the modern man has persuaded himself that nothing is really true, and that all truths are just the convenient opinions of a class or of a nation at a particular moment.

But this disbelief in the existence of a central tradition of human wisdom is the philosophy of the spiritual proletariat. This feeling, which pervades the great urban centers, that all things are relative and impermanent and of no real importance, is merely the reflection of their own separation from the elementary experiences of humanity.

And the bitter, frustrated, and aimless skepticism of the modern man is itself the consequence of the modern disease of which he is the victim.

The Ceiling Is Low

At this point it is natural for you to ask: "Is there anything definite that a teacher or even a school can do in order that the citizen will remember 'the enduring truths about man and his relation with other men,' and how great is my responsibility for guidance as a classroom teacher?" The answer is that time and again the classroom teacher is in the best position to do what needs to be done for a particular youngster. That teacher knows most about him and is closest to him.

However, it is sensible for you to be realistic. The ceiling with regard to what you can achieve in guidance in most schools is still very low. Before we consider practical steps for the classroom teacher, we will do well to look at some conditions that prevent many schools from doing a good job in guidance. Good schools in recent years have been moving toward certain policies that tend to correct the following weaknesses:

1. *Schools need a more comprehensive accumulating record of each pupil.* Of course the best source of information for guidance purposes is the student himself. However, there are factual data not easily obtained by every teacher which often explain why a pupil thinks, feels, and acts as he does. Certainly it is wasteful of time and effort for each teacher to have to discover these facts for himself. Often one teacher knows a fact about a pupil that could be used as an approach by his other teachers if only they knew it. Such facts should be made available in the permanent record. The permanent folder should include a card for recording a good many items—vital statistics, test scores, work experiences, hobbies, interests, sports, education, activities in which the student can exhibit a fine quality of achievement, etc. The folder should also include episodes, especially those from which constructive leads to counselors may stem. Each teacher should feel it his responsibility to do his bit to build up the record of the student.

Finally, it is suggested that from time to time, perhaps once a year, someone must go through the record to discard useless material and to systematize the remainder. The record should be located where it is available to those who need it—classroom teachers, home-room teachers, counselors, and administrators.

A specialist with training in guidance can often be of help to a classroom teacher on problem cases. It may take many forms, as for example, administering a test for which the teacher does not have the time, or interpreting the total picture.[M]

√2. *We must make wider use of tests.* One finds large high schools that have never given a single standardized test—not even in reading, mathematics, or intelligence. The common explanation for not giving standardized tests is that the testing program costs money. If, however, we spend $125 or more per year for the education of a pupil, we should be willing to spend at least one dollar to evaluate in so far as we can what we are doing for him.

We do not mean to suggest that each school embark on an elaborate and costly program. Rather we should hope that more and more teachers will wish to give a good test not as an event but in stride as an important part of the work of some hour, with the emphasis on instructional values.   More than this we should be disposed to place an important test paper in the permanent folder or at least enter the score on the permanent card.   We are convinced that a guidance program to the greatest possible extent needs to operate with factual data.

✓ *3. Schools do not provide enough persons with special technical training to assist classroom teachers with guidance problems.*   The staff of a school should include at least one person professionally trained in guidance procedures.

The guidance specialist should provide in-service training to classroom and home-room teachers.   He should be responsible for keeping the staff informed as to the latest developments in guidance techniques and make certain as far as possible that these are applied. He should be of help to classroom teachers on problem cases that present unusual difficulty.   Above all he should coordinate the efforts of all the teachers on such problems.

✓ *4. Too many schools fail to provide an opportunity for each pupil to receive personal counseling.*   As numerous investigations have shown, in the typical school there are many unhappy pupils who are taking the wrong courses.   They have no challenging plans for their lives; they worry about things; they are convinced that they do not belong; they feel that they have no one with whom they can talk out their troubles; they think that they are moving on an impersonal assembly line of mass production.   This situation is wasteful of precious human material.   In all probability this is the pool from which many of our delinquents, our criminals, and our inmates of mental institutions are drawn.   As such their keep will cost society many times what a good guidance program would cost.

What practical measures can we take that will tend to provide some one who can help the individual student with his personal problems?   The main suggestion is that the school must somehow or other be broken into smaller units with some one responsible for (1) knowing a great deal about each student in his group; (2) seeing to it that other teachers share valuable items of information; and (3) providing personal guidance to each student in his group who may want it.

Some schools solve this problem through the home-room organization.   At least one high school with more than 300 pupils so far as is known, has had only one graduate in jail and that only for one night's detention, in twenty-four years. The home room has in addition to the above specifications the very important element of continuity—a teacher who is adjusted to the group may continue to work for four or perhaps even six years with the same small group. It is probably safe to say that a school which cannot make a home-room organization work, will probably not succeed with any other plan for guidance.

One of the alternatives to a home-room organization is the "core-curriculum." The basic idea is the reorganization of the curriculum so as to provide better general education for all pupils. However, one of the main reasons why the "core-curriculum" is popular with some of our best teachers is the possibility of providing for more and perhaps better guidance. The most common form of the "core" is to teach a correlation of English, social studies, and something of the arts in a double period. Thus a teacher of the "core" is more likely to deal with fewer personalities in an informal workroom setting over a longer period of time. Therefore, other things being equal, more and better guidance can be provided. It is perhaps needless to point out that a "core-curriculum" cannot be a success without gifted teachers.

✓ 5. *In many schools there is still an inflexible pattern of curriculum requirements.* Thus many pupils may be very unhappy in required subjects and have little chance to elect courses where their unusual talents might be nurtured. The fact is that teachers in high school waste time teaching things to pupils that they cannot learn and do not need.

A good school manages by a little adjustment here and there to design a curriculum for each child. Of course the pupil would still work in various groups. This individual program must concern itself not only with all that happens to the pupil in school, but also with the forces that act on him outside. In the lives of most children there are four important factors—school, home, church, and gang—that somehow must be brought to work in harmony for the normal development of the individual child. In some schools the home-room teacher of a small group which normally progresses together for six years is the effective agent for integrating these factors into a sensible program of guidance. However, even the best of schools finds it difficult to design an individual curriculum for every pupil for the reason that many pupils do not seem to know what they can do or want to do.   So school people talk about the *exploratory function* of a school.

The exploratory function by which a pupil may gain self-discovery is important at several levels and particularly in the junior high school.   But it is not clear that it is best achieved by offering the inexperienced pupil a bewildering array of options.   As the philosophic Mrs. Wiggs of the Cabbage Patch says, "Them that's never et turkey don't know how good it is."   Some schools attempt to secure exploration within the school subjects.   For example, in science, social studies, mathematics, etc., the introductory courses for grades seven, eight, and to some extent for grade nine, are *general* in nature, often consisting of sampling units which initiate the pupil in the simple and significant principles of these fields, at the same time offering him a great variety of experiences.   A single subject, if taught well in all its broad relationships, may go a long way toward meeting the curriculum needs of a considerable number of children.   Indeed, even an extracurricular activity may, to a large extent, provide a desirable curriculum for the individual pupil.

Practical Suggestions for Classroom Teachers

It is not the responsibility of a new—certainly not of a beginning —teacher to attempt to reform in militant fashion the guidance program existing in a school.   It is better to see what can be done here and now in a sensible and in a constructive fashion.   Usually far more can be achieved than at first seems possible.   If what you try to do in your area is well considered and demonstrably good, you may safely assume that you will have a surprising amount of support—in the staff, in the student body, and in the community.   To aid you in such efforts we make the following specific suggestions:

1. *Be sure that you use all the data available*.   As you begin your work in a school it may appear that there is no way for you to get information about your pupils from others.   However, inquiry may reveal an amazing amount kept in various places in the building. Even in a small school there may be a permanent folder or card for each pupil.

Then, too, there are schools that build up good records of students but unfortunately teachers do not consult them.   Keeping a permanent record and making proper use of it are two very different things. We give too many tests that are filed and never used in the classrooms to guide instruction. Many teachers find it practical to keep a folder for each pupil, containing important tests and samples of written work, in the classroom. To be sure, there may not be an elegant steel file, but the teacher's desk is usually adequate for the purpose.

Small group counseling can be effective when a common problem, not highly personal, is involved.[L]

✓ 2. *Make objective use of data.* To a curious extent, teachers hold the belief that the pupil should each semester or each year "start over" lest the teacher be prejudiced by low marks, low test scores, low intelligence quotient, or black marks of behavior episodes. A teacher who cannot deal without prejudice with all the facts obtainable before him is not likely to deal intelligently without them. One must plan the school experiences of a pupil on the basis of individual record, observations of behavior, test results, and so on, objectively, much as a physician plans for his patient on the basis of clinical records.

3. *When interpreting data keep in mind the attitude of the social worker and the mental hygienist.*   The general attitude toward behavior problems of the teacher with only traditional training is likely to represent a point of view different from that of the hygienist and the social worker.   According to the best evidence we have, teachers are likely to emphasize as of maximum importance behavior problems which trained psychiatrists consider of relatively little importance.   The teacher views the product and the effect of the classroom situation here and now, whereas the mental hygienist considers the future.   In Wickman's study[1] (see opposite page) the teachers rated transgressions against authority, dishonesty, immoralities, violation of rules, lack of orderliness in the classroom, and lack of application to schoolwork as serious behavior problems.   In contrast, a group of mental hygienists placed the preceding items low in the scale.   They rated as serious the withdrawing, recessive personality and behavior traits; they rated fairly high cruelty, temper tantrums, and truancy.   All of these were rated rather low by the teachers.   To the teacher profanity, smoking, lack of interest in work, disobedience, defiance, and obscene notes and talk are all very grave offenses, whereas such items as excessive suspiciousness, dreaminess, being overcritical of others, sensitiveness, and shyness, which may be overlooked by the teacher, are regarded as danger signals for trouble ahead in the opinion of the psychiatrist.

We should not be excessively critical of the classroom teacher's point of view.   He usually has to plan the work of the day for a large group of pupils.   After all, it is a bit unreasonable to expect him to be unconcerned when a single pupil selfishly wrecks the plans which the teacher has spent hours in making for the good of the group.   The teacher is constantly faced with the possibility of incidents that may seriously disrupt morale, though not involving serious behavior problems; while the psychiatrist is concerned mainly with the problem cases.

The practical implication for your work as a classroom teacher is that valid procedures will involve the techniques and point of view of both groups.   Above all do not lose sight of the remote goals relating to the development of personality while maintaining order in which the work of the school can be done.

[1] E. K. WICKMAN.   *Children's Behavior and Teachers' Attitudes*, pp. 124–125, 136, New York: Commonwealth Fund, 1928.

RATING SCALE[1]

Slight consequence 4.5	Considerable difficulty 12.5	Extremely grave problem 20.5

Type of problem	Teachers' av. score	Mental hygienists' av. score
Heterosexual activity	17.3	9.9
Stealing	17.0	12.5
Masturbation	16.7	6.4
Obscene notes, talk	16.6	8.8
Untruthfulness	15.8	10.3
Truancy	15.6	10.3
Impertinence, defiance	15.0	7.1
Cruelty, bullying	14.8	13.5
Cheating	14.7	10.3
Destroying school materials	14.3	5.1
Disobedience	14.1	6.4
Unreliableness	13.9	10.4
Temper tantrums	13.0	11.7
Lack of interest in work	12.8	9.6
Profanity	12.3	2.9
Impudence, rudeness	12.2	7.6
Laziness	12.2	7.2
Smoking	12.0	2.3
Enuresis	11.8	9.2
Nervousness	11.7	11.3
Disorderliness in class	11.7	3.4
Unhappy, depressed	11.5	16.2
Easily discouraged	11.5	13.4
Selfishness	11.3	11.8
Carelessness in work	11.3	7.1
Inattention	11.2	7.3
Quarrelsomeness	11.1	8.3
Suggestible	11.0	13.3
Resentfulness	10.8	14.1
Tardiness	10.5	5.6
Physical coward	10.4	12.0
Stubbornness	10.3	10.9
Domineering	10.3	13.0
Slovenly in appearance	10.1	7.2
Sullenness	9.9	12.6
Fearfulness	9.7	14.0
Suspiciousness	9.1	16.4
Thoughtlessness	8.7	6.8
Attracting attention	8.5	8.5
Unsocialness	8.3	17.3
Dreaminess	8.3	11.3
Imaginative lying	8.1	7.5
Interrupting	8.0	2.8
Inquisitiveness	8.0	5.3
Overcritical of others	7.9	13.2
Tattling	7.5	8.8
Whispering	7.5	0.8
Sensitiveness	7.0	13.1
Restlessness	6.9	6.4
Shyness	5.4	12.5

[1] Quoted from E. K. Wickman's study, *Children's Behavior and Teachers' Attitudes.*

Children's Behavior and Teacher's Attitudes

The preceding table is quoted from Wickman's study in which 30 clinicians—social workers, psychiatrists, and mental hygienists—and 511 teachers rated the various items. On what issues is the disagreement between teachers and social workers most pronounced? How do you explain such disagreements? Do teachers make issues of too many things?

✓ 4. *You can do a good job orienting pupils to your courses.* Too often the teacher is completely convinced concerning the values of the course he is teaching but never does he stop at the beginning of the course to create in the student this admirable zeal for the task. Seldom do we take the time and effort to show the entering student what kind of courses he is undertaking.

Orientation is an important step when beginning a new unit of work. Effective techniques for this purpose are available. For example, at the beginning of a unit of work, a brief period may well be taken to show the student what values he will get, what abilities are needed or improved, and the main activities of the unit. Some teachers display posters, cartoons, and work of former students on the bulletin board in a manner that creates zest for the new unit. Of course this isn't new in pedagogy. In the long ago it was standard practice to start a unit of work by a general overview of things to come. We seem to have forgotten that establishing the right attitude toward a task is important and that this doesn't just happen without the teacher's planning to bring it about.

✓ 5. *You can capitalize on vocational interests.* Vocational guidance is only a part—for many students an unimportant part—of the total guidance program. Then, too, many persons do not make vocational choices early in life—nor is there a convincing reason why they should. Nevertheless, there are youngsters who have special vocational talents and interests. Moreover, some pupils may discover their special aptitudes if information about a goodly number of vocations is made available.

It is helpful for a classroom teacher to keep a file of his pupils who have vocational interests. Surely it is sensible to capitalize on talents and interests through special assignment—projects, investigations, excursions, reports, etc. This can be done—in fact it is done—by teachers of every subject.

The main goal of a total guidance program of a school is the conservation of human resources.[M]

✓ 6. *You can protect youth against excessive pessimism.* We are much too close to the effects of the war to have a true perspective. It may be that this very age is the period of great opportunities for self-expression and service. For example, there is no reason why anyone should sit down discouraged and weep sentimental tears over the fact that frontier lands are no longer available for discovery. All that a brilliant boy needs to do today is to go to a chemistry laboratory, devise ways and means of doubling the production of an acre, and he will have discovered an acre of ground in a far more comfortable way than his grandfather ever did by the wearying and dangerous trek across the desert plains. Instead of being limited to the opporunities of a small community, the young man or woman nowadays has vocational information over a wide range of territory from which occasionally opportunities emerge. Youth should always keep in mind the fact that the individual person is looking for only one opportunity. The individual youth of merit need not lie awake at night and worry about his own welfare. It is only when we become socially minded and concern ourselves with *all* youth that we strike our depressing problems.

✓7. *You can respect the personality of each pupil.*   This calls for a sincere appreciation of the potential value of the person.   As has been suggested in Chapter II, it demands an unshakable faith that a human being will behave in the right way and grow up to something worth while if only conditions for desirable growth exist.   The teacher's respect for the pupil's personality meets the acid test when the teacher deals with a controversial issue.   The gifted teacher when starting a new unit involving a controversial issue will make clear that while the class may not arrive at a correct solution—perhaps no one in Washington or at the state university knows the answer—every student can achieve the main goal, which is to learn how to work congenially and cooperatively with persons who have very different opinions and convictions.

✓8. *You can establish a mental climate in your classroom that makes it a good place for youth to be.*   Some teachers did a grand job in the days of the depression in the early thirties when perhaps 80 per cent of their pupils came from homes that had inadequate economic support.   In those years the classroom was the only place where some children could find warmth and cheerful companionship.   Again teachers rendered a great service in the war years when the atmosphere in homes was depressed by fear and sorrow.

It is a great mistake for a teacher to fail to realize the many things that cast shadows over the lives of children in normal times.   To suggest only a few, a family may be disorganized by illness, death, or divorce.   Perhaps the most common hazard is lack of economic support.   Even in prosperous times at least half of our families have no margin of economic security.   To the child in the home this can be, and often is, a frightening and therefore a frustrating force.   Investigations provide convincing evidence that poverty is a strong factor not only in such matters as delinquency but also in academic achievement.   The enrollment of classes limited to the dull or slow-learning would be greatly reduced if all the homes represented had adequate incomes.

Then, too, many schools do not offer escape from noise and haste.   Throughout the wearying day children hurry from one hectic situation to another.   The sagacious teacher tries to establish a relaxed atmosphere, a workroom situation where a pupil has at least a chance to work in his optimum rate without undue pressure.   The fact is that far too many people are "cracking up."   While it isn't likely that the school is a causal factor in very many cases, it is nevertheless reasonable to believe that the classroom teacher can provide a situation of good mental hygiene to cut down the incidence of mental deterioration.

Obviously you will not be able to operate with the mental hygiene approach unless you yourself have sound mental health. Whatever the great schoolman, Angelo Patri, says is important and interesting. Therefore note carefully the following quotation:[1]

One of the first requirements of a good teacher is sound mental health. It is not easy to define mental health if there is any doubt of its being perfect. If it is imperfect, there is no doubt about its effect on the people whom it touches. Putting the finger on the difficulty is very, very hard to do with accuracy. But we know sound mental health when we meet it.

The teacher who is in sound mental health can laugh, easily and often. There is no tension anywhere in her body. She swings along easily, a light step, a shining, happy look in her eyes. She takes the mishaps, the annoyances that are daily occurrences in the life of any teacher, with a smile and a shrug and says, "Well, well, tomorrow is another day. We'll begin again tomorrow."

The healthy-minded teacher never bears a grudge. When there is something going wrong, she goes directly to the source and says, "How come? What's to do here? Tell me about it," and—if necessary—speaks clearly, even sharply, what is in her mind, a free clear mind. Once having done so, the matter is settled, as far as she is concerned. She is not going to brood over wrongs, real or fancied.

Nor does the healthy-minded teacher lose her self-control in moments of stress. The usual classroom teacher has hours of such stress, which is the reason why she is not able to lead parents' meetings, sing in the choir, put on a play, and preside at the Young People's Meeting after school hours. But with sound good sense she says, "I'm sorry but my time is fully taken up," and goes her way with a clear conscience—which means with a sound mental outlook.

One of the causes for teachers' mental breakdown is fear—fear of this and that sort of authority that may, if she makes a mistake, punish her with loss of position and salary. This fear can and should be lifted. It is dangerous to the teachers' health, to the success of the school. Supervisors have a great influence over this fear situation. It becomes their duty to study each teacher, learn how to deal with her, and him, so as to not only preserve mental health but to inspire it. Considering that this is one of the topmost requirements of education, it is well worth any supervisor's time and energy to make it his first aim.

9. *You can help your pupils adjust to an imperfect world.* A sound program of mental hygiene suggests that children should not worry too much, or for too long a period of time, over issues for which immediate action by them is not possible. There are

[1] ANGELO PATRI. "Good Teacher Needs Sound Mental Health," Syndicated column, *Ann Arbor News*, Feb. 5, 1948.

Top: Ada has come a long way. She has become acceptable to the group, and there is convincing evidence of the growth of a personality. *Center:* Under the stern exterior, calloused by the hard blows of life, Mother has a warm spot in her heart for Ada. *Bottom:* There may still be trouble ahead, but there is now the suggestion of better adjustment and confident strength.

teachers who argue that their children should not be distressed by the cares and problems of a wicked and disorganized world. Such teachers would provide in the school a temporary refuge from reality. When we consider the fact that most young people now spend from twelve to fifteen years of their lives in school, and that this period is a very large fraction of a total life span, there may be much to be said in favor of a school which will deliberately avoid the task of preparing for life as it is, and provide instead a haven of security. The discerning teacher, perhaps, can avoid the evil in both extremes by devising and illustrating the principles which he wishes to drive home, in situations that are immediate and for which some practical action by the pupil is possible. Shall the members of a school group, for instance, engage in a lottery to pull an organization out of financial trouble? This question children may well debate and decide, for it illustrates a principle that has application to the larger social unit.

Psychology suggests that it is undesirable to stimulate an impulse for which there is no possible immediate outlet in action. Teachers, in a worthy effort to be realistic, may in the end merely recall again and again to the pupil's mind something that had better be forgotten, *e.g.*, the lugubrious tale that is being constantly harped at home, of how Dad lost his money. To teach all the facts relating to the plight of an oppressed people in a remote country would seem to be the clear duty of any teacher dealing with this topic. However, it is well to remember that the typical pupil in our classes cannot do anything about this situation for many a day, and that the emotional indignation involved may not make for mental health, particularly if the pupil is the idealistic type. Far better it would be to motivate him to try to make democracy work in his own home, his school, and his community. The forces tending toward the disintegration of personality are subtle and elusive, as any observing teacher can testify who has noted the struggle which some of his finest pupils have made in an effort to span the gap between their ingenuous idealisms and an imperfect world. Still another illustration is provided in the programs for youth congresses which may sometimes set goals so remote that the net result is a feeling of futility, at the very time when youth should be rolling up its sleeves and going to work to create a better world, with something of the courage and industry that characterized its pioneer ancestors.

10. *You can strive without preaching or moralizing to make an increasing number of pupils socially minded.* Those who in the near future will exercise control in industry, labor, business, and government are now in our schools. They will aid or obstruct the solution of the fundamental problem of combining social responsibility with the possession or control of economic goods. Their contributions will depend largely on the degree to which selfish motives are discarded and social attitudes are inculcated. Alert students of the American scene have pointed out again and again that selfishness is the root of most of our troubles. The school has its share of responsibility for fixing the right social attitudes in our future leaders.

By this time you are probably thinking, "Can the school do this job?" There are at least two partial solutions to the problem of bringing about a change of social thought so that a position of power will be considered an opportunity for a social service; and both of these solutions rest largely on the schools. First, we can build the right attitudes so that more of our future leaders of labor, agriculture, industry, etc., will strive for the higher satisfactions that come through a life of devotion to the public welfare. This suggestion is admittedly idealistic, and probably we can never rely on it wholly; but every effort in this direction will yield valuable returns. Second, the school can increase the number of persons who will vote with understanding, in order that whatever control will be necessary may be secured in the democratic way, without violence, and with enough speed to avoid the devastating effect of an accumulation of unsolved social problems.

SUMMARY

In this chapter we have (1) listed some weaknesses in our school that need to be corrected before a classroom teacher can play a truly effective role in the total guidance program of a school and (2) made some practical suggestions of some things any classroom teacher can do even under adverse conditions. The motion picture entitled "Learning to Understand Children, Part II—A Remedial Program" was produced to help you understand the objectives of this chapter.

FOR DISCUSSION

1. Assume that (1) you are a home-room teacher, (2) a pupil is transferred to your group, and (3) the office can provide you with only three facts besides his name and grade. What three facts would you like?

2. Mention two specific types of help that each classroom teacher should give a new pupil in the school.

3. What relation do you see between a special interest or ability of a pupil and the growth of his personality?

4. What are some of the most common disabilities of mental health that affect schoolwork?

5. Joan Roche, a teacher in the Glendale schools, carefully filed a list of pupil failures. She finds that many of the failures can be classified under the following causes:

Attitude	Performance	Ability and Health
Disorder in class	Poor study habits	Lack of ability
Failure to pay attention in class	Careless mistakes in exact work	Immaturity
Lack of interest in subject	Lack of necessary books, tools, etc.	Poor health
Laziness	Poor work in tests	Poor eyesight
Feeling of inferiority	Failure to make up work	Poor hearing
Fear in examinations	Poor background	
Failure of home to cooperate		
Too many outside interests		
Unexcused absences		

a. Which of the many items listed above are merely symptomatic of a deeper cause?

b. Why do you think there are no items in this table like the following: (1) vocabulary or textbook too difficult, (2) teacher not prepared in the subject, (3) teacher not really interested in the work?

6. The main thing, obviously, is to recognize that the criminals who will terrorize society in the next decade, and the vast number of those mentally ill whose support will tax society to the very limit, are now in our schools. The crucial problem is: What can the school do to identify these people and to take preventive measures. What value do you attach to each of the following suggestions?

a. The school if it houses more than 500 children should establish a clinic for personality and behavior problems.

b. The Parent-Teacher Association should appoint a committee to study the problem.

c. The curriculum and method of instruction should be adjusted so that there will be fewer unadjusted children in the school.

d. Only teachers with the soundest mental health should be employed.

7. You probably agree that a teacher should never pride herself on the fact that she maintains "high standards" by failing 20 or 25 per cent of a class. Under a typical situation, what percentage of failure (as measured by final marks) would you undertake to defend, let us say, in a ninth-grade class in your major subject?

8. Design a plan by which a faculty in a small high school of 200 pupils with eight new teachers could divide up the task of identifying the maladjusted pupils in the ninth grade.

9. How important do you think clothes are in the life of an adolescent?

10. Evaluate the following quotation from a statement made by a member of a board of education: "He is the kind of teacher who ends his pupil-teacher relationships when he turns in his marks."

11. Do you know a high school well enough to venture a guess as to the extent to which its population is unhappy and unadjusted? (Comment: Wouldn't it be a good idea if each student teacher in this group asked one high-school principal about his school?)

12. See again on p. 75 the table from Wickman's study, *Children's Behavior and Teachers' Attitudes*, in which 30 clinicians and 511 teachers rated the various items. A high score in the table means that the item in question was considered serious, a danger signal for the distant future.

   a. Principal Jones said: "I do not blame the teacher. She has to plan the work for a particular hour. If an uncooperative pupil 'spills the beans' so that no one can go forward with work that he can do with profit, she is not going to say 'Never mind, Billy, this won't make any difference in your character twenty years from now.' " Do you agree? Why?

   b. Superintendent Smith said, "I believe teachers are more and more going to employ clinical methods but I don't believe we can do it until we have better records and until we have a lighter pupil load per teacher." Do you know of any schools that are moving in this direction?

Suggested Readings

Broady, Knute O., Lois Pedersen Broady, and Ada Stidworthy Westover: *Orientation and Guidance for High School Pupils*. Lincoln: University of Nebraska, 1947. Pp. viii + 320.
   This book is written for boys and girls in grades nine and ten. You will find in it some good suggestions concerning activities and methods for teaching them.

Cassidy, Rosalind, and Hilda Glute Kozman: *Counseling Girls in a Changing Society*. New York: McGraw-Hill Book Company, Inc., 1947. Pp. xix + 441.
   This is a helpful volume for all persons who have specific responsibilities for the guidance of girls. It is more than that, however, in the sense that it presents a clear and convincing picture of the changing concept of women's role in our society.

Chisholm, Leslie L.: *Guiding Youth in the Secondary School*. New York: American Book Company, 1945. Pp. xi. + 433.
   Prospective teachers cannot all find time in undergraduate days to take a special course in guidance. Yet some training is helpful and for most teachers essential. This book, while not a substitute for a good course, is nevertheless a useful guide to a classroom teacher without specific training in guidance.

Cox, Philip W. L., John Carr Duff, and Marie McNamara: *Basic Principles of Guidance*. New York: Prentice-Hall, Inc., 1948. Pp. 426.
   The authors present guidance as integrating all aspects of school life. Techniques in the fields of health, vocation, avocation, education, and human relations are discussed in detail.

Ellenwood, James L.: *Just and Durable Parents*. New York: Charles Scribner's Sons, 1948. Pp. 1-224.
   Scan the book and you will probably find something interesting and helpful.

Preston, George H.: *Psychiatry for the Curious*. New York: Rinehart & Company, Inc., 1940. Pp. x + 148.

This book is a primer in psychiatry written in charming and intriguing style. You probably won't fall asleep reading it if you start when you are fully awake. If you have not taken a good course in psychiatry this little book will be very interesting and helpful.

SORENSON, HERBERT, and MARGUERITE MALM: *Psychology for Living.* New York: McGraw-Hill Book Company, Inc., 1948. Pp. x + 637.

This is a splendid book for senior high-school pupils. Glance at the table of contents, for there are many parts that you will wish to read.

STRANG, RUTH: *Educational Guidance.* New York: The Macmillan Company, 1947. Pp. xiv + 268.

This is a really fine book on *educational* guidance for the beginning teacher by one of the most competent workers in the field. We suggest that as a minimum you read Chap. VI. It includes reports and appraisals of interviews that are human and captivating. Later you may wish to refer to other parts of the book for specific help.

WARTERS, JANE: *High School Personnel Work Today.* New York: McGraw-Hill Book Company, Inc., 1946. Pp. xi + 277.

For the student teacher who wants to dig deeper into the problems involved in serving as a home-room teacher or as a member of a guidance group, this book will provide many helpful suggestions.

ZACHRY, CAROLINE B.: *Emotion and Conduct in Adolescence.* New York: Appleton-Century-Crofts Company, Inc., 1940. Pp. xv + 563.

This volume stems from the Study of Adolescence set up within the Commission on Secondary School Curriculum of the Progressive Education Association. Various techniques of observation were employed in several public and private high schools and colleges which seemed to have yielded insights into the needs of students that are more comprehensive and more intimate than one can get in the usual faculty-student relationship. The volume gives an insight into those major adjustments in emotion and conduct which young persons have to make as they grow up and which are probably basic to adult adaptations. The book is an important contribution for it will help the teacher gain a better understanding of his problems and more effectively guide the social development of boys and girls.

TEXT-FILMS

The following McGraw-Hill Text-Film on Teacher Education has been correlated directly with Chap. III.

Learning to Understand Children: Part II—A REMEDIAL PROGRAM (23min sd MP). A continuation of the previous film. Miss Brown develops a program for remedial measures which makes use of data collected and utilizes Ada's special interest and ability as a means of giving her self-confidence, and of creating interest in her schoolwork as well as winning her recognition and acceptance by her schoolmates.

Silent follow-up filmstrip based on material contained in the motion picture and textbook offers opportunity for review, testing, application and further discussion of teaching techniques demonstrated.

Top left: Contrast this pupil-teacher relationship with that shown in Chap. 1. *Top right:* Here is convincing evidence that this boy is not vitally interested in a project. On the other hand, it is very difficult for even a good teacher to design tasks that will challenge all the children of all the people. *Center left:* What instructions would you give a class in order that they might carry on when you have to leave the classroom? Have you known of high-school classes that continue to do good work when the teacher was absent several days? *Center right:* "I will make an example of you!" Can you conceive of a situation in which you would employ such a procedure? *Bottom:* How quiet should a well-managed classroom be?

Chapter IV

Discipline as an Aspect of School Morale and Character Education

The fundamental reason why children do not act right is because they do not have the conditions for right action.

—Francis W. Parker

Mr. Jones: "John Williams, I've stood all I can from you. Get out of the room this very minute, and don't come back until you are ready to apologize to me. I never saw anyone in my life who could behave like you have. I've told you time and time again that you couldn't get by me with that kind of conduct, and this time I mean it. Now get out!"

As John was leaving the room in a leisurely fashion, several of the other boys giggled, and Mr. Jones turned angrily to the class. "Who was that I heard laughing?"

The class remained silent. "Come on, speak up."

Silence continued as Mr. Jones scowled menacingly at the group. "All right, since the class seems to think this is so funny, you'll all stay in this afternoon for forty-five minutes. Then we'll see just how funny this is. Remember, the whole class is to report back to this room at four o'clock."

"Harry, pick up that book you just knocked on the floor. What's that? You dare tell me you didn't knock it off? Harry Smith, I saw you do it, and this is the last time I'm warning you about such matters. Next time I'll send you straight to the principal's office, and he'll take care of you! All right, class, silence! Quiet, I say! What is the lesson for today?"

The picture presented in the preceding description is one that is far too common. It is obvious that it could not possibly be defended as a desirable learning situation. Assuming that the subject matter being presented to the class is very much worth while, the total effect is nevertheless made negative by the undesirable concomitant outcomes. The thoughful observer would like to have the answers

87

to many questions, including the following: What caused the pupils to react as they did? How could the teacher have reduced the number of undesirable responses? What should the teacher have said and done?

These questions suggest the three fundamental approaches to the problem of discipline: (1) There is the constructive approach by which we create a situation in which disciplinary difficulties are not likely to arise. (2) There is the preventive approach. Even though the situation is fundamentally not right the teacher can resort to tricks of the trade that cut down the number of undesirable responses by pupils. (3) There is the remedial aspect of discipline. Assuming that something has gone wrong and that undesirable behavior is in the picture, what should the teacher do? This chapter will present only a brief discussion of the constructive approach since Chap. II, "Learning to Understand Children," illustrates, by implication, the main ideas and procedures.

CONSTRUCTIVE DISCIPLINE

The prevalence of disciplinary problems in the classroom of a teacher is symptomatic of fundamental deficiencies in the situation. Any one of a great many things may be wrong. Perhaps the curriculum is obsolete and only remotely related to the basic needs of young people. More often than is realized the trouble can be traced to the economic or the emotional situations in the homes. Frequently, though less often than is assumed, heredity plays a part in individual cases. The mores of the community provide a ceiling beyond which the teacher's ideals cannot penetrate except by accident. The lack of a unifying philosophy of education on the part of the faculty results not only in a lack of teamwork on disciplinary cases but, what is far more important, it deprives the school of the momentum of a tradition of desirable standards and practices. Finally, the teacher's personality may be the basic cause of much of the trouble.

If Bill's undesirable response is the result of two or more of these fundamental causes, mere correction of a specific offense will not carry the beginning teacher very far. It is the point of view of constructive discipline that, when the right conditions exist in the home, in the classroom, and in the community, the amount of misbehavior is reduced to a minimum. Indeed it is not at all certain that all of

"The fundamental reason why children do not act right is because they do not have the conditions for right action."—FRANCIS W. PARKER. Do the conditions seem right here?[N]

the conditions have to be right in order that a teacher may be free from disciplinary annoyances. Beyond doubt, there are a vast number of teachers who secure a very high level of cooperation even in schools and communities where conditions are far from ideal. There are many teachers whose work moves along so smoothly that they need to give scarcely a thought to the corrective aspect of discipline. The point of view of constructive discipline is as idealistic as that of the expert gardener who tries to promote the normal growth of each plant by providing an environment appropriate to it.

At the beginning of this chapter you no doubt noticed the quotation from Parker, "The fundamental reason why children do not act right is because they do not have the conditions for right action." It is probably the most important sentence in this book. Parker's idealistic guide will tend to transform depressing episodes into challenging problems that you can attack with professional zest and handle with the necessary objectivity. Do you accept it as the cornerstone in the structure of your educational philosophy? We urge you to hold on to this idealistic statement whatever may happen in the turbulent exigencies of classroom situations. Without it a lifetime devoted to teaching is not likely to yield the greatest satisfactions, for you would be sailing the pedagogical sea without a true compass.

This positive phase of discipline is fundamentally a program in character education. It is constructive in that it strives to build attitudes and habits that are functional both to the individual and to society. The modern school strives to turn out boys and girls who can make democratic procedures effective by wide participation in the acceptance of individual responsibility. This calls for an indirect program of character education in the classroom based on activities and experiences that develop in the individual habits of self-control based on reason rather than on force and on rules from without.

"Spare the rod and spoil the child" was one of the favored maxims of teachers in the older school. While the rod has disappeared from most schools, the philosophy which caused the rod to be wielded persists in stubborn fashions. It is regrettable that extreme authoritarian control of schools still exists. Then, too, many parents maintain discipline by relying on rules, regulations, and orders supported by strong-arm methods in a day when far more effective methods are available. What both parents and teachers overlook is that dominating behavior on their part tends to be learned by the youngsters.

SPECIFICATIONS OF CONSTRUCTIVE DISCIPLINE

1. *It must be based on "do" rather than "don't."* The emphasis is on practicing right responses and habits.
2. *It must involve a high degree of participation.* If the pupil has a part in creating the conditions under which he works he is less likely to be a disturbing factor.
3. *It must be based on cooperation.* The older form of discipline required a certain degree of cooperation with the teacher but the modern concept of discipline requires a very high degree of cooperation with all members of the group. The modern school seeks to teach pupils that society will have more and better answers for its many perplexing problems if it can operate on higher levels of cooperation.
4. *It must seek social consciousness.* A classroom characterized by excessive noise, discourtesy, and confusion is an undesirable situation, however progressive the school may claim to be.
5. *It must be primarily concerned with changes in pupils.* From the point of view of character education we do not strive for a classroom in which nothing ever goes wrong but we are concerned with the question: What do pupils do about it when a situation is in need of adjustment?

It is not likely that anyone will have serious objections to these general principles. However, the beginning teacher will want to know the practical steps by which he can implement a program of constructive discipline. We turn therefore to a list of practical guides, some of which are so simple and formal that they may appear to be routine matters but which, nevertheless, have far-reaching implications.

PRACTICAL STEPS IN CONSTRUCTIVE DISCIPLINE

Some of the practical steps involved are the following:

1. *Use the school day for work.* It is easier to maintain good order when pupils are busy at worth-while tasks than it is when the hour is devoted merely to the hearing of assigned lessons.

2. *Provide a supplementary library in or near each room.* In far too many cases responsible school officials fail to recognize the extent to which disciplinary problems are due to a lack of instructional materials. Whenever possible use workshop or laboratory techniques, investigations, experiments, projects, etc., in which there is opportunity for problem solving or reflective thinking.

3. *Use the standards of the group as the foundation of your disciplinary measures.* You may need to overlook many undesirable things. Any effort at punishment will be futile if it opposes the standards of the group; *e.g.*, you cannot eliminate cheating from your grade or your school until the group opinion is against cheating. A corollary of this principle is that you must make requests in the interests of the group, never for yourself.

4. *Respect the personality of the pupil.* Employ a procedure that is friendly and informal, but businesslike. Appeal to the personal interests of pupils. Treat every pupil with the same degree of fairness, impartiality, and considerateness.

5. *Whenever possible provide flexible furniture.* The socialized recitation and panel discussions featuring practice in cooperative thinking are very difficult to achieve when pupils sit in formal rows.

6. *Recognize that in general high-school pupils love to work hard at worth-while tasks.* It may not be desirable, certainly it is not feasible, to have pupils do only those tasks in which they are interested; but surely gifted teachers can interest pupils in the things that need to be done.

7. *Stop trying to teach pupils things they cannot learn.* Recognize that many disciplinary troubles, or cases of mental ill health and maladjustment in school, are due directly to our inability to find appropriate tasks for the pupils.

8. *Seek to give every pupil the satisfaction that comes with doing something that exhibits a fine quality of workmanship.* In making an inventory of the human material in your class be sure to list the specific thing which each pupil can do easily and well. A very famous schoolman used the idea suggested here as the main part of his program of character education.

9. *Plan effectively all matters of routine management.* Often the mechanics of the situation stimulate pupils to mild forms of horseplay that develop into serious misbehavior.

10. *Provide a variety of functional extracurricular activities.* There are many student organizations, *e.g.*, student council, camera club, home room, *a cappella* choir, which may serve the special interests of individual pupils and thus divert excess energy into worth-while channels.

11. *Take the clinical view toward problems of discipline.* Remember that the constructive view of discipline holds to the conviction that behavior problems inevitably arise out of wrong conditions for normal growth. In discussing discipline be as impersonal as a physician. When a physician looks down your sore throat he is sympathetic, but it is *your* sore throat. He doesn't go away emotionally disorganized.

12. *Use a variety of teaching procedures.* The long school day can be insufferably boring to young people and they can scarcely be blamed if sooner or later someone does not resist the temptation to start something.

13. *Give pupils a part in planning and appraisal.* In the older school the teacher planned, the pupil did the work, and the supervisor appraised it. The constructive view of discipline holds that this day is passing and that the pupil must have a part in all of these matters.

14. *Build a school tradition of fine standards.* Probably no procedure in character education is more effective in dealing with the pupil who is a behavior problem than to place him with a group of fellows who approve and highly reward the right reaction. You will find it easy to get the correct response in school or camp if "this is the thing to do."

15. *Take every measure possible to improve your personality.* Many teachers never need to give the problem of discipline a thought because pupils like to be under the spell of their personalities. For practical purposes we may compare the warmth of a teacher's personality to the sunlight that brings life and color to a growing flower. Research studies in the area of personality development suggest that there is something the individual teacher can do to improve his own personality.

The day hasn't come when we can afford to forget the statement of the late Warden Lewis E. Lawes that "there is a missing link between education and character which our public schools have not been able to discover."[1] It is clear that he had the conviction that "the faults of education become the problems of penology. The failures of our schools and general educational methods are filling our juvenile homes, our reformatories, and prisons." The question of crime is complicated and one can never be sure that one has identified a primary cause. However, it is plausible that the undue emphasis on negative aims in discipline used in the schools has con-

[1] LEWIS E. LAWES. "The Challenge to the School," *Proceedings of the National Education Association*, 70 (1932), 57–60.

tributed an excessive number of social misfits to the adolescent and adult life of today.   An increasing number of thoughtful citizens are convinced that certain grave social maladjustments today have been due partly to the philosophy of discipline that (1) repressed the interests, personalities, and enthusiasms of pupils, (2) controlled through fear, rules, penalties, and punishments, and (3) placed too

This class is holding an election.   The school's program in civic education is a basic factor in the general morale or discipline of a school.[E]

great an emphasis on passiveness.   In an ideal world this chapter would end here.   But you will discover quickly enough during the early weeks on your first job that the particular universe in which you operate is far from ideal.

PREVENTIVE DISCIPLINE

The beginning teacher needs to be realistic.   There may be some things in a bad situation that you can improve but little, if any. For example, what can you do if (1) Bill's parents are about to be divorced, (2) his mother is incurably ill, or (3) his father's income is wholly inadequate? Moreover, there may be some factors in a given situation that cannot be corrected overnight. For example, it takes time to construct a modern curriculum to replace an obsolete one. In any case a beginning teacher, though he be gifted and idealistic, cannot "go it alone" if those responsible for the philosophy and management of the school have never given serious thought to the constructive phases of discipline, for there must be teamwork. How to prevent disorder in a situation that is not ideal is the practical problem of most beginning teachers.

The following list constitutes a "box of aspirin tablets" to meet such emergency situations. A wise application of these tricks of the trade will give you the necessary time to inquire into some of the fundamental causes that contribute to existing conditions, and in many cases you will be spared the annoyance of facing more serious and perplexing misbehavior. However, the teacher who finds himself in the midst of serious disciplinary troubles should not be deceived into believing that the following suggestions, however helpful they may prove to be, strike at the fundamental factors in a discipline problem:

1. *Learn the names of pupils quickly.* It is helpful to have a task or a variety of tasks ready the first day as the students come into the room and to make a seating chart while they are busy. A teacher should be able to call on any pupil by name within the first few minutes of the first recitation.

2. *Study carefully the seating of the students.* It seems to be true that certain students have a bad effect on each other. A boy who ordinarily is a quiet student may, when seated with the wrong neighbor, start the mischievous spirit in both.

3. *Learn to "ride your eye" through the eyes of your students.* In the early days you cannot often turn your back on the class to discuss maps, write on the blackboard, and the like. In the early weeks you cannot sit much. It is of considerable advantage for a teacher to stand where he can see clearly what it is that each pupil is doing. Try to hear all and see all that is happening in the class all of the time.

4. *Learn to call upon those pupils whose attention is wavering.* It is an easy trick to bring into the fold those who are about to be lost through daydreaming, interest in neighbors, "monkeying," etc.

5. *Be businesslike.* This means that you must have an interesting program of worth-while material for each hour. In keeping pupils busy, provide the greatest amount of variety consistent with good organization. Begin promptly with a suggestion of vigor and close the work on time. If there tends to be crowding and pushing in passageways, step to the door in order to be in a position of advantage. Keep a careful record of absences and tardinesses and cooperate with the office in reporting these in the manner used in the school so that pupils will know where they are expected to be each period of the day. Have a system of

holding every member of the class responsible for all that takes place during the class period.

6. *Make every effort to avoid all suggestions of criticism, disorganization, or anger before the group.* Make your suggestions for improvement in the private conference. Maintain a poise that is characteristic of efficiency and success. Be genuine and, if possible, use a sense of humor.

7. *When a number of the group obstructs the work, the treatment of the case should be calm, dignified, and firm.* If the administration approves, the member should be expected to leave the room, preferably to sit alone in a place provided for such a purpose. At the first opportunity the offense should be dealt with in private conference. If a pupil is interfering with the work of others, go to him quietly and request his cooperation. Send pupils from the class only for serious forms of misbehavior, *e.g.*, obscene language. When you are not certain what to do, do nothing.

8. *Use special occasions to carry over to the pupils the idea that you are interested in them as human beings.* You will find it helpful to attend special assembly programs or athletic events. Many teachers do not recognize what a golden opportunity they have when some of their pupils are sick. In such a case a kindly message, telephone call, or a visit will work wonders.

9. *Stop the little things.* The snowball rolling downhill gathers momentum and size. In like manner many disciplinary problems that seem insignificant in the early stages may become serious. Proper treatment requires good sense and some other means than a "Don't." Avoid too difficult assignments in the early weeks. At the end of each day of the first week list the weak spots of the room.

10. *In the early weeks of your first year of teaching, keep a tight rein.* It is far easier for you to relax your control than to recapture it after the situation has gone beyond your control. This suggestion is especially important in a school that operates with the traditional concept of discipline.

Remedial Treatment for Serious Types of Misbehavior

In the treatment of the more serious types of offenses, which inevitably arise when conditions are very poor, the teacher is professionally obligated to do something to remedy the situation. It is helpful to remember that frustration is often the explanation of misbehavior, for when the road to a goal is blocked the pupil tends to become more aggressive or more infantile. Moreover, unless a teacher exercises great care his teaching will reinforce patterns in which certain pupils will tend to be excessively approved, cruelly rejected, or thoughtlessly ignored. Punishment must never be looked upon as an end in itself, but a means of restoring the individual pupil to normalcy in the group. The clinical technique implies careful diagnosis and an application of proper remedial measures that seem most appropriate in light of the pupil's offense, his personality, and the motives behind his misbehavior. Although no acceptable formula or rule-of-thumb procedure in the treatment of serious offenses can be laid down, successful teachers have found that the following guides help in getting good results:

1. *Isolate the offender from other pupils between the time of the offense and the settlement.* Give the offender no privileges until the case is definitely settled— unless a lengthy investigation is pending.

Here is discipline in grandfather's day as dramatized by a present-day group of youngsters.[N1]

2. *It is often wise to let the offender "meditate" for an hour or so before talking with him.* Particularly should this practice be observed in cases where the pupil is angry or extremely nervous. Make certain, however, that (*a*) the delay is not a mental torture for the offender and (*b*) that the period of meditation ends before school closes when the pupil does not have good mental health. Why?

3. *Be perfectly frank with a pupil.* State the complaint fairly. Be judicial. When one is not absolutely certain of the pupil's guilt, it is often possible through skillful questioning to lead the pupil to convict himself. Do not expect tattling. Seek to determine the facts of the case. Get at the motives behind the offense.

4. *If property has been damaged, a willingness to pay for it, to restore it, or repair it is usually sufficient.* Make certain, however, that the pupil does what he promises.

Should a pupil ever be isolated from a group?[(E)]

5. *Never force apologies.* In fact, apologies are seldom the best form of punishment. Word soon gets around the school that the easy way out of punishment is to "look sorry and say you feel the same"—with fingers crossed. Apologies should never be made to a teacher. It is far better to lead the pupil to feel that the teacher is above holding grudges. Moreover a pupil should come to see that when de does something wrong, he himself is the one who is changed thereby—he is the one who has been hurt.

6. *Do not hurry in decisions regarding the punishment itself.* If the offender has been led to see why he has misbehaved and realized the effect of his offense on others, he will often suggest a penalty himself—usually more severe and far more appropriate than one coming from the teacher.

7. *When the case is settled, drop it.* For every disciplinary case that is closed, be sure the student understands that his record is once more clear and that there is to be no memory of the offense.

8. *Do not publicize offenses and treatment of them before the student body.* There should be no punishment of the whole class for the fault of the few. Never ridicule a pupil except in the case of marked conceit, and then only when you are sure you have a firm hand on the group. For many reasons do not make threats—you may have to carry them out.

9. *An earnest appeal to the opinion of the class is often effective in stopping types of misbehavior that are difficult to investigate.* In many cases you need not be concerned about determining the guilty party.

10. *A visit to the home is often effective.* Do not overlook the chance to utilize the cooperation of a home in which there is teamwork.

97

11. *Classroom teachers should never use the weapon of suspension or expulsion.* This is purely an administrative device. Try to handle your own problems but do not allow them to grow more complex before calling for assistance.

12. *Do not make an issue of something that is trivial.* On the campus of the University of Michigan the famous reply of President Angell to the question, "What makes a great administrator?" is still quoted. He said, "You have to be blind in one eye and deaf in one ear." It is not clear how far the beginning teacher can apply this principle, but the experienced teacher will recognize it as very effective. Presumably it would depend on the extent to which the beginning teacher is really in control of the situation.

14. *The problem that looms like a mountain of disaster at the end of a tired day often decreases to molehill significance after a refreshing period of rest.* As one beginning teacher, humorously but not irreverently, remarked, "God surely had classroom teachers in mind when He put a night between two days!"

DISCIPLINARY PROCEDURE ON PICNICS, EXCURSIONS, AND EXTRACURRICULAR ACTIVITIES

Teachers are called on more and more to sponsor a wide variety of activities in and out of the school, *e.g.*, dances, picnics, hobby clubs, class organizations, athletic trips, and excursions. On such occasions teachers are expected to assume definite responsibilities. In these informal situations the weak teacher is likely to have far more disciplinary difficulties than he does in the classroom. The following suggestions are listed to help the beginning teacher see his proper relation to the public and the school when these occasions arise:

1. Get definite information from administrators as regards your function and the limits of your authority and responsibility. Be sure your status as a member of the group or activity is known and clearly comprehended by the group you are sponsoring.

2. If the picnic, excursion, or activity has been planned by yourself or the group, be sure to let the proper administrative officers know your plans with regard to where you intend to go, who is going, when, and how. This will protect you, the group, and administrators in the event of accidents.

3. Plan all excursions, picnics, etc., carefully ahead of time. Be certain that the pupils have the permission of the home before engaging in activities that are not approved by all parents. Some experienced teachers go through the entire routine with a small committee of student leaders while planning the excursion. This practice is undoubtedly highly desirable, especially if the teacher takes along a small committee of pupils and gives them some participation in planning the proposed excursion and delegates specific responsibilities to them.

COMMON ERRORS TO BE AVOIDED BY BEGINNING TEACHERS

We turn now to a list of errors that are very common in the work of beginning teachers. These errors no doubt tend to contribute to the difficulty of disciplinary problems.

1. A lesson is often rendered ineffectual because the teacher plunges into the work before getting the attention of each member of the class. This is a time when a host of mild discipline problems tend to develop.

This is just one experience in a semester course on social training.(E)

2. In case one pupil makes a mistake, the teacher explains the correction directly to him instead of to all the class.

3. The teacher does the explaining and answering of questions instead of encouraging the class to feel a responsibility for all that goes on during the period.

4. The teacher speaks in a low, unconvincing tone which gives the impression that nothing of importance is happening.

5. Pupils are often seated in straight rows when tables could easily be arranged so as to promote an informal discussion.

6. Teachers allow themselves to be "side-tracked" by irrelevant questions.

7. Teachers parrot the pupils' answers all too frequently.

8. Teachers often use words and constructions far above the pupils' comprehension.

9. Both simple and difficult concepts are left before they have been made entirely clear.

10. The wording of questions is often so poor that two or more attempts must be made before final arrival at the desired statements.

11. Teachers recite the content which the pupils are supposed to have been prepared on, thus lowering class interest.

12. Little idiosyncrasies and mannerisms are developed which detract from the work at hand.

13. Pupils are permitted to *recite* individually to the teacher instead of *discussing* questions with the whole class.

14. Statements of pupils are replied to by a monotonous "All right."

15. Teachers talk too rapidly or too slowly. This practice gives the impression that the teacher is nervous, and the slower pupils are unable to follow the train of thought.

16. Teachers call on a particular pupil before stating the question.

17. Preparation of lessons and collection of teaching materials are often neglected until the last minute.

18. Material placed on the blackboard by the teacher during a recitation period is often ineffectual on account of carelessness in writing and drawing.

19. Teachers frequently fail to take account of the physical comfort of pupils: temperature, ventilation, lighting, seating.

20. Although the teacher does not approve the use of sarcasm, he is not aware that he is using it in devastating fashion.

21. Motivation does not rise above mere entertainment and, therefore, fails to achieve a challenging interest in the task.

22. The teacher draws on college experiences before he has established a firm foundation of fellowship with his pupils.

23. The teacher tries to gear down the difficulty of the task by using "baby talk."

24. The teacher tends to lose control of his temper and fails to see that in the long run a group may be conquered by courtesy.

25. The teacher fails to find out the practice of the school with respect to the manner in which to address the pupils.

It would, we think, be helpful when you have taught a month or so in your first regular teaching assignment to take stock by reading the preceding list again and checking the items that you need to keep in mind for improvement. It is hard for you to appreciate these practical suggestions until you have had considerable experience.

A WORD OF WARNING

The superintendent and principal are also under obligation to respect the mores of the community in which they work, and the

What part, if any, should a student court or a subcommittee of the student council have in the administration of discipline?[(G)]

changes they would like to see put into effect are often blocked by community prejudice and tradition.

If the enthusiastic exponent of the new concept of discipline finds himself in such a situation, there are two common-sense guides: (1) the teacher must operate within the frame of reference used by the administration; (2) the foundations for gradual evolutionary change can be laid in the classroom, if the teacher is tactful, without arousing opposition. This latter step is essentially a long-range program. It is conceivable that it might require years rather than months, and great patience may be needed. A progressive plan that fails is very likely to result in retrenchment and a shift to an extremely conservative position. A school cannot afford to commit costly blunders through the lack of common sense and patience. In brief, "half a loaf" is better than no bread at all.

The beginning teacher need not have excessive fear of the discipline problem. On the other hand he should not underestimate the difficulty. It is indeed significant that an analysis of causes for the failure of beginning teachers as reported in several independent investigations reveals poor discipline as the leading cause in every study. While the real cause of the failure of a beginning teacher may be something more fundamental than the way that he deals with his disciplinary cases, it yet remains true that the persistence of unsolved disciplinary problems provides concrete and therefore convincing evidence to school officials and parents that there is a serious weakness and this they are likely to classify under discipline. An experienced teacher appreciates the many practical suggestions in this chapter. We urge you to read this chapter again just before you start your first teaching position. The sound picture "Maintaining Classroom Discipline," is a realistic film in the sense that it illustrates many of the preventative and remedial procedures.

A Tidbit for Dessert

This chapter really is ended. However, when you finish reading the following two letters you will, we are sure, be glad that this supplement was not omitted. The first letter was written by a teacher new on the job. The other is a reply by a supervising teacher with a discerning mind and a good pen.

An Open Letter to a Supervising Teacher[1]

I am finally prompted to write to you after wondering about the great why of things out here in this fine field that was always lauded to us in hallowed tones. But before you throw this out, and before you turn to quiet the classroom for a bewildered Miss Jones, or whoever it is, wait. I am not really so disgruntled as I may appear at the outset. I still believe all those noble and edifying precepts I was told concerning ideals and sacrifice and the preservation of intellectual integrity. But I also have come to believe certain other things, rather vital too, that I was not told or shown, but that I have since learned. I have learned the full flavor of ignominy and found it far from being sweet. I know this doesn't surprise you. But I wonder if you realize the serious reason behind the necessity for my being humiliated, as I was throughout my entire first year of teaching, by not being able to discipline a classroom. I honestly think you do not. I should dislike thinking you, and others who hold a like position, know why we are forced to submit to such an embarrassment and have done nothing about it in training us. I know you are going to tell me the ability to discipline comes with time. True, it does. It has. But what I would like to see is an avoidance of this awkward period of not having such an ability.

IRKSOME COUNSEL

You will agree there is very little sense, if any, in a superintendent having to counsel a group of new teachers somewhat as follows:

"And now teachers I think you know why I have called you together. I believe you are aware that the discipline problem here is rapidly getting out of

[1] This letter, signed by "One who is puzzled about classroom discipline," appeared in the *Michigan Education Journal*, XV (November, 1938), 128.

control. In view of this disastrous occurrence, and in an effort to remedy this difficulty immediately, I have a set of rules which I expect each of you to learn and enforce on the slightest provocation."

In spite of the fury within one, however, it is best to smile fixedly at such a condition of affairs, and "take it" for the base reason that one must make some kind of living.

Quite definitely I have here set forth a problem—one perhaps nearly hopeless of solution, but nevertheless a situation that should merit some consideration in an attempt toward being solved. Discipline, to my mind, and I believe you will agree, should not be a matter of compulsion, but rather one of persuasion. The failure in accomplishing this control of students seems to lie, not in the natural perversity of human nature, which we cannot blame these students for possessing, but in ourselves (the younger faculty) that we are forced underlings to precepts stubbornly insisted upon by the administrative heads. I realize that no set form, no matter how long established, will help any novice in class control, lists of rules included.

Of course I am aware of my youth and its accompanying foolhardiness, but it does seem that more effective results would be obtained from young teachers were they permitted to achieve discipline in their own way—in a way which they have mastered before they take their first job. Efficient control of a group must come from within, must be allowed to emanate from the personality of the instructor. Now please don't pat my head and say: "Yes, but this technique comes only from experience." That I already know. But what I, and I daresay countless others in a similar predicament, needed was an opportunity to get that experience before we were hired to teach.

VICTIMS OF THEORIES

In the interim, you are thinking, what is to become of the previously well-governed school while we, who lack skill, are getting it by trial and error? Indeed, I can see the folly of too much experimenting and I, too, can predict its demoralizing effect on the student body. Therefore, we must continue with things as they are. But the prime fault continues to lie in the fact that new teachers are turned out victims of mere theory and methods. In my present situation I can do nothing but submit to controlling forces and hope to gain, in the due course of years, a complete mastery of this unhappy problem. For those teachers who are to follow, however, I do hope that not too far in the future our training schools will come to the realization they are turning out puppets that must be manipulated by strings in the hands of already experienced advisers. I further trust they will come to know that we left the doors of our colleges but fifty per cent competent in that we had no practical training in controlling a classroom. Fifty per cent may sound like an absurdly high figure, but pause to consider that subject matter, though it be had in abundance by the instructor, cannot be imparted to a group of indolent and perhaps violently disposed students over whom this instructor can exert little or no restraint or regulation.

The ultimate reason for this being the case seems to repose in the fact that in most all practice teaching courses the potential teacher is hovered over by a critic, and hence the control that is under such a condition achieved is the direct result of the superimposed check afforded by the presence of the critic. I do hope I am not offending you. I think I am not. I feel sure you will do your utmost in trying to alleviate so justified a grievance as I believe this is.

As to the "how" of this solution, that is up to the instructors of the training schools to discover. I am only stating the case, as it seemingly exists, against an inadequately supplied background of training for discipline as *not* provided heretofore by the teacher training institutions of the state. I say of the state, for my colleagues (I refer to the younger members of the faculty) come from various institutions throughout the state and have found themselves in a like quandary.

I do hope you won't judge my dissatisfied comments too harshly. Know this reaction to be one which is the result of my having been belabored throughout the year by irate superiors whose constant cry has been to "man the controls" without my ever having had an opportunity to analyze and study this complex mechanism of discipline in its true proportion. Perhaps, on second thought, these superiors would not appear so annoying and difficult had I come to them sufficiently prepared to meet the demands they have a right to expect. Possibly, were we better turned out, it would not necessitate the time-honored practice of trying to work under the domination of specific and encumbering rules which, to anyone possessed of imagination and initiative, is extremely unpleasant.

If you have found the preceding letter interesting you will surely want to read the following reply written by a gifted supervising teacher.

In Reply to the Freshman Teacher[1]

There is something so disarming in your phrase "the full flavor of ignominy" that even if your letter were couched in vituperative language, which it most certainly is not, no critic teacher could do aught but sympathize with you. The waters of humiliation are indeed bitter, and one can thoroughly understand your impulse to fling the spray, at least, in any convenient direction.

"Discipline" is an unpleasant word in the ears of many teachers and administrators. For some it connotes an unreasonable and unjust use of authority, an iron system that terrorizes the weak and cows even the strong. We shall assume that none of us, including your superintendent, have any desire to see this kind of discipline prevail in any classroom; and we shall further assume that you mean in general what most of us mean by the term "discipline"; namely, the prevalence of a reasonable air of order in a classroom in which interested pupils work on worthwhile activities. Most of us believe that if the last two conditions exist, the first will largely take care of itself. But we won't quibble over terms. What you mean right here and now by a teacher's discipline is her ability *to make pupils behave.* Isn't that it? Very well, then.

REVIEWING THE CASE

For a number of reasons, I am greatly interested in your situation. Before attempting to account for the unhappy condition in which you say young faculty

[1] This answer, by Marion McKinney, appeared in the *Michigan Education Journal,* XV (February, 1939), 276–277.

members find themselves, I want to be sure that I thoroughly understand the points which you make in your letter.

In the first place, you believe that the critic teacher, secure in her own little haven of experience, is quite unaware of the pitfalls which await the beginning teacher; when she refers to "the field" she does so in a tone which invests it with a highly misleading glamour.

You anticipate, and are weary of the banal explanation that ability to discipline comes with time.

The Juggernaut practices of your superintendent infuriate you, and you blame your critic teacher for not having forestalled the necessity for his procedure.

It is your conviction that "efficient control of a group must come from within, must be allowed to emanate from the personality of the instructor." You think you should have found, or learned, or been given this control while you were in training school.

HORNS OF THE DILEMMA

You falter over the sharp horns of the dilemma: The embryo teacher clings to a horn with one feeble finger, casting her eager eye about to detect that pearl of great price—experience; all this with what you call "demoralizing effect on the student body." Over the other horn "hovers" the critic teacher, giving light to the student body, but casting a Stygian darkness over the future well-being of the potential teacher. Yes, you falter, but recover to leap in the next sentence to the generalization "that new teachers are turned out victims of mere theory and methods."

With a complete finality of gesture, you commit the solution of this difficult problem to the instructors of the training school.

Now, my young friend, don't bother reading further unless you will promise to be as honest with yourself as your quite understandably frenzied state of mind will allow.

A BED OF ROSES?

In the first place, did your critic teacher *really* lead you to believe that the teaching profession was a bed of roses? Did she *really* speak of her profession in "hallowed" tones? Confused in your memories, could you by any chance be thinking of some of the generalities that fell from the lips of your handsome young instructor in an education course? All the critic teachers I know are realists. They like this profession and can glow at the vision of its possibilities, but they know the dragons that beset the path of the teacher, and accordingly warn the novice with even boring repetition. Can it be that the principle of learning which applies to children applies equally to adults, and that even prospective teachers will not avail themselves of a learning opportunity until they see an immediate need? Just the other day I was urging a student teacher to show some firmness in her handling of an eighth-grade class. "But," she said, "these children are so sweet—I don't like to come down on them." In vain for me to tell her, but I do, that unless she can come down on them now, her pupils next year, and her superintendent, and in fact the whole town will "come down" on her until she feels, in the salty language of one of my colleagues, somewhat lower than the vest buttons of a snake.

Many a soldier in his brave new uniform has stirred impatiently at the warnings of his superior officer, and thought in his heart that his commander was an alarmist, or that he was becoming a little befuddled.

I can't blame you in the least for growing weary of hearing about "experience." It isn't so very long ago that I learned to drive a car. As I slammed on my brakes, stalled my engine, rounded corners slightly above the curb, I grew to dread what I knew would proceed from my teacher's lips as soon as he could get in a talking position. "You'll get on to it," he would say with a fatuous smile. The really grinding thing about this remark was that I knew it was true; like you, I wanted to see "an avoidance of this awkward period." Learning, skill in any field does not come the easy way. Why, my friend, should you expect to master completely in one semester in a training school the most difficult of all skills, the ability to control yourself and to harmonize your relationships to other people? Your critic teacher would doubtless have told you last year, but you wouldn't have been much interested, that some of us after twenty years of teaching are still struggling to approach the ultimate in what you say students should have mastered before they take their first job.

ON COMMON GROUND

At present I shall skip your next point and go to the following paragraphs in which you discuss what you think constitutes "efficient control of a group." It is here that you strike the root of the matter, the realization that "control of a group must come from within." Here we are on solid ground, and your succinct phrasing of the case saves us much time. Is not the fundamental truth simply this: If the ability to discipline comes from within, the training school can do little for a person who expects to catch on to a scheme of control as he might catch on to a slow freight train? It is my firm conviction that critic teachers do very definitely try to show student teachers their immediate need and arouse within them this inner control of which you speak. And what kind of resistance do they meet? For want of a better phrase I should call it a strong sense of the collegiate, a kind of infantile hang-over. It is as if the college senior, sharply aware that she is about to be pushed from the refuge of the campus, clings with an unconscious tenacity to her sheltered status.

A student teacher whom I was trying to advise, and not in hallowed tones either, said half querulously, "But I don't *want* to act like a teacher. I went to a sorority convention once with one of our alumnae, a teacher, and I decided that I didn't want to be like her."

"NOT AN UMPIRE"

In urging another to handle class problems without referring to me when she was teaching, I had said, "After all, you know, I'm not an umpire." This injustice of mine crushed her so that she had to unburden herself to an operator in a beauty parlor, and thence her sensitiveness was wafted back to me.

"And I just said to him, 'After all, you know, I *am* a college girl.'" Thus spoke in aggrieved tones another potential teacher, whose critic teacher had been moved to suggest a little more discretion in her selection of clothes for classroom wear.

A particularly lively eighth-grade class cut circles around the student teacher. I said to her at the end of the period, "You *must* stop this disorder," and she replied as cheerfully as if I had suggested that she practice the Lambeth walk, "Yes, I will. I'd get a great kick out of it." I didn't stop to ask her why she hadn't availed herself of earlier opportunities for kicks. A few days later I left her and her colleague in charge of the same class. When I entered, near the end of the hour, I still felt that there was something lacking in the power of the kick.

EXIT, COLLEGIATE!

I am not so naïve as to suggest that a few examples prove a general truth, but I am suggesting that the attitude of mind here illustrated is fairly common, even when students are not so gauche as to express their feelings in words. Of course you remember the taunts of Lady Macbeth (Ah, what a disciplinarian was there, my countrymen!). She hit the nail on the head when she reminded her husband that he was like the cat in the adage—the cat who would eat fish but would not wet his feet. The student teacher would like the results which the critic teacher gets, but she would not pay the price if it involved a departure from her student status. In all seriousness I submit for consideration the hypothesis that the "collegiate" and the "professional" spirits do not mix, even with a magician manipulating the glass—and critic teachers are no magicians.

There are other psychological and emotional entanglements in students which effectively block the critic teacher's attempts to arouse and develop this inner control. There is the occasional person with a really cruel vein who seeks to gratify his egotism by exercising authority over children, and there is the exponent of the new, and old, philosophy of futility. This latter kind regard through lack-luster eye the earnest and energetic critic teacher as if she were a none too interesting specimen of the Stone Age. We try to weed out the worst offenders, of course, but a small and not too obvious strain of such inhibitory tendencies can have disastrous results in the unfledged teacher.

And there are with us always the rugged individualists. I suspect, my young colleague, that you are a good deal of an individualist yourself. You speak of effective results which would be obtained if young teachers were permitted to achieve discipline in their own way, and the inference at the end of your letter is plain; namely, that you are one possessed of imagination and initiative.

WHAT DID YOU WANT?

Frankly, what do you want, or what did you want? You imply that your irate superiors did not belabor you until they realized that you were unable to "man the controls" alone. Why did you not, during your first three weeks, utilize your opportunity to achieve discipline in your own way? Three weeks of teaching six hours a day gave you ninety hours—more time than you spent teaching and observing in the training school in a semester. But your critic teacher didn't show you how to man the controls? Stop a moment and consider. Did you try to avail yourself of her help, or were you even then possessed of the kind of imagination and initiative which made the specific "extremely unpleasant"? My guess would be that your present initiative, and you must have plenty, is a mere shadow of the rugged individualism which animated you as a college girl.

ASSORTED SAMPLES

Are you going to insist that your critic teacher should have given you a complete sampling of all the unpleasant situations in which you might find yourself this year? Should she, for example, have incited an eraser-and-chalk riot in her classroom, distributed a generous collection of spitballs, infuriated the biggest boy in the room, and then walked out, signaling to you to enter the combat and bring peace out of pain? This absurd question offends your intelligence, and I apologize for its presence. But again, let me ask what you did want. You speak contemptuously of mere theory and methods, and yet, if you had a fair control of your subject matter, and your critic teacher was able to give you effective methods of presenting it, together with a sane theory about the needs of children, about your profession, about yourself, I should say that you had about the best equipment that would be humanly possible.

I said near the beginning of my letter that I was greatly interested in your situation, and now I'll tell you why. I have of course the professional interest which any critic teacher would have in your article, but I have also a personal interest. My university offered no course in directed teaching, and for that reason I find myself filled with the wildest envy of you. I too had my severe disciplinary problems during my first few years of teaching and—oh, bitter loss—I had no critic teacher to blame.

POSTSCRIPT

P.S.—Why do you suppose that you are getting only about one-half of the salary that you expect to get ten years from now?

FOR DISCUSSION

1. Evaluate the following procedures as techniques for achieving constructive discipline:
   a. Creating many opportunities for pupils to cooperate in activities for the good of the school or class.
   b. Cultivating the kind of school or class pride that will cause pupils to show disapproval of misconduct of associates.
   c. Giving definite instruction in matters of courtesy, sportsmanship, and conduct.

2. Evaluate the following statement concerning what to do with cheating by responding to the following questions: (a) Which reason in the quotation do you believe would make the strongest appeal to pupils? (b) Is there anything the teacher could have said and done that would have been a better procedure?

Miss Rogers discovered that a few pupils cheated when she allowed them to correct their own test papers with a key which she furnished. The first time she met a case of cheating she did not know what to say. She decided to reduce the temptation for the weaker pupils by seizing opportune moments in the weeks ahead to drive home in short incidental comments the substance of the following statement:

"On this test you are going to be allowed to mark your own work. It may be that a few will be tempted to call an answer right when they know it is wrong. You know as well as I do that this is *cheating*. You do not like a cheater on the playground or in the gymnasium, and you do not like a cheater in the classroom, though perhaps you say nothing about it.

"There are several things I want to say about cheating. In the first place I myself will not worry about cheating because very, very few pupils will be so weak. I know great cities that keep large police forces when there are only a few people in these cities that need watching; almost everybody goes about his business and the policeman to the average man is just a good friend who sees that his children cross the street safely or keeps someone from running an automobile over him. In this classroom I do not want to be a policeman to keep you from cheating.

"There are some good reasons why it is unwise for you to cheat. The main reason is that every time you cheat it *does* something to you inside and you can't be quite what you might have been if it hadn't happened. Getting caught by the teacher or anybody else doesn't matter, for *cheating* has caught you then and there. You must live all the rest of your life with yourself, and you will need to respect yourself.

"The second reason is that in this test you will be cheating just one person, yourself, and even a dishonest person would call that foolish. How silly it would be for a boy who is practicing high jumping all by himself in the back alley to say, 'I can jump five feet,' when down in his heart he knows he is doing only four feet.

"The third reason is that if a person were to cheat on this test he would be almost sure to be found out sooner or later. This is the way it works. Suppose you do write in your book that you can do exercise 4 when you haven't really done it. Perhaps a week or so later I will give you another test which will tell me without a doubt whether or not you can do exercise 4. If a boy tells you that he can run 100 yards in 13 seconds, and if later you find out it takes him 15 seconds, you lose respect for him; and it always hurts to learn that someone isn't what you have believed him to be. There is someone at home or at school, indeed in this very room, who believes in you; and you must be as honest as you are believed to be.

"The fourth reason is that so long as a pupil cheats he doesn't give the test a chance to help him. These tests are not given merely to find out how well you can do. We shouldn't need to test you every day if this were all we wanted to know. Their main purpose is to help you to do better. A beginner at golf may be so foolish as to kick a ball that has a bad lie so as to get an easier stroke or not to count a stroke. It doesn't prove that he is a cheater. It merely proves that he is very foolish and that his game will not improve while he plays in that spirit. We can be quite sure that he will keep a correct and honest score as soon as he really begins to like the game and to watch his daily growth. I'd like to have each one of you think of this test as something you need in order to watch your progress."

3. If possible, arrange a conference with, or visit the classroom of, a teacher who is known as a good "disciplinarian." What are the constructive factors in the teacher's practices? Does that teacher have any special "tricks of the trade" for avoiding disorder and inattention?

4. It is suggested that a group of students hold a conference on "The Prevention of Disorder." Make a list of serious discipline cases which you have observed. (In general it is futile for a group to discuss a situation involving a discipline

Some schools think their disciplinary problems are easier because they provide instruction in the social graces.(E)

problem that it has not observed. Why?) Try to indicate, for each, what you would have done, assuming that you were the teacher. Possibly a supervising teacher will be willing to participate in this student conference.

5. Comment on this statement which was made and put into practice by a classroom teacher.

Speaking to the pupils, "I have noticed some of you have trouble behaving yourselves in my class. Up to the present, nothing serious has happened, but before it does, I'm warning you by explaining how I keep my 'black-sheep list.' If anyone disturbs the class, cuts up, or misbehaves, I put them on the 'black-sheep list.' For every first offense I make a black dot to the right of each name. For the second offense, I double the dots, and so on. When I make out your marks at the end of each marking period I check through the 'black-sheep list' and take off as many points from each mark as you have in black dots."

6. "Epidemics" sometimes break out in classrooms and schools, *e.g.*, throwing paper airplanes, spinning tops, stamping feet, defacing desks and walls, hazing, smoking around the building, matching coins or throwing dice, and striking. In general, what procedure would you follow to correct any one of these situations?

7. Should pupils be kept after school for special work for being tardy? for not doing assigned work? for failing in a subject?

8. Describe a specific disciplinary problem that has come to your attention as a student teacher. What methods were used to correct the situation? What suggestions have you as to a better procedure?

9. A high-school senior wrote, "As a rule my teachers are just faces that change from term to term. But the teacher that I like best and the one that is easily the best disciplinarian will never be in that category. She always greets you in a manner that makes you feel welcome, not just another 'kid.'"

What do you think of the suggestion that a teacher's attitude should be that of the gracious host or hostess?

10. A beginning teacher wrote her friend, still in college, as follows:

"Sally just told me this morning that you wanted to know the difficulties that a teacher meets in her first year.

"She probably told you that discipline is my main problem. Many of my pupils are very bright and they don't know how to use their surplus energy and tend to answer questions before the one called upon can respond. In large classes, such a disturbance is very nerve-racking. Then, too, in my large classes I can't speak loudly enough for the whole class to hear. So I just keep quiet until they are quiet and then I continue. This happens about three times each class period. Of course, this wastes much time but I can't think of a better way. When I ask them why they act this way they are very sorry and promise to do better but they forget in ten minutes.

"When I started teaching, I was very idealistic and I thought I could accomplish everything with kindness but I am beginning to have my doubts. I now resort to measures that look bad in theory. I put discipline checks on report cards, I keep some of the athletes from playing on the school teams, I lower their marks on their report cards, or I make them do extra work. The older students I usually keep in during the ninth hour. The little seventh graders I slap with my hand or with a ruler that I have handy on my desk. The situation is I think a little better than it was but I still have a long way to go.

"Well, Ruth, I hope this is what you want and I hope I may see you during your vacation. With the best of luck and good wishes, I am

Sincerely yours,
Alice."

a. What do you think is the main cause of Alice's discipline problems?
b. What measure is Alice employing that you would never use?

11. Jane Dale, turning to her college instructor for advice on a discipline problem, wrote:

"My pupils in senior high-school English are inattentive and disposed to take advantage of every opportunity to create disturbance. For example, I asked one of my classes 'Why did Nero burn the Christians?' and Tony replied: 'Because he thought it would be a good idea to prepare them for the next world,' and Tony was the hero of the hour.

"I can't get these youngsters to hand in homework on time even when I threaten to refer them to the principal.

"In the senior class the students persist in asking me to tell stories of college life. We waste a lot of time. I have considered consulting the principal. But that doesn't seem such a good idea for he may not recommend me for reappointment when he learns of my many failures.

"Do you think that I should try to get advice from the more responsive students in my classes? Any suggestions that you send me will be deeply appreciated."

The following paragraphs will tell you how some experienced teachers in the same school diagnosed Miss Dale's difficulties:

Miss DALY: This is a sad case of a teacher who lacks a sense of humor. The chances are that if she had laughed heartily with the group she could have "cracked the whip" and driven them all the harder for the rest of the hour.

Mr. HALL: I think we are dealing here with a case of weak personality. The continued requests for stories of college life are symptomatic of a lack of respect for the teacher. It may have been a lack of reserve on the part of the teacher or a nervous desire to make good with the pupils.

Miss BATES: Obviously the pupils had no respect for the things they were doing. I would look first into subject matter: Is it a good choice of material? Is it organized as well as it could be? Wouldn't it be possible to find some activity or project that would absorb the energy of most of the pupils for a week or two? If this worked, then I would try to enlist the active interests of some of the others by doing intensive work with them in the conferences that I would seek during the periods of supervised study.

What do you think was the main cause for Miss Dale's troubles?

12. If you have seen the motion picture "Maintaining Classroom Discipline," discuss the following aspects:

(1) Why does Mr. Grimes behave as he does?
(2) Evaluate: (a) "This is the poorest class I have ever taught"; (b) "I'll make an example of you"; and (c) "The whole class will report back here at four o'clock."
(3) Why is a teacher not wise when he (a) uses sarcasm, (b) forces a pupil to "tattle," (c) insists that a pupil apologize to his teacher, (d) makes a threat, (e) refers many problems to the principal, and (f) uses work after school as a punishment?
(4) For what types of misbehavior would you send a pupil to the office?

(5) What's wrong with, "For every offense I subtract 5 per cent from a pupil's grade"?

(6) How would you teach pupils to "carry on" when you leave your classroom?

(7) How quiet should a well-managed room be?

(8) What specific things do you plan to do in order that your pupils may share with you the responsibility for maintaining good working conditions?

SUGGESTED READINGS

EDMONSON, J. B., JOSEPH ROEMER, and FRANCIS L. BACON: *The Administration of the Modern Secondary School.* New York: The Macmillan Company, 1948. Pp. xi + 690.

Here the young teacher will find the wisdom of three schoolmen of long experience. Chapters 10 to 16 will prove especially useful as supplementary reading to certain chapters in this book. For example, Chapter 10 includes a more nearly complete treatment of appropriate penalties.

GOETTING, MARTIN LUTHER: *Teaching in the Secondary School.* New York: Prentice-Hall Inc., 1942. Pp. xiii + 519.

Consult the index of this volume when you are looking for materials to supplement the topics in your textbook. Pages 58 to 67 deal with discipline from a different point of view.

GOLDBERG, HARRIET L.: *Child Offenders.* New York: Grune and Stratton, 1948. Pp. xiv + 215.

This is a very stimulating volume providing samples of day-by-day problems arising in a busy juvenile court. Some day, no doubt, society will be as much concerned about the prevention of antisocial behavior as about disease prevention. This volume speeds the day. There are a great many case studies. We hope you will read at least a few.

PRYOR, HELEN B.: *As the Child Grows.* New York: Silver Burdett Company, 1943. Pp. xvi + 400.

Two brief chapters—Chaps. 12 and 13—although short, contain much helpful material for teachers of the high school.

SHEVIAKOV, GEORGE V., and FRITZ REDL: *Discipline.* Washington: Department of Supervision and Curriculum Development, 1944. Pp. 64.

If you are willing to push through a thicket of split infinitives you will find in this pamphlet one of the most constructive discussions of discipline in pedagogical literature. Nevertheless, it is easy to read; long before the end you will conclude that, while the English is not always accurate, it is curiously charming and appropriate to the content.

TEXT-FILMS

The following McGraw-Hill Text-Film on Teacher Education has been correlated directly with Chap. IV.

Maintaining Classroom Discipline (14min sd MP). This film analyzes common problems met by teachers in the control of class conduct and in the fixing of desirable attitudes. Contrasting methods of handling a class are demonstrated. First, a classroom where schoolwork is neither instructive nor pleasant for anyone; typical kinds of pupil misbehavior are shown. Then the film analyzes this first sequence, showing that the trouble was largely due to deficiencies on the part of the teacher. The important effect of the teacher's personality on the students and on general class progress and behavior is shown. Finally, the film goes back to the starting point and shows how the same class, studying the same material could have been handled successfully by the same teacher. By this study of contrasting methods, basic principles for guiding a class into effective learning are illustrated.

Silent follow-up filmstrip provides statements and questions superimposed over scenes from the motion picture; the frames stimulate worth-while discussion that takes the form of sharing experiences which illustrate and apply the educational theory taught by the textbook and sound motion picture.

Chapter V

Principles of Routine and Classroom Management

A world whose schools are unreformed is an unreformed world.

—H. G. WELLS

THE ORGANIZATION OF ROUTINE PROCEDURE

Most gifted teachers routinize the details and mechanics of classroom management. There are many tasks in teaching that should be done quickly and without noise and confusion. The beginning teacher needs to learn how to reduce them to habitual modes of procedure. There are two main ideas to be kept in mind.

1. *Routine should be looked upon as definitely contributing to the education of the pupil.* To this end pupils and teachers must work cooperatively in getting the matter attended to, either by actual pupil participation or by a pupil attitude which facilitates the doing of the task. The management of the classroom provides a great variety of tasks which pupils can do so as to get practice in cooperation, in acceptance of responsibility, and in many character traits that presumably have carry-over values.

2. *The details must be managed so as to leave pupils and teachers free for the major activities of the hour.* Other things being equal, the better the teacher, the smoother and less obvious will be the routine management.

Fortunately there is no loss in efficiency in wide participation by pupils in classroom management. Most teachers will be able to find at least one pupil in a class of thirty who will be able to do a specific task at least as well as the teacher. There are two types of pupils who respond well to responsibility for little extra jobs of a managerial or routine type that can be delegated to them: the pupil with strong leadership traits—the future Rotarian—and the slow-learning or backward pupil. Hence, the experience values can be spread widely since the teacher can delegate without stigmatizing either the task or the pupil.

115

Suggestions for Managing Routine

To help you select the things that you will routinize and the manner in which this will be done, the following guides are suggested:

1. Routine procedures should be organized so as to yield a maximum amount of experience value to the pupil, the main goal being practice in accepting individual and group responsibility for tasks.

How early in the grades do you think pupils can be taught to help manage the materials in the classroom?[N]

2. Routine procedures should always seek to conserve the time and energy of pupils and teacher for application to the unit that the class is studying or to the major project under way.

3. Care should be taken to select the most desirable routine procedure, and then to use it until it becomes habitual.

4. When evaluating routine procedures some consideration should be given to their carry-over values in other life situations. For example, practice in group leadership would obviously be useful in a great many adult situations.

5. Effective routine should seek to conserve pupil initiative, not destroy it, and should encourage its exercise in harmony with the social activities of the school.

6. Pupil participation, both in setting up the routine procedure and in carrying it out, should be encouraged whenever practicable.

7. Effective routine procedures, already established in a school, should not be changed merely to satisfy the idiosyncrasies of a teacher. Greater educational values should be the chief criterion for any change.

8. Usually, the larger the class, the more necessary is mechanical routine.

9. Effective routine will avoid unnecessary confusion.

10. The pupil should in every case understand how the task should be done; he should understand the advantages to be gained in following certain routines when these advantages are not obvious; and always he should have a part in the appraisal of the quality of workmanship on tasks for which he has responsibility.

FOR DISCUSSION

1. Can you add an item to the preceding list?
2. What is the relation of routine to the problem of discipline?
3. Do you know of any school where routine measures were carried to an extreme? What specific changes would you recommend?
4. Do you know of any school where the mechanics of classroom management were disorganized, lacking in system? If so, what specific illustrations can you cite?

A generation ago, student teachers spent a week or more studying classroom management. Though the topic is just as important today, we try to manage so that you can pick up a little faster what needs to be learned. To that end we now call your attention to a learning device.

On page 118 you will find a check list of a great many items that most teachers would wish to consider routine matters. It will (1) give you an idea of the importance of good management and (2) draw your attention to changes that should be made in a classroom.

We suggest that you use the check list at least once. The idea is that you visit a schoolroom where a teacher and class are in action. In your observation, neglect everything except classroom management and record your judgments on the check list. As you work, ask yourself these questions: Has the matter been attended to with the least expenditure of time necessary for its proper accomplishment? Has the matter been accomplished without unnecessary noise and confusion? Have the pupils and the teacher worked cooperatively in getting the matter attended to, either by actual pupil participation or by a pupil attitude which facilitated the doing of the task? Is the result, as accomplished, good; *i.e.*, is there no way to improve it? Is routine delegated in a way that will yield educational values for the pupil?

INSTRUCTIONAL CHECK LIST ON ROUTINE

Directions: Mark each item of routine on the list as follows: If the item is entirely satisfactory, place a check (√) in the last column opposite it. If the item needs attention, place a cross (X) in the first column opposite it.

Items of routine	Needs attention	Satisfactory
1. *Physical Condition of the Room:*		
a. Adjusting shades to control light....................................		
b. Controlling artificial light..		
c. Regulating room temperature.......................................		
d. Regulating room ventilation..		
2. *Tidiness of the Room:*		
a. Removing waste from desks and floors...........................		
b. Caring for blackboard appearance................................		
c. Caring for bulletin-board appearance............................		
d. Caring for pictures and other decorations......................		
e. Caring for appearance of storecases, shelves, bookcases, maps, and other equipment...		
f. Keeping each pupil's seat or desk neat..........................		
3. *The Movement of Pupils:*		
a. Entering room from other classes...............................		
b. Going to regular seats..		
c. Passing to board or other work place...........................		
d. Getting books, supplies, or other material.....................		
e. Leaving room for other classes................................		
4. *Seating of Pupils:*		
a. Assigning seats to pupils......................................		
b. Revising the seating to meet needs (*e.g.*, seating pupils with respect to working together well; semicircle or hollow square)		
c. Providing for individual needs (*e.g.*, for seeing, hearing)............		
5. *Systematic Procedures:*		
a. Knowing names of pupils.......................................		
b. Beginning all activities promptly...............................		
c. Ending all activities on time...................................		
d. Providing continuous activity..................................		
e. Keeping everybody busy.......................................		
f. Initiating self-direction.......................................		
g. Assigning tasks...		
h. Checking results..		
6. *Handling Materials and Supplies:*		
a. Preparing for their use..		
b. Passing materials and supplies to pupils........................		
c. Collecting from pupils...		
d. Placing in storage...		
e. Passing or collecting notebooks................................		
f. Providing for uniformity in labeling and folding papers..............		
7. *Supplying Instructional Materials:*		
a. Providing for collecting.......................................		
b. Providing for filing and care..................................		
c. Providing for display...		
8. *Making Records and Reports:*		
a. Taking the roll...		
b. Recording pupil marks...		
c. Collecting data for office.....................................		
d. Making periodic reports.......................................		
9. *Courtesy in the Classroom:* Obtaining courtesy in		
a. Pupil-to-pupil relationships...................................		
b. Pupil-to-teacher relationships.................................		
c. Teacher-to-pupil relationships.................................		
d. Reception of visitors..		

You may need to visit a class more than once in order to check all the items that are included. In general it is desirable to use the check list in a classroom other than one in which you do your student teaching. If you happen to be especially interested, you may find it helpful to study classroom management in two extreme situations —one where the teacher is very competent and the other where there is much confusion and inefficiency.

Suggestions for a Written Report

When you have used the check list at least once according to the instructions, then proceed to do the following:

1. Of the routine items which you have indicated as needing attention by marking with an X, select two which you consider important, point out what was unsatisfactory in each, and suggest ways and means of improvement.

2. Of the routine items which you have indicated as satisfactory by marking with a √, select two which you consider important and give reasons for your opinion.

3. Which responsibilities in the check list do you believe can be delegated to individual pupils or committees of pupils?

4. Why is it justifiable to place the item of courtesy in a list of routine procedures?

Time Savers

Let us next consider some aspects of classroom management that seem especially important for a beginning teacher. The following list has been prepared by experienced teachers. Here you find good ways of conserving energy and improving your efficiency.

1. Assigning definite seats to pupils so as to reduce the time in taking the roll; a seating chart is helpful, and in some schools the task of taking the roll is delegated to responsible pupils.

2. Calling on definite individuals rather than waiting for volunteers.

3. Taking up common difficulties in class and assisting individual students after class.

4. Using student monitors to collect and distribute materials and papers.

5. Giving summarized mimeographed statements of future assignments.

6. Reserving library reference material in advance of assignments and placing it in an accessible place.

7. Assigning advanced work in such a way as to decrease difficulties in attacking it.

8. Correcting short quiz papers in class.

9. Using committees of the class to summarize contributions from all members of the class.

10. Giving students adequate instructions concerning the best way to report outside readings or to prepare special papers.

11. Keeping an office hour for consultation with students.

12. Delegating to responsible pupils the task of assisting the teacher in giving special attention to the heating and ventilating mechanisms.

13. Making certain that all pupils can hear what is said in class.

14. Making certain that all pupils can see demonstrations and illustrations.

15. Using inventory tests at the beginning of a unit of work and permitting pupils who have a satisfactory degree of mastery to "skip."

The typical school has plenty of responsibilities if only the teacher will delegate them wisely. Lots of things have to be managed in this classroom.(E)

16. Using the "score card" device by means of which all pupils write brief responses to crucial questions of the recitation instead of developing important issues by means of a conversation with a single pupil.

17. Teaching with a detailed outline of specific objectives of the chapter or of a unit in the hands of pupils.

For Discussion

1. Which items in the preceding list do you think are not used as commonly as they should be?

2. Probably we should give a final word of caution, for it is easy to overdo routine. Many items of routine have little educational value for pupils, and not

all of them should be routinized to the same extent, for the nature and character of some things you have to do in the classroom are such that their educational value for children is decreased when routinized. From the following list pick out those items that should be promptly routinized (a) to a high degree, (b) to some extent, or (c) not at all:

(1) The fire drill.
(2) Forming lines for marching in and out of the building.
(3) Talking in class without holding up hand to get permission.
(4) Leaving the classroom without permission.
(5) Starting a recitation when others are talking.
(6) Getting reference books from the classroom library.
(7) Holding pep meetings preceding a football game.
(8) In determining the mark for a semester, assigning some definite fraction as representing the value of the final examination.
(9) Calling the roll aloud each day.
(10) Dealing with problem pupils.
(11) Obtaining written excuses from parents for pupil absences.
(12) Excusing superior pupils from final examination.
(13) Passing or collecting notebooks.
(14) Labeling and folding papers.
(15) Keeping after school pupils who have done poor work in an English class.
(16) Entering the room from other classes.
(17) Requiring the pupils to say, "Good morning, teacher."
(18) Standing up to recite.
(19) Passing in and out of the assembly room.
(20) Using rules of order in conducting the business of the student council.

AVOIDING DRUDGERY IN TEACHING

No doubt some teachers avoid drudgery by good classroom management. Whether you will find drudgery in teaching, however, probably depends far more on your mental attitude and disposition than on the way that you manage the mechanics of teaching. This fact is illustrated in the following list[1] of guides for avoiding drudgery in teaching:

1. Keep yourself fit for service through special attention to diet, sleep, and exercise.

2. Cultivate friendships outside of the school circle in order that your leisure may bring relief from school interests.

3. Learn to see the humorous side of pupils' activities, as well as those of your associates.

4. Experiment occasionally with new materials, new methods, or new plans of organization.

[1] This list has been adapted from one originally compiled by Dean J. B. Edmonson, University of Michigan.

5. Avoid too much petty "shop talk" outside of school hours.

6. Seek to find something of compelling interest in every pupil.

7. Assume the viewpoint of a specialist toward troublesome pupils.

8. Plan the work of each recitation period in such a way as to keep all pupils efficiently employed, thus avoiding annoying disciplinary difficulties.

9. Plan the work of different classes for several weeks in advance.

The criterion for deciding whether or not a task is to be delegated to Bill Jones depends on what it will contribute to the education of Bill. (Assume that Bill can do the job well enough to meet the needs of the situation.)[B]

10. Give pupils the first chance to supplement, correct, or summarize the contributions of associates in a class.

11. Open classes on time with definite tasks that involve all the class, thus avoiding irritating disciplinary difficulties.

12. Anticipate the difficulties that pupils may have in preparing lessons, thus avoiding an antagonistic spirit on the part of the pupils.

13. Cultivate a spirit of success and happiness in the class or school.

14. Avoid the practice of using every week end for the correction of papers.

Do you recall a teacher of high-school or college days who dissipated his energy by failing to use one of the preceding suggestions?

CORRECTING PAPERS

We turn now to the last item of the preceding list which refers to the proper method of correcting papers. Learning how to correct written work in the most efficient way is one of the perplexing problems of a teacher. A teacher can easily drift into methods that will cause him to take time to read written work that should be devoted to resourceful planning, or he may waste his energy to the point where he is weary and lacking in vigor when the day begins. The grading of an excessive amount of written work is usually a by-product of an obsolete method of instruction and often represents poor organization of the work of the hour, possibly the use of the hour as a recitation period rather than a working period. To illustrate, here is a discussion of this time-worn issue by six experienced teachers:

Miss ALLEN: I correct one-third of the papers each day and throw the rest in the waste-paper basket. The pupils do not know that this is my practice as I never return papers to students. I find, however, that it is a waste of time to examine all the papers every day. Through an examination of the one-third I get evidence as to the quality of the daily preparation of the class. I base my marks on what the students do in class and do not post the marks from the daily papers.

Miss BROWN: I collect the papers every day and correct with great care the papers collected on one day per week. These papers are returned to the students. The pupils do not know the day that the papers are to be marked. I sometimes select the papers of the poorer students for marking every day.

Miss CLARK: I have the pupils exchange papers and correct them according to my directions. After the papers are corrected, the pupils making the corrections are required to sign their names under the mark placed on the paper. These papers are then returned to their rightful owners and later collected by me. I examine carefully the papers for certain days. If I find that a given student has been careless in making corrections, I penalize the pupil by taking a certain percentage from his monthly average. This practice serves to cause pupils to be honest and painstaking in the marking of papers.

Miss DABNEY: I have many of my papers in beginning work corrected by the pupils in my advanced class. I also use the plan of having the papers examined by committees of the class. Occasionally, I correct an entire set. I do not collect the papers every day, but ask that papers be in form to submit, even though I do not call for them. In general, I collect papers twice a week. I do not spend much time on marking papers, as I believe it is possible to evaluate the work of students more accurately by well-organized tests.

Miss EATON: I collect all papers at the beginning of the hour, and correct them before the next meeting of the class. The papers are then returned to the pupils and errors and mistakes discussed. I believe that a pupil is entitled to immediate return of all written work, and I do not approve of throwing aside any material without careful examination. I keep the records of these marks and at the end of the semester the average of the daily marks constitutes two-thirds of the final mark. I find that it is hard work to examine 120 algebra papers each day, but a conscientious teacher must expect to do this. I do not approve of the use of pupil help because this presents temptation many pupils cannot resist. I collect the papers at the beginning of the class hour in order to avoid copying of problems during the class period.

MISS FISHER: I have only a given amount of energy. If I use all of it correcting papers by the midnight lights, I cannot radiate enthusiasm and energy the next day. Moreover, the present-day school requires more thinking and energy than the school in which I began twenty years ago. I feel that the pupils deserve a teacher who enters the classroom confident and rested. I organize my work in units after the fashion of a laboratory course in science. In short, we do most of the work in school and I walk away from the building a free woman. Of course, I take one set home for each class about once a week, and these I spray generously and carefully with red ink.

FOR DISCUSSION

1. State the commendable procedures used by these teachers and list the practices that you consider questionable.

2. Which plan most nearly approximates one that you would approve?

3. Do you think that many teachers lack energy and resourcefulness in their planning as the result of having spent an excessive amount of time grading homework papers in the late hours of the night? Do you recall ever having had a teacher who was a good illustration of this point?

4. In some training programs, student teachers find it interesting to appoint a small committee to interview half a dozen teachers with the purpose of discovering the variation in hours devoted per week to the evaluation and correction of the written work of pupils.

THE PERSONALITY OF A CLASSROOM[1]

One of the phases of a teacher's responsibility often neglected is that of making the classroom a pleasant place in which to work. Successful teachers are usually alert and resourceful in providing an environment appropriate to the activities in which pupils participate; they recognize the importance of giving every classroom a unique personality appropriate to the subject or even to the unit that is being taught.

It is quite impractical to list specific steps you could take to give your classroom a personality. The particular setting of the room

[1] To the supervisor of student teachers: Presumably no justification is needed for including this topic in this chapter. You will agree, will you not, that creating an appropriate atmosphere is a very important part of classroom management?

will depend on many factors, *e.g.*, the age, interests, and abilites of your pupils, the nature of the subject taught, and the specific objectives of the unit of work.

If you are interested in doing all that is possible to improve the appearance of the typical drab and uninspiring classroom, let us take a view of Miss Carr's room in which she is introducing a unit of work on "The People of Mexico."

The details of classroom routine should be managed so as to leave pupils and teacher free for the major activities of the hour.[H]

In the center of a large bulletin board several posters of Mexican bullfights attract notice. Around these are scattered more than twenty post cards of views of the country and its people. On the wall to the right of the pupils appear a number of pictorial maps of Mexico. A table in the rear of the room is used for an exhibit of paper dolls dressed in highly colored Mexican costumes. Among other materials appear Mexican menus, magazines, a newspaper, pottery, and tourist folders advertising the new road.

A little of this material had been posted on the bulletin board prior to teaching the unit so as to give Miss Carr a flying start. She did not like the idea of starting a unit on Mexico with the pupils knowing no more about this interesting country than that it was a

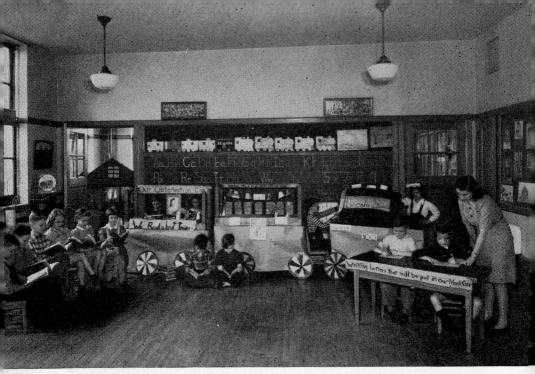

The main goal of good management is to provide practice in accepting individual and group responsibility for tasks. Good management cuts the teacher's load. Many a teacher works himself to frayed nerves by doing things that students could do with educational profit.[Y]

blot of color on the map. When the class entered the room Miss Carr permitted the pupils to walk around and examine the pictures on the walls. Almost immediately the pupils were involved in an interesting discussion in which they were guessing what the scenes might be.

When the discussion seemed to reach the stage of diminishing returns, Miss Carr called the class to order and asked the pupils whether anyone had anything to contribute to the Mexican exhibit. Before the period was half over an art committee was scanning reference books for suggestions. In another corner of the room a committee was planning to make samples of handwork, and a third committee was poring over various catalogues copying the names and addresses of companies and agencies that would furnish free materials upon request.

A visitor to this room would instantly recognize the character of the unit that Miss Carr was teaching. The classroom had been given a setting appropriate for a specific unit of work.

What formula did Miss Carr use? If we asked her how she accomplished this, the answer might appear as follows: "Take ten parts of pupil cooperation and one part of teacher initiative. Season generously with resourcefulness, pour in a few grains of common sense, sprinkle well with enthusiasm, and let simmer in the minds of pupils. Test the mixture in a day or two by looking around the classroom for a change of 'atmosphere,' and then 'cook up a different batch' for every unit."

FOR DISCUSSION

1. Find out from your supervising teacher the nature of the next unit of work for the class. What would you do to change the appearance of the classroom? Your suggestions should be practical to the extent that the changes suggested can actually be made by you and the pupils in the class.

2. Check the personality of the classroom in which you do your student teaching by using the check list on page 128. Keep in mind the fact that here we are not concerned with the teacher's efficiency, the worth of the subject matter, or the value of activities under way. The specific question is: Is this a good place and a good setting for the job the teacher and the pupils are trying to do? It is obvious that you will rate many items that the teacher has no power to change. Nevertheless these matters probably affect the total outcome of their efforts. In any case, it may do much good to draw your attention to such items.

The use of the check list is likely to be more meaningful if several student teachers check a classroom in cooperative fashion. Each student should make an independent rating. By a comparison of his rating with the ratings of other students he may find it interesting to note to what extent they agree as to (*a*) items in need of adjustment; (*b*) items that are excellent; and (*c*) the factors that are beyond the control of the teacher.

A GUIDE FOR USING THE CHECK LIST

1. *The Teacher:*
   a. Attitude toward pupils: has respect for personality of each pupil.
   b. Posture: sits and stands without slouching.
   c. Physical vitality: is enthusiastic, genial, full of life, and radiates an atmosphere of good feeling.
   d. Mental alertness: is sensitive, resourceful and vigorous.
   e. Dress: is suitable; attracts no unfavorable attention to itself. Scrupulous attention to details. It should tend toward the attractive. Smartness counts.
   f. Voice: is soft, well modulated, and clear; not high pitched, rasping, or mumbled.
   g. Manner: is courteous, polite, and cheerful.
   h. Culture: "Imagination sensitive to things of intellectual value and a power of discriminating choice among values that one's surroundings offer, are the chief marks of the cultivated mind."—DEWEY.

CHECK LIST FOR THE PERSONALITY OF A CLASSROOM

Directions: The first item to be rated is the teacher. Note the 10 subdivisions. Check each subdivision in one of the two columns. When in doubt glance at the guide on page 127; then continue.

Item	Needs attention	Satisfactory	Item	Needs attention	Satisfactory
1. *The Teacher:*			9. *Location:*		
a. Attitude toward pupils			*a.* Noises, street, play group,		
b. Posture			and pupil traffic		
c. Physical vitality			10. *Decoration:*		
d. Mental alertness			*a.* Pictures, appropriateness		
e. Dress			*b.* Pictures, number		
f. Voice			*c.* Pictures, position		
g. Manner			*d.* Pictures, condition		
h. Culture			*e.* Plants and flowers, appropriateness		
i. Poise			*f.* Plants and flowers, condition		
j. Absence of physical handicaps			*g.* Plants and flowers, arrangement		
2. *Cleanliness:*			*h.* Walls and woodwork, color		
a. Floor			*i.* Walls and woodwork, finish		
b. Blackboard			*j.* Harmony of room		
c. Desks			11. *Bulletin Board:*		
d. Windows and walls			*a.* Amount		
e. Pupils and teacher			*b.* Quality		
3. *Seating:*			*c.* Placement		
a. Seeing			*d.* Attractiveness of display		
b. Hearing			*e.* Appropriateness		
c. Arrangement			12. *Blackboard:*		
d. Adjustment			*a.* Amount		
4. *Lighting:*			*b.* Placement		
a. Windows, glass area			*c.* Condition		
b. Windows, placement			*d.* Kind		
c. Shades, color			*e.* Eraser and chalk		
d. Shades, adjustment			13. *Built-in Cases:*		
e. Artificial lighting			*a.* Amount		
5. *Furniture:*			*b.* Placement		
a. Pupil desks, type			14. *Storage:*		
b. Pupil desks, condition			*a.* Amount		
c. Teacher desk, type			*b.* Placement		
d. Teacher desk, condition			*c.* Condition		
e. Extra seats			15. *Miscellaneous Equipment:*		
6. *Heating:*			*a.* Amount		
a. Temperature			*b.* Placement		
b. Humidity			*c.* Condition		
7. *Supplementary Materials:*			16. *Visual Aids:*		
a. Amount			*a.* Usefulness		
b. Selection			*b.* Amount		
c. Condition					
d. Arrangement					
e. Modernity					
8. *Ventilation*					

    i. Poise: has ability to maintain self-confidence and self-control.

    j. Absence of physical handicaps: physical form and features are free from annoying defects; is physically fit.

2. *Cleanliness:*

    a. Floor: is free from dust, dirt, and trash; is free from ink spots or other stains. •

    b. Blackboard: is as clean as possible under working conditions.

    c. Desks: are free from trash and accumulations of materials producing unsightly effect; have no ink spots or other blotches.

    d. Windows and walls: are free from dirt, dust, and spots.

    e. Pupils and teacher: exhibit personal cleanliness.

3. *Seating:*

    a. Seeing: pupils correctly seated for nearsightedness or farsightedness.

    b. Hearing: pupils seated with respect to hearing difficulties of individuals.

    c. Light: should be adequate and reduce annoyance and fatigue to a minimum.

    d. Arrangement: provides for a flexible change of seating to meet class needs. In laboratories accessibility is needed for individual conference and guidance.

    e. Adjustment: desks, chairs, or tables should be suited to the size of pupils and to type of activity. Observe extent to which pupils *use* right size, if provided.

4. *Lighting:*

    a. Windows, glass area: should be from $\frac{1}{5}$ to $\frac{1}{4}$ of floor area; clear glass.

    b. Windows, placement: windows should be on long axis of the room and in general to the left of pupils; window heads square and close to ceiling; 4 to 7 ft. dead space from last window to front of room; 3 to 5 ft. dead space from last window to rear wall.

    c. Shades, color: to harmonize with the walls.

    d. Shades, adjustment: hung from center of window and adjustable; note position and condition.

    e. Artificial lighting: no glare, reflection, or harsh shadows; even throughout; rows of lights controlled by separate switches.

5. *Furniture:*

    a. Pupil desks, type: desks, seats, or tables designed to afford a comfortable and convenient working space for each pupil, and space for pupils' books and materials.

    b. Pupil desks, condition: smooth, attractive work surface and in good repair; tidy.

    c. Teacher desk, type: substantial, adequate, attractive; size of top 30 by 42 in.; height 30 in.

    d. Teacher desk, condition: good repair, books and materials neatly arranged.

    e. Extra seats: one or two, for seating visitors (*e.g.*, parents) so as to prevent interfering with work of pupils.

6. *Heating:*
   a. Temperature: thermometer, placed on the wall opposite the windows, should indicate approximately 68°F (maximum 70°).
   b. Humidity: attention to the atmosphere of the room to see that it does not become too dry.
7. *Supplementary Materials:*
   a. Amount: quantity and variety appropriate to the nature of work and number of pupils.
   b. Selection: appropriate to age of pupils and subject taught.
   c. Condition: not torn, broken, or worn so as to interfere with use.
   d. Arrangement: tidy, easily accessible.
   e. Usefulness: materials not obsolete; suited to present-day activities.
8. *Ventilation:*
   Fresh air entering the room at all times. No sign of stuffiness; freedom from undesirable air currents.
9. *Location:*
   a. Noises: room should be undisturbed by noises of street, playground, or adjacent rooms, and during working periods undisturbed by pupil traffic in halls.
10. *Decoration:*
    a. Pictures, appropriateness: carefully selected for the appreciation of pupils and suited to the work of the room; in particular, to the unit being taught. In general, pictures of individuals not recommended, though obviously Shakespeare in an English room, Lincoln in a civics room, and the like would be entirely appropriate.
    b. Pictures, number: too many as bad as too few; two or three should be sufficient.
    c. Pictures, position: attractively placed according to the space to be used and for effectiveness, to be easily seen by those seated in the room.
    d. Pictures, condition: not faded, or worn, or abused, but on the whole pleasing to the eye.
    e. Plants and flowers, appropriateness: select flowers and plants to give color and attractiveness to the room; amount should maintain a proper balance.
    f. Plants and flowers, condition: fresh, free from dead or diseased parts.
    g. Plants and flowers, arrangement: attractively and neatly arranged to give proper balance.
    h. Walls and woodwork: color combination pleasing.
11. *Bulletin Board:*
    a. Amount: minimum 42 by 72 in. Additional amount in proportion to the type of work. Few rooms have an adequate amount.
    b. Quality: good quality of cork or equivalent material.
    c. Placement: on one side; so as not to distract class attention, but easily visible.
    d. Attractiveness of display: materials arranged so as to present a pleasing, symmetrical effect; appropriate to the unit taught.
    e. Modernness: material fresh, up to date, and challenging interest.

12. *Blackboard:*
    a. Amount: minimum of 50 sq. ft. Additional area should be in proportion to the amount of group board work engaged in by pupils.
    b. Placement: on front wall and wall to the right of pupils. Chalk rail should be about 36 in. from floor in junior and senior high schools.
    c. Condition: when not in use, free of all matter not being preserved. Work being preserved should be neatly and carefully arranged.
    d. Kind: fine grain, smooth, black slate. The sections should be from 3 to 3½ ft. wide and about 4 ft. long. The joints between sections should be tight fitting and smooth.
    e. Eraser and chalk: all boards provided with dust trays, reasonably free from accumulations of chalk dust. Erasers should be noiseless, all felt, and in sufficient quantity for class needs.

13. *Built-in Cases:*
    a. Amount: at least one case for display of work or for museum purposes. Total amount should be in proportion to class needs and room balance. Few classrooms have an adequate amount.
    b. Placement and appropriateness: design and placement such as to carry out the purposes. The doors may be clear plate glass or triple strength window glass.

14. *Storage:*
    a. Amount: should be adequate for the units taught in the room.
    b. Placement and condition: easily accessible and not to detract from appearance of room; clean, dust-tight, in good repair, and harmonizing with the rest of the room; all materials stored in an orderly manner.

15. *Miscellaneous Equipment:*
    a. Amount: the minimum and necessary amount should be provided, *e.g.*, pencil sharpener, paper basket, etc. (Radio: provision for plugging in.)
    b. Placement and condition: kept in proper place for convenient use and least disturbance when used; in good repair, attractive, and of good quality.

16. *Visual Aids:*
    a. Usefulness: up to date and carefully evaluated.
    b. Amount: in general classrooms have far too little.

For Discussion

1. How many of the classrooms of your elementary school days suggested detention or custodial care rather than a pleasant place to work? How about your high-school rooms? The classrooms of your college years?

2. Does it surprise you to find items relating to the teacher in the Check List for the Personality of a Classroom?

A Final Word of Advice

Schools differ in the practices of routine management. The way of reporting absence and tardiness is a good illustration. A training program cannot prepare you completely for all the forms which you

In a crowded stiutation like this a teacher would be very inefficient if he did not use effective routine procedures.[N]

will need to fill out when you start full-time teaching. Some of the reports that you will be required to make to the main office or to various persons may seem baffling. It is not wise to worry too much about your clerical duties. However, it is sensible to collect all the forms—preferably in the days immediately preceding the opening of school—and to arrange a brief conference with some experienced teacher who can probably show you in a very short time what to do. Most faculties include teachers who are not only willing but very anxious to lend a helping hand to a teacher new to the school.

GOOD EXPERIENCE

1. If possible get your supervising teacher to delegate responsibility to you for a bulletin-board exhibit that will aid in the teaching of the unit that a class is studying or one that will presently be undertaken. It is perhaps unnecessary to suggest that you may find it desirable to have the assistance of a small committee of pupils. Don't forget to take at least a few minutes to get a pupil evaluation of the exhibit.

2. If you happen to be in your home community—perhaps during a brief vacation—visit a school in session and use one, or

preferably both, of the check lists in this chapter. If it fits the plans of your supervising teacher, make a very brief report of your findings. (Be sure that you do not disturb the teacher or pupils by writing or checking. In general, it is better to check the lists after you leave the building. If there is an item that the check list does not recall, it probably isn't very important.)

SUGGESTED READINGS

BOSSING, NELSON L.: *Progressive Methods of Teaching in Secondary Schools*. Boston: Houghton Mifflin Company, 1942. Pp. xvii + 778.

This book provides many practical suggestions for the beginning teacher. Chapters 2, 3, and 4 are especially good on management technique.

GOETTING, MARTIN LUTHER: *Teaching in the Secondary School*. New York: Prentice-Hall, Inc., 1942. Pp. xiii + 519.

Chapter III entitled "Managing the Classroom" is one that you should read to supplement the discussion in this volume.

PERRY, BLISS: *And Gladly Teach*. Boston: Houghton Mifflin Company, 1935. Pp. ix + 315.

This autobiography of a great teacher, written in a very interesting style and revealing a fine sense of professional zeal, has been a source of inspiration to many teachers. You may wish to keep this book in mind and read it after you have been teaching a few months.

RIVLIN, HARRY N.: *Teaching Adolescents in Secondary Schools*. New York: Appleton-Century-Crofts, Inc., 1948. Pp. xi + 516.

Chapter XI has many practical suggestions for you on classroom management.

Chapter VI

Teacher and Pupils Plan Together

I love to teach as a painter loves to paint, as a musician loves to play, as a singer loves to sing, as a strong man rejoices to run a race. Teaching is an art—an art so great and so difficult to master that a man or a woman can spend a long life at it, without realizing much more than his limitations and mistakes, and his distance from the ideal.

—WILLIAM LYON PHELPS

THEN AND NOW IN PLANNING

If your grandparents were teachers, they no doubt spent a great deal of time writing lesson plans during their training period. Perhaps they wrote three or four pages longhand for a single lesson. Then, too, the lesson plan in that day was pretty rigid in the sense that it had to be built in a certain way and adhered to during the hour of instruction. Many student teachers taught with one eye fixed on the lesson plan. Moreover, many training schools used the same pattern of lesson plan in the various school subjects.

Naturally you ask: Is there anything new? The answer is that some changes have been made; that the lesson plan for today is different from the one that grandfather used. To begin, we are pretty sure that different subject areas call for different patterns. There is no one fixed form of lesson plan. Planning for a chemistry lesson is one thing, planning an activity in general science is something else, and both are different from planning a project in the social studies. Then, too, we don't stick to a lesson plan, come what may. Indeed, we try to teach student teachers today to sense when it is necessary to modify a plan that has been carefully designed. But the most important change is a broader concept of planning. Today we insist that the pupil must have a part. Indeed we realize that pupil planning is an integral part of the learning act. Or, putting it another way, planning has shifted into instruction. So we now minimize the teacher's plans—though he has to do far more than in that distant earlier day—and we emphasize the notion of teacher and pupils planning together.

THE IMPORTANCE OF PLANNING IN TEACHING

The teacher is not the only person who needs to plan his work carefully in order to be effective. An attorney attempts to anticipate and prepare for every move in a court trial; the minister who holds his congregation visualizes the parts of the church service; the sales manager gives careful attention to every step in a proposed selling campaign; and the hostess plans the details of a successful dinner. Two of the best illustrations of planning in modern time are provided by radio programs and the football coach who prepares for the week-end game.

Although most workers in positions of responsibility need to plan, there is probably no type of work where the results of poor planning are so devastating as in teaching. Do not be misled by the occasional teacher with a colorful personality and a resourceful mind who seems to be getting results without careful planning. It is significant that most of the gifted teachers in demonstration schools spend much time and energy planning units of work which they have taught many times and for which the outlines of procedure are very clear in their minds. They realize that pupil growth is, in the last analysis, dependent on the careful selection and the systematic and purposeful arrangement of activities and experiences geared to the level and abilities and interests of each pupil. The importance of planning is also suggested by the fact that some principals still insist that their teachers file, in advance, the detailed plans of every lesson to be taught during the week. In general if a teacher does not have definitely in mind what is to happen when he enters his classroom, very little that is worth while will happen in that period. A plan tends to prevent wandering from the subject. It is a common fault of teachers to waste time on an irrelevant question which interests only a few pupils. A beginning teacher finds it difficult to keep several things in mind at one time. An unimportant disciplinary incident may be enough to cause him to forget a block of material or to change the order so as to lose the connection for the pupils and thus make the hour seem futile to them. Then, too, a well-prepared lesson plan helps to overcome the feeling of nervousness and insecurity so common in the first attempts at teaching.

The typical teacher is decidedly limited in what he can do in planning. He faces the necessity of three, four, or even five daily preparations for large classes; he discharges extensive extracurricular duties and meets a wide variety of community obligations.   While it is extremely helpful to write daily lesson plans during student-teaching days, the teacher on the job must learn to do systematic planning with a minimum amount of writing.   In this chapter you will have practice in writing the kind of lesson plans that are helpful in student-teaching days when one finds it difficult to keep so many things in mind, and we shall describe the practical type of planning that the busy teacher can use when operating with a full schedule of classes.

Three types of planning will be discussed: (1) The work of the year must be outlined in some definite manner; *i.e.*, areas of the curriculum or subjects must be divided into related units.   (2) Each unit must be planned with some care, and this we shall call planning the larger unit.   (3) Each daily lesson must be planned in advance.

Planning the Area or the Subject for the Year

The beginning teacher of a generation ago found his subject already planned for the year; he was given a single textbook that he was expected to follow.   Although poorly trained teachers still use the textbook as a crutch upon which to lean for the sole support of their day's inspiration, its use as a single source is rapidly disappearing.   Creative teachers have discovered that a single textbook is rarely adequate for the needs and interests of all pupils.   Then, too, we need to remember that the tremendous growth in the population of the secondary school has added pupils with low native ability, who are weak in fundamental skills and who have meager cultural backgrounds.   Perhaps this explains why even experienced teachers plan their work anew each year.

The main reason why planning has become so important in the modern school lies in a shift in emphasis or the adoption of new goals. Yesterday's teacher taught subject matter, and factual knowledge was given undue emphasis; the teacher of today is interested also in the social and personal development of the individual pupil.   In grandfather's time instruction was an end; today it is a means to an end—the end being the acquisition of desirable habits, attitudes, and skills on the part of pupils.   It is obvious that subjects become functional only when they serve as bases for setting up situations or providing experiences in an environment that will insure the development of the most desirable attitudes, skills, and habits in pupils. In brief, the various areas of the curriculum must enable us to achieve the fundamental goals of education. Nor can we achieve them unless we know what these goals are.

Since the days of ancient Greece, philosophers have been concerned with what education should do for and to the individual.

Here is a little group in one corner of a classroom planning a project. One of the new things that has come into planning in the last ten years is the notion of teacher and pupil planning together.[M]

Plato advocated an education aimed at the all-round development of the body and soul to an appreciation of beauty and perfection. Aristotle, Comenius, Rousseau, Pestalozzi, Herbart, Froebel, and Spencer each developed a philosophy of education conditioned by the mental climate in which he lived. We also must concern ourselves with planning instruction in the light of the aims of education that are acceptable today in the midst of this changing social order.

In recent times we have had numerous attempts to formulate the goals of public education. Probably the seven goals mentioned

in the *Cardinal Principles of Secondary Education*[1] have been most
widely quoted and kept in mind by teachers when outlining courses
and organizing instructional materials. A more recent report[2]
identifies four aspects of educational purposes as follows:

> These aspects center around the person himself, his relationship to others in
> the home and community, the creation and use of material wealth, and socio-civic
> activities. The first area calls for a description of the educated *person;* the second,
> for a description of the educated *member of the family and community group;* the
> third, of the educated *producer or consumer;* the fourth, of the educated *citizen.*
> The four great groups of objectives thus defined are: (1) The Objectives of Self-
> realization; (2) The Objectives of Human Relationship; (3) The Objectives of
> Economic Efficiency; (4) The Objectives of Civic Responsibility.[3]

We now begin to see what is involved in planning the year's work
in a subject or an area in the secondary school. Two things must
be done before we can do this job: (1) The subject must be planned
in such a way that it will, beyond a shadow of a doubt, make a contribution to one or more of these fundamental goals of education.
(2) The subject or the area must be analyzed in order to identify
the specific contributions that this subject or area may make in
developing in the pupils those particular skills and habits peculiar to
that subject. It is clear that the specific skills and habits that should
be achieved in English will differ from those emphasized in mathematics or chemistry.

But the crux of planning the year's work is to determine how
our broad purposes of general education may be made to function
in the actual teaching situation of a given subject or area. Let us
assume that we wish to teach civic responsibility. Now it is clear
that any purpose in education such as that of "civic responsibility"
is altogether too broad in scope to use as a sole criterion in selecting
subject matter. Civic responsibility is in itself an abstraction and
as such cannot be taught directly. But we can list some specific
skills and attitudes that make for worthy civic responsibility. Then
with these in mind we can plan a course so as to include those activities that will give pupils an opportunity to experience habits of

[1] *U.S. Bureau of Education Bulletin*, 1918, No. 35. The seven goals were, briefly, (1) health,
(2) command of fundamental processes, (3) worthy home membership, (4) vocation,
(5) citizenship, (6) worthy use of leisure, and (7) ethical character.
[2] *The Purposes of Education in American Democracy.* Washington: Educational Policies
Commission of the National Education Association, 1938.
[3] *Ibid.*, p. 47.

civic responsibility. The first task of the teacher then is to determine what the specific characteristics are of the ideal citizen who accepts his full share of civic responsibility. The Educational Policies Commission[1] considers the following to be a summary of the earmarks of one who realizes his responsibility as a citizen: (1) He is sensitive to the disparities of human circumstance; (2) he

What would you do if a chairman continued to insist on the adoption of his particular plan?

acts to correct unsatisfactory conditions; (3) he seeks to understand social structures and social processes; (4) he has defenses against propaganda; (5) he respects honest differences of opinion; (6) he has a regard for the nation's resources; (7) he measures scientific advance by its contribution to the general welfare; (8) he is a cooperating member of the world community; (9) he respects the law; (10) he is economically literate; (11) he accepts his civic duties; and (12) he acts upon an unswerving loyalty to democratic ideals.[2]

[1] *Ibid.*, p. 109.
[2] The Commission has likewise enumerated the objectives of the other three major purposes in its report.

If we accept the preceding list as a satisfactory analysis of the good citizen, the details which link the broad purposes of education and the classroom situation are now altogether evident, for this list of traits suggests to the well-prepared teacher of the social studies a great variety of problems, projects, and activities for classroom use. It may turn out that no two teachers would select the same units to achieve this goal of civic responsibility. There are many acceptable ways of combining a given list of foods into a good meal, and there may be several good roads leading to a common educational objective.

Perhaps you would like to know more about the extent to which the plan for the year should appear in writing. No rule can be given you. Some teachers prefer to read widely and confine their plans to an outline of a few pages. If, on the other hand, you are inexperienced or you find yourself called on to teach a subject in which you are not well prepared, more reading and more written plans may be necessary. In any case you should see, mentally at least, how you intend to relate the broad purposes of education to classroom situations. Furthermore, you should know what basic skills and dispositions you wish to develop in the pupils through your subject or area. Finally, you should have in mind the point or level of thinking from which you intend to start, and a tentative terminal point. The whole plan for the year should be regarded merely as a flexible guide. It has the same function as a general roadmap which shows you that in going from New York to San Francisco you are going to pass through Philadelphia, Chicago, and Denver. When you actually travel the road segment from New York to Philadelphia you will need a more detailed guide, and that is the purpose of the next section on planning, which deals with how to plan the unit of instruction.

Planning the Unit of Work

The wide acceptance of the unit concept has come at least in part as a protest against treating each day's lesson as an unrelated and isolated segment of learning. It used to be a common practice of teachers to make rigid daily lesson plans arranged so as to conform to the interval of the class period. In more recent years, however, we have seen the need for the gradual growth of the individual pupil through participating in experiences that are continuous, integrated, and unified around a central problem or project. Thus the major unit has apparently been the answer to the prayer of the teacher who wanted to get rid of the formal and mechanical type of daily recitations and the excessive use of the question-and-answer technique.

Other advantages sometimes claimed for the unit plan of instruction are:

1. It is easier to provide for (*a*) individual differences, (*b*) directed study, (*c*) socialization, and (*d*) remedial teaching.

2. It is possible to arrange a sensible balance between individual or independent work and cooperative or group activities.

3. The division of a subject or area into units enables the teacher to see the relation of a particular subject-matter area to the fundamental purposes of education, and moreover forces the teacher to weigh values carefully when listing the special objectives of the subject.

4. It permits the teacher to plan activities that change the classroom from an isolated social situation into a vital laboratory of life by basing selection and organization of material on human needs and the persistent problems of life.

GUIDES TO THE UNIT PLAN OF INSTRUCTION

The unit plan takes on many forms in different school systems. Indeed, many names—contract, challenge, job, etc.—are used to identify the method. Probably no acceptable definition of the unit plan could be formulated. However, one can describe what takes place and list the ideals that emerge when teachers employ it. The following basic guides are suggested:

1. *The year's work is divided into a series of related units, each built around some central or organizing idea.* To illustrate, a tenth-grade class may be studying, "Am I normal?"; a seventh-grade mathematics class, "How accurately do people measure in the stores and shops along Main Street in our town?"; an eighth-grade class, "How shall we furnish and decorate the lunchroom in our school?"; a senior-high-school group of girls, "What is the desirable environment for Betty Jane, age three years, in our nursery school?"; an eleventh-grade class, "The westward movement"; and a ninth-grade algebra class, "The four-fold method of expressing number relationships."

When designing or reorganizing a unit, keep in mind the recurring activities in everyday living. Probably the best statement of the persistent problems of people in any age is provided by Frederick and Farquear in the Mississippi State Curriculum Program. The list[1] of nine activities which this study suggests is as follows:

(1) *Protecting life and health:* medical science, life, health, conservation, mental health, safety, protection against disease, accidents, fears.

(2) *Getting a living:* vocations, maintenance, production, distribution, consumption, economy, labor, occupation, industry, unemployment, work, capital wealth, income.

It takes a lot of careful planning to operate a workroom successfully. When the inept see a situation like this, they are likely to conclude that there is no planning.[N]

(3) *Making a home:* parental responsibilities, practical activities, domestic, family, childhood and youth, biological heritage, personal and household regimen, child rearing, private property, conservation of property, sex, marriage, courtship and love, eugenics, housing, food, clothing, "we consumers," parent education, position of women.

(4) *Expressing religious impulses:* morality, religious organization, the church, religious practices, philosophy of life.

[1] J. Paul Leonard. *Developing the Secondary School Curriculum*, pp. 371-372. New York: Rinehart & Company, Inc., 1946.

(5) *Satisfying the desire for beauty:* culture, fine arts, mythology, aesthetics, literature, language arts, charm and good manners.

(6) *Securing education:* mental efficiency, culture, self-improvement, childhood and youth, the school, the press, cinema, the radio, integration of the individual, intellectual vision, how to study, reflective thinking and capacity for work, prevailing ideals, "folkways," and "mores."

(7) *Cooperating in social and civic action:* international relations, social relationships, citizenship, justice, crime and punishment, government, social and public welfare, work, taxation, law, ameliorative institutions, social attitudes, the community, democracy, farm relief, social protection, war, conservation of property, extension of freedom, the constitutions, legislation, population, people, social intercommunication.

(8) *Engaging in recreation:* leisure, enjoyable bodily and mental activity.

(9) *Improving material conditions:* communication and transportation, physical heritage, invention, exploration, discoveries, technological development, science, material traits, scientific knowledge, conservation of material resources, nature, men and machines, power, steel, mastery of material circumstances, expanding the sources of science, adventure and risk, plants and animals, climate, natural wealth, standards of living.

Obviously the number of units constituting a year's work will vary from class to class. Undoubtedly a number between two and twelve is better than a larger number of units. One investigator reports a year's work in biology as consisting of 60 units, but it is difficult to see how such a course could avoid being superficial and fragmentary. It follows that the nature of the project and the maturity of the pupils will have some part in determining the length of the unit. Some teachers have the conviction that a desirable length for a unit is about three or four weeks, though one or two topics in the preceding list of illustrations would undoubtedly keep a high-school class busy throughout a semester.

2. *A well-planned unit includes many and varied activities in which pupils must find, organize, and use facts that throw light on the basic problem which the class is studying.* There should be many things for pupils to do that call not only for physical activity but for a wide sampling of mental life, such as constructing, drawing, carving, pasting, painting, cartooning, reading, memorizing, writing, dramatizing, investigating, and graphing. These activities will range from the simple and easy to the complex and difficult. By spreading the activities over a wide range of both interest and difficulty the teacher finds it easier to adjust to the needs of individual pupils. The slow-learning pupil who profits most through wide

sense experiences has a chance to make his contribution to the thinking of the group by constructing some graphic illustration, whereas
the pupil who reads quickly and widely and who has learned to work
independently may bring in a well-organized report presenting relationships which the others can understand and appreciate but which
they could not possibly collect and organize.

Here we see a student teacher raising a question about one item in a plan that has been
cooperatively developed.   Do you think the students are interested in what she is saying?(E)

   3. *In a well-planned unit much of the time that was formerly called
the recitation period will be devoted to work.*   Obviously an hour in
which pupils collect information, prepare reports, and share experiences is a type of class period very different from that of an earlier
day, largely devoted to questions and answers.   The proponents
of the unit plan have combined techniques borrowed largely from
two sources: (*a*) procedures employed in the science laboratory
and (*b*) the ideals of the project method to be discussed in a later
chapter.

SUGGESTIONS FOR USING THE UNIT PLAN

Having studied the basic guides underlying the unit plan or organization, let us next examine some suggestions that deal with the details. Before trying to teach a unit, use the following check list for evaluating your plan:

1. The unit should be worked out in tentative form with a particular class in mind.

2. The following steps are suggested in planning the unit:
   a. Write the specific objectives.
   b. Try to write a good test covering the objectives or consider other desirable ways of appraising the unit.
   c. List the activities in which pupils may engage.
   d. List the sources of subject matter which pupils will consult.
   e. Write such materials as may be needed to supplement textbook materials.
   f. If guide sheets are employed, write them.

3. In the orientation—perhaps one or two class periods—the time should be devoted to: (*a*) a general overview of the unit and (*b*) teacher and pupils *planning together* a modification of the outline of the unit in terms of the particular interests and needs of the class.

4. It is desirable to indicate the relative difficulty of activities. For example, in a mathematics class it may be possible to employ three lists of problems—an easy one, a harder one, and a more difficult list—each written to give practice in the application of the same set of principles. In like manner activities may be roughly classified as involving different levels of creative work, analysis, and generalization.

5. A good unit should tie in with the out-of-school activities of the pupils. It should utilize the experiences of the pupil in the life and work of the home and the community.

6. If supplementary references are used in a unit the teacher should provide a brief statement at least of the nature and character of such sources.

7. Certain parts of the work should be definitely geared for slow-learning pupils. Directions to such pupils must be definite and specific. They should suggest something to be done. They may well begin with a verb in the imperative: "Read . . . ," "Construct . . . ," "Write . . . ," "Tell . . . "

8. A good unit should have a human episode for motivation purposes. For each unit there should be a springboard provided that is carefully constructed.

9. If a unit is in mimeographed form it is a good plan for the teacher to place clearly before the pupils the outline to be followed in order that they may have a clear comprehension of the problem and in order that they may at that point plan a logical organization of what must be found out in order to solve the problems of the unit. In addition, the presentation by the teacher should motivate the pupils to want to solve the problems of the unit. A series of slides, movie films, graphic materials, or field excursions is desirable machinery of great value at this point.

10. A good unit will leave pupils free to work. They should have a chance to move about, consult with others, go to the library or shops, or on excursions in small groups if supervision and safety can be guaranteed.

11. In a good unit the pupil budgets his own study time and works at his own speed. It is a good plan for the teacher to have a time budget to fix rough limits when various aspects of the work will either be completed or be given a tentative hearing. The teacher keeps out of the way when he is not needed.

12. When possible, give a preview test designed to discover what the pupils know about the given unit of work. Give a test at the end of the unit to determine to what extent the objectives have been achieved.

13. In a unit that is well taught the teacher plans definitely for each class hour.

A Word of Warning[1]

No form of procedure in itself will revolutionize teaching. "It is the spirit that quickeneth." The unit plan like others which preceded it—the problem method and the project method—is a useful tool. But a tool must be understood and skillfully handled if its use is to bring about a superior product. The finer the tool the more disastrous may be the results if it is handled by one who is ignorant of its purposes, possibilities, and dangers.

Principals and teachers in their desire to improve teaching sometimes accept and attempt to use a new technique as if it were a cure-all. A technique cannot solve problems, though it may be directed by the teacher toward the solution of a problem provided that he sees the problem, understands the technique, and gains skill in the use of it. If he fails at any one of these points, there will be failure to achieve the expected results, and he will probably lay the blame on the technique. This is unreasonable. No educational technique can be superior to the personality which administers it. A mechanical device may be made "fool-proof," but education is not on the level of mechanics, and its processes demand intelligent guidance. Courage, thought, and patience will be needed by those who undertake to change their accustomed ways of teaching for new ones, and those who cannot practice all three are likely to be disappointed in a new venture. Those who are willing to draw upon themselves freely, to evaluate results honestly, and to profit by their mistakes, will find adequate reward in the satisfaction which comes from the consciousness of progress.

Major Assignment

1. Make a list of units, say from eight to twelve, that you think would represent a good organization of a year's work in your major field.

2. (Optional for students carrying a heavy load.) Select one of the units listed in the preceding exercise and outline it in some detail, suggesting the main activities and the chief sources of materials for pupils. It is suggested that you hold the time to about three weeks. The creation of new instructional materials is the greatest challenge that a teacher faces, and the competent student will find that this exercise provides good experience.

[1] Reprinted, by permission, from "The Unit Plan of Teaching," *Bulletin* 1, School of Education, College of William and Mary.

Planning the Daily Lesson

It has often been said that the outstanding weakness of instruction in secondary schools is the failure to plan the daily lesson. The teacher operating with the modern point of view will find the task fairly easy, for usually the continuity of the unit will provide enough momentum to determine the details of the next day's activities and procedures. It would be as difficult to imagine an effective daily lesson plan that is not a logical and psychological outgrowth of the two preliminary steps in planning as it would be to conceive of a house without a foundation, a table without legs, or a diagnosis of a pupil's adjustment in school without the necessary data.

The teacher vitally interested in the larger aspects of a year's work will not look upon the task as annoying or burdensome. Indeed, he will do a vast amount of planning, scarcely conscious that he is doing it.

IMPORTANT PARTS OF A GOOD LESSON PLAN

We suggest the following outline, consisting of seven parts, as a minimum to be used in writing lesson plans during student teaching. It is not likely that as a beginner you can neglect thinking through each step very carefully, and making a written record of your decisions, without being unfair to the interests of the pupils you teach during your student days.

1. *Purpose:* Formulate (*a*) the teacher's, (*b*) the pupil's.
2. *Activities:* Include (*a*) the procedures employed, (*b*) the blocks of subject matter.
3. *Time Budget:* State the approximate time you expect to devote to each phase of the lesson.
4. *Illustrations:* Be sure to include a sufficient number.
5. *Questions:* State a few questions that determine and unify the activities.
6. *Assignment:* Make it clear and specific.
7. *Appraisal:* Guide the pupil to a realistic self-appraisal.

Since many of the early lessons taught by beginning teachers are failures because these steps have not been clearly understood, we should consider the details of each part.

1. *Purpose.* The pupil's purpose and that of the teacher may be identical; often, however, they are very different. In general the pupil's aim should be stated in terms of the definite tasks to be

done during the period; often a single sentence for the teacher's purpose will suffice.

2. *Activities.*   List in order of event the things the pupil is going to do during the hour.   For example, if you are a social studies teacher studying the unit on safety you might perhaps wish to list as an activity for the first ten minutes of the hour, "Hearing a committee consisting of Bill, Sarah, and Edith report on the machine used at the county fair to measure the reaction time of drivers." Having listed the activities which would perhaps range in number from five to ten in a good lesson you need to decide what you are going to do and say at each transition point and to anticipate the responses of the pupils.

In thinking about procedures the kick-off is important.   A very large portion of the period is wasted when the teacher moves in a half-hearted fashion and does not get his stride until the period is far along, although afterward he may teach an excellent lesson. He is like a baseball pitcher who enters the game "cold."

Then, too, variety of procedure is important.   Too often the teacher limits himself to one or two procedures for a whole period. The machine-gun, question-and-answer procedure is still common, as is also the lecture method.   It seems strange indeed that even more experienced teachers will turn what might have been a vital period of work and activity into one that is deadly boring to pupils through the endless repetition of procedures which pupils have no part in planning and which lack any degree of variety.   Consider the following list of activities which were all observed in a single class period of 90 minutes:

a. A pupil makes an oral report.
b. Pupils engage in a debate.
c. A dramatization is presented.
d. A motion picture is shown.
e. A talk is illustrated with slides, charts, graphs, maps, postal-card pictures.
f. The class engages in a socialized recitation.
g. Two teams have a contest.
h. The class discusses supplementary reading.
i. A committee demonstrates.
j. Pupils work under supervision of the teacher.

And the list is by no means exhausted.   In any learning situation the resourceful teacher will think of a score of procedures of which she can perhaps use only half a dozen.

3. *Time Budget.* It is worth while in training days to include a time budget in the lesson plan. Its use tends to prevent distraction and aimless wandering. In the early months of teaching, as more and more teaching habits become fixed, this budget idea may gradually be abandoned. Let us be clear on this: there is no suggestion that you operate even in student-teaching days as a slave to a time budget. It is intended merely as a *general* guide. Without it you will, in the early days, run the hazard of being sidetracked by an insignificant question or a discussion in which only a few students are interested.

4. *Illustrations.* Be sure to prepare a generous number of illustrations. It is a comfortable feeling to know that you have more material than you can possibly use. In general, teachers do not illustrate enough. A principle which has often been taught by a teacher is clear in his mind. He tends to be impatient to arrive at the generalization or to point out some relationship. He assumes that the concept is easy for the pupil and he cuts down the amount of illustrative material. He expects the pupil to arrive promptly at a high observation point, but he forgets how many times he has himself traveled the long, tortuous path.

5. *Questions.* A few crucial questions, the "high spots" of the class period, are important. If a teacher finds himself in a situation in which duties are so many that planning is practically impossible, the listing of a few basic questions is about the last part of lesson planning that can be abandoned. These questions serve us as do the signboards on an overland highway. There is some assurance that a school activity "will arrive" if pupils and teachers keep the key questions before them.

6. *Assignment.* The specifications of a good assignment are as follows:

a. It must develop naturally and psychologically out of something the class is doing and must lead into further activity as provided in the plan of the larger unit.

b. It must be planned in cooperation with pupils.

c. It must indicate clearly *what* the pupil is to do, *how* he is to do it, and *why*.

d. It must anticipate difficulties and it must promote good work habits.

e. It must provide for adapting the work to the interests, needs, and abilities of individual pupils.

f. It must use as a springboard the previously acquired experiences of the pupils.

g. It must be tied in with the teacher's plan for motivating the larger unit.

h. When responsibility for a task is distributed, the assignment must be made in such a way that each pupil will be held accountable for his share of the work.

i. It should be made at that part of the class period when interest in that particular phase of the work is highest.

7. *Appraisal.* This phase of planning is discussed in detail in Chap. XIII.

FOR DISCUSSION

1. There are schools whose faculties have voted to give no homework; on the other hand many teachers believe that the assignment of tasks to be done outside of class is very important. On which side of this issue are you? Why?

2. What administrative changes are usually involved if a pupil is to do most of his work in the classroom? How is this topic related to supervised study and to study habits?

3. Extend the list of procedures suggested above under *Activities* (p. 148). Underline those you believe most applicable to the subject you teach.

4. Some teachers plan the hour so that pupils can devote 10 to 15 minutes toward making a beginning on homework. Why?

COMMON ERRORS IN LESSON PLANNING

The following list of errors has been compiled as a result of analyzing lesson plans submitted by inexperienced teachers. An inspection of these mistakes may help you to avoid making them in your own plans.

In preparing the work on specific lessons, teachers have failed to

1. Provide the best illustrative materials available.
2. Include crucial questions.
3. Select the most appropriate aims.
4. Consider the level of the ability and interests of pupils.
5. Consult courses of study and grade requirements.
6. Select the best procedures.
7. Consider the materials in pupils' textbooks.
8. Tie the lesson in with previous ones.
9. Take into consideration knowledge already possessed by pupils.
10. Include an appropriate assignment.
11. Consider supplementary materials in library in making the assignment.
12. Emphasize the main points of interest.
13. Arrange a logical order of activities that would lead toward a realization of the aim of the lesson.
14. Provide for adequate summaries.
15. Make the plan flexible enough to allow the teacher to leave it temporarily and follow pupil interests.
16. Budget the time devoted to phases of the lesson.
17. Provide a means for evaluating the results of the lesson and the teaching.

It should also be pointed out that inexperienced teachers tend to go to one of two extremes in planning lessons—they include either too much or too little in the plan. If too much is included, the lesson is likely to be too formal, or the teacher may get lost in a maze of irrelevant material. Beginning teachers often try to cover too much ground. If the plan is too fragmentary, a whole block of subject matter may be left out. Important illustrations may be forgotten or, even worse, the teacher may run out of something to do before the period ends. The preceding list may be helpful if you use it as a "don't" list to guide you in making a final check on your lesson plans.

A Sample Lesson Plan[1]

TOPIC: CAPITAL PUNISHMENT

Teacher's Purpose: To create or instill an open-minded attitude in the pupils concerning the controversial question of capital punishment.

Pupil's Purpose: To determine what changes should be made in our state law with respect to capital punishment.

I. Short history of the death penalty (Slide film of 10 frames, 5 minutes)
  1. Its underlying motive
    a. In early times
    b. In later times
II. Purpose of capital punishment (Report by chairman of a committee, 5 minutes)
  1. As a deterrent
    a. Does it operate satisfactorily?
  2. As a remedy for certain crimes
III. Right of society to take a life (Discussion by panel of 3 students, 10 minutes)
  1. Projection of this right to other fields than crime
    a. Illustration: Death penalty inflicted in Russia on those holding political views in opposition to those held by the man controlling government
  2. Question of the unreliability of human judgment
IV. Causes of crime (Written review quiz, 10 minutes)
  1. Effects or problems of our social system
    a. Illustration of the congenital criminal and of man as the combined product of heredity and environment
  2. Failure of capital punishment as a solution to crime
  3. How shall we solve or handle these problems?
V. Assignment (5 minutes)
  Prepare a 3-minute talk on the questions: "Who provides the cost of keeping a life prisoner?" "Who should gain by the investment?"

[1] This lesson plan, designed for a ninth-grade class in the social studies, is not intended to serve as a model. Rather, its purpose is (1) to illustrate the essential elements of a plan and (2) to stimulate discussion of its merits and deficiencies.

VI. Conclusion (Discussion by whole class, 10 minutes) Discussion directed to clear up parts I to IV. If necessary or if time permits, use the following questions:

1. What differentiates the so-called criminal class from other classes in society?
2. Under what circumstances might capital punishment serve as an effective deterrent?
3. Has society any responsibility for the committing of a crime?
4. If you were in favor of a law providing capital punishment, and were making a campaign to have such a law endorsed by popular vote, would you like to have that vote taken just before or just after the wide publicity of some gruesome crime?
5. Does life imprisonment reform the prisoner? (Refer to Wickersham report.)

For Discussion

Study the foregoing lesson plan. Was there too much teacher planning? How do you think it would be modified when taught? List its good points; its deficiencies. What specific changes would you make in it?

The Source Unit

So far we have been talking about a *teaching* unit. A teaching unit is ready for you to pick up and take to your classroom (of course to be modified as you teach it by the planning that you do with pupils). A source unit looks a good deal like a teaching unit, but it is something else.

It may be that your mother used to can vegetables in the summer which she would use in a hurry to cook soup for unannounced guests. The can of vegetables was not vegetable soup ready for the table. This illustrates the function of a source unit. It is intended to help a teacher to review quickly and bring up to date some subject-matter area by suggesting (1) a great many activities which he and his pupils can do, (2) typical questions which pupils ask, (3) some of the basic problems and issues, (4) interesting investigations that the more able students can do at that level, (5) list of changes in behavior of students which the teaching of the unit aims to achieve, and (6) sources of up-to-date information with a bit of evaluation of the more important ones.

A good source unit cannot, as a rule, be planned by a busy teacher on the job nor by a tired one after school. Fortunately an increasing number of school boards recognize this job as a technical one, requiring time and energy, by employing teachers in the summer months or by paying all, or at least part, of the cost of attendance at summer sessions or local workshops.

It will be helpful to examine typical source units in your teaching area. Don't forget to locate such source units as may exist in your school when you begin your first teaching.

THE LESSON PLAN MUST CONSIDER METHOD

In this chapter we have considered some suggestions for planning. The next chapter deals with method. You will agree, will you not, that you can't separate these two phases of teaching? For this reason the motion picture, "The Broad Concept of Method, Part I," is geared to the specific objectives of both this chapter and the next one.

A FACULTY DISCUSSES THE LESSON PLAN

We have come almost to the end of the chapter. However, you may wish to read the minutes of a faculty meeting reported here. The record given below is that of an actual meeting. See if you can find a good idea that has not been emphasized in the preceding pages.

PRINCIPAL SMITH: Several teachers have suggested that we devote one of our meetings this year to a general discussion of the lesson plan. I think it will perhaps serve to narrow the discussion if we begin by stating the values that we see in planning the daily work in advance. Mr. Hall, will you start the ball rolling?

MR. HALL: I do not have any patience with impromptu teaching, and that is what it amounts to without a lesson plan. I use my plan for the purpose of keeping in mind the most valuable questions to ask, illustrations to be used in explaining difficult points, and materials which I need to use in teaching a particular group.

MISS COLE: We should not overlook the fact that the preparation of a daily lesson plan is about the only way the teacher has to make certain that each day's work is connected with that of the preceding day. I find the lesson plan particularly helpful in picking up the thread of yesterday's work.

MISS BOYD: I believe we are prone at times to overlook the fact that a daily lesson plan permits greater freedom in teaching. By its use the teacher does not have to worry about thinking ahead when his mind is still on the thing that is going on at the moment. With a good plan I get a feeling of security and assurance that makes my teaching more natural.

MR. LAWSON: Personally, I can't see how a teacher can get more freedom in his teaching when he is chained to a lesson plan. I tossed away my last written lesson plan seven years ago and since that time I've been free to capitalize on the spontaneous interests of my pupils.

MISS HOLMES: Now I am confused. First Miss Boyd claims that she gets more freedom with a lesson plan, and then Mr. Lawson says he hasn't used one in seven years. I know from what I've heard from pupils that each does a fine job of teaching, so I'd like someone to take pity on me as a beginning teacher and explain this point a little more thoroughly.

PRINCIPAL SMITH: To clear up these different points of view we will first have to agree as to the nature of a lesson plan. In other words, should it appear in complete written form, or can it be kept in mind in a general way? Does anyone have a contribution to make on this point?

MISS JAMES: I do not believe in writing lesson plans. I teach five classes a day and if I attempted to stay up at night long enough to write out a plan for each lesson I'd be so tired out the next day that my otherwise good humor would vanish. Moreover, I believe in spending what time I have in collecting materials to enliven my course. I want something new and fresh when I step before my classes, and I'll know how to teach it when the time comes.

MISS ROTHWELL: It may not be necessary to have a written plan, but I certainly want to see my lesson plan on my "mental blackboard" in every detail. Even then I find it necessary to jot down on paper the steps I intend to use.

MISS CUMMINGS: I am fearful of clinging too closely to a plan. The teacher should practice accepting "leads" from pupils. Knowing how to weave pupils' suggestions into a plan and when to discard one's lesson plan previously prepared is very important.

MR. CARR: I, too, am a little afraid of ready-made organizations. However, I do use a plan, but I provide for the maximum amount of inductive development by the pupils.

PRINCIPAL SMITH: These points are exactly the ones I hoped you would bring out in order to clear up Miss Holmes's misunderstanding. You see, Miss Holmes, all of these teachers use a plan, but in different forms. After teaching for several years they have found it unnecessary to use a written lesson plan that has every step completely filled out. In your case you succeed very well in your teaching because you have a plan that you may refer to if you need it. This feeling of assurance permits you to enjoy greater freedom in your teaching. On the other hand, Mr. Lawson and some of our other more experienced teachers have reached a point of diminishing returns in writing out lessons for each class, and they have become so accustomed to teaching that they have changed to the mental lesson plan. I am very sure that Mr. Lawson will do a great deal of planning for tomorrow when he walks home tonight. Miss Rothwell represents more of a mid-point in my illustration. After two years of experience she is gradually decreasing the degree to which she writes her plans in detail. Has this discussion helped to make this clear?

MISS HOLMES: Yes, I realize now that the lack of experience makes me feel that a written plan is best in my case, but I'm already looking forward to the time when I can get away from so much detailed planning. However, I see now that I'll have to continue in this way for a semester or two.

MR. CRANE: It seems to me that there is still one point we haven't cleared up. I don't write lesson plans in complete detail, but I do make it a point to write out each assignment in such a manner that it will be perfectly clear to pupils. Of course the assignment is a part of the lesson plan, and I cannot agree that such an important part of the lesson plan can be trusted to a teacher's memory.

Miss Lester: I believe the assignment should come at the beginning of the lesson and therefore there is no point in writing it into the plan. If every teacher began at the beginning of the period with the assignment it would become so much a part of habit that it would never be forgotten.

Mr. Koomes: I believe the assignment should come at the end of the lesson.

Mr. Crane: I've tried it both ways and have also tried to make the assignment at various times during the hour, but unless it is included in the plan it is either likely to fall "flat," or else the bell rings for dismissal of the class before it is completed.

Miss Hill: I don't believe you can predict at what spot in the recitation the assignment should come. There is such a thing as the psychological point. We teach some new principle and the children see the value of a certain amount of outside practice, or reading in the library, and so at that spot we stop and plan for the supplementary work. This may be anywhere in the recitation or, indeed, it may be the whole of the recitation. In fact, I would go a bit farther and say that if I were using the unit plan I might spend three days making an assignment which would take us two or three weeks to do in the classroom, the library, and at home. Everything else being equal, I would like to support the thesis that the better a teacher is, the more time she is likely to spend on making assignments.

Principal Smith: Miss Hill's point is well worth our consideration. It has been my observation that one of the clearest evidences of the lack of a well-planned lesson is when a teacher forgets this important part of the lesson and then attempts to make an assignment by shouting at the top of his voice as the class is filing out of the room. I do not mean to imply that any of you make this mistake, but I saw it happen often when I served as a high-school visitor for the university.

Miss Hall: Before closing our faculty meeting I should like to say as chairman of the program committee that we are planning another meeting in the near future at which there will be an opportunity to examine desirable types of assignments.

For Discussion

1. Why does the traditional question-and-answer or recitation plan persist?

2. (Optional.) Take notes on two lessons taught by your supervising teacher. Follow the outline for one lesson plan and make a record of the purposes, the activities engaged in, and the time given for each activity. Give some samples of the illustrations used. Note a few of the crucial questions asked, giving your reason for thinking them crucial. Record the assignment given the pupils, note when it was given, and evaluate it.

3. Write a lesson plan you intend to use in teaching, or one that you would be willing to use, placing a copy of the plan in your professional log.

4. Having taught a lesson that you have planned according to the specifications listed, analyze the work with your supervising teacher. The following questions suggest some points to be considered:

    (1) What were the satisfactory elements of the lesson? what were the unsatisfactory elements?

    (2) Were the aims accomplished? How can you tell?

(3) Were the aims such that the pupils see the subject matter of the lesson in its relation to the work of the larger unit or the general goals of secondary education?

(4) Were the questions well worded? How can you tell?

(5) Did the questions provoke thoughtful consideration of the essential subject matter? if not, why not?

(6) Did you take care of all pupils in the class? Was the class exercise a real learning exercise for each pupil?

(7) Did you lose the attention of the class? When did you lose it? Why?

(8) Did the class have a feeling of responsibility for the success of the class exercise? How can you tell?

(9) Was the class at the close of the period ready, psychologically, for the work which is to follow?

(10) Did you make an effective assignment? How can you tell?

(11) Did you apportion the time effectively to each part of the lesson?

(12) Did you get a better appreciation of what teaching is? Are you a better teacher for having taught this lesson? in what ways?

(13) What are the particular points on which you must concentrate to improve your work the next time you teach this lesson?

5. If you have seen the motion picture, "Broader Concept of Method: Part I," consider the following:

(1) Discuss the part of the film that you liked least.

(2) Discuss a pedagogical concept that you think was well dramatized.

(3) What does practice in cooperative thinking involve?

(4) What are the criteria of a good project?

Suggested Readings

RIVLIN, HARRY N.: *Teaching Adolescents in Secondary Schools.* New York: Appleton-Century-Crofts, Inc., 1948. Pp. xi + 516.

If you are interested in learning more about the unit plan of teaching, consult Chap. V.

Planning and Working Together. Bulletin No. 337. Lansing: State of Michigan Department of Public Instruction, 1946. Pp. 191.

This little volume represents cooperative effort to do local planning of curriculum units. The procedures are good and several source units are excellent.

STRICKLAND, RUTH G.: *How to Build a Unit of Work.* U.S. Office of Education Bulletin, No. 5. Washington: U.S. Government Printing Office, 1946. Pp. 48.

This bulletin has been prepared to help teachers select, prepare, and teach units of work. The book includes brief sections dealing with the building of a unit so as to gear it to a required textbook, and with the adjustment of existing units so as to take into account difficulty of content and types of activities.

The Purposes of Education in American Democracy. Washington: The Educational Policies Commission of the National Education Association, 1938. Pp. ix + 157.

One of the most important efforts to state what the schools of the United States ought to try to accomplish. We have here a description of some of the things which the Educational Policies Commission thinks need to be done if these purposes are to be realized.

TEXT-FILMS

The following McGraw-Hill Text-Film on Teacher Education has been correlated directly with Chaps. VI and VII.

Broader Concept of Method: Part I—Developing Pupil Interest (13min sd MP).   This film demonstrates how teacher and pupils may plan together and illustrates important phases of the much discussed concept of group dynamics.   The film presents a realistic picture of the teacher-dominated, lesson-hearing type of recitation, and shows typical effects of this method on student attitudes and achievements.   The film then shows alternative techniques for achieving broader educational objectives.   In an informal workroom employing group discussions, the atmosphere of freedom leads to a suggestion for a class project that is readily accepted by the class.

Silent follow-up filmstrip based on material contained in the motion picture and textbook offers opportunity for additional applications, review of readings in the textbook, and summary.

Chapter VII

The Broader Concept of Method

A passive recipient is a two-gallon jug. Whenever the teacher does not first excite inquiry, first prepare the mind by *waking it up* to a desire to know, and if possible to find out by itself, but proceeds to think *for* the child, and to give him the results, before they are desired, or before they have been sought for, he makes the mind of the child a two-gallon jug, into which he may pour just *two gallons*, but no more. And if day after day he should continue to pour in, day after day he may expect that what he pours in will *all run over*.[1]

—DAVID P. PAGE

No Magic Formula. It is a fallacy to assume that any one teaching method can be used by all teachers to fit all educational materials. Within a single generation we of the teaching profession have been enthusiastic over the problem method, the supervised-study plan, the project method, the contract plan, individualized instruction, and pupil-teacher planning. No doubt every one of the widely publicized procedures has some contribution to make to method, but it is doubtful that any teacher should ever have limited his method entirely to one of these patterns. There is a curious notion abroad that there is only one good way to teach, if it can only be found. Worse still, we are afflicted from time to time by emotional demagogues who insist that some special pattern of method is the final word. The fact that these patterns of method enjoy only a brief hour of glory and then are speedily forgotten suggests the futility of attempting to find a foolproof formula.

In a circular issued by a large automobile-manufacturing corporation, we find a statement that exemplifies this conclusion perfectly:

In engineering, there is seldom just one way and only ONE way to accomplish a given result—nor is there just one BEST way. Generally speaking, I would say that there are about a dozen ways of designing any mechanical device. A dozen of them may be worth developing on the drawing board. A half dozen

[1] This critical and discerning statement by a young and brilliant educator of an earlier day is quoted from his book *Theory and Practice of Teaching*, p. 76. New York: A. S. Barnes & Company, 1849.

One of the ideas in the project is a workroom atmosphere that provides a good situation for each pupil to work.(E)

may be worth building experimentally—four or five may work out satisfactorily in practical usage. And of these four or five there are likely to be two or three designs where it is a tossup as to which is the best.

Problems in education are far more elusive and usually involve more factors than problems in engineering. It is unreasonable, therefore, to expect a specific method for each situation, for there may be many ways of handling that situation. It is important, however, that the prospective teacher be familiar with a few of them. But we must not overlook the fact that there are many common objectionable practices in our schools which have never been advanced into the hypothetical area of debate, and these may be more easily identified by the teacher with the spirit of experimentation and a fair control of basic techniques. To select one of these several correct ways of doing a specific school task and to reject all of the indefensible ways is the persistent and perplexing problem of the classroom teacher. From a great variety of patterns the wise and resourceful teacher will develop a composite method which is appropriate to his own philosophy and personality. The important thing is that you be a student of method through the whole of your professional life.

METHOD RELATED TO THE GOAL OF PUBLIC EDUCATION

In the discussion of planning, we found it necessary to consider methods, for no aspect of teaching can be discussed without taking method into account. For example the persistent agitation for curriculum revision may in part be an unrecognized desire to reform method. Certain it is that a change in methods in most classrooms would effect far more substantial improvement in public education than a change in curricular materials.

Nor can method be discussed without taking into account the fundamental goal to be achieved by education. A method of an earlier day entirely appropriate for teaching pupils how to master subject matter is inadequate for the modern school fundamentally concerned with the adjustment of personality. It will not do to teach as you were taught. It is the shift in our scale of values that necessitates a broader concept of method for the new teacher and requires a reconsideration by the teacher long in the service. It may be true that for the "born" teacher, questions of curriculum and method are relatively unimportant. Few teachers, however, can rely wholly on their intuition and resourcefulness. Witness the fact that the gifted teacher is usually a keen student of method.

FAILURE OF THE OLD CONCEPT OF METHOD

In the traditional discussion of method one finds an emphasis on devices or tricks of the trade, on model lessons dealing with drill and appreciation, on samples of inductive and deductive thinking, on unique patterns of pedagogy, such as the unit plan or individualized instruction, and on directions for teaching delimited skills, such as the placement of the decimal point in long division.

The weakness of the conventional treatment of method is that it fails to give the prospective teacher *basic principles* for solving his instructional problems. To be sure, the beginning teacher usually discovers that he can make a fairly good showing by featuring devices. Thus he becomes more often than not a routine teacher and, except by accident or further training, he does not rise to the level of being a student of method. Even if the older treatment of method were not so futile we would nevertheless be driven to a broader concept of method by the fact that the goals of public education have changed.

THE NEW CONCEPT OF METHOD

What is it that we need to consider in designing a method appropriate to an education that is primarily concerned with adjustment of personality, with the education of emotions, and with the fixing of desirable attitudes?

The first specification for a worth-while school task, whether it be undertaken by an individual or a group, is that it have purpose.[L]

It seems sensible to begin with a consideration of the fundamental *needs* of students in secondary schools, for workers in biology, psychiatry, and clinical psychology suggest the concept of need as the drive or the basis for worth-while educational experiences. In the second place, we shall assume that in a large part of the curriculum the needs of the individual student can by proper guidance (good teaching) be brought to the level of intelligent self-direction toward worthy goals. At this point we shall be much concerned with the students' interests and with the procedures that good teachers employ to make schoolwork interesting. The emphasis in the newer method is more on "why" and less on "how." We shall attempt to suggest procedures for correcting the general shortage, in schools, of experiencing as the necessary basis for symbolism and verbalism.

Finally we shall be much concerned with the techniques for reflective thinking. It is quite clear that society invests in school in order to get more and better answers to the many questions that perplex it. In a world that changes so very rapidly we shall have to emphasize general methods of attack on problems. The old threadbare issue of transfer of training is the crux of the modern curriculum and of the newer method. As far as society's interests are concerned, with the exception of socializing children who do not come from good homes or from desirable communities, the schools might as well be closed unless they can show effective transfer values. We certainly could not justify keeping the schools open by the argument that we are teaching fundamental skills, for schools are falling so far short of what they might so easily do in teaching the skills that in all probability most youngsters without schooling, as an outcome of incidental learning, parents' instruction, and added maturity, could achieve about as well as they are now doing with such inadequate instruction. Since we desire that graduates of the high school shall be able to do effective thinking in problem situations both personal and social, we will need to give careful attention to the techniques that presumably make for reflective thinking.

In presenting the broader concept of method, we will discuss (1) the fundamental needs of secondary-school students, (2) the procedures involved in providing for motivation, and (3) the techniques that are useful in creating situations by which reflective thinking is promoted. And what of the role of the teacher operating with this broader concept? Briefly stated, his task is (1) to study the needs, the environment, and the ability of the pupil, (2) to help the pupil formulate goals that are appropriate, (3) to provide, as far as possible, an environment of experiences that will enable the pupil to achieve his goals, and (4) to guide the pupil in making a valid appraisal of his achievement.

THE FUNDAMENTAL NEEDS OF STUDENTS IN SECONDARY SCHOOLS

There have been some rather comprehensive studies relating to the needs of adolescent youngsters. Unfortunately, as these studies are broadened and deepened, the investigators tend to speak with greater caution.   We can be sure, however, that among the needs that will cause trouble in the education of many youths, if the gaps become too large are the needs for: (1) security, (2) fellowship and companionship, (3) recognition and a feeling of personal worth, (4) new experiences and variety, (5) self-expression, (6) expression

In undertaking a project, students need to decide what information is to be collected, who is to get it, and above all, they must decide how good the sources are.[N]

for special capacities, and (7) the satisfying of various physical demands.

The difference among individuals with respect to adjustment to these needs or drives is a matter of degree, not kind.   Presumably no individual would claim that he has at all times been completely adjusted to his environment.   Always there are gaps that annoy us and tend to make our actions unpredictable.   As the good Quaker is reported to have said to his wife, "All the world is queer except thee and me, and sometimes I think even thee is a little queer."

If it is true as modern education suggests that the concept of need is an activating force in human behavior, if we do whatever we do because the organism attempts to relieve some tension, and if need in this way determines the nature of the effective life, then emotional maturity is obviously the desirable goal of personal and social growth. It follows also that the best way to evaluate the emotional and social development of a student is by his balanced and harmonious control of his needs, wishes, or drives.

EMOTIONAL MATURITY

What is emotional maturity? If we had a scale to measure it, it would register the extent to which a person has grown toward independence, self-direction, self-control, and consideration of others. Furthermore, we are told that the basic idea in emotional stability is "genetic appropriateness," by which is meant the degree to which an element of behavior is appropriate for the level of maturity involved. Some of the common deviations taken to identify frustrations have been classified in three categories: regressions, fixations, and precocious acceleration—terms whose meanings in this connection are self-evident.

What has all this to do with school, in particular with method? You will find a good answer in the following quotation:[1]

Tomorrow morning the school bell rings, children with various degrees of polish and a large assortment of wiggles will fill classrooms equipped with hard, fixed seats; teachers, serene and harassed, will endeavor to wheedle them through the vagaries of a course of study; there are reports to be handed in, parents to placate, boards of education to manipulate, and drugstore coaching staffs to flatter. Why elaborate theories of human need and emotional maturity in the presence of the practical realities of everyday school life?

This tough, skeptical question may be answered by asking other questions. To what extent are the extracurricular program, the administration, and methods and subject matter of instruction arranged to foster the harmonious expression of the basic needs of children? And to what degree is the school concerned with assisting the child to achieve emotional and social maturity?

Does the school give the child a sense of security and achievement, a feeling of belonging and being accepted, a sense of personal worth? Does the school nurture a friendly environment where the pupils may gain greater self-confidence in social adjustment? Or does the school spawn insecurity and defeat? Does it break morale with a burden of inferiority and does it widen a gap of social distance which the child already possesses by virtue of discrepancies imposed by economic

---

[1] Howard Y. McClusky. "Emotional and Social Development," *Pupil Development and the Curriculum*, pp. 92–93. Ann Arbor, Mich.: Bureau of Educational Reference and Research, University of Michigan, 1937.

and home conditions? Does the school give the child the adventure of the intellectual hunt? Does it open new windows in his mind? Does it stimulate his imagination, stir his interests, encourage his curiosity, and give him confidence in his efforts at speculation? Or does it darken his imagination, dull his curiosity, and blot out the windows of his growing mind? Or does it turn him into a trained seal, skilled in jumping through curricular hoops at the crack of the whip wielded by the pedagogical circus master? Or does it freeze his intellectual eagerness and convert the child into an efficient parrot repeating memorized tasks imposed by an arbitrary routine?

Does the school induct the child into the maturity of self-control and independence so that he can take responsibility for his own direction, or does the school establish the child in bondage to his immaturity by making him overdependent on authority dictating fixed requirements unrelated to his real needs? Does the school lead the child to mature development by aiding him to learn that genuine fulfillment and abiding satisfaction come from sharing and cooperating with others? Or does the school confirm the infantile attitude of self-centeredness by emphasizing extraneous awards, and basing recognition on success in competitive contests, and by upholding the ideal of a pedagogical hierarchy of rank based on the feeling that "I'm better than you are because I won first place and you won tenth place," thus diverting his mind from the real task of education and learning?

Is the school sensitive to the hazards of emotional and social development? Is the teacher encouraged to assist the child in overcoming unhappy regressive tendencies, in releasing the hold of emotional fixations which retard, and putting a brake on the child whose personal growth in personality is dangerously accelerated?

Does the school respect the child as a growing organism, not as one who has arrived and therefore needs to be trimmed, but as one who is arriving and needs to be cultivated? Not as one whose life is settled, but as one whose life is projecting from a significant past into a more significant future?

Let the practical skeptic apply the foregoing questions to every phase of the educational task and he will unloose a revolution in many schools and modify the policy of most schools.

The general thesis proposed in the foregoing quotation is that the fundamental concern of the school should be to satisfy adjustment needs, in particular the need for experiencing. If we accept this thesis, then it follows that the satisfaction of human needs is the scale by which we shall have to measure the educational value of the school's activities just as we would if we were evaluating any social institution. It is also clear that the way a student's interest reflects any one of his fundamental wants, desires, drives, or needs is an important element in learning; which is just another way of saying that purpose is one of the keys to method and that motivation is a basic problem of the teacher.

Motivation: A Fundamental Step in Method

One of the crucial questions for the beginning teacher to keep in mind is, "What can I do to make the work interesting to pupils?" It is probably commonplace to say that you will not succeed if the reaction of your pupils is unfavorable. The clever teacher utilizes some of the desirable practices of the successful salesman and the artful dramatist. Much has been written on the psychology of interest. However, when one searches the literature on the subject for specific guides useful to the classroom teacher, the results are meager indeed. A great amount of the literature on motivation can be summarized as follows: Other things being equal, pupils will do better work if the lesson is so planned as to provide for (1) motivation, (2) problem solving, (3) laboratory techniques, and (4) adjustment to individual differences.

A. THE PUPIL'S PURPOSE

We begin our thinking about motivation by noting that, other things being equal, school tasks will be more meaningful and satisfying if we can tie them into what the pupil wants to do.

The pupil's aims should be stated in terms of the definite tasks to be done during the period, and they must be desirable, specific, immediate, and attainable. The pupil's purpose must be founded on the necessary background, the psychological starting point for the lesson. The introduction to a unit is important; otherwise the work may not rise above doing what teacher wants done. In most cases a brief discussion should be started that will give the pupil an active part in exploring related past experiences. Such questions as these will emerge: What is the problem that we want to solve? What do we have to know, or what must we be able to do in order to get an answer? What are the available means of attack? In what different forms do we meet the problem? How will we know when we have a satisfactory answer? What use is the answer after we get it? If the task for the day is worth doing at all, the chances are that the student's interest will be enlisted through such questions, and he should be ready to go to the next step, problem solving.

Before we examine the steps in problem solving we can get a clearer idea of what is meant by intelligent purposing if we read the following minutes of a faculty meeting in which you will find a discussion of the project method:

Miss Green: The chief proponent of the project method is Prof. William Heard Kilpatrick. I had a course with him years ago. The key word in talking about the project method is *purpose* and another cue is "activity which leads to further activity." Other words that I heard again and again and which even now cling to my memory are growth, democracy, self-expression, evolution, and the scientific method. In the course they all seemed to be related and to find their unity in the child's purpose. But in my busy days of teaching, the connections have been lost and I can't seem to put them together again.

Miss Owen: Somewhere I have read that a project needs to be completed "in its natural setting." I don't believe this criterion is essential. My pupils are at present engaged in a project on Latin American customs. We can't have a natural setting, but I am convinced I never had a unit under way that was so vital to the children. The difficulty is that a lot of teachers do not appreciate the fact that the imaginative world may be very real to children.

Miss Clark: I read this definition in a book on education. "A project is a definite and clearly purposeful task, and one that we can set before a pupil as seeming to him vitally worth while, because it approximates a genuine activity such as men are engaged in in real life." I find this definition inadequate. In fact, I think this is not in harmony with Dewey's basic philosophy. I am not interested in focusing attention on an adult world. The needs of later life will probably be cared for if I insure a normal development during the long years of child life. Thousands of children die before they leave school. Why should I point them all for adult life? Aren't we agreed that worthy purposes for the "here and now" are sufficient unto themselves?

Mr. Rowe: Some teachers think that the project method is letting children do as they please. Others define any self-initiated activity of children as a project. Probably such a teacher would insist that a project must be the pupil's choice. I do not accept any of these ideas. Of course a project should offer wide opportunity for initiative, spontaneity, self-direction, and exploration. But children make so many false starts that we run chances of wasting time and encouraging chaos.

Principal Keene: In general I would agree that guidance is essential, but Mr. Rowe needs to remember that a very important part of reflective thinking is the chance to go wrong. It may be that the proponents of the project method have at times overstated their case. Nevertheless, I believe that the outcome has been in the right direction. If I have to choose between two evils I will without hesitation abandon a scheme in which all goals and plans are fixed by the teacher.

Miss Tilden: It is unfortunate that so many teachers have the idea that the project method is a fad—an extreme, inconventional form of pupil activity. The fact is, of course, that good teachers always have believed in careful motivation in order that pupils might *purpose*, in having pupils formulate plans, in encouraging pupils to criticize and accept plans, in stimulating the maximum amount of pupil initiative when carrying out such plans, and in securing judgments in the appraisal of outcomes. These are the significant traits of the project plan. In the last analysis the ideals of the project method are conservative and have long been practiced by all good teachers.

Mr. Allen: I believe this discussion has been helpful in that, by implication, it puts subject matter in its proper place. It is subordinate to the major goal of the "larger method." I do not want to lose my outline of essentials; that is, there is a body of knowledges, a list of skills and attitudes that I must fix in each course. I want my pupils, parents, and colleagues to know that I am not teaching activities any more than I am teaching subject matter. But I must be intelligent enough to provide enough activities to teach subject matter in a way that will insure the educational growth and development of the pupil.

Principal Keene: I think Mr. Allen has put his finger very definitely on some important issues. It is crucial that our attitude toward subject matter be more flexible. I will readily grant that there can be no real freedom when disorder and discourtesty enter into a situation. Freedom at its best implies a greater control of subject matter and in particular of skills. For example, Joe DiMaggio enjoys a greater amount of freedom on the ball field than I do because he knows more baseball. The issue with respect to the project method is not so much a matter of more freedom for the pupil in the conventional sense as greater flexibility in our attitude toward the relation of pupil purpose to subject matter. When a pupil, a group, or a whole class gets under way and gains momentum on a project, fixed patterns of subject matter must be set aside. In short, we must throw the switch and let the train go by. The all-important thing is this: when the term or semester closes, each pupil must of necessity have engaged in a combination of projects that will have achieved the basic objectives of the course.

Miss Tinker: I certainly appreciate this discussion. I thought the project method was just another name for the socialized recitation. I thought it meant to have children take the lead rather than to follow directions. The idea seemed to be to have pupils talk more. Some teachers I know think the phrase is just another term for "motivation" but I now see that this is not true.

Miss Tilden: Why doesn't someone say something about activity? Isn't the phrase "the activity school" still fashionable? Isn't it tied in with the idea of projects? Or is it, too, an illegitimate brain child to be abandoned like the child-centered school?

Principal Keene: Oh! I almost forgot! Mr. Wise, won't you and your committee present your report on the activity school at this time?

Mr. Wise: (reads) What can our faculty learn from the proponents of the activity movement? We must first find out, if we can, what the phrase "activity movement" means. Our committee discovered that the task assigned to us had been done by a committee which had published a report. A committee of the National Society for the Study of Education, which prepared a yearbook entitled *The Activity Movement*, analyzed 42 definitions, 25 curriculums, and 15 books in an attempt to discover the facts concerning the activity movement in which there is more or less agreement. The chairman, W. H. Kilpatrick,[1] who is the leading

[1] W. H. Kilpatrick. "Definition of the Activity Movement Today," pp. 60–61 in *The Activity Movement*. Thirty-third Yearbook of the National Society for the Study of Education, Part II. Bloomington, Ill.: Public School Publishing Company, 1934.

interpreter of the Dewey philosophy, an outstanding teacher, and an exponent of the project method, having analyzed definitions which presumably were the best that the committee could find, selected and pieced together descriptive sentences as follows:

"In a real activity school we see pupils going about their affairs, finding and solving problems, doing real things, creating and evaluating, systematically and understandingly, with the cooperation, participation, and inspiration of the teacher and their fellows. An activity curriculum for any grade of the elementary school consists of a series of activities chosen on three general grounds as follows: (*a*) the interests of the children, (*b*) the immediate needs of the children, and (*c*) the educative values and outcomes of the activity as determined by social needs. It is obvious that an activity curriculum can never be predetermined by administrators and supervisors. Such a conception of the curriculum regards full and complete living in the present as the best preparation for the future. Whereas the conventional school made the acquisition of knowledge and skill an end and thereby smothered the creative ability, the activity curriculum seeks deliberately to foster and strengthen the child's power to achieve and find joy in achieving. It is organized around properly selected problems, projects, experiences (or activities) of the learner. It is a curriculum worked out 'on the spot' by boys and girls under the guidance of the teacher."

From the preceding statement we conclude that the activity movement is a synthesis of good ideas and developing ideals. Impatient with the many defects in an older type of school whose inertia stubbornly resists reform, the proponents try to achieve by evangelism and propaganda many of the educational reforms that the Dewey School of an earlier day tested by the slow process of experimentation. The main assumptions in the activity movement are ". . . that the learner is properly an active being who pursues ends, that each activity means interaction with the environment of people, things, and ideas with which he comes in contact, that the product of this interaction is not only a change in the environment but also a change in the individual, as the inherent effect of the experience is the resultant learning."[1]

Miss Clark: I think, Mr. Wise, that we would have understood your report better if you had read only the last few lines which state the main assumptions. I find that the activity school is easy to understand providing somebody doesn't try to explain it.

Mr. Hard: You hit the nail on the head. We have words, endless words; but few if any ideas. The activity school was demonstrated by Dewey[2] fifty years ago just as he did most of the worth-while ideas in modern education, not excepting the concepts "whole child" and "community school." But mark you, I used the word "demonstrate" in referring to Dewey for I don't believe he proved anything by "the slow process of experimentation." I doubt that he and his staff collected enough verifiable data to fill a vest pocket. Dewey was an original thinker, a prophet, and a super-salesman who induced the University of Chicago to let him have show rooms to demonstrate his model for educational reform.

[1] Kilpatrick, *op. cit.*, p. 66.
[2] Katherine C. Mayhew and Anna C. Edwards. *The Dewey School.* New York: Appleton-Century-Crofts, Inc., 1936. Pp. xvi + 489.

PRINCIPAL KEENE: I am sorry that the time for adjournment comes just when we were beginning to have a little fun.

LᴦᴦX *Basic Concepts Underlying the Project Method.* The ideals of the project method may be listed as follows:

1. The work must be a means of self-expression for the pupil. In any case, the pupil must accept the activity as having unquestioned value for him here and now.[1] The key word is "purpose."

2. There must be practice in problem solving (reflective thinking). Here we need to keep in mind the well-known formula suggested by Prof. John Dewey which will be discussed more fully in later pages.

3. While the investigation will narrow down to finding the answer to a few specific questions, the activity must lead on to ever-widening interests. Two corollaries are: (a) In general, the project requires a larger unit of schoolwork and a longer time than is commonly employed in the doing of school tasks. (b) There is an emphasis on relating knowledge from the various high-school subjects to the guiding and controlling purpose.

4. The unit to be a project must challenge the pupil so that he will be satisfied with nothing less than his finest workmanship. Ideally, the close of the project should find the student an authority on that topic in his group.

5. In general, the unit must require the pupil to consult many sources and to be critical of the reliability of these sources—what books will be helpful, what teachers in the school would be likely to know the information sought, what persons in the community can furnish valid and helpful materials.

6. In the case of a group project, there will be emphasis on planning, on a desirable distribution of labor, on cooperation, on evaluation of results, and on the sharing of benefits accrued.

7. Finally, the project must have value to others. The project at its best is directed toward a social goal.

A Debatable Educational Issue. Before concluding the discussion of purpose we invite your attention to a fork in the pedagogical road where classroom teachers often part company. One group insists that, in an experience program, the pupil always has to be conscious of purposes and interests. Such teachers would try to secure all proposals for projects from the pupils, perhaps even to the extreme point suggested by the threadbare story, "Teacher, do we have to do what we want to do today?" On the other hand, the group that takes the other pedagogical road (shall we say the one to the right!) challenges the thesis that these interests due to fundamental needs are conscious in the incipiency of learning. They

[1] This definition allows a project to be undertaken by more than one pupil. Naturally we must be very critical of any project in which a considerable number of pupils participate, for the obvious reason that the work of some may represent pressure from the group or the teacher.

point out that a boy may be a skillful and enthusiastic tennis player without ever relating his interest in the game to health, to character, to any other conscious need, or they may cite the fact that many youngsters find great pleasure in exploring number relationships far beyond any demonstrable conscious need. This second school of thought agrees that purpose growing out of a conscious need may, indeed, be a satisfactory starting point if a teacher is resourceful enough or lucky enough to be able to provide a situation from which a clearly stated problem or purpose emerges easily and naturally, but they deny that this is always necessary or desirable and they suggest that it is sufficient if the activities in the incipient stage of learning are acceptable to the student. A teacher of this school insists that he can study a problem situation and know approximately what will be satisfying to students; and he does not hesitate to modify their suggestions according to their needs, which he believes he often understands better than they do themselves. Those who look upon the activity movement as requiring emotionalized evangelism rather than painstaking implementation apparently have overlooked a bit of sensible advice given by John Dewey[1] in these words:

> When children are asked in an overt way what they want or what they would like to do, they are usually forced into a purely artificial state and the result is the deliberate creation of an undesirable habit. It is the business of the educator to study the tendencies of the young so as to be more consciously aware than are the children themselves what the latter need and want. Any other course transfers the responsibility of the teacher to those taught. Arbitrary "dictation" is not a matter of words or of form, but consists in imposing actions that do not correspond with tendencies that can be discovered within the experience of those who are growing up. The pupil also makes an arbitrary imposition on himself when, in response to an inquiry as to what he would like, he, because of ignorance of underlying and enduring tendencies and interest, snatches at some accidental affair.

The problem of motivation is so important that we shall need to discuss it further in the next chapter.

B. PROBLEM SOLVING

The hardheaded and intelligent layman probably has some difficulty following the trend of educational progress through a verbal

---

[1] *"The Activity Movement,"* p. 85. Thirty-third Yearbook of the National Society for the Study of Education, Part II. Bloomington, Ill.: Public School Publishing Company, 1934.

thicket of shifting educational slogans. In 1900[1] the faith of school people lay in the Herbartian steps; in 1905, in the cycle plan; in 1910, in the problem method; in 1915, teachers were excited about supervised study; in 1920, the project method promised to solve all our difficulties; in 1925, we had individualized instruction with many different models; in 1930, we became enthusiastic about the

You probably would not guess it but this is part of a physics class working on an outdoor experiment with an automobile.[E]

child-centered school; in 1935, we had great faith in the social studies as the core of the curriculum; in 1940, in learning the ways of democracy; and, in 1945, in education for one world.

The discerning critic of public education will see in this shifting terminology a persistent stream of thought making for educational reform which threatens every five years to break through the stubborn obstacles. There is good reason for believing that the exponents of the problem method, the project method, supervised study,

[1] This series of dates probably represents an oversimplification, but the cycle of educational movements seems accurate enough for our purpose.

and all the rest aimed at <u>one and the</u> same goal: a greater amount of <u>reflective thinking</u>; and that these seemingly unrelated reforms represent a groping to design an education for adjustment and, specifically, an unconscious striving for a greater amount of transfer. By transfer of training we mean that a person will adjust more quickly and effectively to situation *B* because he has experienced situation *A*. This desire for a greater amount of reflective thinking is clearly discernible in the current emphasis on the social studies. In recent times we have looked over the social precipice and noted that the margin of safety as regards making social changes in systematic and orderly fashion was none too great. Hence a frantic emphasis on the social studies resulted, with the hope that our citizens might, as an outcome, vote intelligently on public issues. To the individual the achievement of this goal is of the utmost importance, for it determines whether he will live in a universe of *ideas* or become the victim of *things*. To society, the issue is crucial because on it depends whether we shall have more and better answers to our many perplexing social and economic questions.

In the last analysis, the chief social goal of all schooling is to improve study habits with respect to problem solving. Mere control of subject matter is a very unimportant outcome in contrast with growth in reflective thinking. Many writers in education, and indeed all thoughtful teachers, have been concerned with ways and means of improving a pupil's technique in reflective thinking. The task of the school grows apace as modern science and invention increase our mechanical servants. In this extremely complex situation it is not *change* but the *rate of change* that threatens us. There is little evidence to show that man's mental capacity is keeping step with his scientific progress. The theory of dictatorship frankly challenges the assumption that the complex world created by the technical experts can be operated effectively by decisions arrived at through democratic processes. But we in America presumably are going to demonstrate the possibilities in cooperative thinking, and that requires that the greatest number possible should be taught to think straight in situations that cannot be predicted.

Obviously, it is impossible for the school to teach a pupil what to say and do in all the situations he may later encounter. Moreover, it is inconceivable that we could transfer to the classroom all the situations of life exactly as they occur, particularly those problem situations that a pupil may face in the remote future. Our only hope is that we can teach the pupil how to think, on the assumption that he will be able to transfer these techniques to a vast number of varied problem situations. There is probably very little thinking without some transfer, and certainly transfer is a function of intelligence. Indeed, one may define intelligence as the measure of the manner in which an individual can transfer his training.[1] Hence, a basic problem of the school in the education of an individual is to determine what it can do to make his intelligence function as efficiently as possible.

Curiously enough, we have on the part of a radical group among the educationists the most amazing reliance on the general value of training recorded in the history of education. The systematic arrangement of experiences commonly known as subject matter is held to be of little importance; they rest their program on a series of habits that are expected to do service for situations innumerable. In brief, they would have set up as an end in education a *method* of acquiring meanings, without any considerable organized body of meanings. That is to say, we are going to get swimming lessons with no water in which to swim. Now the literature on transfer of training suggests that we had better look this gift horse in the mouth. We readily admit that the denial of all transfer values resulting from the early fragmentary and superficial investigations never did square with common sense, but we cannot be certain that a particular disposition or skill will transfer to a specific situation.

The Fundamental Question. The fundamental question, then, is how shall we plan for greater transfer? The sensible guess is to teach for conscious transfer of training in all parts of the curriculum where such transfer would be at all natural and possible. The greatest achievement of the social studies in recent years is the organization of courses in units designed to promote reflective thinking. In like manner, to the greatest extent possible the subject-matter materials in every area should organized in problem-solving situations.

[1] It is an amazing and curious fact that the literature on transfer scarcely mentions emotion as a factor though emotion is obviously very important. Witness the extent to which a person with sympathy for the Communistic cause permits his prejudice to color all that he reads or hears. Even a youngster knows that his love for his teacher is likely to transfer to the subject taught.

We must arm ourself with sound principles and methods of problem solving before we attempt to lead our pupils in their attack on these vital questions. We need to begin by giving more practice in reflective thinking on questions that are already vital in the lives of boys and girls. In order to do this we must understand very clearly the process by which thinking takes place. John Dewey's

The seventh grade is not too early to give careful attention to the development of individual study habits.[N1]

analysis[1] of this process, perhaps the best and certainly the best known, consists of the following steps:

1. A felt difficulty.
2. Its location and definition.
3. Suggestion of possible solution.
4. Development by reasoning of the bearings of the suggestion.
5. Further observation and experiment leading to its acceptance or rejection.

To the practical classroom teacher, this formula may seem to be an oversimplification. It needs to be expanded in order that we

[1] JOHN DEWEY. *How We Think*, p. 72, Boston: D. C. Heath & Company, 1910.

may be able to organize school experiences that provide conditions promoting reflective thinking. What are the practical steps that a teacher can take to increase the probability that more thinking will take place?

Practical Guides for Problem-solving Situations. In each of the following guides there is a key phrase to help you remember the specific suggestions:

1. *An Atmosphere of Freedom.* The first essential when setting up problem-solving situations is to establish a free and easy setting. This involves proper physical conditions and an informality of procedure and mutual respect for personality.

2. *Selection of Problems.* Most pupils will need careful guidance to guarantee the selection of a problem that will fit their experiences as well as their needs. The problem must not be too difficult or too easy. It must challenge the student's ability, but it must not be so difficult that it will discourage him.

3. *Definition of the Problem.* Most pupils will need help also on the definition of the problem. Remember that wishes, drives, needs, etc., for most youngsters in the early stages of a learning situation are likely to be buried in a general condition of affairs. It is naïve for a teacher to assume that students are always conscious of vital needs. In general, it is only the brilliant student who can define his problems. The typical student needs to be taught to reject irrelevant facts and to recognize when important data are missing. Once the problem is clearly defined, the pupil should keep the definition in mind throughout the investigation.

4. *The Analysis of the Problem.* The pupil should be taught that his chances of progress are greater if he can take one or more of the following steps:

    a. Break up a problem into simpler units.
    b. Use related ideas bearing on the problem, particularly his own experiences.
    c. Know how to locate source material.
    d. Collect data in a systematic fashion.
    e. Keep his attention focused on the main problem at all times.
    f Fix the habit of seeking important relationships in data.

5. *Formulation of a Tentative Solution.* The efficient thinker may do this step "in a flash" when suggested solutions "pass in review," selecting from them the most promising hypotheses for further study; but the typical student will need help in evaluating

tentative proposals and in selecting the most promising line of investigation. This step not only provides but requires practice in scientific guessing, for life is certainly too short to follow down every clue in all problems. In general, it is desirable at this point to require a student to write a definite statement of the tentative hypotheses and techniques to be employed.

6. *Treatment of Data.* Organization of data is an aid to memory. Teach the pupil to use efficiently the various tools for expressing facts or data, such as systematized tables, charts, and graphs. The student should arrange hypotheses in order of probable worth and consider each in turn. Stimulate pupils to review hypotheses and to express the progress made to date in concise, clear language, both oral and written. Outline future procedure or the "next step."

7. *Test of Hypotheses.* In this step the student should experience the essence of open-mindedness. Allow free discussion of each suggested solution. Encourage each pupil to participate, to bring up additional ideas, and to suggest the rejection of unpromising proposals by the use of cause-and-effect relationships. Encourage comparison of findings.

Among the other useful steps that the student can take are:

a. Check hypotheses by applying experimental tests, by critical observation, and by consulting competent people.

b. Compare with similar situations.

c. Maintain an unbiased frame of mind.

d. Suspend judgment until hypotheses have been tested.

e. Develop the disposition to be critical of opinion, of traditional procedure, and of persons with final solutions.

f. Seek new evidence to modify a concept, principle, or definition.

8. *Finding the Solution.* The student should arrive at a conclusion based on the evidence and the data secured. A common error of teachers is made at this point when they permit the student to drop an investigation without a clear-cut and definite written statement indicating the point he has reached in his thinking.

9. *Application.* Both satisfaction and meanings are increased when the pupil successfully applies the newly learned principle, concept, or skill to some immediate problem situation. It is the way to "clinch the nails" in learning, and it is reasonable to assume that the chances of getting transfer of training are increased thereby.

In order to operate successfully with the new concept of method, you have to have good materials and lots of them. Incidentally, one of the serious handicaps is that most class-rooms are not built with adequate storage space.[N]

C. LABORATORY TECHNIQUES

Other things being equal, schoolwork will be more interesting and meaningful if the day is used for work and the classroom takes the form of a workshop in which laboratory techniques are employed. The main ideas involved in the laboratory form of instruction are:

1. *The Use of Part or All of the Class Hour as a Work Period.* Pupils are allowed to work individually or in small groups on the same or different activities.

2. *The Enrichment of School Experiences by a Greater Amount and Variety of Equipment and Materials.* In many schools and certainly in the literature there is now available a wide range of visual, auditory, and manipulative materials.

3. *A Decreased Emphasis on the Recitation.* There is less of the machine-gun fire of questions and answers. Discussion tends to be limited to those topics that are of value to the whole group, and occurs perhaps at the beginning of the unit for orientation purposes or near the close as a means of summarizing, taking stock, or drawing together the significant findings and implications.

4. *The Changed Role of the Teacher.* The teacher's function in this new role is to guide and assist the pupils in solving a problem or in investigating a project. Presumably, a good part of the hour is a free-study period which gives the teacher an opportunity for pupil conferences. Too often a formal recitation is dominated by a few pupils or, what is even worse, by the teacher. The laboratory method gives every pupil opportunity to have the help and guidance of the teacher.

5. *The Greater Socialization of Pupils.* The evidence seems fairly clear that pupils work in more relaxed fashion when they take part in small friendly groups than they do as members of large formal classes. It is highly probable that the flexible furniture of a laboratory contributes to this socialization.

6. *Greater Provision for Reflective Thinking.* It is argued that in the laboratory form of recitation it is easier to get pupils to look on their work in terms of the solution of a problem, and that the doing of a series of unrelated routine tasks is avoided. It is probable that the detailed study guides so commonly employed by teachers who profess to use the laboratory form, help by gearing the pupil's work to the solution of a problem.

7. *Individualization of Instruction.* In the laboratory form of instruction assignments are outlined for rather long periods. Such units have, as the unifying idea, a concept, skill, or appreciation which the pupil is expected to achieve. In most cases the teacher tries to make these assignments flexible and varied so as to make adjustment easier to the varying abilities of pupils. A common device is to make assignments on three levels, easy, hard, and still harder. In that case the easy assignment probably defines the minimum essentials for the task. Even when assignments are on one level provision can be made for the progress of pupils at different speeds. The free period referred to earlier provides an opportunity for the teacher to confer with superior pupils on special projects, and to examine written reports on these differentiated assignments.

8. *More Provision for Supervised Study.* Believing that numerous and vivid illustrations are to be preferred to a formal description when one is attempting to make a concept clear, a list of activities is presented to give meaning to the phrase "supervised study."

The faculty of a certain school appointed a committee on supervised study. The committee asked their fellow teachers to visit each other and to note good examples of class activities illustrating good techniques of supervised study. The list which appears here is a report of their investigation to the faculty. This extensive array was collected during a single week in a high school of fewer than 400 pupils. Though a general inspection of this list now will meet our purpose, you may wish to refer to it later for specific suggestions.

CLASS ACTIVITIES ILLUSTRATING SUPERVISED STUDY

1. The pupils were reading subject matter to get the "guide posts" or topic sentences. In another class the teacher called this activity "writing the key phrases."

2. The pupils were reading subject matter and making summary statements of the unit.

3. The class was divided into groups to prepare questions on different units. The questions were later given to the rest of the class to answer in class discussion.

4. Pupils were furnished definite goals or questions, the answers to which they were seeking. These goals were in the form of mimeographed materials.

5. The pupils were reading materials for the purpose of writing paragraph headings for each paragraph.

6. Topics were assigned for writing short paragraphs. The teacher was checking as they wrote.

7. Large problems were divided into smaller units in class. Then the smaller units were attacked, and the problems were thus solved.

8. Individuals prepared the next day's lesson under the direct supervision or, at least, available guidance of the teacher.

9. Ideas given by pupils from outside reading were summarized and outlined on the blackboard and were later copied into the notebooks. The teacher insisted, "This is not supervised study, but is supervised learning."

10. Extra textbooks for supplementary reading were given out according to the ability of individual children and then help was given each reader in getting and arranging the main points read.

11. The teacher was helping the pupils in the reading period to use indexes to find the material wanted.

12. Pupils were drawing and studying cartoons on current events to help the individual understand and enjoy cartoons.

13. Pupils weak in French were grouped together and were writing verbs, grammatical forms, etc., for drill. Strong pupils were doing extensive reading from library books, French magazines, etc.

14. The whole class was writing answers in French to questions on the text matter. The teacher compared members of the group as to time and accuracy. She walked about helping individuals.

15. The whole group was reading an assigned amount in French. Pupils wrote on paper the word they needed to look up. The teacher showed how too much thumbing of vocabulary could be avoided.

16. Class was writing in the foreign language, during class period, an exercise to which the group study had been directly leading.

17. Pupils kept a "record sheet" or "score card" of their work in class. The teacher at various times walked among pupils, inspected record, and cleared up difficulties as they appeared.

18. Committees of pupils were busy ranking sets of papers and getting ready to report to the class. The teacher tried to work with each of the committees.

19. The teacher first gave the pupils exercises directed toward the correction of some particular fault and then worked with them individually to eliminate that fault in their own themes.

20. Pupils were engaged in silent reading in class to "guess" at the meaning of strange words by studying context. The teacher was "visiting" with pupils who needed individual help.

21. Themes were being corrected in class. The group at each table apparently had a very competent chairman.

22. In this class themes grew out of the discussion. They were written in class with the teacher going about to give help either in mechanics of writing or in choice of content itself.

23. Pupils under direction performed in several different ways an activity involving the same as-yet-undiscovered principle. They compared results and tried to find the governing principle.

24. Pupils were reading in order to answer questions that had been placed on the board.

25. Pupils made a sketch or cartoon illustrating a description.

26. Pupils were finding out what x authors say in answer to a specific suggestion placed on the board. Later the discussion was directed toward gleaning the truth from conflicting evidence.

27. Pupils were outlining a plan for collecting data on a problem in the social studies.

28. Pupils were locating places on an outline map.

29. Pupils were drawing a bar, line, or circle graph expressing important relations.

30. The teacher gave a timed test, during which she walked among the pupils noticing faulty technique or common errors.

31. Pupils wrote a summary of class discussion, the outline for which was on the board.

32. The class was divided into four groups and each group was asked to rank five papers in order of excellence.

33. Pupils were asked to read x pages and to list crucial sentences fitting the outline which the teacher had written on the blackboard.

34. The class undertook twenty minutes of supervised preparation of the next day's assignment of sentence analysis, immediately after the work had been thoroughly explained by the teacher. Pupils, by raising hands, could usually secure the personal attention of the teacher. The aid given was not based on the one sentence causing trouble, but on similar examples, numerous enough to give thorough drill on the point in question.

35. Drill in the use of principles discovered and in their extended application took the form of short groups of examples to be done individually in a given time, the period allotted being such as to keep the brightest busy. The checking of results after a small number of examples had been done prevented the growth of wrong habits, while giving the examples in groups provided the possibility of each individual's working at his own rate. Keeping of scores by individuals added interest and incited enough rivalry to bring forth real effort.

36. Thirty minutes was spent in a "laboratory correction" of themes after exchange of papers. The teacher placed on the board a specific list of corrections to be made and then assisted individual pupils who raised questions. After the return of the papers to owners, the themes were rewritten for the next day's assignment under teacher guidance.

37. In studying a phonetic sound, the symbol for the sound was written on the board and the pupils were asked to read a certain passage and underline all words with that sound. The teacher circulated about and aided pupils. Later this was followed by general discussion.

38. Pupils read aloud a new passage of French and then studied it with the aim of being able to give synonyms in French and a brief résumé of what had been read. The teacher was free to help all those who desired help with difficult constructions or idiomatic expressions and to watch the ways in which pupils worked.

39. The teacher used the developing method with the phonetic study in all but first-year classes. The pupils learned a sound and, instead of making a homework assignment of listing a number of words with the same sound, the exercise was done in class. In this way no errors were made—at least, no written errors—for pupils selected only the correct words for their list on the blackboard.

40. Special reports were being given by students and by teachers. Students were required to take notes. The teacher discussed the notes later with the individual pupil in supervised study; thus developing a technique for note taking and, in particular, training pupils to sift the important from the unimportant.

41. Pupils with the teacher were working out a technique for the steps to follow in making a diagram, a chart, a graph, or a map. The teacher was going from one pupil to another and offering suggestions to improve the technique employed in making the graphic presentation.

42. The teacher in geometry was using cards on which exercises were written. The class was divided into several small groups. Each group was given a card on which was one exercise. It was the responsibility of each group to put a good figure on the board and prepare an excellent proof. The teacher gave help to "needy" individuals during the study period. Any member might be called upon, so it was desirable for each group to be sure that *every* member could recite, since at the end the class decided which group had made the best showing.

43. The class was selecting words that needed to be defined. Five steps were employed: (*a*) Each pupil attempted to formulate his own definition. For each word, one pupil was sent to the dictionary to get a definition. (*b*) The teacher worked with individuals, pointing out good or bad practice. (*c*) The class pooled their efforts. They selected the definition agreeable to all (including the report from the dictionary). (*d*) They copied the accepted definition in their notebooks.

(*e*) Each pupil used the word in a sentence to illustrate its proper use. In the meantime the teacher was at the elbows of individual pupils.

44. A class employed six steps in learning to make outline maps: (*a*) The class had in notebooks rules previously worked out, few and simple, for drawing outline maps. (*b*) Pupils attempted to draw a map before rules were applied. (*c*) The pupils discussed the application of these rules to the map to be drawn, noting errors made in the map just done. The teacher discussed common mistakes with all, and less common ones with individuals making the mistakes. (*d*) A second map was drawn in class. The teacher worked with individuals in the supervised study period. (*e*) The best three maps were selected by pupils who walked about to view the maps. (*f*) Then followed "merciless" criticism of the best one selected. These criticisms were constructive.

45. A class in social studies used these nine steps in a period that illustrates supervised study in an excellent form: (*a*) The class had studied such topics as Teapot Dome Affair, Disarmament, and Unification of Germany which they decided could be studied by cartooning. (*b*) The class discussed phases of the question which needed to be set forth in the cartoon. (*c*) Cartoon ideas for the subject were suggested by pupils and teacher. This was done to aid members having little originality. (*d*) Cartoons were drawn in class. (*e*) The class viewed all cartoons and selected the best three. The class criticized the best cartoon selected. (*f*) The pupils wrote down desirable rules for drawing cartoons in the future. Their suggestions were based on previous criticisms. (*g*) A committee was appointed to codify rules. They were instructed to seek aid from the teacher. (*h*) The rules were mimeographed and a copy was given to each pupil.

With the influx into the secondary school of great numbers of pupils of wide differences in intellectual capacities, the study method has come to be of great significance in guidance and teaching. Recent surveys of home conditions in both rural and urban areas point to the school itself, with its library facilities and equipment, as being the most nearly ideal and most logical place for schoolwork on the part of the pupils. These factors, and the tendency of teachers to move away from a single textbook, have in many instances decreased the amount of required home study. The implication for the classroom teacher is to make each class period a place for serious work. The beginning teacher must, therefore, be familiar with methods used to guide pupils in their development of good study habits. The name "directed study" or "supervised study" has come to denote such a technique.

In supervised or directed study, pupils work as individuals or in small groups on assigned or chosen tasks while the teacher is *actively* engaged in observing methods of work, checking results, and giving needed assistance to the individual or to small groups without disturbing the other members of the class. Teaching conditions must be such that they give the teacher an opportunity (1) to observe the technique of study used by each pupil, (2) to check the results of pupils, and (3) to suggest type errors and more effective methods of attack.

An effective directed-study period involves definite planning by the teacher. Although it is obviously impossible here to consider all the teacher activities that might be included in a program designed to promote better study habits, the following list may suggest the nature of the teacher's work.

TYPICAL ACTIVITIES OF TEACHERS IN DIRECTED-STUDY PERIODS

1. Observing pupils at work in order to diagnose poor or faulty habits of study.
2. Showing pupils how to use dictionaries, tables of contents, glossaries, indexes, etc.
3. Pointing out ineffective methods of study employed.
4. Supervising the preparation of written work; *e.g.*, making outlines, constructing tables and graphs, completing exercises in manuals.
5. Assisting pupils to summarize material studied.
6. Explaining mimeographed guidance outlines for study containing definite goals and pertinent questions.
7. Helping pupils select topic sentences, "guidepost" sentences, key phrases, and key words from printed matter.
8. Explaining the assignment in detail to a pupil or group.
9. Conferring with pupils and suggesting *definite* ways to improve habits of work.
10. Helping pupils set goals to attain during the period.

The supervised-study plan represents a genuine effort to use the school day for work by modifying the recitation so as to include a study period and to decrease the burden of homework. Directed-study techniques are being widely used, particularly in the junior high school, where little outside preparation can be justified.

A Good Workshop. In general, a good laboratory lesson may be described as one in which (*a*) the work is individual and the pupil is at work on a problem, (*b*) the teacher serves as a consultant—he does a good deal of work at the pupil's elbow—and (*c*) the student lives through certain experiences and emerges with one or more concepts or general principles. As has already been suggested, one of the significant advances of nonscience studies in recent years is the increasing tendency to organize the work of the hour after the fashion of the laboratory sciences.

We should note in passing that the teacher who makes good use of the unit plan modifies the recitation period so as to include a study period. As stated earlier, in supervised study, pupils work as individuals in the classroom during the period on assigned or chosen tasks while the teacher observes methods, checks results, and gives needed assistance to individuals or to small groups without disturbing the other members of the class. Obviously the results of such work can best be checked and methods can best be observed when the results of the work are in tangible written or graphic form. The task assigned should usually be of the same general type as that assigned for individual and unsupervised homework, and it may well consist of a portion of the advance assignment.

D. ADJUSTMENT TO INDIVIDUAL DIFFERENCES

Other things being equal, school tasks will be more interesting and more meaningful if the work is adjusted to individual differences.

We have dealt with the adjustment to individual differences in the discussion of laboratory techniques, but certain additional facts need to be listed. We need to realize that the problem is growing more acute by virtue of the fact that a vast number of pupils with very low skills in the fundamentals of reading, computation, etc., are entering the secondary schools. In the classrooms of small high schools and in the larger schools where homogeneous grouping is not attempted, the range of ability has greatly increased; nor has the problem of individual differences been solved for those schools that have adopted homogeneous grouping. Thus, a typical slow-learning group in the seventh grade may present the following ranges: in I.Q., from 70 to 110; in reading ability, from grade level 3.0 to 10+; in computation, from grade level 3.0 to 10+; and, even in schools that use almost no failing marks, the chronological age may range from twelve to eighteen years. Such a group may include an excessive number of pupils who are unadjusted because of personality traits, thus presenting a most perplexing array of individual differences.

From the point of view of motivation, as has been suggested elsewhere, one of the most important things to strive for in planning a unit is to provide tasks for each pupil that are not too difficult, yet difficult enough to provide a real challenge. Interest apparently is promoted by tasks which are hard enough to call forth the best one can do. If the pupil is to find real zest in the task, the hill to be ascended must be as steep and as long as he can climb under his own power.

What are the practical steps for providing challenging tasks within the range of each student's ability? No one list would get wide endorsement by experienced teachers. There is, of course,

Agricultural education, and especially the 4-H clubs, have long demonstrated the importance of activities and projects as motivation in a sound educational method.[B]

homogeneous grouping but that confronts us with a debatable issue. There are excellent textbooks that provide materials at several levels of difficulty. Probably the activity program is the best answer, for, in a worth-while project it should be possible for pupils to contribute each according to his ability; but it takes a good teacher to keep the competent student from running away with the project and to protect the weak student against the devastating feeling of inferiority that comes when he realizes that the years have gone by and he has gained very little. In the next chapter you will find many helpful procedures that successful teachers have long used. A vivid illustration is provided by the motion picture entitled, "Broader Concept of Method: Part II—Teacher and Pupils Planning and Working Together."

A Bit of Advice

In this chapter we have tried to keep in mind the conditions in schools as they are in this transitional stage. Since the statement of the broader concept is highly idealistic, there is danger that you as a beginning teacher will be overwhelmed by a feeling of hopelessness when you recognize the gap between what you would like to do and what you can achieve. Some perplexing problems may weaken your faith in your fundamental philosophy of education. Perhaps you can hold on to your idealism if you keep in mind that very few gifted teachers, even with nation-wide reputations, are resourceful enough to demonstrate the ideal method day after day.

For Discussion

1. Observe three lessons with the purpose of identifying situations that offer excellent practice in reflective thinking. Describe each situation briefly. As an optional part of the assignment list the factors in the situation that helped to promote thinking.

2. Can children be taught to enjoy hard and disagreeable tasks? Defend your answer and, if possible, illustrate. Is there a conflict between interest ("sugar coating") and discipline ("iron")?

3. Do pupils come to your subject with antipathy or phobia? If "yes," how would you go about securing a fair amount of interest and reasonable effort? For securing interest, what special techniques and devices are more effective in your major subject than in other school subjects?

4. A teacher said, "The old rascal 'transfer of training' is going to stage a comeback disguised as 'education for adjustment.'" Do you agree? Explain.

5. If you could plan and do your high-school work over, what changes would you make?

6. Is it the responsibility of each teacher to help pupils develop correct study habits and work skills? What inferences might be drawn from an observation that some pupils make high marks but waste their time in the library and study hall? How is the following observation symptomatic of poor classroom teaching and planning? It was noted that pupils were noisy in the study hall and library. They wasted a large portion of the period and, when requested to use the time as a work period, many claimed they had already finished their study.

7. Have you ever seen a useful classroom library in your major field? If so, tell in a general way what it contained. What specific change would the presence of a classroom library make in teaching procedures?

8. To what extent is individualization of instruction desirable and feasible in the subjects that you expect to teach?

9. What are some of the factors that determine the amount of freedom that may be given to pupils in permitting them to plan and select the activities of a class?

10. Discuss the place of the workbook in the area in which you teach.

11. (Optional.) Consider the following comments[1] and criticisms of the activity movement by outstanding educators:

12. If you have seen the motion picture, "Broader Concept of Method: Part II —Teacher and Pupils Planning and Working Together," consider the following:

   (1) Discuss the part of the film that you liked least.
   (2) Discuss a basic principle of teaching that you think was well dramatized.
   (3) Should Mr. Evans be standing in a situation where he is giving practice in cooperative thinking?

BOYD H. BODE: "The failure of the activity movement to straighten out its basic psychology is chiefly responsible for the prevailing confusion, and for the phobias that have developed against 'imposition' by the teacher, against 'subjects,' and against the introduction of 'described' situations. In its reaction against the admitted evils of traditional education the movement has taken the 'reconstruction of experience' as a kind of slogan and has suffered the penalties that normally go with the use of slogans. More specifically, it has failed to appreciate the permanent values in traditional education, particularly with respect to 'logical organization of subject matter,' and the need of a more basic conception of social values in education. Consequently, it has laid itself open to the charge of being random, and also—despite its emphasis on cooperative enterprise and free interchange of thought—of being 'social' only in a superficial sense of the term . . . The trouble lies, not in the basic idea or purpose of the Activity Movement, but in the development of its program. Despite its protestations to the contrary, it has been too much disposed to treat the pupil as a detached unit. Whether this disposition springs from a reaction against the formalism of traditional education, or from a sentimentalism generated by theological or psychological notions regarding the nature of childhood, or from a plain inability to understand the educational implications of our changing civilization, it seems clear that the Activity Movement must make its underlying philosophy more articulate if its present promise is to come to full fruition."

ROSS L. FINNEY: "For centuries teachers have seldom been satisfied with themselves unless they could succeed in concocting something difficult and uninteresting for children to 'grind over'—a movement that has finally culminated in the 'problem solving' objective even for the masses of modern democracies . . . Modern democratic society certainly does require its quota, though a relatively small one, of 'problem solving' thinkers to function as its leaders of thought. It needs a majority who are capable of following such leaders. But it also needs an overwhelming majority who can participate, through an imitative, *memoriter* substitute for thinking, in the established institutions of civilization . . . Informal education . . . is good medicine for the duller masses. It interests them, keeps them out of mischief, and imparts the kind of habit-stuff out of which the institutions can be fabricated to order; but it is not adapted to providing modern civilization with its relatively few, but absolutely necessary, 'problem solving' thinkers.

[1] *The Activity Movement*, Chap. V. Thirty-third Yearbook of the National Society for the Study of Education, Part II. Bloomington, Ill.: Public School Publishing Company, 1934.

"For evaluating the 'activity movement' therefore an elaborate description of the stunts practiced under that verbiage is quite unnecessary and irrelevant. The important question is not the nature of the stunts but the nature of the *students*. If they are only the mediocre minds out of which democracy flatters itself that it can make 'equals' let the 'activity movement' proceed merrily; by such schooling that kind of minds can be regimented and habituated to the institutions of civilized society; and that is about all that can be expected to be accomplished . . . Perhaps, after all, that is really the way to educate the mediocre masses of a democracy."

FRANK N. FREEMAN: "Self-activity or wholehearted participation by the child in learning is a necessary condition for effective learning. But no magic formula for securing this desirable condition exists. Certainly an 'activity program' does not provide it. Appropriate activities may be used as a partial means of stimulating learning, but they are not the only, and probably not the most effective means."

a. What ideas in the foregoing arguments do you reject?

b. What constructive suggestions do you find?

13. With respect to reflective thinking consider the following: Superintendent Hilton said, "Democracy can probably get more and better answers by relying on a program of educating the emotions than by an effort to get the masses to think straight. Reflective thinking is fine so long as not too many people are hungry. The human being will sacrifice longer for an emotionalized ideal than he will for a rationalized value."

a. What do you think?

b. Does Superintendent Hilton operate with a philosophy of democracy or of dictatorship?

SUGGESTED READINGS

BARR, A. S., WILLIAM H. BURTON, and LEO J. BRUECKNER: *Supervision.* New York: Appleton-Century-Crofts, Inc., 1947. Pp. viii + 879.

> If you are willing to do a little "digging" you will find some practical suggestions on how to improve the work habits of pupils.

DEWEY, JOHN: *Experience and Education.* New York: The Macmillan Company, 1938. Pp. xii + 116.

> There is some reason for believing that Dewey wrote this book to straighten out the thinking of some of his disciples who misinterpreted some of his earlier writings. He is, as you would expect, critical of both the old and the new education. Here is a sentence that common sense will support: "Again, experiences may be so disconnected from one another that, while each is agreeable or even exciting in itself, they are not linked cumulatively to one another." And here are two that should be very interesting in some quarters: "Unless experience is so conceived that the result is a plan for deciding upon subject matter, upon methods of instruction and discipline, and upon material equipment and social organization of the school, it is wholly in the air. It is reduced to a form of words which may be emotionally stirring but for which any other set of words might equally well be substituted unless they indicate operations to be initiated and executed."

KILPATRICK, WILLIAM HEARD: *Foundations of Method.* New York: The Macmillan Company, 1925. Pp. xi + 383.

> A helpful and stimulating treatment of the broader problem of method presented by the author in conversational style. This book has profoundly influenced a whole

generation of teachers. You will be surprised to see what up-to-date ideas Kilpatrick
was teaching before you were born. Two of his more recent statements are the articles
"We Learn What We Live," in *Childhood Education* for October, 1948, and "The Education We Need: The New versus the Old," in *Childhood Education* for September, 1946.

LAFFERTY, HARRY M.: *Sense and Nonsense in Education.* New York: The Macmillan
Company, 1947. Pp. vi + 202.

This is a very playful volume written by a teacher with a grand sense of humor and
the ability to write a riotous sentence. The author makes it abundantly clear that the
problems of teaching are not nearly so dull and pedantic as they are often made to
appear. The author locates himself on the leftist-right scale as "a little bit north of
South Carolina." Between the lines of this boisterous nonsense the reader will find
nuggets of curbstone philosophy. The volume does not have much practical value for
the classroom practitioner, but it is splendid vacation reading, and it won't be in the
category of a mailman taking a walk!

TEXT-FILMS

The following McGraw-Hill Text-Film on Teacher Education has been correlated directly with Chap. VII.

*Broader Concept of Method: Part II—Teacher and Pupils
Planning and Working Together* (19min sd MP). Continuation of *Part I—Developing Pupil Interest.* The film demonstrates several major ideas in modern educational theories; as
for example, how to teach cooperative thinking, how to get a
project started, and how to complete it. As the project
develops, students learn to work together in functional groups,
to make and carry out plans cooperatively; and to present
recommendations in the form of a final report that represents
cooperative thinking. Evidence of reflective thinking and self-
expression, plus a growing ability to evaluate properly things
learned as a result of experience are some of the more important outcomes of this project. Techniques shown in this
film are readily applicable to other class situations in which
students share in planning and carrying out their work.

Silent follow-up filmstrip provides statements and questions superimposed over scenes from the motion picture. The
discussion of the frames elicits a variety of experiences that
illustrate the basic principles discussed in the textbook and
dramatized in the sound pictures.

Chapter VIII

A More Interesting and Challenging School Day

Once upon a time the animals had a school. The curriculum consisted of running, climbing, flying, and swimming, and all the animals took all the subjects.

The Duck was good in swimming, better in fact than his instructor, and he made passing grades in flying, but he was practically hopeless in running. Because he was low in this subject he was made to stay in after school and drop his swimming class in order to practice running. He kept this up until he was only average in swimming. But average is acceptable, so nobody worried about that except the Duck.

The Eagle was considered a problem pupil and was disciplined severely. He beat all the others to the top of the tree in the climbing class, but he had his own way of getting there.

The Rabbit started at the top of the class in running, but he had a nervous breakdown and had to drop out of school on account of so much make-up in swimming.

The Squirrel led the climbing class, but his flying teacher made him start his flying lessons from the ground instead of from the top of the tree down, and he developed Charley horses from overexertion at the take-off and began getting C's in climbing and D's in running.

The practical Prairie Dogs apprenticed their offspring to a Badger when the school authorities refused to add digging to the curriculum.

—G. H. Reavis

Of course many children—perhaps most of them—like to go to school. The conventional cartoonist who invariably pictures the opening day as a despised event is not on the beam. Nevertheless, we who operate schools have far too many dissatisfied customers. Far too many out-of-school youth—tens of thousands—look back upon their school days as insufferably boring. This need not be. We are not going to be content by pointing out that a good teacher can make almost anything interesting. There are specific teaching techniques and curriculum provisions which help to make the school day interesting and at times even exciting for youngsters.

Nor are we going to be drawn into the age-old debate of "sugar coating versus iron." There is no conflict between interest and effort. Every school day a vast number of pupils somewhere work with zeal at tasks which are hard.

Some procedures which help to make the school day more challenging have been discussed earlier and need only to be listed here with a brief comment for each.

School can be fun! Here is a class on a field trip, concerning which Ethel Nordling of the Earle Brown School, Minneapolis, says, "The project was a perfect culmination of our year's work."

1. *Specific objectives.* We believe that definiteness of goals makes for interest, cuts down distaste for school subjects, gives direction to learning, and helps to solve the problem of the crowded curriculum. The main reason why the curriculum bucket is always running over is that we do not have specific objectives—not even the "must know" for our courses. Far too often no one in our classrooms knows what is to be achieved. We can think of no better way to make a substantial improvement in our schools than for teachers to provide pupils and parents with at least a rough list of the things to be mastered in each unit or course. Children, like

adults, are more interested at their tasks if they know what they are expected to do and why.

2. *Better planning.* The right kind of planning gets results for it enables the events of the hour to move on schedule, guarantees variety, and avoids exceeding the span of attention to a single type of mental experience. In far too many schools, teachers and books change every year without a respectable course of study, without supervision, and with no provision for the right kind of planning.

3. *Learning aids.* Other things being equal, the interest and understanding of pupils will be increased by teaching that provides extensive sensory experiences. When it is at all natural to do so, utilize concrete things that the student can see and feel and handle. Even in the later grades, emphasis can be placed on dramatics, excursions, and visual aids.

It has often been pointed out that children in the early grades of the elementary school are alive and alert, whereas in the later years they tend to be passive and unresponsive. One explanation of why children go into "deep freeze" somewhere in the middle grades is that sense experiencing is reduced too much and the shift to symbolism is far too rapid. A teacher who has taught a concept or principle many times is likely to forget the many experiences that he had before he fully understood it. The common error is to provide too few illustrations. This factor is so important that a whole chapter in this book is devoted to audio-visual aids.

4. *Selection of students with special aptitudes for the task to be learned.* It is not difficult to interest a student in that for which he has a native flair. Long ago a great teacher, Colvin, said, "We must stop teaching people what they cannot learn." We have many pupils studying algebra and geometry who can never be interested except by excessive cost of time and effort. Such students might well be guided to more appropriate mathematics courses. In brief, we must sooner or later do some sensible sorting and screening in terms of abilities and needs for certain things that we are trying to teach. The high school should provide opportunities for pupils who have special interests and abilities. In fact the early identification of talented youth and their proper culture is one of the two major responsibilities of a school.

5. *More achievement testing.* This factor also has been covered. Suffice it to say here that if tests are used in the right way—largely

for instructional purposes—the pupil will like them and the school day will be more interesting.

6. *Organizing a curriculum unit in terms of ability to do.* "Learn today and use or demonstrate tomorrow" is a good pedagogical maxim but extremely difficult to apply day after day. The general suggestion is that the pupil who is unadjusted in the traditional

In the future, schools will probably give more attention to the early identification and proper culture of youth with special talents.[M]

academic course needs to be placed in a rather small world—a workroom setting—in which things need to be managed, so as to demonstrate or utilize the principles that we aim to teach him. It is the only way to keep meanings ahead of manipulation and to build for confidence by avoiding confusion and frustration. We are convinced there should be and can be more doing and less reciting in our classes.

7. *Using students as assistant teachers.* We do not give students enough practice in leadership by having them appear before the

class or before a subgroup with the responsibility for driving home some specific point of the lesson. Far too many students leave school who have never had this valuable experience in all the years spent in elementary and high schools. Moreover, a little of this type of work often results in rapid growth in confidence and interest in the work. One teacher uses the commendable technique of staging a short ceremony during which he inducts five especially competent students as assistant teachers for the duration of the unit. Incidentally, more often than one would guess, it is possible to find a few students with greater control of the skill or subject matter than the instructor. We have all urged wider participation by pupils. We wonder if many of us have made good use of this very simple procedure. In any case here is a technique which should be more widely used and which is just as easy to apply in the teaching of Latin as it is in a science.

8. *Instructional materials more nearly self-teaching.* These are hard to find. However, some textbooks and especially courses offered by correspondence have been designed to be more nearly self-teaching. The person who wants very much to study such materials may need the guidance of a teacher, but he doesn't want too much interference. He doesn't want the time of a teacher one hour a day five times a week!

The strategy is to place more responsibility on the student for his own education. Too often in the typical classroom the disposition of the pupil is "I dare you to teach me." Perhaps we can manage things so that a student who wants an education will feel that he must do something about it. An increased emphasis on the guidance function and wider use of instruments for the discovery of aptitudes and abilities should tend to place the responsibility where it belongs—on the individual student. We are convinced that the school day will be more interesting if this happens.

9. *The use of humor.* Traditionally the use of humor by teachers has not been encouraged. Can it be that we have taken ourselves too seriously in the classroom? All the fun and excitement should not be outside of a school. Of course humor can be distracting and inappropriate. It can miss fire with youngsters; but this need not be the case.

So much by way of introduction and summary of what has been discussed earlier. We come now to some fundamental procedures

that require more detail. Other things being equal, a class hour will
be more interesting if the teacher plans so as to employ (1) a variety
of procedures, (2) wide participation, (3) the socialized recitation,
(4) growth of meanings and concepts, and (5) awareness of success.

VARIETY OF PROCEDURES

To maintain interest, the class period must be characterized
by a change of pace, of materials, of methods, and of physical

Classwork can be exciting without being the preliminary to horseplay.

and mental environment. Perhaps the most outstanding trait of the
human mind is its craving for a change in experiences. Symptomatic is the relatively short span of attention of audiences or of
groups in a classroom. No doubt the explanation of the high degree
of interest and satisfaction achieved by the movie and the radio lies
in the fact that it provides changes in mental experiences.

It is significant that in the depression years one could find 90 per
cent of the homes equipped with radios in a community where more
than three-fourths of the people were on some form of relief. So
close has the radio come to being added to the necessities of life:

food, shelter, and clothing.   To a lesser extent, the movies and the automobile for recreational purposes are approaching inclusion in the list of necessities.   The explanation is that they provide for variety of mental experiences, and they provide a lot of it within a short period of time.   The psychology of interest applied by the movies and the radio carries a lesson for the classroom teacher. Other things being equal, to make an hour of work interesting you must plan the show so that it will have a good many acts.   One can find teachers with the ability to make their work interesting who recommend that the lesson for a period should be planned so as to employ from five to ten different procedures.   Too often the teacher limits himself to one or two procedures for a whole period.   The question-and-answer procedure, for example, is still common, as is also the lecture method.   Most teachers recognize the importance of variety, but they fail to see the great range of possible procedures. The following list, which could be extended indefinitely, suggests the possibilities for a teacher who wishes to avoid the very bad habit of restricting his work to a few procedures:

1. The pupils sing a song, as for example, a spiritual in Latin.
2. The pupils do a three- or four-minute drill on important skills to be fixed in English, mathematics, science, Latin, etc.
3. The class engages in a rapid oral review.
4. The pupils take a "spot" test, written.
5. A pupil makes an oral report.
6. A committee reports to the rest of the class.
7. Pupils engage in a debate.
8. A dramatization is presented.
9. A teacher demonstrates.
10. A pupil demonstrates.
11. A committee demonstrates.
12. A teacher lectures.
13. A film is presented with comments.
14. A talk illustrated with slides is given.
15. A talk illustrated by charts, graphs, maps, pictures, and the like is given by a pupil.
16. The teacher reports on test papers given the preceding day.
17. The pupils take a standardized test.
18. The pupils score a set of test papers.
19. The teacher reports on common errors found in test papers.
20. The teacher does some remedial teaching to prevent errors.
21. The group engages in a socialized recitation discussing the best plan for the development of a class project.
22. Pupils and teachers discuss a basic question.

Here enjoyment rises to a high level.[N]

23. The teacher reads orally.

24. Several pupils who are good readers read to the class.

25. Pupils and teachers discuss practical applications found in life or in general reading.

26. Two teams have a contest—the application is not limited to spelling and mathematics classes.

27. Groups of pupils play games as a part of certain drill lessons.

28. The class discusses supplementary reference material.

29. A committee reports an interview with a local citizen on some point at issue.

30. The class considers the written report of a class excursion.

31. A period is devoted to the laboratory form of recitation including attention to study habits of individual pupils.

32. A period is devoted to leisurely reading on supplementary topics.

33. The teacher makes an assignment.

34. The pupils discuss the assignment and anticipate difficulties and plan reports of source materials.

35. A free period is provided when pupils may make graphs, charts, or other objects useful as illustrations.

WIDE PARTICIPATION

Other things being equal, students will be more interested in the thing they are doing if the plan provides for wide participation. A recitation of the traditionally formal type often presents a curious distribution of such participation as it provides.   For example, in a class taught solely by the question-and-answer method, it is not uncommon for one-sixth of the class to make more than three-fourths of the total oral and written responses.   Much of the teaching in our schools is still done by this method, and it will be worth your while to investigate the extent to which uneven distribution of participation prevails, even in the classes of better than average teachers.

The following are symbols that will make it easy for you to make such an investigation:

SYMBOLS FOR A MEASURE OF PUPIL PARTICIPATION

c+ called on and responded correctly (without hand raised)

c— called on and responded incorrectly

co called on and gave no response

v+volunteered and responded correctly

v— volunteered and responded incorrectly

q   asked a question

g   group responded

cb called on for board work

vb volunteered for board work

tp teacher-pupil conference initiated by teacher

pt teacher-pupil conference initiated by pupil

pp pupil-pupil conference

On page 200 is a picture of what happened in a class taught by a history teacher.   The technique used to obtain this record is very simple.   One enters a class at the beginning of the period. When a name is called, it is noted and a line is drawn, along which one writes the correct symbol for each pupil response.

To guide you in your study of pupil participation in lessons of a rather formal type we suggest the following exercises.

FOR DISCUSSION

1. Use the foregoing data as a basis for your answers to the following questions:
a. What is the sum of the responses by Elva, Mildred, Sue, Kelley, and Jones? What percentage of the total is this?
b. Is Miss Brown's "zone of fire" directed to the front line? to the rear row? How would you describe her zone of fire?
c. How do you think the intelligence test scores of Alice, Bob, George, Fred, Charles, Jim, Wendell, Bill, Jones, Ruth, Sue, Mildred, Elva, Esther, and Kelley would compare with the average score for the class?
2. Using the symbols suggested here, or some modification of them, study the distribution of participation in each of two class periods.   You will need to arrange

for your visits with the teacher. You should sit where you can see the face, especially the eyes, of each pupil. In general, it is desirable to select two classes in which the activities are in sharp contrast. Write a brief statement of your findings. In particular, what type of teacher does the picture of participation suggest?

3. It has been said that teachers commonly instruct their classes in such a manner that one-tenth of the class does more than half of the talking. Do your data support this indictment?

TEACHER..............

Esther	Elva	Mildred	Sue	Charles
tp	q	c+	v+	q
pt	cb	v+	c+	q
	vb	c+	c−	
	c−	c+	c−	
	c−	v−	v−	
		c+	q	

Ruth	Jim	Kelley	Alice	Bob
q	pp	c−		c−
pp	pp	c−		
pp		v−		
		v−		
		v+		
		c+		

Wendell	Bill	Jones	George	Fred
c−	c−	c+		cb
	c−	c+		
		co		
		q		
		cb		
		vb		
		c+		

4. Is it necessary for a pupil to talk or to write on the blackboard in order to participate in a recitation? Do you participate in a football game when you are in the bleachers? Do you participate in the giving of a play when you are in the audience?

5. Miss Adams began her lesson as follows: "This morning I read on the front page of my newspaper a proposal by a government official that affects the welfare of all of us. I want each one of you to write your guess as to the proposal, and to write a sentence suggesting how it affects us. Later I will ask you to write on other questions and I want you to leave your papers on my desk at the end of our period."

Miss Stowe began as follows: "I read in my morning paper of a very interesting proposal by one of our high government officials. Who has a guess as to the topic which caught my eye? Edward, we will hear from you."

Which teacher do you think secured the larger amount of participation? Why?

THE SOCIALIZED RECITATION

A partial answer to the problem of providing for wider participation is provided by the socialized recitation. The socialized-recitation method includes practice in cooperative thinking as well as the better types of question-answer methods.

The main purposes of the socialized recitation are to develop techniques useful in group work, to stimulate reflective thinking, to

School should be fun, but it need never be at the expense of fellow students.

supplement previous knowledge, to encourage creative expression, to develop desirable social attitudes by providing practice in a large variety of socialized situations and above all practice in the techniques of cooperative thinking.

As a method, the socialized recitation does not follow any set pattern of procedure. It is subject to considerable modification and is easily adaptable to all subjects in which the recitation normally plays an important role. If represented on a scale of "degrees of socialized recitation," the procedure in the classroom might indeed range from a just-noticeable point above zero, in which the teacher permits a few questions to be raised by pupils and answered by others, to a point high in the scale, in which the recitation is completely socialized and carried on by pupils in accordance with democratic procedure. The transition from the formal recitation to socialized recitation is largely a matter of infusing life into the classroom by introducing worth-while activities, and of encouraging pupil expression with the aim of making the classroom a unit of dynamic group life.

In the pure form of the socialized recitation the members of the class elect a chairman, executive committees, and special committees. It is the task of the teacher to set the stage and guide the work of the committees into the most fruitful channels. A partial list of teacher and pupil activities follows:[1]

Teacher Activities:
1. Planning
   a. Of the organization of the class.
   b. Of the distribution of the tasks to give each a varied experience.
2. Supervision of the leaders, chairman, and committees.
3. Cooperation
   a. With the group, as one of them in making decisions.
   b. By contributing material to the discussion when essential.

Pupil Activities:
1. Presiding over the class organization.
2. Conducting discussions.
3. Planning distribution of work among the class as a member of a committee.
4. Making reports.
5. Volunteering pertinent material from experience.
6. Asking informational questions.
7. Making both destructive and constructive criticisms.
8. Summarizing.
9. Cooperating with the group.
10. Assuming responsibility for tasks.
11. Initiating activities.

The degree of pupil activity, freedom, and informality is dependent on such factors as maturity of the group, previous practice in self-direction, interest, and spirit of cooperation of pupils. The success of the teacher in the use of the socialized recitation will depend to a very large extent on his ability to weigh these factors and to adjust the activities of the hour to them.

[1] This outline was suggested by a former student, M. L. Robertson.

Here these youngsters relive a scene in one of the Lincoln trials.   Most children, and as a matter of fact, grownups, enjoy dramatization.[E]

THE GROWTH OF MEANINGS

Other things being equal, interest is easier to build up if we can begin with something that the pupil has partially experienced. Herbartians used to call this basis the apperceptive mass.   But this is only the starting point; the next step is to provide new experiences that will add meanings to the old and cause the concepts to grow. Perhaps you now begin to see what Kilpatrick means by the phrase, "activity leading to further activity," and Dewey by "the reconstruction of experience."

The activities and the materials must be realistic and must have a direct bearing on felt needs.   They must have something to do with present-day problems and happenings.   However, we should not make the mistake of assuming that a problem that is vital for adults is necessarily of great interest to children.   For example, teaching the topic of investments to an eighth-grade class in arithmetic is easily justified on the criteria of social usage; nevertheless, it may be very difficult, and not at all necessary to get a class of fourteen-year-old girls excited about stocks and bonds.   In general, interest in an activity will depend on the extent to which the materials have a direct bearing on problems which the pupil considers vital to his needs here and now.

A further implication of method is that the printed materials employed must not be "over the heads" of pupils. The material must be written not only *for* the pupil but *to* the pupil. Many authors of textbooks give special attention to vocabulary difficulty, but we still have a long way to go in cutting the gap between authors and pupils. Special attention should be given to the reading problem which lies at the root of many difficulties that pupils have in the various school subjects. Moreover, the teacher of every school subject must be a teacher of reading. The fact that a pupil is a fairly good reader in social studies does not guarantee that he is also a good reader in general science or of art materials. Our textbooks are getting larger and larger but it is an intriguing fallacy to assume that many slow-learning or dull pupils can read a "wordy" book. Materials that such pupils are expected to read, and to be able to do, must be written in simple English, with brief paragraphs and short sentences. Keep in mind, however, that the difficulty of a sentence depends far more on the extent to which the ideas have been experienced than on the length of the words or of the sentence.

AWARENESS OF SUCCESS

The ability to do something in an activity produces, in the long run, an interest in it. For example, pupils like to compute if they know how. One reason pupils like standardized tests, if they are administered in the right way, is that the degree of success is so definitely measured. An important pedagogical implication is that a teacher should break up the activities into tasks which are small enough to enable even the slow-learning pupils to tell whether they are making progress, for one of the basic challenges in life is achievement. It does not follow that schoolwork should be highly competitive, but certainly the pupil should be provided with means for measuring his progress. In a later chapter on appraisal, the need for awareness of success is illustrated by self-appraisal techniques.

GUIDES TO SECURING AND MAINTAINING INTEREST

There are certain practical guides which are by no means mere tricks of the trade and which teachers find useful in securing and maintaining interest. The most important of these suggestions are:

Do you think this project would be fun for youngsters?[B]

1. *Manage the situation so as to avoid mental and physical annoyance.* If you seat your pupils where they can see and hear everything that goes on in an attractive room in which the temperature is comfortable and the lighting adequate, you have taken an important step toward an effective program of motivation. Then, you should avoid mistakes that annoy pupils, such as (a) making assignments unnecessarily long, (b) being too impatient to get to the difficult parts on the assumption that the advanced work is more interesting, (c) assuming that it is normal for pupils to be bewildered and lost for a while, that "something may snap" in the pupil's mind, and that then all will be clear, (d) assuming that pupils have an adequate grasp of basic concepts and skills, (e) looking at the slow, even though serious, student as a pest, and (f) taking for granted that the pupil already realizes the value of the subject and hence making no effort to convince him of its value.

2. *The right attitude toward the subject is at least a start on the road to interest.* Many pupils come to a subject with an antipathy for it. Some are disorganized by fear of the subject, and still others come with the attitude that the subject is not very important and is surely not worthy of serious attention and effort. They have heard (a) that the subject is difficult, (b) that Dad or Mother, who is per-

Outdoor science under the guidance of a great teacher can be as rich an experience as schools offer.[D]

haps quite a person, didn't do well in it, (c) that the subject has little practical value, (d) that many pupils fail the subject, and (e) that "our family" can't do the languages, sciences, etc. Also, they may have been taught previously by an untrained teacher who did not like the subject, or by one who at the moment was busy revising some other part of the curriculum. The teacher should try to secure the cooperation of the home so that parents will in incidental moments picture the subject as being desirable.

3. *Exhibit or simulate enthusiasm for the work.* Unfortunate indeed is the adult who has not had at least two or three great teachers from whom he could catch some of their infectious zeal. The teacher without wasting time should suffuse the period with good cheer and sociability. If he has troubles, he should leave them at home, for youth deserves something better than can be provided by a sick or a troubled teacher.

4. *The teacher who has a fine control of subject matter will learn rather easily how to bring back to the fold the pupils with wandering attention.* Moreover, a broad background of subject matter insures an extra challenge to the small group in each class possessing a deep, permanent interest in that area.

5. Materials of instruction should be developed at a fairly rapid rate. It is common for a teacher to get into a vicious circle: the pupils do not understand; the teacher slows down the work; the pupils lose interest; he retards the work still further, with the result that the work drags. You probably have heard very, very few people who are leaving a movie say, "I didn't understand what was going on"; but you have heard many students say this as they were leaving classes in high school and college. The motion pictures and the radio have taught us that a good deal of material can be crowded into a relatively short period of time.

6. Interest is stimulated if recitations are conducted in such a way as to utilize the element of dramatic surprise. A mother who says, "John, if you do a good job mowing the lawn this morning I'll have a surprise for your dinner," is applying an effective principle in motivation and one that far too few teachers use in their daily work when they fail to plan lessons so as to give the unexpected a chance to happen. One of the most interesting teachers who taught for many years at the University of Wisconsin so planned his demonstration lessons as to provide a surprise for his students in nearly every meeting of the class.

A STUDY OF ATTENTION

We present now an objective device for studying the extent to which a teacher can gain and hold the attention of his class. Ad-

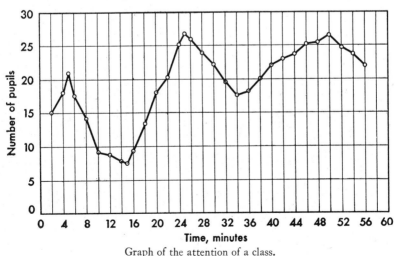

Graph of the attention of a class.

mittedly the device can be used only with a rather formal type of recitation.   But you will learn something if you practice this technique several times.

Miss Grove visited her friend's class in American history.   On a horizontal scale she plotted the minutes of recitation and on a vertical scale she showed the number of pupils at full attention. She sat on the side lines where she could see the face of each pupil. She counted the pupils who were on the job at the end of each two minutes.   The graph gives us a picture of the class in terms of its attention.

FOR DISCUSSION

1. What were the two high points?
2. Do you think the class made a good start?   Why?
3. Is it true that many teachers use the first 15 or 20 minutes of a recitation for "warming-up" purposes?
4. Some psychologists tell us that the attention span for complete concentration on a narrow mental function is very short.   You can get evidence on the validity of this statement by arranging with some teacher to observe her class and constructing interest graphs.
5. Miss Grove had learned to write on the chart the activities that caused the curve of attention to rise or fall.   She found that the low spot in this particular recitation was caused by "a committee of pupils making a poorly prepared report." The first high point occurred at the end of 25 minutes.   This was when a pupil showed a photographic copy of a paper published the day after Lincoln's assassination.   The second high point was reached when the teacher was making the assignment for the next day.   Some teachers can be classified by means of interest graphs.   What kind of curve do you think you would get from the "hearing-of-the-assigned-lesson" type?
6. (Optional.)   Secure permission to visit and draw an interest graph for each of two recitations.   You will need to sit where you can see the face, especially the eyes, of each pupil.   Your supervising teacher may wish you to do this assignment in the hour when he is teaching the section in which you are to do most of your directed teaching.

THE CRUCIAL FACTOR: THE CURRICULUM

The fact is that we have not yet come to grips with the factor that makes the school day boring to about 40 per cent of the high-school population.   We refer to a curriculum that doesn't fit.   In your high-school days you probably liked school and you may not have noted the large number of students in your classes who never "knew the score."   Such pupils will never be satisfied with a purely academic program.   Many of them have the ability to render valuable services with a bit of special training.   Witness the fact that several hundred thousand boys held important semitechnical jobs during the war as a result of something that they had learned *after* they left the regular schools.   We must provide a more realistic curriculum for the large number of persons who will continue to be absorbed fairly early in life by industry, trade, farm, and business.   We must

There is no trouble about providing for individual differences in a garden project.   The range in difficulty is from the simple manual tasks to problems requiring careful thinking in the application of scientific knowledge.[E]

give our boys and girls greater security in practical affairs.   Since there are in our high schools these large groups of pupils whose needs cannot possibly be met by traditional courses, the sensible thing to do is to provide good courses with very different goals and experiences for groups with different needs.   If the school does not classify students according to needs, then you can divide your class into two groups and teach units on two levels simultaneously.   It should not be too difficult to teach two classes in the same class hour—every teacher in a one-room country school has to teach a good many groups at different levels. Obviously you would need to use the workshop techniques described elsewhere. Furthermore, as has been suggested earlier, we must somehow do this in a manner that does not stigmatize any group.

There is here no implication that the traditional courses will be less important in the future than they have been in the past. Since the turn of the century the high school has been facing a double responsibility. It must train for leadership in communication, science, mathematics, and the other learned fields, and it must provide a broad education in terms of effective citizenship, in the home, the community, the state, and the world. It is not a question as to whether special attention shall be given to either the college preparatory group or the noncollege group; both jobs must be done.

Another practical suggestion for enriching the curriculum of a small high school is to arrange for correspondence courses that are now provided by some eighty colleges and universities. A vast number of men and women took such courses in remote places all over the world during the war years. It would seem that pupils in the small high school would have a much better chance to succeed in correspondence courses than men in the armed forces for the reason that the local teachers might service such work in the fields that they happen to be teaching. Since the teacher of a small high school has only a few regular students, the implementation of a correspondence course for one or two extra pupils would obviously not be an impossible task. In fact one city in Michigan (Benton Harbor) has provided correspondence courses for high-school pupils for a long time. In that school there are in some semesters only two or three pupils who wish to take some special course, as, for example, trigonometry, and yet these may be the very ones who should take such a course. To provide a teacher for so small a group is very expensive.

Many persons do not realize that more than two-thirds of all high schools are small, with certainly fewer than 200 students and probably fewer than eight teachers. Such small high schools enroll in all more than a million pupils. We feel, therefore, that our recommendation is of a good deal of importance. It is gratifying to note that to an increasing extent school boards are arranging to provide correspondence courses when they feel that instruction by a teacher is too expensive.

Using Community Resources

As you recall your earlier school days, do you agree with the following criticism of schools expressed by John Dewey?

From the standpoint of the child, the great waste in the school comes from his inability to utilize the experience he gets outside the school in any complete and free way within the school itself; while, on the other hand, he is unable to apply in daily life what he is learning at school. That is the isolation of the school—its isolation from life. When the child gets into the schoolroom he has to put out of his mind a large part of the ideas, interests, and activities that predominate in his home and neighborhood. So the school, being unable to utilize this everyday experience, sets painfully to work, on another tack and by a variety of means, to arouse in the child an interest in school studies.[1]

To use materials and persons from the community would seem to be the best way, not only to motivate some of the units, but also to enliven them with realistic problems. Thus there would come to be a two-way flow in school and community relationships.

It is to be noted that the human resources should not be overlooked.

In almost any community there are people who can and will take a little time off from their regular duties in order to cooperate in teaching some unit in the high school. For example, the local insurance agents can be used in rotation over several semesters in a way that will keep the unit on insurance up to date without proving to be a burden to anyone, and with little danger that a particular agent will take unfair advantage of other agents. The managers of banks are usually highly cooperative and willing, especially immediately after closing time, to confer with a class in mathematics. Cooperation can also be secured in most cases from persons whose business it is to give advice on making out income tax reports.[2]

In the smaller cities (of less than 4,000) it is a good idea to keep a record of the persons in the community who will not only be able but willing to help in the instruction of some curriculum unit. Obviously such a record should be kept in a central place, built up, and kept up to date by the teachers.

It must be admitted that there are units in the curriculum for which the use of community materials is not only difficult to arrange but is even artificial. If not well managed, such efforts may become a nuisance to everyone concerned. Probably a great deal

[1] John Dewey. *The School and Society*, p. 67, Chicago: The University of Chicago Press, 1915.

[2] *The Role of Mathematics in Consumer Education*, p. 20. Washington, D.C.: Consumer Education Study, 1945.

of very valuable school time is now wasted by too many excursions that are poorly planned. Nevertheless, the suggestion that teachers use what is going on in the community as their laboratory material is sensible.

The Teacher's Part in the Community School

The meaning of the phrase "the community school" is vague to many teachers. Perhaps it was unfortunate that this overworked phrase was ever introduced, for the idea which it is intended to convey is simple and sensible. Before we turn to the teacher's part let us consider the following definition:[1]

> The purpose of the community school is to help meet the major social problems of our day; namely, the development and practical implementation of a democratic philosophy in local communities and the nation at large. In the community school, children, teachers, parents, and local community groups cooperate in the development of the school program. Children study such areas of community living as *health, home making, recreation,* and *industry* as a regular part of their school curriculum. They make excursions into the community. They study the national and world aspects of local problems. They explore the many questions vitally concerning them which they read about in newspapers, hear over the radio, or see shown in the cinema. They study how such problems are being met in other localities in the nation and the world. They seek to cooperate with adult groups to improve local health, safety, recreational and other conditions. The community school is thus not only concerned with children's studying about life. It is concerned with children actually working with adults toward the improvement of democratic living.

Let us be clear on one point. When using the phrase "community school," we do not assume that all pupils should be educated to live in that particular community. The fact is that a rather small fraction of adults continue to live in the communities in which they attend school. The idea in the community school is that the activities of the community are the most practical resource for enriching the curriculum. Using the community resources is fairly easy in some subjects, as for example, in the arts, in science, in the modern languages, and in the social studies. It is more difficult in others, as for example, Latin and mathematics. But even in these fields a good teacher would deny that it is impossible.

Values in a Community Study. There are many reasons why a comprehensive knowledge of the community is valuable to a teacher.

[1] Samuel Everett. "Challenge of the Community School," *Michigan Education Journal,* XVI (February, 1939), 279.

The statement that "a teacher should know the community" is more than a mere corollary of the fact that he should know his pupils. In making a community survey the teacher can kill two birds with one stone, for not only will he be doing the very things that will make him more of a person when it comes to dealing with his pupils, but he also will be getting experiences and collecting materials that will make him a better classroom practitioner. The teacher who keeps an eye on the community will discover human and physical resources that may be used to improve instruction and put greater vitality and reality into the curriculum.

The teacher should know what forces play on the pupil, not only to understand better why he responds in the way he does, but also to learn at first hand the cultural pattern to which the pupil must adjust, at least temporarily. Obviously the pupil will profit most when his courses in school include essential experiences. He will be more intelligent in thinking about the social relationships and problems of his community and, through practice in cooperative participation, he will be better prepared to take an intelligent part as an adult. Even if the pupil moves to another community, as he almost certainly will in two out of three cases within five years of graduation from high school, the local community is the springboard conveniently available for inducting a pupil into the larger concept of society.

The community, too, will profit because its needs and deficiencies will become known and it will have more citizens who are concerned that something be done about them. The community will come to take pride in a school that seeks to minister to its needs. It is not uncommon for committees of laymen from business and other groups to undertake a community study or project that originated in the classroom of the local high school.

Probably the one who profits most by the study of the interplay between the resources of the school and those of the community is the teacher for there is no better way for a teacher to gain zest for his work, to grow as a person, and to keep alive, than by a community approach to his curriculum problems.

How to Begin. In communities where the curriculum has for the most part been limited to book learning within the four walls of the classroom, the intelligent teacher will do well to take the first step without making an event of the procedure, taking it in full stride as a part of the regular work of some class. For example, a mathematics class in the junior high school may with profit undertake to investigate with what precision people measure in "our town" or "along Main Street," and the chances of an unfavorable reaction on the part of citizens to a study of this type are very low. The science class may perhaps be interested in making a study of the local water supply and the social studies class in the housing problem.

In the second place, a teacher playing a lone hand in using community resources should not undertake too wide a study. Rather, he should concentrate on a very simple but well-defined problem. The study will grow and spread to related problems fast enough, for an investigation of this sort usually uncovers more questions than it answers. For this reason it makes little difference which aspect of the community the teacher selects, so long as it is thoroughly worth while for pupils.

On some community studies it is desirable for the whole faculty, or at least a considerable part of the group, to work together. Momentum is gained by an accumulation of resourceful suggestions. The task can be distributed so as to economize time and energy, and many otherwise deadly faculty meetings can be enlivened when the data are assembled, interpreted, and applied in curriculum revision. Here, too, it needs to be recognized that almost any one of a wide range of community problems may be selected for the initial investigation. Among those that have yielded helpful findings when undertaken by whole faculties are the following:

1. The number of young persons in the community between the ages of 17 and 21 who are neither at work nor in school.
2. The types of work undertaken by the members of the last five graduating classes and their reactions to the curriculum.
3. The extent to which the school meets the community needs.[1]
4. To make an inventory of court cases of delinquency involving pupils enrolled in school or who have recently left school.

Using the Data. Care should be exercised to make certain that the data will be useful in the future. The average tenure of teachers in small school systems is short—less than $2\frac{1}{2}$ years. Many teachers do not stay long enough to analyze the wealth of curricular

---

[1] In the city where this sentence was written there is a project under way in which all citizens were asked to serve as volunteers to work with the teachers in a comprehensive evaluation of the schools.

Often school could be more interesting and more exciting if the teachers used the resources of the community—especially if the persons who are able and willing, come and help teach a unit. Don't you think these students find it interesting to discuss oriental culture with this Japanese student of American birth?(M)

materials that exist at their very door. There should be one or more central places where data and illustrative materials gathered in the community may be kept up to date in systematic fashion. From time to time all teachers should be informed by the principal or a special committee in faculty meeting, or through mimeographed bulletins, as to what materials have proved valuable in instruction. In some courses it may be entirely appropriate, and good experience for both pupils and teachers, to spend parts of class periods in classifying and cataloging the community's educational resources.

ILLUSTRATIONS OF COMMUNITY SURVEYS[1]

In order to get a clear notion of a teacher's relationship with his community consider next a few samples of simple studies. Each represents the first experience of the investigator in this type of work. Unfortunately it is not possible for us to do more than to sketch the procedures; nor can we provide you with more than mere fragments of the complete findings for each study.

[1] To the supervising teacher: The discussion of this section may need to be kept brief in the busy days of student teaching.

1. *A Study of Materials Available for Instructional Purposes.* This study was undertaken by a teacher and the students in one of his classes. They interviewed residents of the village and the surrounding farming community. They received some help from other teachers and from the reports of their pupils who undertook to investigate specific parts of the problem. In this small town of 1,250

Science is more meaningful for this student because she has had an opportunity to see some of the equipment used by Thomas A. Edison.(E)

persons an amazing number of experiences available for curriculum enrichment were uncovered. We now direct your attention to three outcomes:

a. The pupils made a long list of industrial processes and business practices that they would like to study. The immediate result in one class, not even taught by the investigator, was that the class took nineteen field trips instead of none as was the case in the preceding semester. The class made an excursion to study each of the following: old log buildings, frame buildings, camp site (Indian), automobile factory, cattle ranch, creamery, dairy farms, general farms, poultry farms, pumping station, Ford's Greenfield Village, ice-cream factory, lumber yard, saw mills, table factory, violin factory, water works, State Capitol, Michigan State College. One of the main outcomes was the increased interest on the part of the parents and the pupils in the work of the school.

b. The class organized a school museum including such fascinating articles as the following: a water carrier, a spinning wheel, a loom, a clock made by the first clockmaker in America, colonial pots and kettles, Indian relics (Indian baskets, meal bowl, dugouts, stone weapons, peace pipe), World War equipment, a broad axe, ox yoke, mastodon skeleton, old guns and cutting weapons, powder horns, old newspapers (one of them dated the day after Lincoln's death), a German Bible 200 years old, and a wedding outfit over 100 years old.

c. The investigator was amazed to learn the number of citizens who possessed some special knowledge of topics that for the most part were taught in some class in the school. He placed a list of

TOPICS AND AVAILABLE SPEAKERS

Topic	No. of speakers	Topic	No. of speakers
Agriculture (general)	5	Meats	2
Aviation	2	Milling	1
Banking	2	Music:	
Business	1	Vocal	4
Carpentry	1	Instrumental	4
Cooperative organization	1	Oil refining	3
Dairy	3	Plumbing	1
Dentistry	1	Poland	1
Education	6	Printing	2
Engines, internal combustion	1	Recreation	3
Farm animals	1	Religion	4
Gardening	2	Sanitation	3
Guidance	3	Sales	2
Health	4	Shop practice, woodworking	3
History of the town	8	Telegraph operator	1
Insects	3	Travel:	
Insurance	4	Florida	2
Irrigation	4	Europe	1
Italy	1	Cuba	1
Journalism	2	Canada	1
Law	1	Mexico	1
Literature	1	Welding, electric	1
Machinery, power	1	World War	4
Management, cooperative	2	Y.M.C.A.	1
Marketing	2		

the topics, together with the names of available speakers, in the school's card catalogue of instructional materials. His list included 47 topics and 108 speakers.

Considering the size of the town this list is truly amazing. It may be added that the investigator did not include sixteen formal organizations that were willing to supply speakers regularly for various school occasions.

2. *A Study of Housing Conditions.* A teacher studied the housing conditions of his pupils in a town with a population just under 12,000. The procedure involved an inventory that was filled out by 458 high-school pupils. Since the information was collected as a part of projects carried forward by students and the responses were for the most part unsigned, it may be assumed that the facts were not willfully distorted. An interesting aspect of the investigation is that the teacher remained under the general impression throughout the investigation that living conditions in this town were really quite good, though 8 per cent of the houses did not have regular disposal of garbage, 10 per cent did not have adequate fire protection, 17 per cent had no indoor bathrooms and toilets, 60 per cent still used wood as fuel for cooking, 60 per cent had no telephones, and only 30 per cent had refrigerators of any kind—all this in spite of the fact that as many as 70 per cent of the families owned their own homes and 31 per cent had lived more than ten years in the houses which they occupied.

The pictures most common in order of frequency were "Lone Wolf," "Last Supper," "Song of the Lark," "Springtime," "Blue Boy," "End of the Trail," "George Washington," "The Angelus," "Age of Innocence," "Sir Galahad," "Boy with Rabbit," "The Windmill," "Old Ironsides," "Flower Girl in Holland," "Whistler's Mother," and "Lincoln."

3. *The Reading Tastes of the People of a Community.* In a town of 1,300 people, a teacher of English tried to find out what the people in his whole school district read during a given month. The local newsdealer and the local druggist both provided him with the name and number of each magazine and newspaper sold during the entire month. He next secured from the postmaster some confidential information, provided at great inconvenience, concerning the reading material that had passed through the post office during that month. Finally he included all materials checked out at the school

and adjacent libraries by people in the community. The main generalization, a very comforting one to school people, is that we need not be unduly disturbed by the salacious magazines displayed in lurid fashion on our newsstands, as is evidenced by the following table:

A homogeneous group is having a good time reading materials at their level.[E]

Type of publication	Num- ber sold	Two highest frequencies
Magazines:		
Occupational	1,353	*Michigan Farmer* (302); *Farmer's Wife* (166)
Home magazines	711	*Country Home* (125); *Household Magazine* (110)
Cultural	336	*Pictorial Review* (91); *American* (80)
Sex-story magazines	88	*True Story* (30); *True Confessions* (22)
Detective, adventure, western	65	*Master Detective* (9); *True Detective* (8)
Religion and politics	57	*Christian Herald* (15); *Social Justice* (14)
Sports	39	*Scouting* (9); *Hunting and Fishing* (8)
Radio, stage, screen	24	*Radio Guide* (7); *Real Screen Fun* (5)
Newspapers	1,225	Local paper (432); paper of neighboring city (225)
Miscellaneous	86	*Good Stories* (65); *Pythian Tidings* (45)

We may note that, while the people of this community bought a total of 3,984 magazines and newspapers, only 177, less than 5 per cent, are classified as radio, stage, screen, sex, detective, western, and adventure types. We are not suggesting that these materials are altogether objectionable for young people. Rather, we are pointing out that, even assuming they are undesirable, the total amount of such reading is a small fraction of all that was read in this community.

4. *Number of Volumes in Home Libraries.* This investigation was carried out with the same children involved in the preceding study. Any teacher in that school should find the facts in the following table interesting and illuminating.

NUMBER OF VOLUMES IN HOME LIBRARIES

Number of Books	*Pupils Reporting*
No books	19
1– 20	220
21– 60	402
61–110	93
111–150	18
151–200	37
201–300	20
301–500	18
501–850	2
1000	1
Not reporting	50

There were 19 children who reported that they had not a single book in their homes; 220 more reported that they had fewer than 20 books. A total of 641 said they had fewer than 60 books in the home, including even catalogues of mail-order houses. We must not conclude, however, that these children were completely cut off from educational influences at home, for 834 (more than 94 per cent —a truly astonishing figure considering the type of town) reported that they had radios in the home.

THE TEACHERS' PART IN CURRICULUM REVISION

At present there is widespread interest in the revision of the high-school curriculum. Among the conditions that make this a crucial problem are (1) the ever-widening gap between the traditional academic curriculum and the needs of pupils who will have to adjust to a world that is becoming small so very fast, (2) the promotion to the high-school grades of a vast number of pupils who are low in ability, skills, and cultural background, and (3) the inappropriateness of the professional education of teachers for the new scale of values in education that fixes as primary goals such matters as the integration of personality, attitudes, behavior, and the education of the emotions.

Alumni remember for many a day some small part that they had in the school operetta.[E]

At the outset, it will be gratifying to note that a clear understanding and sensible application of some of the broader concepts stressed in earlier chapters give you a good start on curriculum revision. For example, if you know a good deal about your pupils, their needs, abilities, interests, satisfactions, and dissatisfactions; if you know something about your community, its resources and mores; and if you have clearly in mind the general goals of education, you are already a long way down the road. In fact, curriculum revision will not be a brief journey but a continuous one that you travel as a matter of course. Recognize that the product of your first efforts, while undoubtedly good for the producer, may not be worth much for the consumer, the pupil. You cannot begin some fine morning by just sitting down and revising the curriculum. You have to grow to the task.

It may happen that even in the early months of your first year of teaching, you will find yourself a member of a curriculum committee, struggling with the problem of how to get started. It is easy to get lost in a thicket of words when one begins reading the numerous books and articles dealing with curriculum revision, and in the early stages you will need to limit yourself to a few simple, practical steps.

1. *State in simple terms the kind of school that you will aid in building.* In the small school you may have to do this thinking by yourself, though for obvious reasons it would be much better if you could formulate such a statement as the outcome of cooperative thinking by the whole faculty. To be concrete, let us assume that you arrive at a list of statements something like this one:

a. Our school community should be as close to real life as we can make it. We will seek to bridge the gap between school and daily living by an interplay of the resources of the community and the school. Many of the classes of our school should find meanings for the students in the world in which they now live.

b. The general patterns of conduct in our school should be shaped by cooperative thinking and action of students and faculty. We should develop the understanding of the meaning of democracy by providing democratic experiences in the life of the school.

c. Learning situations are not incidental nor are they wholly teacher-assigned tasks, for learning is a cooperative adventure with the teacher as the experienced guide.

d. The school should seek to develop the ability of the pupil to recognize problems; to master, so far as he can, the techniques of problem solving; and to fix the disposition to solve the problems he meets in systematic fashion and to the extent possible by employing the method of science. We will strive to provide workrooms with a friendly and informal setting where these problems may be solved.

e. The primary aim of the school is to promote the growth of each individual. Subject matter is to be mastered, not as an end in itself, but as a means to more worth-while living. Outcomes are to be sought in terms of a broad understanding essential for effective adjustment to a modern world which we hope will be governed by resourceful thinkers, not by chance nor by the whims of dictators.

Fragmentary as this list may seem to you, it is nevertheless a start on constructive thinking about the curriculum.

2. *Make available a fairly good professional library.* There is no good reason why the teachers in a small high school remote from a

college or university library should struggle without important books. Practically every small town has its book club for the distribution of recent books of fiction. By a little cooperative action, teachers can utilize this plan in keeping themselves up to date on professional literature at little expense.

3. *Formulate the specific aims for the courses which you teach.* Relate these to the general objectives of education, to the full program of the school, and to the needs of your pupils and the community. Try to consult several lists that you have reason to believe are carefully prepared.

4. *Arrange for systematic and cooperative planning.* This involves not only students but teachers in related areas as well. In some systems the authorities have encouraged teachers each week to use one or more hours of the school day for group planning.

5. *For each area, select a few activities.* Choose those that (*a*) have a vital bearing on the progress of mankind, (*b*) provide worth-while experiences for most students, and (*c*) can be taught by realistic materials.

6. *Choose carefully the most desirable forms of appraisal.* The details of this step are presented in Chap. XIII. Too often the emphasis in evaluation is on the pupil's work, to the neglect of a critical appraisal of the teacher's method. Curriculum revision is, or at least should be, quite as much concerned with method as with the selection of materials.

7. *Visit once a year a school that has undertaken a carefully considered innovation.* If possible, discuss the implications of your observation in a subsequent faculty meeting. The outcomes of such visits are better when undertaken by a committee. In a few school systems, whole faculties have undertaken such visits, delegating the tasks of teaching for the day to representatives of the student body. Needless to say, such sweeping delegation of responsibility will yield valuable experiences for pupils only when a great deal of time and energy has been given to careful planning.

8. *Check your work with good practice.* You may be able to consult one or two experts. In any case you can check your thinking by noting the trends in recent textbooks or in a few courses of study that have been carefully constructed. A great many sins are committed in the name of curriculum revision, of which one is endless duplication. When you organize a new unit or revise an old one,

remember that a good many persons have probably worked on that same job and that you may be able to profit by their experience. Don't waste time rediscovering America; rather, begin where the other person stopped. Too often teachers without sound scholarship or with little ability to organize materials for children start from scratch, thus ignoring available materials.

Too often schools snuff out the creative spark. On the other hand, creative work may be done anywhere in the curriculum when a teacher knows how to fan this spark. In some schools gardening offers a fine opportunity.[L]

SOME COMMON ERRORS

There are many ways in which teachers and administrators waste precious energy and valuable time in the effort to improve the curriculum. Some of the most common errors are:

1. Centering the attention at the beginning of a unit on subject-matter materials rather than on general and specific goals.

2. Rationalizing by refusing to be critical of one's practices and offerings.

3. Maneuvering to secure a vested interest for one's special subject.

4. Accepting as authentic the work already done by other school systems and committees, or that found in textbooks.

5. Failing to secure the frank criticism of pupils, parents, and intelligent citizens.

6. Failing to make use of the best textbooks.

7. Writing a course to fit a particular textbook.

8. Failing to recognize that curriculum revision is a continuous process or at any rate a long-time job, and trying to complete the job in a month or two.

9. Undertaking a task that is too difficult in the light of one's teaching load.

10. Copying uncritically the existing outlines and syllabi, rather than undertaking a comprehensive investigation.

11. Assuming that curriculum revision does not go beyond adding new units and eliminating obsolete ones.

12. Failing to recognize that, in the modern school, there are all sorts of boys and girls whose educational needs may be very different from what one's own were.

13. Failing to recognize that the curriculum consists of all the experiences which are influenced by the school.

For Discussion

1. Consider your own high-school days. Estimate the percentage of pupils who found school not interesting. (You may wish to have a committee summarize the opinions of your group.)

2. We suggest an informal panel on the topic: The most interesting course or unit that I studied in high school.

3. There are school people who believe that a teacher can be just as efficient in teaching a very large group, let us say 50 to 70 pupils, as a teacher who has from 20 to 25. The fact is that teachers do from time to time have to teach big classes. Here is a list of procedures employed by one teacher who, hour after hour, taught large classes:

The teacher organized classroom routines so that

    (1) Pupils assisted in roll taking, distributing materials, etc.

    (2) Upon arrival, pupils set immediately about prescribed work.

    (3) Small groups were formed for special drill, projects, etc.

    (4) Student leaders helped to direct small group activities.

The teacher organized subject matter for the course

    (5) Into units for easier administration, assignment, checking.

    (6) Into specific goals, guided by pretest results.

    (7) Into assignments differentiated upon ability levels.

    (8) Into assignments specified on work sheets or workbooks.

    (9) Into new-type tests for checking mastery of units.

Time saved in routines and memory testing was devoted to

    (10) Much individual help and supervision of slower pupils.

    (11) Stimulation and direction of brighter pupils.

(12) Emphasis upon diagnosis and remedies of weaknesses.

(13) Serious efforts to direct concomitant learnings.

(14) Training all pupils in self-control and self-direction.

a. Which of these procedures would appeal to you as worth trying in case you should get an assignment to teach a large class?

b. Try to visit several times a class that includes more than 50 pupils. Note what procedures are employed that are of special aid in teaching large classes.

c. Miss Allen, teacher of a commercial subject in which she has 80 pupils per class, said, "The statement that a teacher can be just as efficient teaching large classes as small classes is just as true as the statement that two can live as cheaply as one. They can, but not so long!" What did Miss Allen have in mind?

d. Do you agree with any one of the following statements? Which? Why?

(1) A school with oversized classes cannot do effective work in guidance.

(2) Most of our educational reforms, such as knowing more about the individual child, the activity program, and emotional adjustment, are contingent on a reasonable teacher load.

(3) Except for socialization purposes the ideal school is one pupil per teacher. In practical situations we should approximate this ideal as closely as the budget of the community will permit.

4. A teacher reports that he asks each student to write in what way, large or small, he can show leadership in the class sometime during the semester. Then he provides the situation that will enable the student to "take charge of something or somebody." Do you think this is a desirable and feasible procedure?

SUGGESTED READINGS

BENJAMIN, HAROLD: *Under Their Own Command.* New York: The Macmillan Company, 1947. Pp. viii + 88.

Perhaps you would like a sample of the serious thoughts of the author of *The Saber-Tooth Curriculum.* It is a little book of high idealism on the role of education in a chaotic world, written by one of the finest in the teaching profession.

DOUGLASS, H. R.: *The High School Curriculum.* New York: The Ronald Press Company, 1947. Pp. viii + 661.

This is one of the good books on the high-school curriculum. You probably won't have time to read it all in student-teaching days. However, glance at the Table of Contents and the Index. You may find an excellent discussion on some topic or activity that you are studying, for example, personal and family living, extracurricular activities, guidance, and "core-curriculum."

ELDRIDGE, PAUL: *And Thou Shalt Teach Them.* New York: Sheridan House, 1947. Pp. 273.

In this book you will find a series of human episodes written in futuristic and impressionistic style. The author assumes that a New York City high school is a representative sample of America!! Nevertheless, there are some significant episodes that a discerning person might see in almost any high school. Most of the author's characters suggest disgusting little boys with dirty minds in grown-up bodies. If you are a busy teacher, don't take the hazard of starting to read it now. "No kidding"—you will probably find it fully as interesting, and in spots surely as repulsive, as some of the popular novels. The total effect is fine idealism abundantly spattered with mud.

LEONARD, J. PAUL: *Developing the Secondary School Curriculum.* New York: Rinehart and Company, Inc., 1946. Pp. xi + 560.

This book represents a progressive-education school of thought about trends in curriculum revision. Teachers of the social studies will find much of the volume interesting and useful. For the busy teacher in some other field we suggest, as a beginning, Chaps, 12, 13, and 16.

PEDDIWELL, J. ABNER: *The Saber-Tooth Curriculum.* New York: McGraw-Hill Book Company, Inc., 1939. Pp. xiii + 139.

It is possible that school teachers, time and again, take themselves too seriously. If you should ever slip into that sad state, you will find in the little book, *The Saber-Tooth Curriculum*, a wholesome corrective. It is not only good fun—in fact riotous in spots— but the discerning author makes many sly and sagacious comments on the curriculum. J. Abner Peddiwell is, of course, the fictitious name of the author with the playful pen. Seven out of every hundred readers (so the rumor goes) can figure out who the real author is.

WILLIAMS, E. I. F.: *Horace Mann, Educational Statesman.* New York: The Macmillan Company, 1937. Pp. xii + 367.

This book is a biography of one of America's great educational reformers. Chapter XVI, "The Man and His Legacy to the Schools," is very interesting; it suggests the contribution of Horace Mann to his time and to the solutions of educational problems of our day.

Chapter IX

Three Important Competencies of a Teacher

Every artist was first an amateur.

—EMERSON

A teacher who doesn't know how (1) to use a textbook, (2) to apply modern psychology in designing effective drill, and (3) to ask provocative questions may not be the poorest teacher in a school system, but he surely cannot be a very good one. This chapter deals with these three important competencies of a teacher.

THE PROPER USE OF A TEXTBOOK

For over a generation, some prominent educators have, by implication at least, stigmatized the use of a basal textbook. In this period, a great deal of nonsense has been written and spoken about its place in instruction.

In discussing the issue, textbook or no textbook, we need to consider three related questions:

1. What area of the curriculum do we have in mind? It is one thing if we are considering the social studies where sequence and continuity as yet play no great part; it is a very different matter if we are thinking about an introductory course in a foreign language or a senior-high-school course in physics or geometry, where logical and psychological order are of great importance. We are not implying that even a first-year course in German or Spanish cannot be greatly enriched by supplementary aids, or that a course in the social studies consisting largely of American history should be taught without a textbook, but we are insisting that the subject or area to be taught has a bearing on the place of the textbook.

2. What type of pupil do we have in mind? If we are thinking about the dull and the slow-learning, we shall soon enough discover that he is likely to be confused by different discussions of the same principle and even by two or more summaries or outlines of the same points.

3. What type of teacher is to guide the pupils without a basal textbook? And some subsidiary questions are: Has he had fundamental training in this area or is he a made-over football coach? How heavy is his load? Does he really have time to plan and to collect enriching materials? In the case of the untrained and the overloaded teacher, it is a very poor textbook that is not better than

One reason why many teachers fail to use the textbook in the right way is that they have no supplementary materials. However, much can be obtained by clipping, filing, and evaluating materials from current magazines that often include more recent and more meaningful materials than textbooks.[M]

no textbook. It is significant to note that in more cases than not, teachers who hold to the no-textbook theory show an utter lack of fundamental training. The competent teacher, who has a well-considered plan for the teaching of a unit which he believes better than any now in existence and which he wishes to subject to careful systematic trial, should be given not only permission to proceed without a textbook but every aid and encouragement.

The real issue is not textbook or no textbook, but the desirable method of using one or more textbooks. The stigma of the use of a textbook is probably a by-product of our desire to put subject matter in its proper place. What we really should condemn is the way in which textbooks are misused and our failure to educate prospective teachers in their proper use.

The following practical steps making for more effective use of a textbook can be suggested:

1. *Organize a simple guide sheet for each unit or chapter.* This should serve to guide the student in the definition of the problems of the course, suggest activities and methods of attack, refer to helpful supplementary reading materials, and provide him with specific goals of the unit.

2. *Make available enough copies of three or four supplementary textbooks.* Perhaps no suggestion has contributed more toward improving instruction than the concept of the classroom library. When this technique is employed, the guide sheets must be worked out carefully and in some detail.

3. *Appraise the textbook now being used in terms of the objectives of your course.* Where are the gaps? Which parts are not up to date? Which parts should be omitted? What developments, reviews, and summaries will really prove useful?

4. *If possible, use textbooks that are fairly recent and up to date.* Too often teachers proceed to utilize mimeographed materials that are crude and incomplete, and reflect poor scholarship; in short, materials that present clear evidence that those responsible for them did not know of the existence of much better materials.

5. *Exercise care in the selection of the textbook.* This step will be developed in some detail in the following section.

PLAN FOR THE SELECTION OF TEXTBOOK

It is very common for a beginning teacher to be appointed a member of a committee to which is delegated the task of selecting a new textbook for some course. The following procedure is suggested as a means of eliminating the books not worthy of a detailed study; hence, it may be used as a set of practical guides for securing a brief list of books and as an aid in making a final selection. The idea of a score card is probably not valid for the same reasons that have been pointed out in discussing the use of a score card in rating teaching personality; in any case, if one is employed, it should be made in terms of the local situation and designed for the special course.

It is far better to develop a simple and brief check list by taking the following steps:

1. Secure a statement from a few experienced teachers of their criticisms of the textbook to be replaced.

2. Prepare a brief statement of recent trends with respect to the aims and the scope of materials of the course.

3. Request the publishers to furnish samples of available textbooks, and examine each of these in terms of the goals of your course and the problems that you believe to be most crucial and interesting to students, the scholarship reflected by authorship, and the local community needs.

4. After the best five books have been chosen, ask each teacher who will use them to make a critical comparison of them by utilizing a simple check list that will reflect the high and low spots on such items as:

   a. Quality of cover, binding, and mechanical make-up.

   b. Quality of paper.

   c. Quality of printing (type, illustrations, etc.).

   d. Kind and value of teaching aids (review exercises, drill exercises, text material, bibliographies, etc.).

   e. Appeal to pupils (based on an examination of three or four pages on the same subject in each book. Note the vocabulary, illustrative material, style, study helps, etc.).

   f. Accuracy of scholarship (based on an examination of the treatment of a few difficult topics in each of the books).

   g. Extent of the use of results of available educational research.

   h. Skill and resourcefulness of the author in selecting and organizing materials in terms of the aims and objectives of the course.

5. Recommend the first and second choices to the superintendent of schools on the basis of the data submitted.

How to Teach with a Hopeless Textbook. If you are realistic you will realize that you may have to teach with an obsolete textbook. Moreover, in a small school there may be a very poor library and little reading material in your classroom. Is there anything you can do? Yes, indeed! If the textbook is too bad it may drive you to a really fine procedure. We suggest that you keep a file with a folder for each chapter or unit. In each folder you can place a wealth of materials clipped from magazines, newspapers, government bulletins, and free materials. Even in a small school in a remote community, parents throw away a lot of fine curriculum materials. Perhaps on your way to school you see a stack of magazines awaiting the collector. Some of these probably contain more vital material on the topic you are teaching than can be found in your textbook. Pupils and parents can be interested in the project and a stream of helpful material will flow into your classroom.

But this material must be systematized. Five hundred magazines in your classroom will be of little use unless you clip and file properly. How will you get the time needed for this job? The

answer is: use the class hour as a work period in which pupils working in groups evaluate, clip, and file materials for a chapter (or a
unit) in which they are interested. The task can be managed so as
to have very great instructional value, perhaps the best that you
can design. For example, one gifted teacher takes two weeks near
the end of each year during which his class operates an assembly
line as follows: (1) each group of pupils will inspect a folder for one
unit; (2) they evaluate the materials; (3) they throw some away;
(4) they rearrange others; (5) they add some that were overlooked.
In brief they put the folder in proper shape for the next class. It
is obvious that the procedure is a grand review of the year's work,
and it is perhaps unnecessary to say that many of the pupils (and
some of their parents) do a lot of outside work and beg for more
time to devote to the project.

A Sound Psychology of Drill

The educational psychologist concerned about making school
tasks interesting does not rule out drill. Let's admit that much of
the drill material in textbooks is boring and meaningless. Nevertheless, among the most interesting tasks for pupils designed by a
school are those in which they are engaged in drill that they understand and believe worth doing. That observation, we think, holds
for any subject from art to Latin. If this is true then we had better
examine modern educational psychology to see what it says about
drill.

There is some confusion in pedagogical literature as to the
place of drill in the modern school. There are still persons who
campaign for the activity program with more emotion than understanding. With very few exceptions, there should be no drill on
things that are not clearly understood. However, there are some
fundamental skills that need to be driven to a high level of proficiency in order that time may not be wasted in learning them in
the first place.

Perhaps we can dispel some of the confusion by considering the
following:

1. *Drill is a very important phase of all learning.* If an attitude
is to be fixed, a concept to be clearly and fully developed, or an item
of information learned to the point of automatic response, or if some
specific skill is to be acquired to an efficient degree, drill—and much

of it—will be needed.   If a boy lies and cheats, he does so because he has learned it.   That is to say, he has experienced drill exercises on these matters.   The fact that he has learned to be dishonest suggests that he could have learned to be honest if only honesty had been practiced.   The fixing of attitudes, contrary to general opinion, involves extensive drill.   We may note in passing that in adver-

Here is another scene from the Lincoln trials.   Apparently the children are not disturbed by the fact that a girl is taking the part of a judge.   Again, drill made this project successful.[E]

tising and in propaganda, drill is the basic technique for fixing attitudes.

2. *Repetition is not of itself annoying.*   Unfortunately many teachers are of the opinion that repetition is in itself annoying. The evidence, we believe, marks this as a mistaken notion.   If you wish to please a child with a bedtime story you may tell him one that will enable him to experience again the events of his own day. The favorite stories of children, "The Three Bears," and "The Little Red Hen," and so on, all involve much repetition.   Every

masterpiece of music is built on the principle of repetition. A sports fan who has watched a champion football or baseball game hurries to buy a paper in order that he may experience again the exciting events of the contest. If these illustrations are not sufficient, then consider the individual who has recently had an operation. Repetition with all the gruesome details is not annoying to him. This last illustration is needed in order to avoid the conclusion that repetition is satisfying only when the experience has been accompanied by pleasure. Probably the unmotivated reviews so common a decade ago were distasteful and wearying to pupils, but in the ideal drill situation there is never exact repetition of a specific response. The violinist may play one exercise fifty times a day for a week. Yet during no two times that he plays it is his mind-set exactly the same. He improves one thing and then another in his effort to obtain perfection and automaticity. As long as it takes a fair degree of effort for him to play the exercise and as long as he can make some improvement, repetitions are interesting to him.

3. *We need more effective drill.* Sufficient evidence has accumulated to establish pretty clearly that, in general, pupils leaving our schools have acquired very incomplete mastery of the fundamentals in writing, speaking, reading, and computing. The business world and the colleges have long complained of the results; their contention seems now to be fairly substantiated by the more accurate measures of ability of pupils afforded by results of standarized tests.

We do not mean to imply that conditions have been getting worse or that pupils are not attaining the skill that they did in the "good old days." We feel sure that improvement has been made, but we are nevertheless convinced that our schools generally can do a very much better job of teaching the skills than they have been doing, especially as regards precision in scholarship.

PRACTICAL GUIDES FOR DRILL

It is a very real problem of the modern teacher to make certain that the drill materials function better. The new psychology of drill furnishes helpful guides that have become widely accepted in theory, but thus far have not been extensively applied in the practical classroom matter of constructing functional drill materials.

1. *Drill must follow understanding.* On this point the new psychology of drill speaks quite clearly. Pupils are likely to learn more easily and to remember longer if we drill that which they understand. In general, the steps of a process should be thoroughly learned before the formal drill is started. The fundamental principle in teaching is that experience must precede any effort to make a process automatic. The excessive formalism which characterized courses of an earlier day violated this basic guide.

2. *For drill to be effective, the pupil should have a desire to learn the thing practiced.* A normal person will practice the things that he believes to have value. The following devices can be used to convince pupils that the habits of accuracy in speech, writing, etc., are important: (*a*) the teacher should set a model of precision; (*b*) it should be recognized that precision pays in the business world; (*c*) pupils should be familiar with definite standards based on present conditions. Meanwhile, (*d*) make the standard low at first and gradually raise it; (*e*) permit no errors other than an occasional slip of the pencil. Other things being equal, when a pupil is convinced of the instructional values of certain habits he will be more than willing to practice.

A few additional guides for motivating drill are: (*a*) use numerous devices for variation of procedure; (*b*) teach the most interesting aspects of a particular skill early; (*c*) keep in mind that a skill practiced in a natural setting—that is to say, if it has purpose—will be enjoyed more; (*d*) provide activities whenever you can, rather than passive seeing and hearing; (*e*) remember that the interest and enthusiasms of the teacher are likely, in part at least, to be transferred to the pupils.

3. *Drill, to be effective, must be individual.* Practice exercises must be so organized and arranged that each pupil can work by himself, find his own level of skill, and spend his time drilling on his weak spots. Pupils must be allowed to travel at their own rates so that the bright ones can work ahead without waiting until their classmates catch up, and the slow ones can take the time they need without being forced to go ahead until they are ready.

4. *A drill exercise must be specific.* If you wish to teach a pupil "how" to locate the decimal point, build a drill lesson that will give practice on this one thing and let him know in advance what is

being practiced.   Each part of the drill exercise should apply to a
unit skill.   Indiscriminate drill is wasteful of time and energy.
Drill on specific skills in which pupils are weak will yield better
returns than "just drill."

   5. *In general there should be much practice on a few skills rather
than a little practice on each of many skills.*   In most subjects we try

A student interested in industrial arts is scarcely aware of the hours he spends in practicing
fundamental processes.   The reason is that meaning runs ahead of drill.(M)

to teach too many things.   In arithmetic, for example, we give
practice on fractions with all kinds of queer and difficult denom-
inators, whereas we undoubtedly should be wiser to put more
practice on the few fractions with which the world does its computation.

   6. *A drill exercise may well be serviced by a scoring technique so
that the pupil may watch his daily growth.*   It is little fun to play golf
without a score card or to watch a baseball game when you do not
know the score.   Why should we neglect so sound a principle of
learning in our classrooms?   The use of a scoring device does not

mean that pupils should always be competing with their fellows. Undoubtedly the schools have greatly overdone competition in the past and the emphasis may properly be placed upon cooperation. A pupil can be guided, however, so that he will be just as much interested in comparing his record for the day with his own achievement on preceding trials, as he would be in exceeding the score of a classmate. A pupil should know his degree of success in reaching a goal immediatley after practice.

7. *The practice should be staged so that the pupil will realize the pleasurable outcome of achievement.* Knowledge of achievement is one of the greatest challenges and satisfactions for either child or adult. When the pupil becomes a student of his own growth, the problem of motivating drill is solved. It is advisable, therefore, to have with the drill a record system which will show the pupil his progress from day to day and from unit to unit. The standards should be difficult enough to present a challenge to the learner.

In any case a pupil should have a definite goal to aim at—he should know what mastery is expected. The goals or standards for drill exercises must be reasonable, based on what children have actually done, and should be established for three, four, or perhaps five levels of ability.

Psychologists and superior teachers assert that drill materials should be self-scoring. Answers must be provided for the pupil at the time he is taking the practice. The argument for providing the answers in case of drills for *skill* seems sound. The pupil needs to know the correct response here and now; next day or next week, when the teacher has had time to mark the papers, the learning situation will have grown "cold." For the pupil to correct a wrong response by means of the desired response before him is an exercise of the right mental connection in a setting possibly more vivid than his original response. Interchanging papers, as is so often done, may be allowed, but the mind of a pupil who has really caught the zest of learning, is on his own paper while he marks the paper of another. There is annoyance and he misses the chance, while his interest is keenest, to see what he should have written.

The objection to the common practice of the teacher's reading the answers is that some pupils hear incorrectly. There are, then, practical reasons why pupils should be provided with answers on drills for skill.

The question of cheating arises. The tradition is that the teacher scores all the papers and gives all the marks. Here is an opportunity to teach a real lesson in honesty that will "run on its own power" and keep going when the artificial control of the teacher is removed. If a pupil will cheat himself in marking his own paper, you may be reasonably sure that he is already cheating in other respects, as for example in homework. Perhaps you are merely catching him more frequently.

The fact is that pupils do not cheat themselves. A fine old man, the soul of honor, in the early days of his golf practice when his ball had rolled into a particularly unfavorable position, was observed to kick it slyly into a more favorable position. It was later noted that he had neglected to count the "foot stroke" in his total score. Could it be said that this grand old man was a liar and a cheat? Surely not, for as soon as he became interested in the growth of his own game—in his daily improvement—he could be trusted to keep an accurate score. In like manner pupils at their tasks may be relied on to use answers honestly as soon as they have become students of their own growth.

8. *Only right practice makes for perfection.* In terms of habit formation, there is, perhaps, little difference between a wrong response and a correct one. This means that drill is a process by which errors are fixed as well as correct responses. Therefore effective drill must give repetition for correct responses.

There are a number of important techniques involved in securing correct responses in drill exercises:

a. Be sure pupils understand the exact form which they are to repeat.

b. Supervise all drill closely until the right habit is established, since this step insures correcting errors before habits become fixed.

c. Make sure that pupils have not forgotten the process since the last drill.

d. Establish one skill before introducing another.

e. Proceed slowly in the early stages of habit formation.

f. Make accuracy the main issue at first.

g. Do not attempt to change habits already formed unless you are absolutely sure they are bad.

h. Form habits in the way they are to be used.

i. Follow diagnosis with sufficient drill on the specific difficulty to overcome it.

j. Do not prolong drill on a specific difficulty to the point where pupils lose sight of the whole process of which this difficulty is a part.

9. *Drill material should make possible the diagnosis of individual disabilities.* Exercises can readily be constructed and grouped so that individual troubles can be located in little time. Errors should be corrected before habits become fixed. The popular terms "diagnostic" and "remedial" are recklessly used in advertisements and even in textbooks. Much of the drill material appearing under these labels is in fact no better than the unmotivated reviews so common in earlier publications.

10. *Practice should be distributed in diminishing amounts and at increasing intervals.* Too often we teach a skill once and for all, and leave it with the hope that pupils will have mastery. But there must be systematic recall in a motivated setting or mastery will always be low. This is a very important principle. It involves laying out the whole program of drill for a course, making certain that there is the proper practice at desirable intervals.

The important specifications of drill materials intended for review are: (*a*) from time to time drill should be given on the entire process; (*b*) drill should be given frequently and in small units; (*c*) examples in each unit of drill should be in the order of difficulty and the range should be wide enough to challenge the abilities of all pupils.

DRILL CAN BE FUN!

A device[1] that provides for pleasant repetition of materials to be learned can be constructed rather easily and inexpensively. One of its advantages is that it tells the pupil when he is correct and does not depend upon the presence of the teacher. It is particularly useful because it is adaptable to many types of materials. Changing materials on the board merely demands taking off the series of cards and clipping on the new set. The pupils or teacher can prepare the cards. One may use questions and answers, equivalents, and various stimulus-response pairs; *e.g.*, in the teaching of reading, on the one side may be cards with pictures of various objects and on the other side may be the written or printed words associated with the pictures. (See diagram on following page.)

The operation of the board is well within the grasp of the primary grades and offers interest for much older pupils. To illustrate

---

[1] The interesting drill device shown here, and this description, were provided by W. A. Williams, a graduate student at the University of Michigan.

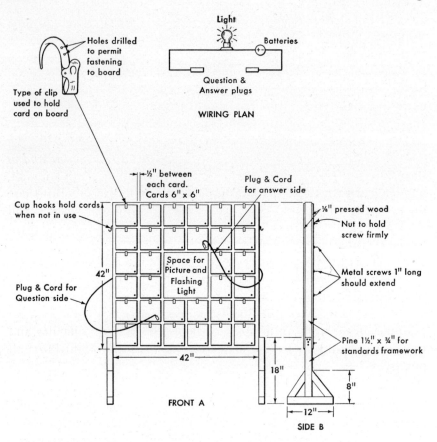

Light

Batteries

Holes drilled to permit fastening to board

Type of clip used to hold card on board

Question & Answer plugs

WIRING PLAN

½" between each card. Cards 6" x 6"

Plug & Cord for answer side

Cup hooks hold cords when not in use

⅛" pressed wood

Nut to hold screw firmly

42"

Space for Picture and Flashing Light

Metal screws 1" long should extend

Plug & Cord for Question side

42"

Pine 1½" x ¾" for standards framework

18"

8"

FRONT A

12"

SIDE B

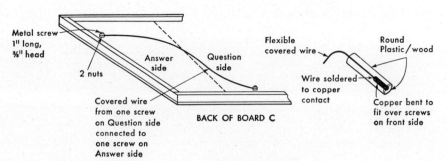

Metal screw 1" long, ¾" head

Flexible covered wire

Round Plastic / wood

Answer side

Question side

2 nuts

Wire soldered to copper contact

Covered wire from one screw on Question side connected to one screw on Answer side

BACK OF BOARD C

Copper bent to fit over screws on front side

All screws on Question & Answer side not included but wired like example shown

Drawing suggests how drill device may be made.

how the board works, suppose there are questions on the left side of the board and answers on the right. The pupil takes the plug (and cord) from the left side and places it over the contact on the particular question. Then with the plug from the right side of the board he searches the answer group, touching each answer contact. When he contacts the correct answer, a light goes on. The writer used a

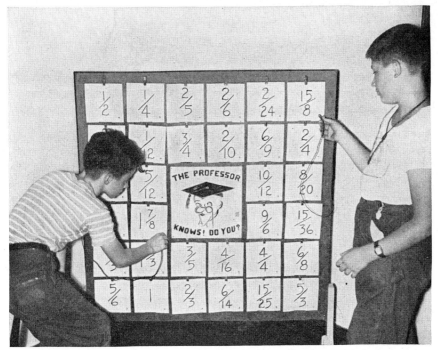

Drill device used with fractions. It may be used in any subject merely by substituting a different set of cards.

picture of a professor and titled it, "The Professor Knows;—Do You?" The eyes were cut out and a translucent material placed over them so that when the light went on the professor's eyes glowed. The professor was located in the center of the board.

It is necessary that the wires which connect the paired contact points on each side of the board be fastened so that they may be changed. Pupils soon learn which contact points are paired and the drill is not so effective as when they have to study and search for the answer. The back of the board is made removable for this purpose.

This teacher not only knows how to ask questions that stimulate reflective thinking, but also gives his pupils time to think.[G]

THE ART OF ASKING A GOOD QUESTION

The efficient teacher knows how to ask questions that stimulate or even goad pupils to do reflective thinking. A good question should be concise. The common fault of questions asked by teachers is that they include parenthetical phrases which confuse the student.

It is helpful to consider the *types* of good questions. Francis D. Curtis has provided an excellent list[1] for science teachers. In the following pages you will find a slight modification of his list that is likely to be helpful to you and to teachers of all subjects.

1. *Comparison or Contrast.* This type of question involves the enumeration of likenesses or differences which may be arrived at through reflective thinking.

Example: What is the difference between weather and climate?

2. *Decision For or Against.* All questions involving a choice or an indication of preference. Questions are classified in this group if the answer requires a weighing or preference of factors or conditions involved. If the answer is arrived at without such weighing of factors or use of judgment, the question is classified as one of recall.

Example: Do you think it is correct to call the Wright Brothers the inventors of the airplane?

[1] FRANCIS D. CURTIS. "Types of Thought Questions in Textbooks of Science," *Science Education*, XXCII (September–October, 1943), 60–67.

242

3. *Application in New Situations.* The employment of principles or other knowledge in a particular situation or problem with which the student has not heretofore been confronted.

Example: Suggest ways of correcting a bad case of reverberation in a hall or church.

4. *Classification.* This type of question involves comparison of two or more things in order to (*a*) place them in a predetermined group based on similarity, differences, or other relationships, or (*b*) define a group.

Example: What kind of change occurred in each of the following: ice melted, sugar dissolved in water, milk soured, warm pop foamed out of bottle, zinc dissolved in acid?

5. *Relationships Including Cause and Effect.* This type of question requires the student to perceive the interdependence or connection, either objectively or in the mind, between phenomena, conditions, or other data.

Example: What is the relation between friction and the efficiency of a machine?

6. *Example or Illustration.* A type of question wherein the learner is asked to give an example of a type or principle not found in context. This type is usually the converse of classification. Diagrams called for (if they are not a reproduction of an illustration in the text) are classed in this type.

Example: Describe a case that you have actually witnessed where inertia was a disadvantage.

7. *Statement of Aim.* Questions involving the author's aim or purpose in the selection or arrangement of materials.

Example: Why is the author interested in the history of elements?

8. *Criticism.* In this type of question the pupil must judge as to the adequacy, correctness, or relevancy of a situation, statement, or diagram. He might also be requested to judge his own work or the work of another person.

Example: What are your main sources of error?

9. *Inference.* This type of question requires the student to draw inferences, or deduction from data, using as starting points previously learned facts, laws, principles, or other data.

Example: From the data presented, what do you think will happen to Niagara Falls in the next 500 years?

10. *Discussion.* This type of question involves consideration of controversial questions, and argument for the sake of arriving at truth or clearing up difficulties.

Example: Discuss the most important proposal before the United Nations during the past year.

11. *Outline.* This type of question requires that the pupil give a preliminary sketch or plan of some procedure that might be enacted, or material that might be written.

Example: Outline the activities of the conservation program in your state.

12. *Definition and Explanation.* This type includes any question wherein the pupil is asked to give the exact meaning of some word, phrase, or statement, or to make the definition clear.

Example: How does a siphon work?

13. *Recall.* Any "recall" question will require an answer that depends chiefly on the use of memory. In this type of question the answer must have been given in the textbook, and the pupil is required only to recollect what is in the assigned reading. Questions often classified as simple, selective, and evaluative recall come under this classification. If additional mental processes are involved, such as drawing conclusions or making observations, they shall hold precedence over recall in determination of type.

Example: What do you consider the three most important inventions of the nineteenth century, from the standpoint of the expansion and growth of transportation?

14. *Summary.* This type of question requires the student to make a résumé of principles or facts; *i.e.*, a concise rewording of major or important ideas involved in any area of experience.

Example: What were the big ideas in Chapter 67?

15. *Observation.* This type of question requires the student to arrive at an answer as a result of direct observation at the time the question was asked.

Example: Examine the carrot. Where are the buds located?

16. *Formulation of New Questions.* This type of question includes those wherein the pupil is asked what question or problem comes to his mind, or is asked to formulate a new question.

Example: What questions occurred to you while doing this experiment?

For Discussion

1. Observe a class and write down about five questions in the exact form in which each was asked. Consider for each question: Is it good? If not, how should it have been stated?

2. Describe a situation that illustrates the poor use of a textbook.

3. From your own school experience select and describe a drill procedure that was wasteful, boring, and ineffective.

4. Try to find a good teacher who operates without a textbook. Visit the class often enough or interview him to get what you need to describe the procedure employed.

Suggested Readings

Bossing, Nelson L.: *Progressive Methods of Teaching in Secondary Schools.* Boston: Houghton Mifflin Company, 1942. Pp. xvii + 778.
   Chapters 7, 8, 9, and 10 deal with planning and method. Chapter 17 is entitled "The Project Method." Teachers will find the discussion of the assignment and the art of questioning very helpful.

Edmonson, J. B., Joseph Roemer, and Francis L. Bacon: *The Administration of the Modern Secondary School.* New York: The Macmillan Company, 1948. Pp. xi + 690.
   For a convincing statement on the importance of the textbook as an instructional tool, see page 391.

Rivlin, Harry N.: *Teaching Adolescents in Secondary Schools.* New York: Appleton-Century-Crofts, Inc., 1948. Pp. xi + 516.
   Chapter VII provides one of the best discussions that you can find on the proper use of questions.

Chapter X

· *The Slow-maturing Pupil*

We know that every child is an individual and that he travels by his own tailor-made time schedule.

—Arnold Gesell

A Typical Dull-normal Pupil[1]

According to school records Bill is a dull pupil. For years he has been unhappy in school and his parents have been troubled and humiliated by the fact that he does not keep step with his more able classmates. Because there are a good many boys and girls like him, it is worth while to find out a little more about Bill. By considering his case we may see why it is important that we do something about the schooling of the dull pupil, and we may see how to go about solving the problem of teaching him.

Bill has had more than his share of bad luck. In the first place, he was born into a world in which most people are not dull. If all of Bill's companions were like him, the world might not be so interesting, but it would be a more comfortable one for him. In the second place, either Bill's father or his mother, though a normal parent, probably had some wrong great-great-grandparents; for undoubtedly heredity plays a part in Bill's difficulties. He is blamed for many things that he does merely because he is made that way. In the third place, Bill is forced to go to a school in which the curriculum has largely been handed down from the traditional school whose chief aim was preparation for the professions. It puts great emphasis on the ability to read a page with understanding, and to deal with abstract symbolism which has little meaning in the life situations that Bill meets.

---

[1] To the director of student teaching: It is necessary in this chapter to use the objectionable terms "dull-normal" and "slow-learning" for the reason that they are in professional literature. Obviously, these terms should never be used by a truly professional worker in the presence of pupils or in dealing with parents. In the opening pages of this chapter we define the slow-maturing student by a description of a typical case.

Our academic high-school curriculum tends to be bookish, superficial, and lacking a practical basis which in the earlier days was
supplied to the pupil in the more fundamental vocational activities
carried on in the home or on the farm. The public still seems to
assume that the academic curriculum of a high school is the real
road to an education. In school Bill forever finds himself in situa-

The slow-maturing student differs from others in degree, not in kind.

tions where his weaknesses are often in the spotlight and his strength
is usually concealed.

For Bill does have his strong points. He is not dull in doing
many tasks outside of school. He knows how to deal with people;
he is intelligent when something goes wrong with the automobile;
he is faithful and responsible for tasks that are assigned him at
home. If he is asked to do three things while his parents are shop-
ping in town, he will not only do these tasks faithfully but he will
think of some others and do those to the satisfaction of the rest of
the family. He is very different in this way from his older brother,
Joe, who has never had any trouble in school. When the parents

ask Joe to do a task while they are out, he may fully intend to do it before they come home, but actually they will find him buried deep in a book and the assigned task undone.

Bill hates school and he would like nothing better than to do some of the things that he can do so well. If Bill had lived in an earlier generation he probably could have dropped out of school and gone to work on the farm or in the mill, the bank, or the store. But today there is little hope for Bill before he reaches the age of twenty. He is caught in a trap, in a school that does not fit his needs.

This year he is in the senior high school, trying to do Latin, history, English, and geometry. His work is probably not much worse than it was in earlier years, but he faces almost certain failure in two or more subjects. In the senior-high-school work, the materials are rigorously organized, and because the door of college entrance is so near, teachers are now more reluctant to give passing marks that are not deserved. In the early years Bill's teachers passed him along in the hope that he might do better in a later course. As a matter of record Bill has not received any failing marks in the early years, but he could not possibly have earned the passing marks which he received. If the dull pupil were kept in a grade until he deserved passing it might be necessary to hold him there five or six years. It is obvious that when two pupils, one six years old and one twelve years old, are together in the first grade, the situation is not good for either. Many teachers have learned that it is unwise to withhold promotion until the tasks of a grade can be done. So it has come about in many schools that the chronological age of a child is the only factor that is especially significant in promotion. If you tell me how well a boy can read or do problems in arithmetic, I cannot possibly guess what grade he is enrolled in: he may be in the third grade or he may be in the tenth. But if you tell me how old he is in years and months, I can make a fairly accurate guess. Probably a dull pupil learns more from his fellows that are at the same stage of social development while moving through the grades than he would learn if he were kept with children much younger than he. I have no quarrel with the philosophy that causes children to be promoted regardless of achievement; but teachers and parents should know the tremendous problem of adjustment that is involved when boys and girls arrive at the senior high school without a reasonable control of the fundamental tools of reading, spelling, composition, and arithmetic.

Now Bill has never been fooled by his promotions. He has always realized that he was not actually understanding what was going on and that he was not getting anywhere. The bad effects of the fear of failure have been present all these years. He has

Reading is an important factor in the success that pupils have in all academic subjects. This applies to all pupils, bright or dull.(D)

become fairly clever in making it appear that he does understand. He finds expression in associating with companions who, like himself, are not doing well in school and who cause discipline problems in every classroom in which the teacher's hand is not firm. A very bad factor in Bill's development is the conviction gradually driven home to him that he is not a perfectly normal human being. In recent years he has more or less tried to play up to the part that he is different. This is probably one of the evil outcomes of school machinery which puts so much emphasis on credits, examinations, and marks.

It is hard to realize the blighting and destructive effect on a boy or girl who has really been trying, of a barely passing mark in every school subject. But up to now, the worst break in luck that has come to Bill is a bit of gossip that his mother brought home. It had something to do with an intelligence quotient, something about an I.Q. of 78. Bill this year has a teacher who gave her class an intelligence test. The teacher does not know how to deal with pupils, dull or bright. She was employed because she is a local girl, the cheapest teacher that could be hired for the job and the daughter of a man who is the close friend of a prominent local politician. She is not well trained and did not herself know the meaning of a score on an intelligence test. She found out that such scores do in fact predict with high accuracy how well a boy or girl will do in schools as they now are organized. She thought this was very wonderful and, in an unguarded moment, she told one of her friends that, after all, nothing much could be expected of Bill because he had an I.Q. of only 78. This news trickled home to Bill's mother and the damage was done. Bill is now convinced that he is surrounded by the prison walls of an intelligence quotient from which he cannot possibly escape. To him an I.Q. is final and fatal. It is a pity that this unwise teacher did not realize that tasks in school are only a small part of the life of a boy and the life of an adult. She should have known that intelligence tests, helpful as they are to an intelligent and well-trained teacher in dealing with the schoolwork of a boy or girl, do not measure more than a small part of the tasks that people have to do. She should have known that their scope is far too limited to measure the needs of life. Intelligence is much broader than most people realize. Life offers the opportunity to learn an infinite number of things, but fortunately does not require that we learn them all. Some of these things you and I learn easily, but we are dull and stupid in learning most of them. We do not have an intelligence test with a range that is as wide as life. If we had one, I think Bill would make a very satisfactory score. A careful study of Bill's ability by a competent teacher might easily reveal something in Bill that is far more valuable to society than anything Joe, who has always had high marks in school, can do. This idea, if driven home to Bill, might have changed the whole pattern of his life. In fact, there would be fewer pupils considered dull if there were fewer unintelligent teachers.

Bill is not a dull pupil, and thousands of boys and girls today labeled dull are not dull at all.   The term "dull" is a most unfortunate one and should never be applied to an individual pupil by either parents or teachers.   It is not the only unfortunate term that has been used in dealing with Bill.   This same teacher not only talks glibly about low I.Q.'s but refers to her pupils as "dumbbells," "dumb clucks," "dumb bunnies," and "boneheads."   Recently I visited this teacher's classroom.   She met me at the door saying, "You mustn't expect much of this class.   This is a dull group." The work of the hour fully met her prediction.   One can easily see why boys and girls who find themselves in such classrooms soon become emotionally sick.   It is to be hoped that teachers will come to have the point of view of the following quotation: "All who reach the high-school door are bright boys and girls, bright in social values or bright in the two great commandments, or bright in manual skills, or bright in the knowledge of art and the production of beauty, or bright in the ability to bear silently and without complaint the great burdens of life, or they may be school-bright alone."   This writer makes the clear distinction between school-bright and life-bright.   The facts of learning do not, I think, support the details in the quotation but the point of view is a very wholesome one for parents and teachers.   Parents and teachers do grave injury and injustice if they ever become discouraged with a pupil of sound character who tries to do his school tasks.

DEFINITION OF THE DULL-NORMAL

The psychological classification under which pupils whose intelligence quotients lie within some defined range, *e.g.*, 80 to 90, are designated as dull-normal is too restricted for the practical classroom teacher.   The fact is that the members of a class selected by this criterion do not stay nicely put within the limits of the range adopted.   Moreover, this definition is an oversimplification, for there are many factors besides stupidity which may cause a pupil to be classified in the minds of his teachers as slow-learning; *e.g.*, glandular disturbances, interference of emotional factors, interplay of pupil attitudes, defective hearing, poor eyesight, fatigue, economic insecurity, ill-health, poor habits of study, and inferiority complex. It is a better procedure to define the slow-learning by employing a descriptive technique that presents a total picture of many measurements and recorded observations.

Here, we are not dealing with pupils who lie extremely low in the scale of ability. In the large cities, at least, such pupils are often assigned to classes labeled "special education," and the pedagogical literature for such groups is not only extensive but highly technical. Rather, we are concerned with the pupils who sit in our classes and are promoted semester after semester but do not appear to achieve a worth-while degree of mastery of the subject matter taught.

IMPORTANCE OF THE PROBLEM

There is good reason for believing that the fundamental cause of widespread dissatisfaction with the curriculum lies in the fact that the existing curriculum has not been created for, nor adjusted to, the lower levels of intelligence. In recent years vast numbers of pupils of low ability and low skills have been swept into our high schools. In practice we have a new philosophy of education which is concerned with the normal growth of every individual child and which strives to provide the most desirable setting for each personality. One of the practical outcomes of this philosophy is that the passing mark as concerns achievement in secondary schools has become a myth. Then, too, pupils of grades seven, eight, and nine are not dropping out of school at the same rate as they did ten years ago. As a result we have in the later grades of the secondary school an enormous piling up of educational laggards. A competent teacher of world history, Latin, geometry, or a commercial subject will admit that he is not achieving very much with tenth- and eleventh-grade children who have reading skills typical of the average pupil in the fourth or fifth grade.

It had taken us centuries to build a curriculum for the superior pupils, but overnight we faced the problem of designing a curriculum and an appropriate method for this onrushing crowd of inferior students. One can go into practically any high school, small or large, and find a goodly proportion of the pupils attempting to do tasks which in difficulty are four or five years beyond their mental ages. The slow-maturing pupils constitute a large percentage of all the pupils in our schools.

It is not likely that our institutions and our democratic experience will be destroyed by outside forces. Rather, they are threatened from within our own borders when we neglect to provide an appropriate education for the vast crowd of unadjusted pupils who are now passing through our junior and senior high schools. One

reason why this nation is becoming so politically and socially volatile
lies no doubt in the fact that a vast number of young people are going
through our schools without learning to do their own thinking when
confronted by problems involving alternative solutions.   In America we are set on the path of solving our problems by the democratic
method implicit in a government under the control of the common
man—a system dedicated to the scientific way of seeking out the
facts, threshing out the issues in the full view of free discussion,
and applying each new increment of knowledge for the common
good, with the consent of, and by the collective aid of, those who are
the recipients of its advantages.   In the United States, at least this
is our faith; but we are certainly on trial before the world, and it is
one of the major tasks of our educational system to see to it that this
ideal is given a fair testing.   It is not being given a fair test today,
and it will not be given one later unless every voter is provided with
at least as much education as he can absorb.   One should add that,
even so, we may not succeed in the experiment; but it is surely the
only hope.

Though space does not permit us to discuss all the reasons why
the problem of the dull-normal is one of the most important before
school people, it seems necessary to consider at least briefly the
following circumstances:

1. The dull pupil as a human being with only one life to live is
entitled, quite as much as his more able brother or sister, to an education which provides for his normal growth.

2. The problem of the dull pupil is very closely tied up with the
problem of crime.   It appears that the slow-maturing group supplies far more than its share of delinquents, inmates of prisons, and
institutions for mental and nervous disorders.   Competent students
of mental health persist in pointing out to us the bad effects of the
frustration which results when pupils are for years placed in competitive situations where they cannot understand.

3. We must give attention to the needs of the dull in order to
maintain a reasonably efficient instruction of the competent and
bright pupils.   Any teacher who in a modern classroom attempts
much adjustment of her teaching procedures to the wide range of
ability represented by unselected pupils has, to a large extent,
jeopardized the opportunity for thinking on the part of the brilliant
student.

FACTS AND PROCEDURES

The main thing to remember in teaching slow-learning pupils is that it requires supremely fine ability. Research to date has certainly not provided separate and unique lists of principles of learning for the dull-normal. However, we are likely to make a more sensible adjustment of general principles to the needs of the slow-learning if we keep constantly before us the facts concerning the dull that are fairly well established either in professional literature or by observation of teachers who are especially successful in teaching them. In this connection we shall present a list of facts and after each include some of the implications for method.

1. *The dull differ from the normal not in kind but in degree.* The dull are not divided from the normal and the bright by sharp lines of demarcation, for the same characteristics are found in all. We cannot say that the dull lack any one trait, such as memory or judgment. For any amount of a given trait a large number of pupils can be found who exhibit it. There is no absolute lack of any one thing which is always found in a bright person. In brief, the curve for each trait, mental and physical, is continuous. In view of these facts one can take the wholesome position that all pupils with whom we deal in this discussion are perfectly normal human beings.

The fundamental problem of method in dealing with the dull-normal is one of mental health. Research suggests that even in educated adults there is difficulty in learning when the mind has been suffering or when it is disorganized by fear. What, then, must be the effect on dull children who have been frustrated all their school days in subjects which teachers, parents, and friends assert are essential to living useful and happy lives. He becomes a victim of the devastating effect of the "I can't" factor. The cleverest of teachers will slip and discourage the child, probably unconsciously, if he does not have a genuine faith that the pupil can learn to do worth-while tasks. The damage is done by the attitude of a teacher, who may live in a different universe, even though he never says a word implying that the pupil is stupid.

Schools should not develop the dullness complex in pupils by creating in them a feeling of inferiority. Consider what must be the inmost feelings of a child when the school, the one agency sup-

posed to minister to his special need, has labeled him dull and has
implied that he cannot achieve well in any mental activity requiring
more than slight intelligence. Is it any wonder that such a pupil
comes to regard himself as hopelessly handicapped and drops out as
early as he can, disappointed, depressed, probably embittered, and
seeking some way to compensate his weakness and to satisfy his
craving to achieve something?

In the educational guidance of the dull pupil we must remember
that the main challenge for him as well as for the gifted student is
achievement. We need to inventory the tasks of school and life in
order to select those that are simple and important, and to guide the
dull-normal so that he will find these tasks and be prepared to learn
how to do them. By great good luck he may happen to find a niche
in society that he can fill with satisfaction to himself and benefit to
others, but in schools as they are now organized, the great probability is that he will find his satisfaction in ways not socially acceptable. His great desire is for attention and approval that he fails to
get in school. When he finally quits school he resorts to fighting,
bragging, loudness, recklessness, etc.; even crime lures him.

The dull child is likely to be an impulsive, happy-go-lucky extrovert, often a problem child because he does not fit into a universe
so largely dominated by introvert teachers. The school's recent
recognition of the importance of an activity program and its concern
about emotional adjustment, both inside the classroom and out, are
evidence that at last school people have come to accept extrovert
behavior as an essential part of child development. We are beginning to suspect that the population of the world is predominantly
extrovert, with a school system predominantly introvert. Peda-
gogically we have been seeing that the method can no longer be a
pouring-in, but must now be a drawing-out process if the pupil is
to be guided to a proper adjustment of his personality.

What can a teacher do to understand and improve the mental
health of the dull-normal? He can take an inventory of himself
and consider these questions: (*a*) Am I content to call a child dull
without attempting to find out whether his trouble is sheer stupidity
or some remediable cause? (*b*) Have I enough common sense to see
the value of taking the child where he is and allowing him to develop
from that point in a way that is normal for him? (*c*) What can I
learn about the child that will help me to understand his particular

needs? And how, then, can I build my school subject or the work of my grade to fit in with his needs?

Remember, too, that the slow student usually is afraid of your subject. Try to secure the cooperation of the home so that parents will in incidental moments picture your subject as being desirable. The unfavorable attitude toward your subject may have been fixed by casual remarks to which parents at the time attached no particular importance. Tactful comments on the part of cooperating parents can lead children to picture your subject as being desirable rather than something that should be dreaded.

2. *The dull are usually mentally immature for their group.* The mental age of the slow-learning pupil is likely to be less than his own chronological age, and the average of slow pupils in a class is almost certain to be far less than that of the group. In schools that attempt to classify pupils in homogeneous groups and label certain sections "slow" and others "bright," the average of the chronological age of a seventh-grade slow group is likely to be about one year and eight months *more* than the average of a corresponding bright section; while the average of the mental age of a slow section is almost certain to be at least one year and six months *less* than the average of a bright section.

The implications as regards method relate to the fact that one can go into almost any school, large or small, and find a goodly number of the pupils who are expected to do tasks which in difficulty are from two to five years beyond their mental age. In dealing with dull groups, the conventional classification of subject matter by grades is futile. A unit of work may be quite as difficult for dull groups in the ninth grade as for dull groups in the seventh grade. Delay the teaching of a task to a dull pupil as long as is feasible. With dull pupils never do today what you can put off until tomorrow. Maturity is a better teacher of dull pupils than you will ever be. Remember that a dull pupil is mentally immature and may do successfully and with satisfaction the simpler tasks of an earlier grade. For example, a fairly satisfactory solution to the problem of teaching arithmetic to dull pupils in the eighth grade can be found in supplying them with books written for grades five and six, under a bright new cover labeled "Mathematics for the Eighth Grade." Maturity and added experience will later make easy many tasks that now are difficult. In brief, the principle of delay is very important, always keeping in mind of course that whatever really needs to be taught must be taught before the pupil drops out of school.

Directions for such pupils as well as any other material that you wish pupils to read must be written in simple English. The dull should have a careful explanation in very concrete and definite terms of all fundamental parts of the new work. Daily assignments should be distinctly and plainly set forth and should never be involved. Daily demonstration in supervised study periods of how to go about preparing the lesson is essential. Short unit courses should be developed with distinct divisions, each having definite objectives. Opportunity should be provided for oral and written expression in their simplest forms.

3. *Strong drives and interests are weak in slow-learning pupils.* They fail to make plans, and their method of attack not only is poor but gets under way slowly. Although one finds superior students who are able to perform a task well, even though it is poorly motivated, an inferior student rarely can. Motivation should come from the genuine drives of pupils rather than through artificial pedagogical tricks and devices. Though motivation with dull students may be more difficult than with superior children, it is all the more important. In general, work that cannot be reasonably and immediately motivated should seldom be attempted. All of us, in teaching very dull pupils, have observed their great interest in doing something they can master. It is pathetic to see the effort that dull pupils put forth, perhaps even on tasks not worth while for them, in order to achieve some measure of success and approval. Every unit of work for the slow student should contain a purpose that he can understand, accept, and appreciate.

In directing study habits of the dull pupil, try to substitute a definite goal for intentions that are usually good, but vague. Probably no one trait is more characteristic of the dull pupil than the aimlessness of his movements in attempting to study. Try to get him to do something that is definite. Do not expect the slow pupil to be a self-starter. Do not be disturbed by low ability but by failure to achieve normal growth for whatever powers may exist.

Do not assume that the dull pupil is a lazy pupil. The chances are that you have not learned his real needs or identified the basic reasons for his condition. It is very interesting to note that in no investigation of the causes of dullness or slow learning has the investigator listed "teacher has weak foundation," and "teacher was indifferent and showed lack of interest," as causes of pupil failures. School systems do not always provide adequate instructional material, textbooks, classroom equipment, space for class groups, and teachers who know appropriate methods and who have the

Dr. Charles Eliot has the good idea that sensory experiences are basic to verbalism and, in particular, to reading.[N]

necessary skill in diagnosing individual cases. Yet each of these causes has surely been among the real ones.

4. *The slow-learning pupil is usually very weak in reading.* In schools that have homogeneous grouping the average score on a widely used standardized reading test for all the pupils in the seventh-grade sections labeled "dull" is likely to be not higher than the fifth month of the fifth school year. Further evidence of weakness in reading and also in arithmetic is found in the following table.

This table, we believe, presents a representative sampling of conditions as they exist in many schools. Note the large number of children in this group whose ability to read is not above the norms for third-, fourth-, and fifth-grade pupils and remember that the average or norm of any skill, whether it be baking an apple pie, playing bridge, or correcting engine trouble in an automobile, is likely to be too low for use.

It is probable that the slow-learning pupil is very low on all basic skills, such as ability to write and to speak what he needs to write and to speak. We know he is low in computation. How-

PER CENT OF 144 DULL SEVENTH-GRADE PUPILS AT VARIOUS GRADE LEVELS IN
FUNDAMENTAL SKILLS

Grade level	Per cent of pupils at particular grade level in	
	Reading ability	Ability in arithmetic
Second..................	1.4	1.4
Third..................	4.2	6.9
Fourth..................	29.9	20.8
Fifth..................	41.0	46.5
Sixth..................	18.7	16.7
Seventh..................	3.5	6.9
Eighth..................	0.0	0.0
Ninth..................	0.0	0.0
Tenth..................	0.7	0.0
No record..............	0.6	0.8

ever, we are here especially concerned with reading because that is still a basic tool in all school subjects and is most important in the modern school where a pupil who hopes to do satisfactory work needs to read extensively.

The dull pupil is extremely weak in forming associations between words and ideas. If he is asked to name a series of words at random he usually mentions one word of a kind only, whereas the bright pupil immediately lists many words in a particular group. Not only is the number of words inadequate, but the relationship between words is not recognized.

In attempting remedial reading at the secondary-school level, the following five techniques[1] are of major importance:

[1] These suggestions stem from the author's experience as the director of a summer-school clinic concerned with secondary-school pupils who exhibited wide discrepancies in reading and arithmetic.

a. Provide a new and stimulating reading environment. This principle has been applied in remedial arithmetic at the secondary-school level by surrounding students, who are very low in arithmetic skills, with computing machines. Not that anybody believes experience with computing machines will improve computing ability with a pencil, but rather this device is employed to motivate a driving interest in number relations. When you initiate a remedial program with a pupil, it is a good idea to do something to rock the pupil off "dead center." Thus it may help if you change the reading picture for the pupil in drastic fashion, perhaps by placing him in a room with noninstitutional furniture and surrounding him with

Visual aids are especially helpful when teaching the slow-maturing pupil. Here is a group with a wide range of ability in which the dull make fine contributions to class projects.[L]

new and attractive instructional materials. Try to find books which are written at his level on activities that he likes, and which have beautiful illustrations in them. Most important of all, provide him with a teacher who will use effectively the factors of interest and social approval.

b. Begin where the pupil is, with regard to both his control of the mechanics of reading and his interests. The angler usually does not have much luck in fishing "where they ain't." The slow-learning pupil is caught in a circle of low reading skill, narrow interests, little drill, and little progress in reading. One must get dull students to read something, and we must not be too much concerned about quality. You may need to begin with the big-little books and adventure magazines, and study carefully the strong forces that play upon the growth of a pupil's vocabulary. You will discover very soon that his interests outside of school have a very marked bearing on a child's vocabulary. A recent study shows that pupils whose school marks in mathematics, social studies, English, and general science would classify them as very poor students were found to excel the average students in their classes in their knowledge of detective and comic terms. It was found that greater word learning resulted from motion pictures, gangster stories, and from comics than from articles based on science, invention, and travel. A second study shows that very wide reading of articles and stories of gangsters, the "funnies," and the screen produced a high degree of voluntary mastery of related words. A reading list that seems to be especially satisfactory with inferior students of the tenth grade suggests

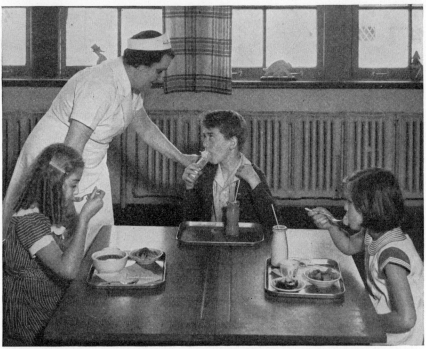

The school cafeteria can be a phase of the instructional program, especially in the teaching of some things that all citizens should learn. It should be more than a place to eat.[L]

that the interests of the dull run to romantic and adventure narratives, to stories that have action and vitalized situations. To interest them, poetry must have a swing to it. To an increasing extent, books, not only in the reading field but the other school subjects, are being published without grade labels; this obviously makes it easier for a teacher to find materials that are adjusted in difficulty to the abilities of the slow-learning pupil.

    c. Provide an experience basis. Meaning for the dull-normal pupil must run ahead of verbal statements and symbolism. If you wish the dull pupil to understand a word, a phrase, or a symbol you must provide definitely that he live through some experience as a basis for the meaning of the word, phrase, or symbol. Difficulty in reading is not so much a matter of long words and long sentences as it is unfamiliarity with ideas.

The pupil should not read very much before being required to make some physical or mental response. It is futile to use a wordy book to explain ideas and projects if the pupils cannot read.

d. Avoid stigma. The general guide is, do not have a pupil read aloud until he wants to read, but be sure to manage the situation in such a way that he will want to read to somebody. If you can increase the audience, all the better. Then, too, remember that whatever is read aloud to a class should be well read so as to give pleasure to the listeners. In some classes you may have to read the material yourself the first time or two. Try to spot early in the year the good readers in your class, and let each read aloud a part of what needs to be read. Try to draw in the poor readers by letting them read the parts of which they are sure. This suggests that much of the material used in remedial reading should in form be close to plays and the techniques close to dramatization. In any case, it is unwise to let students stumble through remedial reading materials, because it provides undesirable models and stigmatizes the performer.

e. Recognize that the teacher of every school subject needs to be a teacher of reading. Specialists in remedial reading insist that it is not merely a question of teaching reading as a sort of general skill, but that it is necessary for the science teacher, the mathematics teacher, etc., to teach the pupil to read the particular type of material that appears in these subjects. So long as the high-school curriculum is organized according to subjects there will be special vocabularies that need attention. In remedial reading it is helpful to teach the meanings of words that are new in the next unit to be read, either orally or silently, before you ask the student to do the reading. If you will build reading materials in your special school subject which motivate the activities, which are in themselves worth reading, and which explain the new words you are going to use anyway, you will be making a contribution to reading improvement in your school.

5. *With regard to sensory and motor capacities, the dull are not far from the normal.* It is of course very difficult to make scientific tests of sensory capacities in the case of dull pupils because such tests require the ability to understand and to follow directions, which at once involves intelligence. Moreover, the failure of dull children to learn lessons which the bright learn with ease may not be due to the lower acuity of sense organs but to the inability to organize and interpret such sensations as they do have. At any rate it appears that, both in and out of school, tasks which involve motion and physical coordination are fairly easy for the school-dull to learn. In an investigation in which the various trades and professions are ranked in the order of scores on a psychological test, machinists, taxicab drivers, and other groups which deal with motion or which require good physical coordination are relatively low in the scale. It appears that tasks involving motion are far

lower in difficulty than such abstract tasks as reading and understanding a paragraph.

The fact that the dull are nearer the norms in sensory acuity
than in intellectual ability appears to be a matter of common
observation. What large football squad does not have its brilliant
player who in schoolwork is excessively dull?

Assigning dull students to art projects for most of the school day isn't the answer even
though good teachers of the arts adjust their materials to the slow maturing.[L]

It is not clear, however, that school people have used this fact
in an intelligent way. For example, there are cities that are
attempting to meet the needs of the dull pupil by assigning him
daily three or even four hours of industrial arts. We are not saying
that many tasks in this field may not be easier than tasks in some
other school subjects. Nor are we implying that individual pupils
may not with profit be given very generous assignments in industrial arts. But the notion that this type of work does not require
intelligence and that it is a get-education-quick cure for the dull
student is fallacious. Similarly, the desirability of wholesale assign-

ment and enrollment of dull pupils in commercial courses should be challenged sharply and further investigated.

The dull pupil needs to be taught by concrete things that he can see and feel and handle. Abstract ideas are too difficult. Emphasis should be placed on dramatics, excursions, and visual aids. Other things being equal, a situation that is explained by something which can be seen and manipulated is more easily understood and appreciated by the dull student. Schools of today are particularly fortunate in the wide use of charts, slides, diagrams, graphs, cartoons, models, motion pictures, dramatics, and the like. Through the mediums of clay, wood, crayon, and paints abstract ideas are made real. These pupils, therefore, should have ample opportunities to make things.

The material must be characterized by activities. The observing teacher notes that the dull pupil is often very competent in doing things. He may turn in a notebook with excellent drawings or collections. In mathematics he may make an excellent transit with a mechanical building set. The main implication, with regard to method, is that laboratory techniques employed in a classroom which resembles a workshop are likely to prove fairly successful when teaching the dull.

6. *With respect to instincts and emotions also, the dull approach much nearer the norms than they do in intellectual traits.* It is not any deviation in instincts and emotions that differentiates dull from bright, but the control of those which make desirable social relations possible. Patterns of behavior in the dull tend to be determined by impulse and immediate satisfaction without conscious purpose or much consideration of consequences.

There is at least one important pedagogical implication in the fact that the tides of emotions run about as strong in the inferior as in the bright. Since dull children differ from the bright far less with regard to emotions than they do in the higher mental processes, the emphasis in their curriculum should be on appreciations rather than on mastery of facts, principles, and skills. There are those who would place the emphasis for the inferior child on the practical, that is to say, on the three R's. It would seem far safer to place it on the three H's, the hand, the heart, and the head, in the order mentioned. Begin with the hand since experiences are basic in the learning of the dull; proceed to the heart because effective action must be rooted in attitudes, and dispositions rest primarily on emotions; leave the head for last because for the dull experience must run far in advance of generalization. In common practice, schools start with the reverse order and seldom get beyond a futile effort to educate the head.

There is a widespread assumption abroad that the enriched curriculum is to be designed for the gifted child and that a drill program

Teachers of courses in the arts have always employed visual aids.[N]

on the practical is the salvation of the dull. In the absence of scientific evidence, the writer challenges the soundness of such a program, (1) because the dull probably have had plenty of drill on the fundamentals in the traditional curriculum, or the three R's, and yet have achieved very low mastery; (2) because an enriched curriculum, with an activity program as a means and with the emphasis on attitudes, would be more nearly in accord with the fact that the dull approach much nearer the bright with respect to instincts and emotions than they do in intellectual traits.

7. *The higher mental processes differentiate the dull pupil from the bright.* His mind, instead of being systematic and orderly, gets

as cluttered up as a slovenly housekeeper's kitchen. Many teachers say that the dull pupil is poor in reasoning, but this statement is so general as to be meaningless and we need a more detailed analysis of the fundamental differences between the dull and the bright.

It is very difficult for dull pupils to detect an absurdity in an illogical statement. They make such absurd mistakes that their lack of ability in self-appraisal is often taken by the teacher for deliberate disobedience, when the truth is that the dull pupil does not know he is wrong. The reason is easy to see: though the recognition of the meaning of a single word may be a very simple mental process, the combination of words to form a thought unit is a complex mental process on a higher level of mental ability; and we should not be surprised if the dull are poor in manipulating two or more thought units.

Dull pupils are limited with respect to imagination. They have difficulty in projecting themselves into a situation of which the parts and relationships have not all been experienced. They cannot easily utilize vicarious experiences and supply elements to fill gaps. If you want a pupil to learn a new word, a broad concept, a general principle, or a precise definition, the best way, perhaps the only one, is to have him live it through some concrete experiences. For the dull, and probably also for the bright, even a definition should be a summary of his experiences.

The dull have an inadequate memory. It is a common observation of classroom teachers that the dull pupil may with prompting or suggestion give the correct response to a simple question and a moment later may reply to the same question as if he had never heard of it. It is this fact that has led teachers to conclude that the dull are very low in memory. Granted that the association of elements, an important factor in recall, is weak, nevertheless the opinion of teachers that dull pupils are extraordinarily low in recall may need to be modified. The evidence is fairly convincing that when a given task has been learned to a high level, forgetting is not so great as we have commonly believed.

Most important of all, the dull pupil has difficulty in generalizing. To him, inductive experiences are merely just one thing after another in which he fails to recognize the identical elements. In the inductive development of a principle or a concept the dull pupil will need more illustrations and a greater variety of them. The way to make an illustration meaningful is to tie it to his interests and experiences.

But the dull pupil is often without the everyday knowledge and contacts that normal children just naturally acquire because of their varied interests. The result is that, in the practical task of teaching a new idea to the dull, one often cannot find anything to which to relate it. As one investigator has suggested, the dull pupil "has ears and hears not, eyes and sees not."

Dull students have a short attention span. The period of complete concentration on a specific mental task for all pupils, dull or bright, is shorter than is commonly recognized. The mental craving for change, for variety, is one of the clearly marked traits of the human mind. Herein lies the chief reason why the radio and the motion picture make a fundamental and universal appeal. But comparatively, the bright have a much longer span of attention than the dull, particularly on the side of voluntary or active attention in contrast to passive attention. The dull simply cannot stick to a thing very long. Several factors contribute to this defect. Among the important ones are narrow interests, restricted curiosity, difficulty in assimilation, and trouble with language symbols.

The pedagogical implication of this fact is that we must see to it that, physically and mentally, the dull pupil has a great many different tasks in an hour. Every class period should be characterized by variety. Call on the dull pupil frequently, perhaps for simple mechanical tasks or for answers to questions that require mere acquiescence. Watch him so closely that his attention has little chance to wander. Study him so as to aid him with specific directions and encouragement at each small step of progress he makes.

Finally, the main implication of the differences with respect to the higher mental processes relates to the old, old question of transfer of training. To the excessively dull, life tends to offer one problem after another in an infinite series in which no two problems seem to have anything in common. It is the teacher's task to help him recognize patterns by pointing out that "this is like that."

As has been suggested, in the modern theory of transfer of training we no longer deny that there is transfer but we ask the question, "How can we teach this concept, skill, or principle so as to increase the probability that the pupil will use it when he meets it again under a greatly changed situation?" Since we have discussed transfer elsewhere, no further comment is needed here.

8. *The dull-normal usually responds well to responsibility for little extra jobs that can be delegated to him.* Tasks in the management of the routine of the class, such as taking care of musical instruments and athletic equipment and keeping the record of them, are often simple enough for even a student who is not bright to do well. These little odd jobs, so time-consuming to the teacher, are sometimes just the thing needed to interest dull pupils. They like to do extra little things that to them are important. The taste of success means so much to them.

In conclusion it should be pointed out that investigations relating to the dull and the slow-learning pupil provide a basis for optimism. With an appropriate curriculum and method he can be taught. Most important of all, the road to making good citizens of the dull and the slow-learning seems to be open.

For Discussion

1. In speaking to his teachers concerning slow-learning and unadjusted pupils Superintendent Hayes said, "Unless we give special attention to the problem of the dull-normal, we will continue to lose the public's confidence and support, overlook one of our most important leads for curriculum revision, fail to advance our knowledge of educational psychology as rapidly as we might, and cause our nation to become more and more volatile in response to social panaceas."

In the discussion that followed, Miss Adams, the teacher of the social studies, said, "All that you need to do to realize the importance of this problem is to turn on the radio and listen to the panaceas that are proposed for our social ills. I am convinced that the schools face a hard task if we are to turn out a sufficient number of citizens who can and will find the right answers to our problems by thinking."

Miss Smith said, "The unadjusted pupil in our school is a constant threat to our program of public relations. We are piling up dissatisfied customers year by year. To me it seems a bit unreasonable to expect persons who have been unhappy in a school for four years to graduate and thereafter be loyal boosters for the school's program."

  a. Which of the four results mentioned by Superintendent Hayes do you think are valid? Why?

  b. Do you know of a school that has been forced to take drastic measures of retrenchment? Was the accumulation of "dissatisfied customers" a factor in the situation?

2. Assume the ideal high school. For what reasons would you be willing to fail a pupil in a ninth-grade subject? How many times would you fail him on the same semester's work, assuming that you could see no improvement in the conditions that caused the first failure?

3. If possible visit a slow-learning group in a school that attempts homogeneous grouping. Describe the special curricular materials and methods employed.

Suggested Readings

Burt, Cyril: *The Backward Child.* New York: Appleton-Century-Crofts, Inc., 1937. Pp. xx + 694.

This book is the most thorough and systematic study available dealing with the backward child. It is far too detailed to be used as an introduction to the study of the problem but it has great value for the mature worker.

Carroll, Herbert A.: *Mental Hygiene.* New York: Prentice-Hall Inc., 1947. Pp. v + 329.

Chapter 11 entitled "The School and the Community" comes very close to being a "must." In it you will find a splendid discussion of the factors that condition the mental health of pupils and teachers. It is interesting and easy to read. We suggest that a committee of student teachers make a brief report of the main ideas in the chapter and that you follow through with a panel discussion in one of your conferences on student teaching.

Children in a Democracy. General Report adopted by the White House Conference on Children in a Democracy. Washington: Government Printing Office, 1940. Pp. ix + 86.

This brief report of the second session of the White House Conference on Children in a Democracy presents a clear picture of the present situation of children in America and contains 98 recommendations intended to stimulate interest and effort toward a realization of the ideals of the American people for our children. Among the important chapters are "The Child and the Family," "Religion in the Lives of Children," "Educational Services in the Community," "Protection against Child Labor," "Youth and Their Needs," "Conserving the Health of Children," and "Children under Special Disadvantages." The report is an important addition to educational literature and it is suggested that for most classes it will be worth while to have a committee report based on this document.

Landis, Paul H.: *Adolescence and Youth.* New York: McGraw-Hill Book Company, Inc., 1945. Pp. xiii + 470.

Since the ceiling with regard to achievement of the excessively dull and the slow-maturing pupil is low, the social adjustment and the acquisition of the competencies of good citizenship are obviously of enormous importance in the education of such students. This book quite properly puts the emphasis on the social and the psychological elements. The reader's attention is directed to a study of how the social processes impinge on the developing organism.

Merrill, Maud A.: *Problems of Child Delinquency.* Boston: Houghton Mifflin Company, 1947. Pp. xxiii + 403.

This is an excellent volume written by a competent student of child behavior who has had wide experience with juvenile court cases. Perhaps in its scope the book goes beyond the needs of the classroom teacher, but it provides a fine insight into problem cases that a home-room teacher in a typical school would meet time and again. The book would be especially helpful to a teacher who has had little training in sociology and psychology and who is obliged to operate in a school system that does not have on its staff a person trained in special guidance techniques.

Chapter XI

Audio-Visual Aids for the Classroom[1]

A single picture often conveys more than volumes.

—O. S. Fowler

The idea of visual education is not new. We are told that Pythagoras, about 2,500 years ago, drew geometric figures in the sand when making his demonstrations. The first illustrated textbook appeared shortly after the invention of the printing press. Reading was taught in the early New England schools with the aid of pictures. The good teacher has long used maps, charts, globes, diagrams, models, flat pictures, dramatizations, the blackboard, the bulletin board, collections of specimens, exhibits, cartoons, posters, and a variety of laboratory equipment.

The thing that is new about this type of education is that the number of visual and auditory aids in teaching has increased tremendously in recent years as new developments in electrical engineering have opened up greater possibilities for their use. Moreover, research studies of learning and a vast experience in schools of the armed forces have suggested that these supplementary aids not only are useful to enrich and vitalize teaching but probably improve its effectiveness.

Within the last few years new forms of visual and auditory aids have appeared, each one having a definite educational value. Among these are the silent and sound motion picture, radio, phonograph, school museum, stereograph and stereoscope, lantern slides, filmstrip, opaque projector, and sound slide film.

It was natural that the Army and Navy should go all out for training aids, for millions of men had to learn a lot in a hurry. They were given plenty of money and adequate personnel to do the job. Their imagination and resourcefulness, implemented by vast

[1] In this chapter, I am indebted for suggestions to F. D. McClusky, Joe Park, and Howard Batchelder.

sums, resulted in a classroom which looked different from the typical academic classroom and which was a far more exciting place for the learner. Whatever the historian may say about the schools of the armed forces, they convincingly demonstrated the very great possibilities of more effective learning by the use of training aids, which we shall call learning aids or instructional aids.

Here is an honest-to-goodness picture of a girl doing her homework on the back-yard fence, a type of visual aid that dates back to the cave dwellers.[D]

Let us be clear on one point. Training aids as used in the armed forces mean a great deal besides something on a screen. It would take many pages to list even a small fraction of the different training aids. However, here are a few: (1) films (movies and filmstrips —both sound and silent); (2) two-dimensional graphic devices (photographs, posters, cartoons, diagrams, scale drawings, graphs, maps, charts, graphic portfolios, etc.); (3) three-dimensional objects (models, mock-ups, sand tables, dioramas, terrain models, real objects, etc.); (4) auditory aids (phonograph records, devices simulating sound, etc.); (5) special devices (mock-up of a pilot's compartment, Link Trainer, model topography classroom, miniature planetarium, globe with blackboard surfaces, pinball machine, etc.); (6) printed materials (books, manuals, bulletins, pamphlets, periodicals, etc.).

The basic assumption underlying audio-visual aids is that learning—clear understanding—stems from sense experiences. The pedagogical guide is: Whatever is to be mastered should be learned in its natural setting, or in a situation that is staged as close to the real situation as possible.

Perhaps you think, "Well, that's all right for the sciences and the arts but how can you do this in the social studies?" The answer is that teachers to an increasing degree are simulating real situations. Thus, for example, a school may hold an election for officers of its student council. In the assembly the various candidates, with the utmost seriousness, discuss the duties of the officers of the council as they see them. This may be followed by discussions in the home room in which supporters of the candidates present the various platforms; and, finally, there is the use of a school ballot. We can and do make instruction realistic at times but we do not do it often enough. The main reasons are: (1) in general, teachers do not have the time to plan; (2) too often we do not have the equipment; and (3) sometimes we do not have the vision.

The main idea of a strong program in audio-visual aids is the same as that which underlies the settings for good activities in the first grade. For example, what would a good first-grade teacher have in her room if she wanted the children to do a good job in reading and talking about rabbits? The obvious answer is a couple of rabbits. Most teachers will perhaps admit that too often our rooms lack equipment—that they are so barren as to suggest mere detention or custodial care of children. Then, too, many schools operate on the assumption that a subject in high school can be taught in any vacant room. We hope you will change that by providing films and gadgets and by covering the walls of classrooms with posters, cartoons, etc., all of which drive home the main ideas of the unit that is being taught. In short, we hope you will manage to have the "rabbits" in your classroom.

A BIT OF HISTORY

The basic principles in the training aids program are, of course, far from new. In the long ago, Johann Amos Comenius (1592–1670) in *Orbis Pictus* (*World in Pictures*) wrote as follows:

And let the things named them be shewed, not only in the picture, but also in themselves; for example, the parts of the body, clothes, books, the house, utensils,

A map helps these children to understand and remember facts in geography.[E]

etc. . . . things rare and not easy to be met withal at home might be kept ready in every great school, that they may be shewed also, as often as any words are to be made of them to the scholars.

Thus at last this school would indeed become a school of things obvious to the senses, and an entrance to the school intellectual.[1]

A couple of centuries later Pestalozzi objected vigorously to teaching words and phrases that children do not understand. Consider the following:

In Europe the culture of the people has ended by becoming an empty chattering, fatal alike to real faith and real knowledge; an instruction of mere words and out-

---

[1] This quotation appears in the Preface of the Eleventh English-Latin edition published in London in 1728 and reprinted by C. W. Bardine, Syracuse, in 1887.

ward show, unsubstantial as a dream, and not only absolutely incapable of giving us the quiet widsom of faith and love, but bound, sooner or later, to lead us into incredulity and superstition, egotism and hardness of heart. . . . Everything confirms me in my opinion that the only way of escaping a civil, moral and religious degradation, is to have done with the superficiality, narrowness, and other errors of our popular instruction, and recognize sense-impression as the real foundation of all knowledge.[1]

The statement is so prophetic of the present utter chaos of Europe that a superstitious person might be tempted to say Pestalozzi had a premonition of Hitler, et al.   More recently, Charles W. Eliot, then President of Harvard, attacked our reliance on the printed page by emphasizing that the meaning of concepts and principles should to the greatest extent possible stem from sense experiences. As everyone knows, many teachers in the early grades have long been "visual education" minded.   Nevertheless, we need to make greater use of sense experiences when staging learning situations.

We believe that this area, if intelligently cultivated in the years ahead, might yield a real improvement in our schools.   It could happen that any city, state, or teacher education institution which neglects this problem may find itself outmoded ten years hence. However, before we go all out for a program in learning aids, we should recognize that we can go off the deep end in many places. Here, for example, are some common ideas about learning aids that may need to be modified or even discarded before a sensible program can be provided.

PHONY IDEAS	REFUTATION
1. When you do find a good film you should dismiss a lot of classes in order that all the students may see it.	1. We might call this the shotgun technique. Since you have a good gun it seems reasonable that you will hit something if you scatter over a wide area. The whole school on exceptional occasions may, of course, need to see a film. But in general, a film needs to be geared to a specific objective in a unit of instruction.

[1] In a letter quoted by ROGER DE GUIMPS, *Pestalozzi, His Life and Work*, p. 233, New York: D. Appleton & Company, Inc., 1890.

2. Training aids, as used by the military, are limited to the teaching of science and the arts, and, therefore, they are of no great interest to teachers of other subjects.

2. The Army uses training aids with great success in teaching attitudes, as for example, morale and the traits of a good soldier. Learning aids should prove to be especially useful in the social studies, in fixing the dispositions that make for good citizenship.

3. The phrase, learning aids, refers largely to sound films.

3. As has been suggested, sound films, while used in fantastic numbers, are nevertheless a small part of the total program of training aids in the schools of the armed forces.

4. The way to make a big improvement in the existing program of visual aids in the school system is to secure a lot of surplus property.

4. Much of this will have no useful purpose in our schools. The task of judicious selection will be very difficult, and in many cases the teacher will not know how to use some of the materials.

5. We can develop a good program of learning aids without a research program.

5. A good learning aid is one which stems from a classroom need and which has been tested to see if it is better than any other known device. Before an aid is released for wide use it should have the "bugs" taken out of it. Without systematic studies of pupils' responses our teachers will be overwhelmed by much useless material.

6. Learning aids are useful mainly in teaching skills and in giving information.

6. As has been suggested above, they may prove equally useful in teaching attitudes. In schools of the armed forces specific attitudes and dispositions—

PHONY IDEAS

REFUTATION

those related to good housekeeping, morale, discipline—are driven home by visual aid techniques that are illustrated in civilian life by certain aspects of bond drives and advertising campaigns.

7. A learning aid is an end in itself.

7. This fallacy is perhaps obvious and yet some teachers lose sight of the fact that a learning aid is only a means to an end.

8. A large city should develop a department of audio-visual aids separate from the curriculum.

8. There is no justification for a learning aid that does not implement some objective of the curriculum. In efficient administration the program will be subordinate to the curriculum.

9. A learning aid is a substitute for a teacher.

9. A good program of learning aids increases the importance and responsibilities of a teacher. In common practice a teacher may perhaps take his class to see a film and seize the opportunity to relax or even take a nap. When properly used a learning aid frees the teacher for his task of guiding the learning process.

10. The teachers of the various school subjects have little to contribute to a program in learning aids.

10. In a good program many valuable ideas will come from classroom teachers. Moreover, teachers, especially those in industrial and fine arts, will produce many useful aids when they realize the possibilities, and are given necessary materials and the time in the school day to make the aids.

PHONY IDEAS   REFUTATION

11. The supervision of a program in learning aids is an extra job that can be undertaken along with a full teaching load, not unlike the sponsorship of an extracurricular activity.

11. It is inconceivable that a teacher or even a committee whose members are teaching full time could guide a program of consequence in a large school, and obviously not in a city system.

12. With proper guidance the staff can do at very little cost all that the Army and Navy did with training aids.

12. As has already been implied, some things can be done without much cost, but a really fine program will cost money— lots of it.

13. Learning aids are just a passing fad—all we need to do is to ignore the present emphasis and to wait it out.

13. We shall always have pupils who have difficulty grasping abstract ideas. Competent teachers will always be aware of this fact and they will try to do what they can to provide vivid illustrations. A good school will see to it that learning is not unnecessarily difficult.

14. All we need to do to solve the problem of learning aids is to get the legislature to appropriate one or two million dollars to buy visual aids.

14. At least one state has passed such an act and in the surge of interest for visual aids others may follow. A considerable fraction of such sums may be frittered away by the numerous districts in buying visual aids that will not fit specific units in the curriculum, and in a short time the materials may be stored on shelves—if there are shelves.

15. The problem will be solved if enough teachers take professional courses in visual aids.

15. No doubt such courses are helpful but they are not sufficient to create and maintain a vital program in visual aids.

Underlying the preceding discussion is one important guide. It is, that there is not much chance of making a substantial beginning on a good program in learning aids unless at the same time we make provisions for selecting, testing, and utilization. How shall we get started toward an effective program in learning aids? There is a step that every school should take:

The faculty of a school should have a standing committee on audio-visual aids. Nearly every faculty has a few members especially interested in visual aids. They should be encouraged to develop their hobby. Working as a standing committee they can make themselves exceedingly useful to a school. There was no implication in a preceding section that the teachers of a school can do nothing without a development unit nor that everything connected with visual aids costs a great deal of money. That is, of course, far from true. No doubt the school principal who spent some of the war years teaching in the schools of the armed forces on more than one occasion had the thought, "How much Miss Allen on my staff in fine arts and Mr. Jones in industrial arts could contribute to social studies, mathematics, the languages, etc., if we had this kind of audio-visual aids program under way!"

The efforts of such a committee might well utilize the imagination and resourcefulness of certain students who also are greatly interested in visual aids. The practice now followed in some of our schools of giving a small group of students the bit of special training necessary for their participation in the management of the visual aids program might well become more common. Certainly students profit by such experience.

The numerous services that a standing committee on visual aids, which in some schools is called a projection committee, can render to a faculty are perhaps obvious. At any rate, only a few will be listed here.

1. Avoid undesirable duplication. We are told that a Michigan school showed a movie on the use of the micrometer to the same students three times in one day!

2. Provide teachers from time to time with a brief list of really useful materials. There are not as many valuable movies and film-strips as the catalogues suggest. Obviously useful material that is

A student committee on audio-visual aids, consisting of pupils that engage in this activity as a hobby, can be of great service to a school.[L]

free or that can be obtained at low cost should be featured in such a list.

3. Help the classroom teachers to manage visual aids. There are many possibilities. For example, students who make audio-visual aids a hobby will be not only competent but pleased to show how to thread a machine and how to make adjustments in projecting a picture.

4. Improve the ways that teachers use visual aids. Although many teachers make good use of visual aids it is also clear that much which is now done in the name of visual aids is a waste of time and money. As has been suggested, a good filmstrip should be used in a unit to achieve a specific objective. In common practice many movies and filmstrips are shown without even a preview. The movie in far too many cases is the resort of a lazy, tired, unprepared, or overworked teacher. In brief, there is much to remedy.

5. Exercise a caretaker function of the visual aids now possessed by the schools. If there is not a central place in the building for aids used by more than one department, the equipment tends to be lost and new teachers especially may not learn for a long time that it exists.

A standing committee, such as is here suggested, might well use at least one faculty meeting early in each semester to discuss its continuous survey and its recommendations relating to proper utilization of visual aids.

SOME BASIC GUIDES FOR USING CLASSROOM FILMS

This brief section is probably the most important one in the chapter. We are going to suggest a few basic guides for the effective use of classroom films. First, however, we need to note the three criteria of a good educational motion picture (or filmstrip). It must (1) be geared to the specific objectives of a curriculum unit, (2) result in more interesting and more effective teaching, and (3) make the teacher's job easier.

If you accept the above criteria for a good educational film, then we may suggest the following guides as basic:

1. Keep your list of good films up to date for each course that you teach. Remember: (1) the catalogues are fat, (2) there are as yet in most subject areas only a few good educational films.

2. Preview every film that you haven't seen and make sure it does a job that you want done.

3. Prepare your students by telling them what the picture does and what they are to note with care.

4. Do not compete with the theater. Note that the word "entertainment" does not appear in the criteria for a good educational film.

5. Make sure the mechanism is in order. Do not wreck a good picture by bad lighting or poor sound.

6. Follow up the film. This may take the form of a discussion or a debate of one or more issues, some application, carrying out a project suggested by the film, or at least a simple evaluation.

LOOKING INTO THE CRYSTAL BALL

We are convinced that the filmstrip, especially the type which elicits responses of the student, has great possibilities for improving the curriculum. There are good reasons for believing that a teacher can make a significant improvement in his work by the wider use of filmstrips. The filmstrip, or slide film, consists of a series of frames that may be projected on the ordinary wall of a classroom. The room does not need to be darkened. It has the very great advantage that a single slide or frame may be held on the screen or wall for a period of time that is adequate for careful study. Other things being equal, a filmstrip is of most use if it is built into a unit to achieve a specific objective. Moreover, a group of related filmstrips can give continuity in the development of a curriculum unit.

Fortunately, the writing of the script for a filmstrip is not too difficult for a resourceful teacher. Teachers with imagination who have a favorable school situation and time in the school day to do the job, may, in increasing numbers, be disposed to experiment with filmstrips. If this should happen, the total number of teachers in our larger cities will be more than adequate to provide a complete set of filmstrips for every curriculum unit that can be illuminated by this technique.

However, the design and construction of filmstrips need much investigation and experimentation or it will get out of bounds. Already there is a flood of filmstrips—a few good and the rest bad or useless. The construction of a filmstrip geared to the specific objectives of a unit is an excellent problem for an individual or a group in a summer workshop. It is also conceivable that some boards of education will come to realize that this job is worth doing in school time. Thousands of miles of screen materials were made in the war training program by high-priced personnel with no other duties. The lessons for peace also are, for all the children of all the people, difficult to learn and they too call for vivid—even expensive—instructional aids. It is perhaps unnecessary to say that the evaluation of a filmstrip should be in terms of its contribution to classroom instruction.

SOME PRACTICAL SUGGESTIONS

One very clear fact should be evident as one glances at a list of audio-visual aids. It is: the majority of these aids are available to all teachers regardless of the size and location of their school. Some of the most commonly used visual aids are those that require little or no outlay of money. We are not implying that schools should for one moment hesitate to buy the more expensive visual and auditory aids if they have the money to do so. Undoubtedly there is a very real need for most of this equipment in classroom teaching. Our plea is for more teachers to develop and use those aids which are available; and the fact remains that a vast number of aids are found in the smallest school and in the most remote community.

The following is a list of suggestions pointing definitely to greater use of the wide variety of visual aids commonly found in all schools and communities:

1. The school journey or field trip holds infinite possibilities for enriching instruction on practically any subject. Indeed, every city, town, and farm community contains a wealth of material of so exhaustive a nature as to defy a

To the greatest extent possible, meanings should stem from sense experiences.(B)

mere list of things that pupils should know more about in order to understand the society in which they live.

2. Many schools have built up a fine collection of museum materials through the cooperation of parents, pupils, and teachers. These materials often consist of old newspapers and magazines of historical interest, objects associated with pioneer life, and various forms of collections, *e.g.*, minerals, samples of farm crops, flowers, and stuffed animals and birds.

3. Probably every community contains a few outstanding people who know more about some phase of life than anyone else around. Doctors, lawyers, busi-

nessmen, former pioneers, travelers, and many others may be classified as a group which has accumulated "special information" during the course of their lives. This group represents a part of the resources of every community from which teachers may draw in order to enrich classroom teaching. Usually such persons are willing to share their views and experiences with pupils on topics that are appropriate to the lesson or unit being taught.

At the risk of some duplication we now present a list of important audio-visual aids with two purposes in mind: (*a*) to make this list available to you at some future time when you may wish to use it to check the things that are available in your community, and (*b*) to correct the erroneous impression that the only visual aids are slides and films, for motion pictures and slides have come to fill the center of the stage at the expense of cheaper, but perhaps just as important, items.

A List of Visual Aids

Apparatus	Drawing	Post card
Aquarium	Field trip	Print
Blackboard	Filmstrip	Sand table
Bulletin board	Flat picture	School museum
Cartographic map	Globe	Slide
Cartoon	Graph	Specimen
Carving	Map	Stereoscope and stereograph
Chart	Model	Television
Collection	Motion picture	Textbook and reference book
Demonstration	Opaque projector	illustration
Diagram	Painting	Time line
Dramatization	Photograph	Writing

THE SYSTEMATIC USE OF AUDIO-VISUAL AIDS

Let us assume that the administration of your school is willing to provide you with much of the necessary equipment with which to begin an audio-visual education program, *i.e.*, motion-picture projectors, silent films, slide projectors, filing cabinets, bulletin boards, and the like. But this does not include all of the necessary audio-visual aids for a successful program. You must plan to accumulate for your own classroom use such other important aids as cartoons, graphs, flat pictures, photographs, postal cards, and clippings. It is here that most teachers fail to make the most use of audio-visual aids and it is here that you will strike the first problem, which is to keep all this material in some form where it will be available to you and the pupils. Many classroom teachers have hit on a file for audio-visual aids as a partial solution for this problem. In a small school you may not be able to purchase an expensive filing cabinet, but your pupils will be able to provide a box for arranging the labeled materials. Do not overlook the valuable experiences that pupils get when aiding you in the administration and organization of visual aids, not to mention the time it will save you.

The teacher who guided this project long had pursued puppet shows as a hobby. If you do have a choice of extracurricular activities in your first year of teaching, better choose something that is fun for you.[N1]

GRAPHIC AIDS[1]

One of the most common of the visual aids is the statistical graph. The widespread use of pictorial and graphic techniques for the presentation of quantitative data in newspapers, textbooks, and

[1] For a more complete treatment see the chapter, "How to Picture Number Relations," in *Mathematics in Life*, by Raleigh Schorling and John R. Clark. Yonkers-on-Hudson, N.Y.: World Book Company, 1946. Some classes will wish to skip the remainder of this chapter. However, a shocking number of teachers leave training schools without the ability to use graphic aids in correct form.

scientific reports is sufficient reason for teaching the interpretation and making of simple graphs. For many people these two skills may be more important than penmanship and spelling. The teachers of all secondary-school subjects should know the right ways of making graphs which may be used to depict existing economic and social conditions, to make enlightening comparisons between masses of statistical data, and to prophesy future conditions.

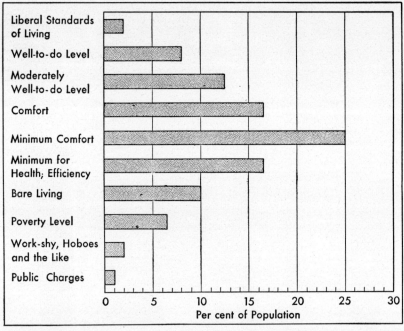

Population classified by income. This graph shows that 2 per cent of our people have incomes sufficient to support a liberal standard of living, 8 per cent are at the well-to-do level, etc.

Unfortunately many teachers, while completely convinced of the importance and interest value to pupils, do not in fact realize that graphic presentation is a waste of time, and perhaps even harmful, unless precise standards of workmanship are observed. The graph is fundamentally a tool for expressing number relationship, specifically to picture relative size by expressing ratio. The development of mathematical concepts, the very purpose for which the graph is employed, often fails when the activity does not rise above a "messing around" with colors. The mathematical skills and concepts must be given careful attention in order that the social interpretation for which the graph is undertaken in the first place may emerge accurately enough to justify undertaking the study. We repeat that what the teacher needs to remember about graphic presentation is that there are precise standards which, while perhaps not observed by all graphic technicians who prepare materials for newspapers or magazines, are nevertheless coming to be accepted very rapidly by the public press and by publishers of books. These standards should be taught to children in order that they may be intelligent in the interpretation of such graphic materials as appear in the public press.

For ordinary purposes the teacher will employ only simple graphs, the most useful of which are the bar, the circle, and the line. The following sections present a set of specifications of each.

1. *How to Make a Bar Graph.* In interpreting data one type of graph may be better than some other kind. The bar graph is the simplest when you wish to picture a series of ratios. Thus, if you wish to show graphically that *A* is 2½ times as large as *B*, and *B* is 3 times as large as *C*, then it would seem desirable to use a bar graph.

In drawing a bar graph, follow these steps:[1]

1. Plan the vertical spacing of your graph on the paper,
   a. Allow room at the bottom for the title.
   b. Plan the number of bars, making the width of the bars and the spaces between them equal.
   c. Allow room at the bottom for the scale and its label.
2. Plan the horizontal spacing of the graph,
   a. Allow room at the left for the names (or dates) of the items which are represented by the different bars.
   b. Choose the scale for the bars so that you can get the longest bar on the graph.
3. Decide upon the order of the items and write their names in the space allowed at the left. (Do you think it will improve the graph if you arrange the items in order of size, with the longest bar at the top or at the bottom?)
4. Mark off the scale at the bottom of the graph and label it.
5. Draw the bars according to scale.
6. Write or print the title of the graph at the bottom. The title should be brief, interesting to other persons, and carefully lettered.

[1] *To the Teacher:* Emphasize accuracy and neatness. Some schools provide pupils with rolls of narrow gummed tape for making the bars. In using tape, pupils avoid some of the work which is too exacting, without losing the important mathematical values. The tape may be bought in several attractive colors in most cities. It is fairly inexpensive and it improves the appearance of most graphs. Some teachers motivate the appreciation of standards by posting, in order of excellence, a set of graphs.

The preceding steps are for making graphs with the bars horizontal. At first all your bar graphs should be made that way. When graphs are made with the bars vertical, the points to be taken into account in planning the vertical and horizontal spacing are of course different, except for the title at the bottom.

2. *How to Make a Circle Graph.* A circle graph is one way to show the relation of a part to the whole and the relations between

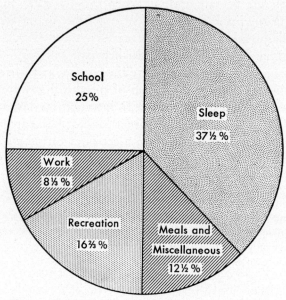

Circle graph showing how, on the average, a class spent the 24 hours of the day.

the different parts. There are certain basic skills that the student needs in order to do acceptable work. You may need to review and in some cases to teach the fact that a complete rotation is 360 degrees, and also how to draw with the protractor an angle of a required size. The pupil should be able to compute what fractional part (preferably what per cent) one number is of another and know how to find a part (or per cent) of 360 degrees.

In making a circle graph, follow these steps:

1. Find the total of the quantities to be represented. The complete circle (360°) always represents the whole.

2. Find the fractional part (or per cent) that each quantity is of the total. Check to be sure that the sum is 1, or 100 per cent.

3. Multiply 360° by the fractional part for each quantity. This gives the size of the central angle for each quantity. The sum of all the angles must be 360°.

4. Construct central angles of the sizes just found to represent the different quantities.

5. Label the sectors to show the name of the quantity represented by each. It is usual to state also the size or amount of each quantity, or what per cent it is of the whole.

6. Provide a title that tells what the graph is about.

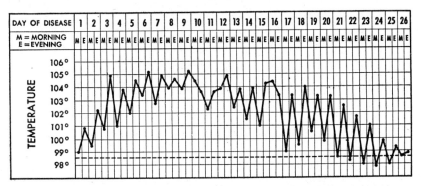

Temperature chart of a typical fever patient. This is a line graph showing the relation between the readings of a temperature scale and the hours of the day.

A well-made circle graph should be easy to read. It should show clearly what quantities are being compared and what are the relations between them.

3. *How to Make a Line Graph.* A line graph is used to show fluctuations in some variable in relation to a second variable. A temperature chart is a good illustration of a continuous curve because for any given time shown on one scale there is a corresponding temperature, though it may not in fact have been measured. The line graph is often used in the public press and by teachers when a bar graph should have been employed. For instructional purposes some deviation from precise mathematical practice may be justifiable.

In making a line graph, follow these steps:

1. You need two scales: a horizontal scale and a vertical scale. It is important to choose each so that your graph will be the size and shape you want.

2. Label each scale clearly to show what it represents. It is not always necessary to write every number for values which are measured by a scale.

3. You need a table of the data to be represented. The data must be arranged by pairs; one item of each pair is the number or date for the horizontal scale, and

the other is the number or quantity to be shown on the vertical scale.   Each pair is used to locate a point on the graph paper.

4. Points must be located and dots placed on the graph paper before the line can be drawn.   This is called "plotting the points."   A point is plotted by means of each pair of numbers in the table.   One of these two numbers tells how far to count on the horizontal scale, and the other tells how far to count on the vertical scale.

5. After all points have been plotted, they are connected by straight lines (or in some graphs the points are connected by a smooth curve).

6. The title of the graph should be clearly written.

7. Accuracy is essential and neatness is important.

For Discussion

1. If there is an audio-visual committee in your training school, it might be well to invite a member of that committee to one of your conferences on student teaching to acquaint you with the available materials and the procedures.

2. If you like the criteria for a good educational film given in this chapter, then you had better make a list of the good screen materials in the subject (or subjects) that you plan to teach.   The list will not be easy to make, and unfortunately in most subjects, it will be very *short*.

3. Here are four steps to be used as a general guide for using a classroom film: (1) preview the film, (2) prepare students for the film, (3) present the film, and (4) follow up with class discussion.   In two or three sentences tell what you would do in each as regards steps (2), (3), and (4).

Suggested Readings

Audio-Visual Guide (Formerly *Film and Radio Guide*).   Newark, New Jersey: Educational and Recreational Guides, Inc.,

Cook, Dorothy E., and Barbara Borden: *Educational Film Guide* (Formerly *Educational Film Catalog*).   New York: The H. W. Wilson Company, published annually.

Cook, Dorothy E., and Katherine M. Holden: *Educational Film Guide*, Section Two, "Filmstrips."   New York: The H. W. Wilson Company, published annually.

Dale, Edgar: *Audio-Visual Methods In Teaching*.   New York: The Dryden Press, Inc., 1946.

DeBernardis, Amo: *The 1946 Audio-Visual Projectionist's Handbook*.   Chicago: Business Screen Magazine, 1946.

Educational Screen.   Chicago: The Educational Screen.

Goetting, Martin Luther: *Teaching in the Secondary School*.   New York: Prentice-Hall Inc., 1942.   Pp. xiii + 519.
     Chapter 12 deals with visual aids.

Hass, Kenneth B., and H. Q. Packer: *Preparation and Use of Audio-Visual Aids*.   New York: Prentice-Hall, Inc., 1946.

Journal of the A.E.R. (Association for Education by Radio) Chicago Association for Education by Radio.

Levenson, William B.: *Teaching Through Radio*.   New York: Rinehart & Company, Inc., 1945.

McKown, Harry C., and Alvin B. Roberts: *Audio-Visual Aids to Instruction*, 2d ed.   New York: McGraw-Hill Book Company, Inc., 1949.

PETERSON, HOUSTON (Editor): *Great Teachers*.   New Brunswick: Rutgers University Press, 1946.   Pp. xxi + 351.
  This book is a collection of firsthand accounts of great teachers, written by former students.   Since the authors are persons of unusual abilities, the main contribution naturally is on the problem of early identification of pupils with special talents and the proper culture of such gifted youngsters.   There is not enough in the book that deals with the day-by-day techniques of teachers to warrant including it in one's required professional reading.   However, you will find it sufficiently interesting if you read it a bit at a time on a long train journey, and it would not wreck your idea of a vacation.
See and Hear (International Journal of Audio-Visual Education).   Chicago: Audio-Visual Publications, Inc.
WITTICH, WALTER A., and JOHN G. FOWLKES: *Audio-Visual Paths To Learning*.   New York: Harper & Brothers, 1946.

Chapter XII

Extraclass Duties of a Teacher

Of all the work that is done or that can be done for our country, the greatest is that of educating the body, the mind, and above all the character, giving spiritual and moral training to those who in a few years are themselves to decide the destinies of the nation.

—THEODORE ROOSEVELT

THE EXTRACURRICULAR PROGRAM

To begin with, let us make an inventory of what you believe about the form and functions of an extracurricular program in a school. The accompanying list of issues will direct your attention to those aspects that are most significant.

Directions: Read each of the following issues carefully and then place a check mark[1] in that column to the right which you think best answers each question.

Issue	Yes	No	Question
1. Should the teacher recognize extracurricular work as an integral part of his duties?			
2. Should sponsorship of activities be considered an "extra" load because they are not strictly curricular?			
3. Should an activity be an end in itself; *e.g.*, a social club purely for the enjoyment of members?			
4. Should activities always be teacher-supervised?			
5. Should supervision be definitely directive with the teacher acting as the recognized leader?			
6. Should activities meet outside of school hours?			
7. Should activities be so organized that any interested pupil may join without invitation?			
8. Should activities contribute to the welfare of the school at large; *e.g.*, a music club which furnishes music for school affairs?			
9. Should the student who is not able to keep up in his academic work be required to give up his extracurricular interests?			

[1] In case a student does not wish to mutilate his book, he may write the numbers from 1 to 25 in a vertical column in his notebook and proceed to write his responses as suggested. It is assumed that a class discussion will evolve from this exercise.

Issue	Yes	No	Question
10. Should every pupil be required to join some activity?			
11. Should a supervisor possess the veto power?			
12. Should an activity be directed largely by pupils?			
13. Should school time be regularly devoted to these activities?			
14. Should clubs be allowed the added group loyalty and interest that come from an elected membership?			
15. Should the failing student be allowed continued participation in activities?			
16. Is the teacher's opportunity for character development greater in extracurricular work than in the classroom?			
17. Should activities relate definitely to the curricular work of the school?			
18. May extracurricular activities be entirely independent of curricular work?			
19. Should each activity handle its own finances and pay the bills it incurs?			
20. Should money be raised by individual activity dues?			
21. Should membership in activities be entirely a matter of personal decision?			
22. Should boys and girls no longer in school be encouraged to participate in extracurricular activities?			
23. Should a general school tax be employed in financing the extracurricular program?			
24. Should honor clubs be based solely on scholarship?			
25. Should pupils weak in leadership qualities be permitted to continue in an office to which they have been elected?			

PURPOSE

In much the same way that blackboards, textbooks, physical education, and instruction in music came into the school to fill a need, extracurricular activities have been accepted as a necessary and vital supplement to the more formal curricular program of the school. The extracurricular program is the response to the demand that the school furnish more than mere academic instruction, that it give preparation for life by providing experiences in the broader phases of community living and intelligent citizenship. There is of course no reason why the various school subjects should not provide most of this training, but in the typical school the modification of the curriculum does not keep pace with the needs of pupils, and therefore the extracurricular program is a convenient tool by which an obsolete and inadequate curriculum may be modified. It is a good deal easier and quicker to bring a new experience informally

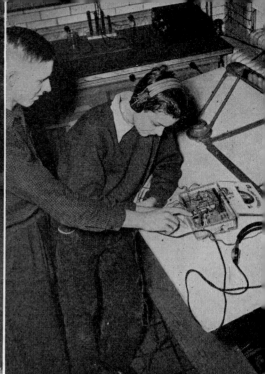

If a school is not too small, music activities and a science club help to provide talented youth with tasks that challenge them.(D)(E)

into a school by the side door labeled "extracurricular" than it is by the formal front entrance, "curricular."

The philosophical argument for extracurricular activities in the high school is precisely the same as that underlying the whole educational program. In this area we also strive to minister to the needs of the individual and of society. In brief, each activity should fulfill a pupil need and justify its inclusion in the program by contributing to some general social objective of education. Among the significant social and psychological needs that an extracurricular program may be expected to meet are the following:

1. *To Develop the Whole Child.* Through a well-balanced extracurricular program that is properly integrated with the curricular offerings, the school is in a position to place equal emphasis on the social, moral, mental, and physical development of the individual, and thus increase the chances of realizing the newer aim of the modern school, the development of an integrated personality. The main problem of the school is to provide enough opportunities for self-expression.

Granted that much of that which is offered in the name of extracurricular activities should be incorporated in the regular work of the school, there yet remain some practical problems. For example, a typical student in a senior high school takes four or at most five school subjects. In general, these four subjects cannot satisfy the worthy special interests of all the pupils. Assume that a boy is much interested in photography and that this hobby would contribute in a desirable way to his development. Perhaps one of the school subjects, *e.g.*, science, could and should include a unit on photography. However, such a unit would not be likely to reach all the pupils of a school interested in photography, nor would it be easy for the boy in question to keep in touch with this activity throughout the period of his schooling, whereas a camera club operating as an extracurricular activity can serve the needs of all the pupils who can profit by this experience. Thus we see that the typical academic program of four subject-matter courses in which the pupil is enrolled during a single term or semester is at best an inadequate provision for ministering to his specific needs and interests. It is here that the flexible extracurricular program supplements the academic offerings and provides for the development of special talents, interests, and abilities. Through a variety of activities the slow-learning pupil as well as the alert pupil may be given increased exploratory opportunities that serve to make his life more meaningful.

2. *To Develop the Good Citizen.* Desirable social habits such as individual responsibility, constructive leadership, and effective resourcefulness are more likely to be discovered and given scope in an extracurricular program than in classes that tend to be conducted on a basis of assignments by, and recitations to, teachers. When properly organized, extracurricular activities provide laboratories in which pupils can be initiated gradually into the duties of citizenship.

3. *To Develop Worthy Recreational Interests.* It is generally recognized that both youths and adults have a dangerous amount of leisure time and that the continued decrease in the number of working hours for all is almost certain to make practice in the wise use of leisure a fundamental concern of the school. The need has become acute for developing constructive avocational and recreational interests which are immediately useful to the pupil and which will carry over and serve to enrich the leisure hours of his adult life.

Thus it is seen that the extracurricular program is a direct outgrowth of three things: (1) the changing social and economic condi-

Beginning teachers are often asked to be sponsors of the school's publications. Even if you have training in journalism, it might be a good thing to watch a high-school staff in action and learn what the main duties are.(E)

tions; (2) a better understanding of the psychological needs and characteristics of the adolescent; and (3) the lag in the reform of the secondary school curriculum.

THE SCOPE OF THE ACTIVITY PROGRAM

Several factors enter in, to determine what a school should offer in the way of extracurricular activities. The work of other agencies in the community, school plant facilities, and the training of the teaching personnel are illustrations of some of these determinants. In most schools, however, a well-balanced and adequate extracurricular program is built around (1) student civic activities, (2) academic clubs, musical organizations, and hobby clubs, and (3) interscholastic and intramural athletic teams. This classification will be expanded to give some idea of the variety of activities which it includes.

1. *Student Civic Activities.* The student council, home room, assembly, and class organizations all may offer experiences leading to a better understanding and appreciation of democratic processes. In these activities pupils help determine the policies and the pro-

grams. They plan and present assembly programs. The individual pupil learns how to conduct a meeting in approved parliamentary style. He learns that the "common good" should transcend selfish interests. The meetings of the home room and of class organizations and the election of representatives to the student council, athletic board, and assembly committee provide practice in the operation of democratic machinery and the exercise of the student franchise in the school.

Here we must pause to call attention to a fatal hazard to the effectiveness of an extracurricular program in giving practice in democratic living. It is that a faculty will not really trust the sound judgment of a student body. It will time and again outmaneuver a student group with the worthy but mistaken purpose of avoiding impending error. It is not likely that by secret and unsigned ballot students will come to a wrong decision, provided there has been adequate discussion of all the facts and issues involved. The writer, having served as principal for eight years of the Lincoln School of Teachers College and the University High School (Ann Arbor), does not recall a single decision stemming from an all-school forum that seemed wrong to the faculty. When students of a high school have a real part in planning and managing a wide range of extracurricular activities, they quickly, say in a few years, become mature enough to realize that some aspects of the school's administration cannot be completely delegated to students. In such a school there will be few silly statements implying that "the students run the school" and "handle all discipline cases." The undercurrent of faith or lack of faith in a student body is so extremely important that it in the end determines the effectiveness of the program in democratic living.

2. *Academic Clubs, Musical Organizations, and Hobby Clubs.* Academic clubs grow out of, supplement, and enrich subject-matter courses in which pupils express special interests. Among typical academic activities in the extracurricular program are foreign language clubs, science clubs, mathematics clubs, vocational clubs, fine arts clubs, library clubs, English clubs, and student publications.

In general, a faculty may well challenge the desirability of a club operating in a school subject. Too often such a club is the instrument used by ambitious departmental teachers to dispense propaganda, or it is a device for motivating extra work. Then, too, the materials of unusual value and interest provided by club programs should probably be an integral part of the curriculum of the school in order that all pupils may benefit by these experiences. The school orchestra, band, glee clubs, and small musical units are typical extracurricular activities providing valuable experiences that would be difficult to include in formal courses.

In many schools a few teachers are selected by the staff as advisers to the student council. Would you know how to be a constructive force rather than a dictator in a scene such as you see here?[(N1)]

Hobby clubs likewise grow out of expressed interests and are organized to develop special talents. They provide increased exploratory opportunities for pupils but, unlike academic clubs, are usually not closely related to subject courses. A wide range of interests finds expression in such organizations as model airplane clubs, outdoor clubs, camera clubs, radio clubs, and rifle clubs.

  3. *Athletic Organizations.* Health, the worthy use of leisure, and the development of habits of service, loyalty, and teamwork, with their concomitant attitudes, are among the more evident values in

the athletic program of a school. Teams in football, basketball, baseball, hockey, track, swimming, tennis, and golf usually represent the school in interscholastic competition. However, since membership on these teams is generally restricted to the superior athlete, the need is acute for the organization of activities so that all pupils may share in the benefits of a physical education program. "Every pupil a player," the general principle that should govern the organization of the intramural athletic program, calls for a variety of organized play groups. In addition to the games listed in the interscholastic program, there are many intramural sports, such as boxing, tumbling, ping-pong, and archery, in which many boys and girls may engage.

Varying in extremes from ping-pong to football, from an informal meeting of a social program committee to an executive session of the student council, from flying model airplanes to a rendition of the *Poet and Peasant Overture* by the orchestra, we find operating in all these activities the basic principle that "the school exists for the development of the pupil and the welfare of society."

THE ROLE OF THE ACTIVITY SPONSOR

There is no guarantee that the extracurricular program will either possess a general educational value or fulfill an important need in the pupil's life unless each activity is properly organized and directed. Obviously the most important factor in the success of a club or organization is the sponsor. The teacher in training should not overlook the importance of preparing to direct at least one or two extracurricular activities before completing the period of student teaching. In many secondary schools today the extracurricular program is scheduled during a regular period of the school day, and teachers are expected to regard sponsorship of activities as a definite part of their work in the school. In selecting new teachers, superintendents and principals are placing increased emphasis on ability and willingness to assume responsibilities in connection with the school's extracurricular program. It is evident that preparation for sponsorship must be considered an important aspect of professional training and equipment.

Teacher-training institutions recognize the value of preparation for the supervision of extracurricular activities. Among the courses now available, that have a relation to the activity program, are those in the theory of extracurricular activities, in guidance, character education, music, debate, journalism, and dramatics. Participation in such campus activities as athletics and literary clubs provides foundational training for directing similar activities in high schools. If possible, a student teacher should arrange to serve as an assistant sponsor in one or more of these activities in the period devoted to professional education; in any case he should observe as many activities in action as time will permit.

QUALIFICATIONS OF THE ACTIVITY SPONSOR

The following questions may help you to appraise your fitness as the sponsor of an assigned activity. If you find any checks in the column indicating a negative response, try to determine what you can do to prepare for the task.

SELF-APPRAISAL BY AN ACTIVITY SPONSOR

Directions: Consider each item carefully and place an X in the appropriate column opposite it; *e.g.*, if you think you welcome suggestions that improve your efficiency, place an X in the column marked "Yes" after item 3.

Qualities	Yes	No
1. Have you had some special training that has prepared you for the responsibilities as a sponsor of this particular activity? If not, are you willing to learn?		
2. Are you interested enough in the activity so that it is likely to develop as a recreational hobby for you?		
3. Will you welcome suggestions that will improve your efficiency as a sponsor?		
4. Do you plan to cooperate with sponsors of other activities and with your principal?		
5. Do you think that you can manipulate the total situation so that pupils will like to have you as a member of the group?		
6. Are you acquainted with the general principles that should govern the administration and supervision of extracurricular activities?		
7. Do you understand the specific aims and functions of the club you will sponsor?		
8. Do you see in this activity opportunities for such guidance as may be suggested by the terms "self-expression," "leadership," and "mental health"?		
9. Have you any plan for appraising the value of this activity for the participants? for the school?		
10. Do you deal effectively with social and informal teaching situations?		

ORGANIZATION OF THE EXTRACURRICULAR PROGRAM

Extracurricular activities vary somewhat widely in the range of experiences provided, but certain fundamental principles of organization and supervision are sufficiently broad to guide the extracurricular program in all schools. The beginning teacher needs to know these principles in order to give the proper aim and direction to the activities he is likely to be called on to organize and sponsor.

Here is practice in democratic action. Are you convinced that cooperative thinking can be utilized in the management of a school?[N1]

Principles of Organization:

1. The extracurricular program should be strictly under the guidance and control of the school. Final authority as regards the organization of new activities and the plans and policies of organizations should be vested in the faculty. Each activity should be supervised by a faculty sponsor.

2. Activities should be organized for specific purposes. In particular, those should be encouraged that (*a*) grow out of and serve to enrich curricular work,

(*b*) fulfill an immediate pupil need, (*c*) have carry-over values in adult life, and (*d*) produce significant values to society.

3. There should be a wide variety of activities in order that the needs of as many pupils as possible may be met. Extension of the extracurricular program should be gradual and will be influenced by the type of community and its agencies, the school plant and equipment, the curriculum, and the training of the personnel of the school staff.

4. The sponsors of the different organizations should, by cooperative thinking, arrive at a common policy to be observed in the supervision of all activities. Unless the program is integrated, by which we mean that the activities rise out of projects and units that are related to each other and to the general curriculum, a school day may become very hectic for both pupils and teachers. The fact is that many buildings house two institutions, the school of the academic curriculum and the school of the extracurricular activities. In order that all the programs may be tied together the teachers have to come to certain general agreements.

5. Activities should be inexpensive for the individual pupil. All business accounts should be budgeted through a central organization, and a definite and specific means provided for checking and disbursing funds.

6. Participation of all pupils should be encouraged. Membership should be voluntary, but limited to the extent that a proper balance is maintained between the curricular and the extracurricular activities of each pupil. Some schools operate with a "point system" so as to insure wide participation. Under such a plan a pupil carrying a full quota of points when elected to still another office must give up some other responsibility.

7. There should be a definite time allotment provided in the regular school program for all activities.

8. Provision should be made for periodic appraisal of the services and values of the extracurricular program to pupils and to the school. These values should be publicized.

Principles of Supervision:

1. Each activity sponsor should have some special knowledge of, interest in, and enthusiasm for the activity he is supervising.

2. The sponsor should see that the policies and plans of the activity harmonize with the principles of organization, the philosophy of supervision, and the policies governing the functioning of the extracurricular program in the school.

3. Supervision should be in the nature of guidance and cooperative leadership rather than complete domination or direction by the teacher. Pupils should be given as much opportunity for self-expression, choice, freedom of opinion and action, and initiative as is consistent with the nature and purposes of the organization and the maturity of its members.

4. Each activity should have an advisory board consisting of a faculty sponsor and officers of the organization. Opportunities for leadership and positions of responsibility should be distributed among all members.

5. Records of pupil participation in extracurricular activities should be kept by each sponsor, and excellence in participation should be recognized by the school.

6. The purposes of the activity should be clearly understood by both sponsor and pupils, and cooperative appraisal of the work and progress of the activity in terms of these purposes should be made from time to time.

EVALUATING EXTRACURRICULAR ACTIVITIES

To what extent are activities in the extracurricular program meeting pupil needs? What tangible evidence is there that the

A beginning teacher who undertakes to direct an operetta or any activity in play production should probably have special training or a very special talent in the area.⁽ᴱ⁾

activities are enriching the curriculum? What is the contribution of activities to the development of the "good citizen"? These are some of the important questions that must be answered before teacher effort and public cost in maintaining the extracurricular program can be truly justified. The terms "fads" and "frills" may be all too appropriately applied to some of these supplementary activities unless it can be shown definitely that they are accomplishing the purposes for which they were set up. The values of these activities cannot be taken for granted; the responsibility for determining whether the ascribed values of the program are real or imaginary rests in part on the sponsor of the activity.

The beginning teacher needs to know how to use at least a few of the more satisfactory appraisal techniques that sponsors have found helpful in measuring the benefits and values of pupil participation in activities. Specifically, information is needed that will reveal the extent to which an activity (1) meets a felt need in the pupil's life, (2) functions in making the school a happier place in which to work, (3) is properly organized and sponsored, and (4) produces desirable changes in pupil behavior. Before other values can safely be inferred this basic information must be determined.

The suggestions for appraisal that follow by no means cover all aspects in the evaluation of the extracurricular program. However, the use of these simple techniques will reveal whether outcomes which have been assumed to exist have actually been realized.

1. *Appraising the Individual Club.* The criteria in the list on page 303 are based on the principles that should govern the organization and supervision of extracurricular activities. The evaluation sheet has been constructed to give the sponsor a convenient method for determining whether the techniques employed in directing the organization are thoroughly consistent with the best principles governing the administration of all extracurricular activities.

2. *Observational Techniques.* The use of informal techniques in appraisal was considered in more detail on earlier pages. An extended discussion will not be necessary here, for the same procedures can be employed in the measurement of the outcomes of extracurricular activities. Indeed, their use is particularly helpful in determining changes in pupil behavior and interests that are likely to grow out of membership in activities. To illustrate, the sponsor of a photography club whose patience is at times considerably overtaxed by the persistence of pupils who repeatedly ask for more frequent meetings and more reading references about amateur photography, who carry their newly developed interests into the classroom and their curricular work, and who spend a great share of their leisure hours taking and developing more and better pictures, need not worry about securing a valid appraisal of certain worth-while outcomes of that particular activity. On the other hand, if pupils are frequently absent from meetings, if activities are entered into in a half-hearted manner, or if pupils refuse to serve on club programs,

CRITERIA FOR JUDGING THE INDIVIDUAL CLUB

Directions: On this list, "5" is the highest rating that can be given, and "1" is the lowest. For example, if the group spirit is properly developed, check with an X in the "5" column opposite that item. At the end of the list, state whether you think the activity is very effective, effective, or poor. Where check marks appear in the first three columns, considerable attention should be given to improving the activity with respect to that criterion.

Criterion	1	2	3	4	5
1. Is the sponsor capable, sympathetic, enthusiastic?					
2. Are purposes evident?					
3. Is interest sustained?					
4. Is the club approved by school authorities?					
5. Has the activity been organized to meet a definite pupil need?					
6. Is the membership limited to pupils enrolled in school?					
7. Is the club open to all expressing an interest in it or possessing the ability to profit by membership?					
8. Does the club meet at school, during school hours, and at regularly scheduled times?					
9. Are fees limited and stated in advance?					
10. Are programs planned and approved in advance?					
11. Do club activities grow out of curricular work?					
12. Does the club foster helpful school morale, a spirit of service and cooperation?					
13. Are the business meetings of the club conducted in accordance with approved parliamentary practices?					
14. Are positions of leadership and responsibility open to all on an elective basis?					
15. Are positions of leadership and responsibility distributed often enough for all to receive training?					
16. Does the club work correlate with regular schoolwork?					
17. Is the club well organized, well supervised, and satisfactorily financed?					
18. Does the club promote cordiality between pupils and teachers, and between school and home?					
19. Is the proper use of leisure time encouraged?					
20. Is the group spirit consciously developed?					
21. Are records of participation properly kept?					
22. Are financial reports made and reported to the proper authority?					
23. Are purported values adequately appraised?					
24. Are special talents and abilities given expression?					
25. Are ideals of fair play and leadership rightly developed?					

there is need for further inquiry into the weaknesses that surely exist somewhere in the organization.

3. An Opinionnaire on Pupil Interest. A sponsor may use an opinionnaire to encourage constructive suggestions aimed toward the enrichment and improvement of an activity. Interest is a fundamental motivating factor in all extracurricular work, and

It is sometimes hard to draw the line between an extracurricular activity and a project that involves the whole school. Here is a Christmas project that required lots of sagacious guidance by teachers.

worth-while outcomes rarely if ever grow out of activities which pupils regard as uninteresting or which they feel possess no values. Since pupils often hesitate to express honest opinions in conversation with teachers, the use of the unsigned opinionnaire is a legitimate approach in determining the personal reactions of students, for it safeguards their identity. An analysis of these views may reveal in an organization weaknesses that otherwise might not come to light.

Though the content of the opinionnaire should vary with the age group to which it is directed and the nature of the activity to be appraised, the accompanying sample will serve to illustrate the application of this technique.

WHAT IS THE GOOD CITIZEN?

The end product of all schoolwork, curricular and extracurricular, is good citizenship. The modern school is considered a miniature society, a community in itself that initiates pupils into the desirable activities of the larger society. In some home rooms, pupils are encouraged to analyze the qualities of the good citizen and to practice those habits that tend to improve the good tone of the school

PUPIL OPINIONNAIRE

Directions: Do not sign your name. Make your statements concise and to the point, and be perfectly frank. Think through your answers before putting them in writing, and be sure each answer expresses what you really feel.

1. Did you attend all the meetings of this club?........... (Check) Yes___No___
2. Have you participated in the activities of this club as
   much as you would like to?......................... (Check) Yes___No___
3. Would you like to be a member of this club next year?.. (Check) Yes___No___
   Why?.....
   ....
   Why not?.....
   ....
4. Among the activities of this club, which have you enjoyed most?...........
   ....
   ....
   least?.....
   ....
5. As regards the meeting of the club, check the answers you think best apply to each of the statements below:
   a. Are too long___; too short___; the right length___.
   b. Held too often___; not often enough___; at correct intervals___.
   c. Are very interesting___; fairly interesting___; boring___.
6. What suggestions might the club adopt in order to be a more effective organization?.....
   ....
   ....

and help to create better working conditions for all. Needless to say, the greatest benefit of such a plan comes during the period when the list of traits of the good citizen is being formulated. The requirements for good citizenship that were analyzed, defined, and accepted in various home-room groups of a secondary school follow:

OUR REQUIREMENTS FOR GOOD CITIZENSHIP

Cooperation: is helpful on a school problem; cares about the school as a whole.
Fellowship: is friendly; adapts himself; is thoughtful of others.
Sportsmanship: knows the rules and does not take advantage; is a fighter to the end; is not a boastful winner; can lose without alibis; is honest.
Responsibility: does his job well and on time; accepts a post willingly; is punctual; sees a thing through.
Sense of Humor: is good natured; is not always tense; is cheerful; is a good person to be around.

Courtesy: is thoughtful of others; shows special consideration for women, children, elders, etc.; has kindliness of heart rather than observance of formal rules.

Workmanship: is not satisfied with poor quality; appreciates a task done at an artistic level; values highly expert guidance and knows where to find it; does a job to the best of his ability.

Pep: is a self-starter; has ideas; has initiative and enthusiasm; is energetic; has an interesting and colorful personality.

School Spirit: supports the school activities (paper, games, council, orchestra); believes this to be the best school, but offers criticism to make it better.

For Discussion

1. Could the preceding definitions be made to have meaning to all pupils of the high school, even those enrolled in the seventh grade of the junior high school?

2. Assume that this school offers honors in three areas: scholarship, athletics, and citizenship. Do you think that a student ballot could and should be used to determine which pupils should receive honors in good citizenship? With the same assumption do you think that a group of children could and would choose those who are the most entitled to recognition? Specifically, do you think that a choice by the pupils would be as valid as one made by the teachers?

3. A home-room teacher said, "Such a citizenship ballot will cease to have great value when the pupils are satisfied with the definitions." What do you think that teacher meant?

4. Principal Hart: "I believe that it is undesirable for a teacher, a group of teachers, or a class to rate Bill by the use of such questions as, Is he honest? Is he cooperative, etc." Do you agree? Why?

ILLUSTRATIONS OF FORM AND FUNCTIONS OF EXTRACURRICULAR ACTIVITIES

The discussions that have been grouped to form this section were written by six high-school pupils[1] who occupied positions of leadership in their school. The activities, it will be noted, represent important aspects of the extracurricular life of the school. The discussions by these pupils indicate the organization, functions, and values of these activities from the student's point of view.

The Homeroom
FRANCES ORR

The homerooms are the basic units of the University High School. Two Student Council representatives are elected from each homeroom, some school

---

[1] There has been a bit of editing with regard to the mechanics of expression but none to modify the ideas of the youngsters. All the pupils were students in the University High School, Ann Arbor, Mich. Perhaps you recognize one or two names, for all are now very effective citizens in adult life and several have achieved national recognition for competence in their fields. Obviously, no great amount of time should be spent on the remaining pages. Perhaps you will read them as you would articles in a magazine.

contests are between them, and every student belongs to one of them. As the students enter the school in the seventh grade, they are placed in a homeroom and given a teacher who "belongs" to them through both junior and senior high school. There are two homerooms for each grade: one for girls and one for boys. The groups are small—20 to 30 pupils.

To a very large extent the homerooms are managed by the students. The usual officers are in charge. They, in turn, appoint committees who work out home-

Here is a committee in an English class preparing a program for a school assembly. Looks as if this is a good situation for teaching good habits of work.

room projects. In my homeroom there have usually been scholarship and citizenship committees which study and discuss these subjects in detail. In addition, there are always committees on homeroom programs, assemblies, and special projects. The activities of the homeroom outside its own group consist of an annual assembly program for the entire school, occasional parties for other homerooms, and charity work. At present most homerooms prepare Christmas baskets for needy families under the direction of the local Family Welfare Bureau. One group is providing milk for the entire year for one family. Incidentally, we do not know and do not want to know the name of a family—we operate with a fictitious name—but the family is plenty real to us.

The activities which the students participate in during any one home-room period are varied. The schedule of an average week is: Monday, announcements and study or committee meetings; Tuesday, study for those not at Council or *Broadcaster* meeting; Wednesday, business meeting for Council report, project discussion, etc.; Thursday, study for senior-high-school groups and original programs for younger groups; and Friday, assembly.

By far the most important part of the homeroom system is the teacher. Because of her long and intimate contact with the students, she is able to give invaluable aid in matters relating to choice of a vocation and the solving of personal problems.

The homeroom, being a small group which carries on many activities, affords a fine opportunity for the development of leadership; it enables the individual, by working with other pupils of his own age, to become better acquainted with more people than he would if he saw them only in classes; and it gives the student an intimate adult adviser.

STUDENT GUIDES
STANLEY MOORE

Many schools have certain types of office work, more or less routine, which can be handled efficiently by trained student help. In the University High School there is an organization which handles just such duties. It is called, appropriately enough, the Student Guides.

The club has a limited membership of fifty, from grades nine to twelve. Under its officers, the president, vice-president, secretary, and a faculty adviser, the group holds its meetings every other week, discussing problems which arise, planning programs for future meetings, handling its elections, and taking care of new memberships.

Eligibility for membership in the Student Guides is determined by citizenship. A mark of "4" or "5" in citizenship disqualifies a guide for half a semester. While there is no scholarship requirement, the organization places a guide on the reserve or inactive list if his academic work is unsatisfactory, because the club feels that such a guide really needs the time for study rather than service.

The services performed by the Student Guides include the collection of absence slips each hour from every classroom, receiving telephone calls and delivering messages to pupils and teachers, running errands to the campus and elsewhere, operating the mimeograph machine, and similar duties. Nearly all visitors to the school are escorted through the building by a guide who explains the physical equipment, the activities, and the organization of the school. In brief we interpret the school to visitors. They seem to prefer a pupil's interpretation and certainly this experience gives us an overall picture that I would regret to have missed.

Each guide is available one hour a week, an hour which would otherwise be spent in the library, for service in the office or wherever he is needed. To reward good service, a system of pins was inaugurated recently. On admittance to the organization a guide is given a silver pin which is the possession of the school and is accepted as a loan for the school year. After three successive semesters of uninterrupted service the pin is exchanged for a gold one which is the permanent possession of the guide.

GIRLS' ATHLETIC ASSOCIATION
BETH O'ROKE

Extracurricular sports for girls in the University High School are directed by the Girls' Athletic Association, which is made up of all the girls who have participated in athletics. The Association has a directing board composed of four officers and a manager for each sport.

There are interclass tournaments for such team sports as baseball, and hockey, and instruction and meets for swimming, badminton, and similar sports. The girls are awarded points for engaging in these activities, and also for participation in sports not connected with the school. At the end of the year, junior and senior high school numerals and letters are awarded to the girls, according to the number of points they have earned.

The school calendar includes some combined athletic and social events. The Association's years open with a treasure hunt given by the G.A.A. board for the new girls in school. The fall season ends with a hockey spread, at which the losers of the tournament provide the entertainment. In spring the girls of the Huron League schools meet for a play day. The biggest event, the G.A.A. Circus, comes a few weeks later. The year ends with the annual picnic at the island, when the retiring officers are succeeded by those who have been elected for the next school year.

The girls' sports program in the University High is considered very successful. The plan of having one manager directly in charge of one sport avoids conflict of student authority; many types of activities are offered for girls of all abilities; instruction and practice, as well as games, are offered; most of the girls in school take a part in the G.A.A.; and they all enjoy it thoroughly.

Sports for Boys

PHILIP NEWMAN

Athletic sports at the University High School are divided into three programs; junior high school intramural, senior high school intramural, and senior high school interscholastic. These programs have different functions, involve different students, and have divergent purposes.

The junior high school intramural program involves speedball, basketball, and baseball. The program is directed by the athletic council, a body composed of a boy from each homeroom and a chairman. It is this group that is responsible for the schedule and its administration. Before the opening of the season for each sport, junior high school students sign up if they wish to participate. Captains are then chosen, and they, in turn, pick their teams.

The senior high school intramural program is organized on a different basis. The sports are touch football, basketball, and baseball. This program is also directed by the athletic council. The main difference is that the teams are class teams, one for each of the last three grades.

The senior high school interscholastic program is intended to provide specialized training in certain sports. The five sports now included in this program are basketball and swimming in the winter, and tennis, golf, and track in the spring. These teams are coached by the two members of the high school department of physical education and by student teachers.

From the students' point of view the main achievement of these programs is their provision of vigorous and enjoyable recreation. This is especially true in the intramural programs, where competition is less important than in the interscholastic events.

The Place of High-school Publications

STANLEY M. SWINTON

I am the editor-in-chief of a high-school newspaper. Our paper is similar to thousands of high-school newspapers, and, like them, it has a number of functions which could be accomplished through no other medium and which justify its existence.

First of all, *The Broadcaster* (which is the name of the paper) informs. It lets the student know what is going on and tells him what other homerooms, teams, and classes are planning and doing. Then, it informs the parents of what goes on in and about the University High School. Incidentally this is why we refuse to print a so-called "gossip column"; the average parent reads the high-school paper thoroughly, and gossipy references to his child can cause endless complications and embarrassments.

Other groups informed by the high-school paper include the alumni, other schools—for we exchange papers with some eighty-odd institutions—and the various people who are interested in education and have had themselves put on the mailing list. Also, in our case, the paper is used by students in the School of Education of the University of Michigan.

The second function of *The Broadcaster* is to give practical training in journalism. There are approximately fifteen active members of the staff. These fifteen, under the supervision of the editors, write their stories, work on rewrites, correct galley proofs, write heads, and help make up the paper. As far as possible we have students perform these tasks in the same way as they would be done on regular daily or weekly newspapers. Besides this technical knowledge the reporters get experience in dealing with people.

Another, although slightly less important point, is the way in which the high-school newspaper helps to influence public opinion. The value of the paper in this respect, however, must not be overestimated, for the editorials constitute one of the least read sections of any paper; and since the average high-school student is gripped by a mighty urge to appear sophisticated, his pseudo-sophistication makes it difficult to point or change an opinion.

A fourth purpose of the newspaper is to furnish a record. The only complete history of the school is to be found in the files of the newspaper.

Other publications which our school supports are the school annual, *Nunc Dimittis;* an annual literary publication, *Pegasus;* and a handbook which explains the customs and rules of the school to new students and to visitors.

Most important, however, among the University High School publications, is our newspaper; for it informs, points public opinion, furnishes a record, and gives practical journalistic training.

The Value of a Student Council

GEORGE W. DANA

In a conversation several weeks ago, a teacher from a school where there is no student council told me he felt that any such council would be influenced, even overruled, by the faculty. He wondered, therefore, what advantage there might be in having one. Having gone to University High School for six years and having taken the Student Council quite for granted, I was aroused by his comments. After giving the criticism some thought I was by no means ready to agree with that teacher, and I even felt that his objection could be neglected in determining the value of a council. The value does not lie in what the council can do for the school—the school would undoubtedly run fully as well without us—but in what the council can do for the students.

In working with the council and in having an opportunity to voice their opinions on school matters the students gain not only an awareness of school problems, but also the ability to express themselves—something all modern schools are trying to give them. The representatives to the council learn to accept responsibility in carrying matters from the council to their homerooms and from their homerooms to the council and from the council on occasion to the faculty and to the assembly of the whole school.

As in any modern organization that participates in policy making, the greatest part of the council's work is done through its committees. We have the following committees: assembly, social, safety and building and grounds, bulletin board, eligibility, and lost and found. The names of these committees indicate their functions. The assembly committee must arrange programs which will satisfy junior and senior high school students and the faculty; the social committee has charge of planning an adequate social program for the school; the safety and building and grounds committee organizes and carries out monthly fire drills, and in the past has solved the problem of traffic congestion in front of the school by arranging with the police to have the school block open only for one-way traffic at the close of each half-day when parents are driving past to get their children. In this work it is to the students that the council gives its greatest benefit, by giving them the chance to work together and to cooperate with people outside the school in solving their problems and in carrying out their duties.

For Discussion

1. What are the purposes of the home-room organization?

2. What changes would you like to see made in the extracurricular offering of the high school that you know best?

3. If you had to plan your own high-school days, what change would you make with regard to your participation in extracurricular activities? For this question it may be worth while for a committee to interpret the responses obtained for the whole class.

4. Assume that you had been assigned, without previous experience, to one of the following responsibilities: home-room adviser, chairman of the pupil-teacher assembly committee, auditor of the bookkeeping phases of extracurricular organizations, adviser to the senior class, dean of girls, chairman of the testing committee, adviser to student guides, adviser to publications. What steps tending to increase the value of your services could you take?

5. One writer labeled the assembly the "town hall" of the school. What do you think he meant by that?

6. Some student teachers, having consulted the suggested readings at the end of this chapter, prepared a list of different types of activities that are commonly found in our high schools. Each then selected one activity and prepared a brief manual of practical suggestions to aid a teacher who might be assigned without experience to the supervision of that activity. Finally, they appointed an editorial committee and arranged to finance the mimeographing of copies of the composite report. This exercise should not be undertaken by a class unless it has the disposition to devote a good deal of time and effort to the projects.

7. As you read the two problems that follow, determine the basic principles of organization and supervision that were missing in each case.

Problem A

Superintendent Brown dropped into Principal Newcomer's office and engaged him in general conversation. During the course of the conversation, Mr. Brown asked Mr. Newcomer how his program was coming out financially.

"Rotten," replied Mr. Newcomer. "The publications staff will have a debt of $600 to carry over to the next year."

"Why, what's the trouble?" asked Mr. Brown.

"Well, some of the money was stolen from the manager's desk; two sponsors insisted in keeping their activity funds in the bank as separate accounts; and there was no definite system of bookkeeping on the part of the staff. When the manager received a telegram that he had been elected to teach in college next year, he left the staff with all the responsibility; so now, no one knows just how we stand, or anything much about it."

   a. Who should be held responsible for this state of financial embarrassment?
   b. What action would you suggest to Principal Newcomer as a possible solution to the problem?
   c. What system of financial administration and bookkeeping would you suggest?

Problem B

Teacher A confided in Miss B, a colleague, that her work with the French Club was not moving so smoothly as she would like. In fact, some of the members had rebelled against paying an assessment of 75 cents, which she had set as a membership fee. Miss A said that of course they must pay it, because there was no way of resigning from the club once a pupil had joined.

There was trouble too, with some of the members because their parents thought there was too much foolishness going on in the club. Pupils were refusing to serve on the program, and many were not satisfied with the meetings because the officers Miss A had appointed were called the teacher's pets.

   a. Just what was wrong with Miss A's French Club?
   b. What method of fixing membership fees would you suggest?
   c. How would you proceed to convince parents that an extracurricular activity is worth while?

SUGGESTED READING

BELL, HOWARD M.: *Youth Tell Their Story.* Washington: American Council on Education, 1938. Pp. 273.

This is a book that emerged from a survey made under the direction of the American Youth Commission. The picture of the plight of youth is painted in vivid and graphic fashion. Many laymen have read this volume; the well-read teacher cannot afford to miss it. Among the urgent social problems which the report throws into sharp relief are the necessity of equalized educational opportunity; the need for finding employment for youth when they emerge from school; the recognition of youth that economic security is their most urgent personal need; the importance of giving more attention to guidance; the lack of appropriate and adequate vocational training; and the need for community planning for youth.

Bulletin of the National Association of Secondary-school Principals: "The Student Council in the Secondary School," October, 1944; "The Assembly Program in the Secondary School," November, 1946; "Camping and Outdoor Education," May, 1947; Curriculum Trends in the Secondary School," November, 1948.

EDMONSON, J. B., JOSEPH ROEMER, and FRANCIS L. BACON: *The Administration of the Modern Secondary School.* New York: The Macmillan Company, 1948. Pp. xi + 690.

A book with lots of common sense; better take a look at Chap. XVI.

FRETWELL, ELBERT K.: *Extra-Curricular Activities in Secondary Schools.* Boston: Houghton Mifflin Company, 1931. Pp. xix.+ 552.

A comprehensive discussion of the whole field of extracurricular activities: the home room, class organizations, student council, the assembly, clubs, student publications, athletics, finances, and commencement. This book is old, but it was a pioneer volume by a grand teacher. Much of that which is fine in extracurricular programs today stems from Fretwell's vision.

McKOWN, HARRY C.: *The Student Council.* New York: McGraw-Hill Book Company, Inc., 1944. Pp. 352.

This is a helpful book by one of the constructive thinkers in this field.

National Association of Student Councils: *The 1948 Student Council Handbook.* Washington: National Education Association, 1948. Pp. 144.

This handbook is sponsored by the National Association of Secondary-school Principals.

School Activities. The national extracurricular magazine. Published monthly (September–May) by School Activities Publishing Company, 1515 Lane Street, Topeka, Kan.

Although no specific reference is cited, the magazine will be found helpful to the sponsor of activities and the home-room teacher. In addition to the usual discussion of general problems in extracurricular activities, assembly programs, plays, and special occasion activities are included in the various issues during the year.

SPEARS, HAROLD: *The Emerging High-school Curriculum and Its Direction.* New York: American Book Company, 1948. Pp. xii + 416.

The author is an alert worker in the secondary field. The book is a revision of an earlier edition and deals with problems and experiences in curriculum reorganization. Chapter VIII, "Growing the Curriculum out of the Extracurriculum," is one that student teachers should read; and Chap. VI, "The Problem of the Small High School," will interest many a beginning teacher on his first job.

SPEARS, HAROLD, and C. H. LAWSHE: *High School Journalism.* New York: The Macmillan Company, 1939. Pp. xvi + 464.

Here is a document you will need if and when you are given responsibility for publications.

The Extracurricular Library.   New York: A. S. Barnes & Company.

This library consists of a set of handbooks, each devoted to a consideration of some phase of the activity program. The titles are indicative of the areas in which the individual teacher may be particularly interested.

BORGESON, F. C.: *Elementary School Life Activities.*
COLLINS and CHARLTON: *Puppet Plays in Education.*
DRAPER and CORBALLY: *Extracurricular Credits.*
DRAPER and SMITH: *Intramural Athletics and Play Days.*
EVANS and HALLMAN: *Home Rooms: Organization, Administration, and Activities.*
JOHNSTON, E. G.: *Point Systems and Awards.*
JONES, GERTRUDE: *Commencement.*
LeCOMPTE, PEARL: *Dramatics.*
MACDONALD, MARGARET: *The Class Organization and Activities.*
MEYER, H.: *The School Club Program.*
MEYER, HAROLD D., and S. M. EDDLEMAN: *Financing Extracurricular Activities.*
MURPHY, CAROBEL: *Thrift through Education.*
POUND, OLIVA: *Extracurricular Activities of High School Girls.*
POWERS, FRANCIS: *Character Training.*
STEVENSON, IDABELLE: *Safety Education.*
VINEYARD and POOLE: *Student Participation in Government.*
WAGNER, M. CHANNING: *Assembly Programs.*
WELLS and McCALISTER: *Student Publications.*

Chapter XIII

The Broader Concept of Appraisal

Greeting his pupils, the master asked:

What would you learn of me?

And the reply came:

How shall we care for our bodies?
How shall we rear our children?
How shall we work together?
How shall we live with our fellowmen?
How shall we play?
For what ends shall we live? . . .

And the teacher pondered these words, and sorrow was in his heart, for his own learning touched not these things.

—CHAPMAN AND COUNTS[1]

The baseball pitcher who in the midst of a great series of games asked his folks over the radio, "How'm I doing?" stated a fundamental problem. In all types of work we have to measure the product. The automobile factory has a proving ground as a laboratory in which rigid tests of many qualities, such as efficiency, are applied. An alert and conscientious teacher will continuously appraise the progress of his pupils, the efficiency of his own instruction, and the effectiveness of his school.

The task of appraisal in the classroom is obviously more complex, for many factors affect pupil growth. In the secondary school of an earlier day about the only instrument available for measuring the achievement of pupils was the formal examination. Recently, school people have been intrigued by the many significant contributions of standardized tests; *e.g.*, achievement in some of the basic skills, such as reading and arithmetic, can now be measured with great objectivity and high reliability. Indeed, a teacher in the

---

[1] J. CROSBY CHAPMAN and GEORGE S. COUNTS. *Principles of Education*, p. ii, Boston: Houghton Mifflin Company, 1924.

One of the new things that has come into the concept of appraisal is that the student has a part. Here we show a student who has written a story for the school paper, and she is being guided to an appraisal of it before she submits the story.[E]

modern school who does not make use of some of the new testing techniques available as side lights on the problem of instruction is either poorly trained or badly misguided.

There are, however, good reasons for believing that we are entering a new phase of appraisal in which a much broader concept will challenge the efforts of teachers. What are the main ideas in this new concept of the appraisal of the instructional efficiency of a teacher?

1. Of major importance is the notion that the pupil will have a part and that his appraisal will be done in terms of goals that to him are desirable, definite, immediate, and attainable.

2. The new idea of evaluation is more comprehensive, for by it we try to measure some things that are more significant than the pupil's control of items of information. We try to get evidence on the heretofore intangible outcomes. Then, too, we are more concerned that the pupil shall understand something he has learned than that he remember it. We emphasize understandings and appreciations. In instruction we are likely to hear often such cue words as "why," "how," "interpret," "apply," and "explain." We

try to get evidence on behavior that is socially significant. We go beyond standardized tests and essay examinations in appraisal, and we recognize the inadequacies and weaknesses in traditional marking systems.

3. We seek to evaluate what the pupil does in terms of goals that are appropriate to his abilities and interests. We try to take more things into account. In particular, we are concerned about social and personal goals. This implies that the teacher must know more about the pupil, his home and community background, his physical and mental health, his educational experiences, his emotional development, his level of skills, and his intellectual maturity. We want new instruments which will define the goals more clearly and which will identify desirable changes in behavior. In brief, we try to measure growth. As you would infer, we are more reluctant to use measuring devices without considering their probable effect on the pupil being tested.

4. The discerning workers in schools recognize the importance of greater specificity in the statement of teacher objectives. The traditional classification of the aims of a high-school subject as practical, disciplinary, and cultural is, although valid, so inadequate as to be meaningless as a guide to the teacher in the selection of materials. A list of specific items which the pupil is expected to understand and to be able to do at a high level of mastery is of great value alike to pupil, parent, and teacher.

5. We have some excellent standardized tests. To be sure, those in wide use in general are tests that measure skills. However, they measure improvement in skills that are of fundamental importance.

6. We recognize that appraisal is a continuous process. Measurement is not something that we can accomplish by a spot survey of a class, a school, or a city. We need to investigate changes in pupils over a longer period of years by reexamination of the same children. The significance of a change is determined largely by the pupil's capacity and the level at which he is operating. For this reason we interpret test scores in the light of analyses of descriptions of the pupil based on recorded observations of behavior in a great variety of situations.

We turn now to a consideration of some of the procedures involved in this more comprehensive notion of appraisal.

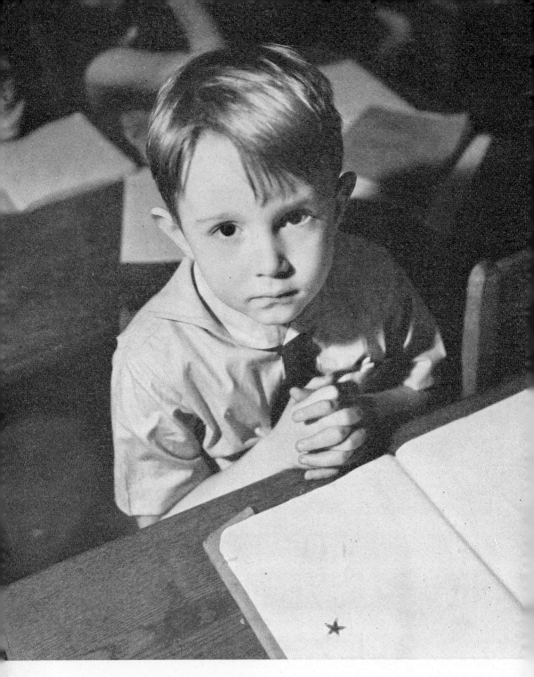

Why do you think thousands of teachers have chosen this picture as their favorite? What does this fact imply about teachers?[N]

PUPIL SELF-APPRAISAL

The sample form of a Report on Progress on page 320 represents the cooperative effort of a teacher and his pupils. Before the appraisal form is marked by the teacher it is used as a basis for classroom instruction, during which each of the goals is interpreted. In the discussion the pupil may suggest a simpler definition or may even cause a goal to be rejected or added. The pupil is then given an opportunity to appraise his own growth by checking the appropriate column in the space at the right of each goal.

Appraisal of pupil growth is next undertaken by the teacher, who bases his judgment on test scores, general classwork, observations of pupil behavior, and analyses of notebooks, themes, projects, etc.

If there is a wide gap between the pupil's appraisal and that of the teacher, a conference between pupil and teacher is in order, with the purpose of bringing their two ratings closer to a valid measurement. Such a conference may reveal that the teacher has misinterpreted some of the reactions of the pupil, or the pupil may discover that he has failed to understand what is involved in one or more of the goals.

What are the advantages in the use of this method of appraising pupil growth in the school? (1) It is a descriptive report that is more meaningful to a pupil. Instead of reporting "poor" or "excellent" for so broad an area as English, social studies, or the like, it shows more nearly the pupil's status in terms of the important skills, attitudes, and knowledges that are essential goals of each subject area. (2) It undoubtedly serves as one of the most convenient methods for acquainting pupils with the aims in subject-matter areas. (3) It makes appraisal more objective by focusing attention on specific items. (4) The goals motivate pupils in their efforts to attain them because they are definite and understandable. (5) The report stimulates pupils to be critical of their own progress and provides experiences in self-appraisal. (6) It contains space for teacher comments; .e.g., suggestions for improving work, etc. In short, it is a step in the direction of a constructive, descriptive, and diagnostic appraisal of pupil progress.

MORE SPECIFIC TEACHER AIMS

Did you ever take a course in high school or college without ever knowing its *specific* objectives? Unless you had a good textbook and

MATHEMATICS DEPARTMENT—REPORT ON PROGRESS

Grade..............   Name........................

                        Date.................   Date....................

Mathematics goals	Pupil's estimate				Teacher's estimate			
	Needs atten- tion	Nor- mal	Good	Ex- cel- lent	Needs atten- tion	Nor- mal	Good	Ex- cel- lent
Growth in:								
1. Control of basic skills..........								
2. Understanding of fundamental ideas......................								
3. Ability to apply fundamental principles...................								
4. Ability to solve problems.......								
5. Understanding of necessary vocabulary..................								
6. Understanding the idea of rela- tionship....................								
7. Ability to express himself mathe- matically...................								
8. General power and mathe- matical experience.............								
9. Ability to read..............								
10. Ability to generalize..........								
Social goals								
Growth in:								
1. Ability to follow directions.....								
2. Sustained attention...........								
3. Cooperation................								
4. Individual responsibility.......								
5. Accuracy of results...........								
6. Precision of statement........								
7. Systematic procedures........								
8. Ability to work independently...								
9. Critical attitude toward reason- ableness of results............								
10. Openmindedness—delayed judg- ment.....................								
11. Resourcefulness—ingenuity, inventiveness...............								
12. Impersonal attitude toward criticism...................								

Comments:

                        Teacher's Signature......................

                        Parent's Signature......................

a competent teacher, you probably found it very annoying. In many classes pupils are not aware of specific goals. They are likely to have the frustrated feeling that they are being taken on a "snipe hunting" expedition. Some parents, too, would like to be let in on the secret. To be sure, if the teacher commands the confidence of his students, the general attitude is, "Teacher knows where we are

Information and skills that are needed in a school activity are more likely to be understood and to be remembered.[D]

going and it must be all right." However, too often the teacher— new to the job, struggling with a fat book, and lacking any course of study or supervision—does *not know* the specific objectives. Surely someone in a classroom should know where they are going! Ideally the students in every course should have a list of *specific* objectives.

A definite goal toward which to work not only stimulates growth, but in addition makes measurement of the amount of progress toward that goal easier, more exact, and more meaningful. "To save money" is, to be sure, a goal, but at best it is an indefinite one for which measurement would be difficult. By changing the statement to read "To save $50," the goal becomes tangible and exact measurement of progress is possible. Moreover, other things being equal, the activity is more challenging because it is now directed toward a specific end.

On the opposite page, we provide a sample list of *specific* objectives for a course in mathematics for the seventh school year. Just as an aerial photograph reveals the important features of a landscape and their relationship to each other, a list of specific objectives provides a perspective for basic concepts and fundamental principles. Fortunately, an increasing number of lists of specific goals for teachers of the secondary-school subjects are appearing in pedagogical literature. Of course you will find different patterns. It is, however, fairly common to classify specific objectives under the headings: (1) information, (2) skills, and (3) attitudes. The outline for mathematics is a slight modification of this and uses the headings: (1) vocabulary, (2) skills, (3) principles, (4) formulas, (5) concepts, and (6) attitudes. In this illustration we do two things: (1) we show a few items under each heading and (2) we suggest the total list under each heading.

By glancing at the following list we see that the specific objectives of a year of mathematics consist of about 120 new words, 40 skills, 24 principles, 11 formulas, and 12 attitudes—a total of 227 goals. Perhaps such a list seems formidable to you. However, many of these ideas have been developed partially in earlier grades and are listed in order that they may be strengthened. A list of specific objectives for almost any high-school course could be written on one or two pages and would certainly not look as ominous as a thick textbook.

Some of the useful purposes of a list of specific goals for the teacher are:

1. *To Provide a Way for the Teacher to Keep a Course Up to Date.* The construction of such a list will force him to reconsider values and cause him to have a much broader view of the place of subject matter in the modern school. Even if he does not have the time and energy to build such a list from the ground up, he can take the best list of specific goals he can find in professional literature and adapt it to the needs of his own class and his own community.

2. *To "Let the Pupil In on the Secret."* In any case the pupil will find the list helpful as a device for summary and review. As has already been suggested, some parents will find it gratifying to learn that the fundamental principles, basic concepts, and new words to be learned in a whole year of instruction in a course are actually few in number.

An Outline of Essentials in Seventh-grade Mathematics (Excerpts)

A Guide to Pupils, Parents, and Teachers

VOCABULARY*

Be Able to Illustrate Each

FIRST SEMESTER	SECOND SEMESTER
Amount of turning	Accounts
Angle	budget
acute	cash
obtuse	checking
opposite	expense
right	savings
straight	Altitude
Approximate	Amount
Average	

*About 60 words each semester.

PRINCIPLES*

Be Able to State and Illustrate Each

FIRST SEMESTER

1. Graphs may be used to picture numbers.

2. The ratio of one number to another means the one number divided by the other.

3. "Per cent of" means "hundredths times."

4. To find an answer to the nearest tenth, carry the answer to hundredths, then express the number of tenths to which it is nearest.

SECOND SEMESTER

1. Interest is equal to the principal times the rate times the time.

2. In computing interest on notes, banks use 360 days to a year and 30 days to every month.

3. The number of square units in any surface is the area of that surface.

4. The area of a rectangle, a square, or a parallelogram is equal to the base times the height.

*About 12 principles each semester.

FORMULAS*

Understand and Be Able to Use

FIRST SEMESTER

1. $x + y + z = 180°$

SECOND SEMESTER

1. $i = prt$
2. $A = bh$
3. $A = s^2$

*Only one the first semester and ten for the second.

ATTITUDES*

Strive For

FIRST SEMESTER

1. Accuracy.
2. Neatness.
3. A disposition to be systematic in keeping records and accounts.

SECOND SEMESTER

1. Appreciation of geometry in nature, architecture, and art.
2. Precision in statement.
3. An attitude of inquiry —"getting at the bottom of things."
4. Annoyance with vagueness and incompleteness.

*About 6 each semester but all 12 get some emphasis throughout the year.

SKILLS*

Be Able to

FIRST SEMESTER

1. Use a table to find desired information.
2. Interpret graphs.
3. Make a neat, accurate bar graph and line graph.
4. Find the ratio of one number to another.
5. Recognize equal ratios.
6. Supply the missing part of a ratio when an equal ratio is given.

SECOND SEMESTER

1. Substitute given values in a formula and compute the result.
2. Find the interest when the principal, rate, and time are given.
3. Fill out a check.
4. Indorse a check.
5. Read and interpret promissory notes.
6. Balance simple cash accounts.

*About 20 each semester.

CONCEPTS*

Give at Least Three Illustrations

FIRST SEMESTER

1. Ratio
2. Average
3. Angle

SECOND SEMESTER

1. Area
2. Bisecting
3. Formula

*About 10 each semester.

3. *To Orient a Beginning Teacher.* Indeed, it would seem to be the obligation of the school, when assigning a subject to a teacher without preparation or with meager preparation, to provide him with a blueprint outlining the objectives to be achieved rather than the pages of a book to be covered.

4. *To Serve as a Check List.* As will appear in the following paragraph, the pupil needs such a list to protect him from the danger of serious gaps in his basic training in a given field.

The Danger of Gaps. Schools that undertake to experiment with a "core-curriculum" discover very quickly that pupils tend to raise questions, undertake projects, and engage in activities stemming from subject-matter areas in which the teachers are deeply interested and well prepared. For example, if a group of children is assigned to three teachers, one of them trained in the social studies, the second in instrumental music, and the third in science, nearly all of the really worth-while activities that the children will undertake and execute with a driving zeal will relate to social studies, music, and science, and there will almost inevitably be a dearth of experiences in the other significant areas of the curriculum. Even in an experimental situation the basic preparation of a teacher largely determines the curriculum.

Further evidence on the high probability of devastating gaps in the education of pupils is provided by the widespread lack of adequate training in fine arts in American schools. No doubt the chief reason for this deficiency is that our teachers have not had adequate training in this field. A competent teacher, aware of the danger of leaving gaps with regard to fundamental principles and concepts, will wish to escape vagueness in the minds of pupils by keeping constantly before them the definite things he wishes to accomplish in a given semester or year.

A final question arises: Does a list of specific objectives make for rigidity in the curriculum? The fact that it is definite does not necessarily imply less flexibility. In fact, we are more likely to change something when we know what it is we can change. In any case a really good teacher will think of the outline as a general guide —a servant rather than a master.

MARKS AND REPORT CARDS

What can be done to improve methods of recording for the school office or for reporting to the parents a summary of pupil growth? In a school employing conventional marks, a pupil is given a report card containing a list of subjects, each followed by a per cent, number, or letter. Thus Bill's report card might read as follows: English, 92; Geometry, 64; American History, 76, etc. In a different school, Bill's report card might contain *A, B, C, D,* or *E,* in place of the per cent scores.

Just how is this appraisal of Bill's progress to be interpreted? A closer examination of the report would probably reveal an explana-

While it is wise for you to hold to a considered program of diversions, your work itself may provide that which will keep you young. Here, for example, is an idealistic youth working on a project that for him has abiding values.[N]

tion to the effect that *A* equals excellent or that 64 represents poor work; but is this summary meaningful? Does it reveal the basis on which Bill was appraised? Does it interpret progress by indicating what he should strive for? Is there even the slightest indication as to *why* he has failed in geometry? In short, is it an objective and constructive appraisal of Bill's growth and development in the school? To answer such a question, one must inquire, "Pupil growth in what?" Obviously in English, geometry, etc. But is even this a satisfactory statement? Actually, it is an evasion of the real problem; for, after all, are we not concerned primarily with the pupil's growth in knowledge, skills, attitudes, and patterns of conduct?

Yet no mention of these items appears on the pupil's report. Instead, we are told that Bill is "poor" in geometry. Consider the feeling of futility of a patient upon visiting the doctor, if he were told simply, "Your health is poor." Fortunately, the medical profession has devised more nearly perfect instruments for diagnosing the complexities of the human organism. Likewise, one of our important tasks in teaching is to devise more nearly perfect instruments and techniques for diagnosing and summarizing the status of pupils in terms of growth in knowledge, skills, attitudes, and social behavior.

An Indictment of Report Cards. There prevails a consensus of opinion that the traditional report card has failed to keep step with the more progressive changes in education and, more specifically, that we have underestimated the importance of the report card as an interpreter of the school. The main deficiencies may be listed as follows:

1. *The pupil tends to work for marks.* If he accepts these as his real goals his work will not rise above superficial scholarship.

2. *Marks are injurious to the mental health of the pupil.* They promote unwholesome competition in the classroom resulting in antisocial qualities; *e.g.*, selfishness. There is also the danger of superiority and inferiority complexes, to say nothing of defense mechanisms and the general mental strain caused by fear of low marks. Then, too, we should be concerned by what happens to the mental health of a pupil when we insist on standards of workmanship which for him may be unattainable.

3. *Marks fail to encourage the very desirable habit of self-analysis.* They cannot readily be used for diagnosis. A general average of numerous items obscures many things which a parent would like to know and which the pupil should know. The typical report card for the secondary school has little to say about such fundamental matters as study habits and social traits.

4. *Letters and numbers fail to picture all the aspects of pupil development.* In particular, marks do not reveal to the parent or the pupil the goals of general education or the specific objectives of the subject.

5. *Conventional marks lack reliability and validity.* It must be admitted, however, that, contrary to general opinion, the ability of a teacher to take a series of papers and rank them in order of merit with respect to the goals the teacher has in mind is highly reliable. Traditional marks are too often based on an inadequate sampling of a pupil's work, and the personality of the pupil may color the marks awarded.

6. *Conventional marks are too inflexible to be readily adapted to the general character of our high-school population.* The shift from a homogeneous body to a

heterogeneous one has placed a strain on the marking system which now clearly reveals its many weaknesses.

The Specifications of a Good Report Card.   The new techniques of appraisal may be illustrated by studying a report card in the light of the following specifications.   Conventional marks and the method of reporting to parents cannot function properly in the progressive, democratic school until revised in such a manner that they will

1. Place equal emphasis on the mental, social, and physical development of children.
2. Eliminate comparison of the individual pupil with the achievement of the other pupils in the class.
3. Indicate the aims of the school and the general objectives of education.
4. Report the achievement of the pupils in relation to the specific aims of each subject.
5. Diagnose the pupil's difficulties, and follow with suggestions for improvement.
6. Provide for pupil self-analysis.
7. Consist of a personalized message to pupil and parent.
8. Indicate the relation of the pupil's present status in terms of requirements for graduation.
9. Provide supplementary notices to parents of failing or unsatisfactory work.
10. Be attractive in composition, appearance of printing, and quality of paper.

A Note of Warning.   The preceding set of criteria is highly idealistic.   There are very few school systems that employ the type of report card suggested here, though fortunately many schools are moving in that direction.   It is significant to note the increasing number of schools that have undertaken to substitute an appraisal letter to the pupil or a conference with the parent for the traditional report card.   Unfortunately, in most cases these are quickly abandoned when the schools discover that they have inadequate clerical service.   What really happens is that too many schools are abandoning marks altogether, thus failing to recognize that "more marks" are needed when traditional marks are discarded.   Presumably a poor report card is better than none.   The solution for the problem of finding an adequate substitute for the traditional marks and the report card is not an easy one, and certainly not one that will be quickly provided.

Above all, the beginning teacher must be realistic about marks and report cards.   It is not your responsibility to reform the marking system of a school before you are emotionally adjusted to it and the new community. Rather, it is your job to do the best you can with the existing system without expressing or even implying excessive criticism, thus biding your time to the day when your feet will be on more solid ground and when you can undertake to work cooperatively, perhaps in your second year of service, with other members of the faculty for constructive reforms. The real danger is that in the end you will do nothing about it!

STANDARDIZED TESTS

The construction of standardized tests is one of the most important contributions to education. The well-informed teacher knows that today there are available excellent standardized tests for measuring the abilities that are of fundamental importance in the development of a pupil. Reading, computation, sight, hearing, penmanship, and spelling can be measured with high or at least satisfactory degrees of precision; in the high school there are also some highly useful tests in various subjects; *e.g.*, those in algebra and functional competence in mathematics for better living.

School people have not been very discerning in their attitudes toward standardized tests. In the early days many teachers were exceedingly gullible and seized avidly numerous hastily developed tests that frequently had been designed by untrained workers in graduate courses. Millions of tests were given to children and were often scored and filed away without being used for instructional purposes. Then, too, broad interpretations that competent designers of tests never intended were made of the findings. Although one can find, even today, high schools where teachers have been so cautious as never to use a standardized test, in the first decade of the standardized-test movement teachers in general were not sufficiently critical of the validity of them.

Recently the pendulum has swung in the opposite extreme and today many alert teachers are excessively critical of standardized tests. One can find schools with competent faculties whose principals forbid their use. The moment the limitations of many standardized tests were pointed out, some teachers jumped to the conclusion that all tests were undesirable, forgetting altogether that the value of a movement must be judged by its best product rather than by its worst.

The intelligence test especially is under fire today. Competent workers have always known that an intelligence quotient, even if carefully determined and predicting with amazing precision how well the pupil will do the academic tasks of schools with their present emphasis on symbolism and verbalism, does not in fact predict how well this pupil will do all the infinite tasks of life that lie outside the academic world. When this fact was suddenly thrust on teachers, they seemed to lose perspective with regard to the legitimate use of such rests.

But there is another reason why teachers are losing faith in intelligence tests. One group of research workers has taken the children of dull parents, placed them in highly desirable environments, and presto! the children have high I.Q.'s; and it turns out that the dull parents have bright children. With regard to these startling research findings, the cautious teacher will demand much additional evidence, for, as Terman[1] is reported to have pointed out, if the implication is true that dull children can be made bright merely by taking them away from their parents and placing them in ideal homes, it would be the most important discovery in and contribution to education in a thousand years. The fact remains that if, through careful administration of several widely used intelligence tests to seventh-grade pupils, we determine that Dora's intelligence quotient is 80 and Bill's is 140, we can predict with high precision the academic record that each of these pupils will make during the next six years of schooling in any one of at least 90 per cent of our junior and senior high schools as they are now organized. The implication is that an intelligence test, if sensibly used by the teacher, beyond question will provide helpful side lights, and that the intelligence quotient is merely one of many important facts that a teacher should know about a pupil to narrow the areas of guessing. The word "sensibly" in the preceding sentence implies that information about the intelligence quotient should not be given to pupils or allowed to seep home to parents, for the good reason that neither pupils nor parents are able to see this lone factor in its true perspective.

A similar case, though obviously not quite so strong, can be made for the use of the better type of achievement test. In spite of the extreme reactions to various standardized tests in some quarters, the wisdom of using or constructing tests dealing with specific skills

[1] *School and Society*, L (July 29, 1939), 135.

seems undebatable. It is obviously unintelligent for a teacher to struggle blindly with a pupil who exhibits special disabilities in computation and reading when tests are available that might yield illuminating information on his difficulties. There is good reason for believing that the unfavorable reactions to all types of standardized tests is transitory, and that presently teachers will come to accept as legitimate the use of tests for instructional purposes. On this assumption you can take the following practical steps:

1. If there is a testing bureau or an exhibit of tests conveniently located, examine carefully several tests in each of these fields: intelligence, general achievement, reading, and computation.

2. Also examine critically one or more standardized tests in your major and minor fields.

3. Examine one or more good manuals that accompany standardized tests.

4. If a standardized test is given at any time while you are a student teacher, participate in administering it, in scoring it, and most important of all, in interpreting the findings.

In the last step you should try to answer such questions as these: What does the test measure? What does the test show about the class considered as a group? What do the pupils' responses to various elements of the test mean? What facts of value did I learn about the individual pupil? What can the teacher do as the result of the information gained from the test to aid in the growth of the individual pupil and to improve instruction for the group?

To guide your future work with standardized tests we now direct your attention to the following facts relating to standardized and informal tests:

1. *Many teachers have been critical of the traditional or essay type of examination.* The chief deficiencies are that (*a*) it involves too much writing and not enough thinking, (*b*) the sampling of a unit is so limited that the pupil's ability is not measured, and (*c*) it has been shown that the scores of an essay examination are not sufficiently objective to make for high reliability.

2. *Examinations, especially of the older type, are usually not popular with teachers.* Some of the reasons are that (*a*) examinations encourage the cramming of facts rather than a broad understanding of basic principles, (*b*) when semester or term marks depend largely on formal examinations, there is at once a premium on dishonesty, and (*c*) the marking of examinations tends to be injurious to a

teacher's health.   It is easy to see that what 150 pupils may write on even a 10-minute test will require much time and energy of the teacher.

3. *To correct some of the defects of the traditional type of examination, workers have developed the standard test and the informal test.* These employ the newer procedures such as matching, multiple response, rearrangement, computation, construction, identification, correction of errors, deduction of conclusions from given facts, translation, true-false, and completion.   Some widely used standardized tests are designed so that they can be machine scored; they are multiple response—usually—with five choices.

In general, tests are classified as (*a*) the old or essay type, and (*b*) the new, including both teacher-made and standardized types. The standardized test refers to carefully devised tests for which norms of achievement have been obtained.   It takes a great deal of time, energy, and thought to construct a worth-while standardized test; and obviously this is not the responsibility of a teacher with a heavy load.

4. *The functions of examinations have been enlarged.*   The old form of examination had a stimulus value ("stimulus" being derived from a Latin word meaning "ox goad"), since a teacher who felt himself slipping could always bring the woolgatherers back to attention by the threat of an examination.   The old form of test, commonly referred to as the "essay type," gave training in the use of the English language and practice in organizing material to bear on a specific discussion.   Standardized tests are used not only to measure achievement but also to suggest standards of accomplishment.   A teacher may, and probably should, use examinations to reach all of the following aims: (*a*) to discover how much a pupil knows at the beginning of a unit, (*b*) to provide a highly motivated drill and a basis for remedial and corrective work during the instructional period, and (*c*) to discover the extent of an individual pupil's achievement at the end of the unit.   They may also be used to reveal the necessity for reteaching to some pupils.

5. *Tests are often classified as survey, diagnostic, and instructional.*   These terms are often recklessly used.   In general, a survey is a rough measuring instrument which reveals what a pupil does with reference to norms on rather large unit skills, but does not show in what details he is weak.   A diagnostic test shows the nature and

character of a pupil's weaknesses. An instructional test, as the term implies, is any test that is given to the pupil with the main purpose of teaching him some specific items.

6. *The chief value of a test, aside from instructional purposes, is in the diagnosis of a pupil's work to discover the errors that are made.* Too many tests are administered, scored, and filed away. A careful study of test results should reveal type errors and should suggest what teaching needs to be done and which of the pupils can profit by special teaching.

7. *The phrase "nonstandardized" or informal test usually refers to a test constructed by the teacher in which the newer testing techniques are employed.* The most popular type perhaps is the true-false test which is often avidly seized by teachers when they first become interested in standardized tests. It is easily constructed, administered, and scored, and children usually are interested. However, a true-false test, while it may have value for instructional purposes, is a weak instrument for measurement and practically worthless in interpreting the meaning of an individual pupil's response, for it involves guessing.

8. *The teacher should have a set of criteria for selecting a few tests for use and study from the many available.* Among the items that need to be considered in determining the value of a test are (*a*) validity, (*b*) reliability, (*c*) objectivity, (*d*) ease of administration and scoring, (*e*) the existence of norms or standards for the evaluation of results, and (*f*) the availability of equivalent or duplicate forms.

Validity refers to the goodness or general merit of a test. The technical definition is "the degree to which a test or examination measures what it is intended to measure."

Reliability refers to the uniformity with which a test measures. A better term is "consistency." The technical definition is "the degree to which a test measures whatever it does measure." Reliability refers to the degree of correlation existing between the scores made by the same pupils of the same class on Form A and Form B, when both forms have been given within a short interval of time. More simply, the degree of reliability answers this question: To what extent is the picture of the class which we get today by giving Form A like the picture which we shall obtain by giving Form B tomorrow?

Reliability is expressed in terms of the coefficient of correlation which, for this use, is called the "coefficient of reliability." For measuring the work of individual students a test should have a reliability coefficient of .80 at least. There are only a few basic tests that, when given to classes, yield coefficients half of which are above .85.

Objectivity refers to the degree to which identical results are secured when the same papers are marked by equally competent persons.

Ease of administration and scoring must be assured by a carefully constructed manual to accompany the tests. There are a few manuals so well written that competent teachers wholly unfamiliar with the directions can after a short inspection proceed to administer the test under standard conditions.

Strictly speaking, the terms "norm" and "standard" are not synonyms. Norm usually refers to the average or median accomplishment, whereas a standard is usually an arbitrary goal higher than a norm.

Grade norms refer to the averages or medians of the scores made by pupils in the different school grades. Sometimes these norms are established for the end of the school year, but the tendency is to establish them for the tenths of a school year. Beginning with September 15, a tenth of a grade is added for each month. Thus, a score of 85 on a section of the Stanford test would correspond to 7.4 grade. This is another way of saying that, in general, children at the end of the fourth month in the seventh grade, or about January 15, tend to make a score of 85. The phrase "tend to make" means that the median score is 85. The median is that score above or below which half the scores are found.

Percentile scores are the scores below which certain per cents of the scores fall. For example, if a score of 40 is the 80th percentile, then 80 per cent of the students fall below this mark and of course 20 per cent would, in general, fall above it.

At least two equivalent forms of the same test are essential if growth or progress is to be measured.

The teacher needs to be very critical of standard tests. Many of them have not been carefully constructed; some, in wide use, have very low reliability. The measures of validity of some of the widely accepted tests are rough and vague; in the case of a majority of them there is no evidence that there actually have been studies of validity.

9. *The attitude of pupils toward examinations has undergone a marked change.* In general, pupils have come to like examinations that are used in the right manner. One of the most effective devices for motivation in a number of school subjects is the new-type or informal instructional test. When tests yield impartial and objective results and when tests are specific, detailed, and diagnostic in character—and in particular if the instructional function is stressed —pupils enjoy taking them.

10. *The cheapest test is not necessarily the best test.* Ordinarily school officials are excessively critical of the cost of a test. They fail to realize that a few cents spent for a good standardized test is certainly an excellent investment when compared with the total cost of the school's services to the pupil. If a task, say the teaching of a course in mathematics, is worth doing at a cost of $25 to $35 a year, then it would not seem unreasonable to spend ten cents each year to see how well the job is done.

GUIDES FOR A TESTING PROGRAM

The preceding list of facts suggests the following procedures to be used in employing tests:

1. *A teacher should be cautious in selecting a test.* Keep in mind the various items that need to be considered in rating a test. Subject all claims for validity, reliability, and values as an instructional tool to systematic study. Your appraisal of a test should be based on classroom use.

2. *Do not start too broad a testing program.* It is better to use and study one test at a time than to give numerous tests without careful consideration of each.

3. *In the use of standardized tests, place the emphasis on instructional value.* There are tests in high-school subjects now available that employ excellent procedures for teaching and reviewing some of the basic principles and processes.

4. *Practice interpreting what a test reveals.* Too many tests are filed away by administrative officers or supervisors without utilizing what they reveal. The teacher should study (*a*) the degree to which individual items have been well taught and (*b*) the extent to which an individual pupil has mastered each item.

5. *Give a standardized test strictly in accordance with the printed instructions.* A test should be given in an informal manner so as to make certain that children do not become tense. On the other hand, if comparison with norms is to be made, the conditions must be uniform.

6. *Do not make the giving of a standardized test an event.* Rather, it should be all a part of the day's work. It should be possible for a teacher, when schools can

afford to do so, to give ten or more standardized tests in a school year without having the pupil especially aware of an extensive testing program. Avoid excessive publicity in initiating a testing program.

7. *Do not weigh heavily a pupil's response to a standardized test in determining the mark of a semester.* To do so would encourage cheating and decrease the satisfaction that pupils normally have in taking such tests. They should be used to throw light on a pupil's achievement.

8. *Make certain, when you give an experimental trial to a standardized test, that you do not permit it to modify your objectives, unless you are sure that the test measures desirable things.* The surest means of driving a thing into the curriculum is the continued use of a test which involves that thing.

9. *Keep a permanent record of the responses and total scores of individual pupils.* This will enable you to compare the performances of a class with that of similar classes in preceding semesters. The norms as published in manuals to accompany standardized tests are for groups widely selected. It may be quite unfair to compare a class in a particular situation with these general norms. Perhaps the pupils should be held to a much higher achievement; on the other hand, the standard, if arbitrarily fixed by those who constructed the test, may be much too high.

10. *Practice making informal tests which employ the newer techniques of testing.* It is desirable from time to time to place tests of the newer type on the blackboard or to distribute them in mimeographed form for instructional or review purposes.

11. *Include the old form of test in your program for the semester or year.* The old form of test commonly called the "essay" type has some real values that should not be discarded, among them being, that (*a*) it requires the pupil to organize his thoughts and gives him training in expression and (*b*) it can be made by a teacher with far less expenditure of time and effort than a standardized test. Its limitations are that (*a*) two teachers would probably not give the same mark to a pupil's paper—indeed the same teacher might not give the same mark to two successive ratings, (*b*) the sampling of a pupil's knowledge or skills is much too small to be reliable as a typical random sample, which is what it will have to be to give a true measure of achievement, and (*c*) it is very easy for such an examination to be made up hastily and without careful consideration of the real objectives of the course. This might easily cause a pupil to be given a low mark in the course when actually he had done the work that was of real importance.

OBSERVATIONAL TECHNIQUES

In earlier chapters we have discussed observational techniques used to collect significant facts about pupils. We return now to observational techniques in order that we may look at them from the point of view of appraisal. In recent years observational techniques have been gaining in popularity as means for collecting valuable data regarding changes in pupils. As the term implies, the behavior of pupils is observed and, if possible, their verbalizations and reactions are recorded as they occur in significant social situations. These reports are collected in the form of anecdotes and summarized in a Behavior Journal. The temporary method and treatment of these data are shown on the following sample form:

ITEMS FOR USE IN THE BEHAVIOR JOURNAL

Date	Incident	Interpretation
Feb. 26......	Bill is interested in reading books on etiquette and correct manners. He checked out two recent books on that subject.	(To be supplied in each pupil's individual data sheet
Feb. 27......	Bill remarked in class, "I think the boys should wait first for the girls to leave the room after class is dismissed." John remarked, "Aw, let the girls take care of themselves."	when the pattern of his behavior has been clearly established.)
Feb. 28......	Henry tore up his report card. He said, "I hope the school burns down."	
Feb. 28.....	John tripped Mary as she walked past his desk.	
Mar. 1......	Helen refused to play with the others. She said, "They don't like me. They make fun of me."	
Mar. 1......	Bill suggested we have a unit on "Good manners." Tom and Mary each made a short talk and agreed with Bill. Everyone except John and Cecil voted to plan a unit on etiquette. Cecil said, "I hear enough of that stuff at home."	

Verbalizations are very important and should be noted if possible, since they often furnish the basis for a more valid interpretation of the particular behavior reaction.

The final form of the Behavior Journal differs from the content here illustrated to the extent that all the recorded incidents relating to each pupil are collected on one or several data sheets or in a folder, and interpreted in the light of the total picture of that pupil. Obviously, the more observations of a particular pupil with recordings of both negative and positive reactions, the more valid is likely to be one's interpretation. Teachers who attempt to work on a scientific level often keep a Behavior Journal consisting of several pages for each pupil. Recordings are either inserted directly on each pupil's sheet, or brought together from a miscellaneous Behavior Journal as shown in this section. The data sheet for each pupil finally becomes a series of significant word pictures that are obviously of great value for purposes of guidance.

Without question, the keeping of these records becomes another task for the teacher but, if we expect to apply clinical techniques, we must expect to devote more time and energy to diagnostic, remedial, and clinical procedures. When the lack of time and energy makes the continued daily use of the Behavior Journal for all pupils impractical, observations and recordings may be limited and concentrated on problem cases. As a matter of fact, with the cooperation of playground supervisors, athletic coaches, home-room teachers, scoutmasters, parents, and others, it is possible to compile considerable data about a few pupils in a remarkably short time. The folder of the individual pupil then becomes a depository for the information collected from the various teachers who deal with him. Obviously, the longer these records of individual pupils are kept, the more valuable they become in contributing a fund of information upon which guidance decisions may be based.

As has been suggested earlier in this volume, the materials in the folder of an individual pupil are likely to become voluminous and miscellaneous in character, and to some extent meaningless. It is therefore necessary as a practical step for someone from time to time to survey the total record and to take stock by writing a brief abstract that will reveal in a glance to other teachers dealing with the pupil the significant phases of the general picture. Often the home-room teacher is the logical person to undertake this service.

Measuring the Intangible Outcomes

One of the important aspects of the broader concept of appraisal is that we have become concerned with more than achievement in subject matter. We recognize that mastery of subject matter is only one aspect of education and we try to identify changes in important social and personal traits. We speak of such attitudes as cooperativeness, tolerance, and scientific-mindedness as intangible outcomes, presumably because we cannot measure these directly by paper-and-pencil tests and express changes in precise and standard units. An individual may know all the answers to a test measuring cooperation and yet be an uncooperative person. The real measure of interests, attitudes, appreciations, work habits, and study skills is the behavior of the individual. After all, the old farmer had a pragmatic and effective test of laziness when he identified his hired hand hoeing corn in a remote field by saying, "I think that's him over there. But if he moves, it's a stump."

We need to dispel the erroneous notion that we are helpless in appraising changes in intangible outcomes. The world of practical affairs identifies these social traits in an efficient manner when selecting persons for positions where these traits are believed to be important. Children exhibit a discerning intuition when they classify the new teacher as a "good sport" or a "friendly" person on the first day

A project like this may provide self-expression and the release of tension for pupils and teacher.(M)

of school. Nor is the task of appraising an intangible outcome one of enormous difficulty. A mere fragment of behavior may be highly symptomatic of the presence or absence of an important social trait. As has been suggested, the important phase of the technique is to be sure that we have an adequate sampling in the form of a series of behavior episodes providing the general pattern of the personality with respect to the trait. We now provide two illustrations. The first represents an effort to measure scientific-mindedness and the second, an attempt to measure growth in tolerence. The student teacher is expected to use these illustrations later as samples in his own effort to measure intangible outcomes.

Techniques for Measuring Scientific-mindedness. The ordinary textbook provides a source of facts and hypotheses, often undocumented and certainly questionable in validity. With respect to such material we may ask the following questions about the pupil:

1. Has he the disposition to want the facts?
2. Does he arrange facts in systematic fashion?
3. To what extent does he check on source materials?
4. Does he accept the first and perhaps the only statement of cause and effect?
5. Does he compare the conclusions of various authors?
6. Is he able to detect prejudices and fallacies?
7. Does he seek the opinion of competent persons in the school or in the community?
8. Can he identify issues?
9. Does he pick out arguments that are intended to mislead?
10. Is he disposed to ask "Why?" and "How?" whenever it is sensible to do so?
11. Is he resourceful when suggesting possible solutions to a problem?
12. Does he insist on checking a solution that seems to be correct?
13. Does he form opinions for himself and does he know how to design ways of testing them?

A series of observations of an individual with respect to one or more of the types of questions suggested in the preceding list should throw a good deal of light on the degree to which he is becoming scientifically minded.

Other appraisals take the form of setting tasks involving inductive thinking based on experimentation in the laboratory, and checking source materials in the library. Moreover, in some areas it is feasible to construct tests in functional thinking that consist of a series of statements revealing wide gaps between the presentation of facts and the conclusions drawn.

The Appraisal of Growth in Tolerance. Bertrand Russell[1] makes the interesting suggestion that the way to teach tolerance is to provide pupils with eloquent statements drawn from historical materials in favor of positions that no one now holds. In any case, if we are going to measure tolerance we will have to assume that it exists in

[1] BERTRAND RUSSELL. "Education for Democracy," *Education Digest*, IV (April, 1939), 1–4.

some amount and that the school knows how to increase this trait. In scanning the Behavior Journal of a pupil we need to raise such questions as the following:

1. Does the pupil admit that others have a right to positions, opinions, customs, and habits that differ widely from his own?
2. What is his attitude toward the people of other nations and, in particular, of other races?
3. To what extent is he bitter and antagonistic toward persons who represent different social strata?
4. To what extent is he aware of prejudices that were inculcated by an early environment?

To an observing teacher the pupil will almost certainly reveal the answers to some of these questions in his English themes, debates, and presentations of reports, particularly if they are assigned so as to reveal the fundamental opinions of pupils on questions of this nature. Opinionnaires may be constructed and included in specific units in English, social studies, and foreign languages to reveal the sensitivity of pupils' feelings toward other groups; for example, in relation to their customs and beliefs. Then, too, the socialized recitation will throw considerable light on the extent to which the attitude of tolerance is characteristic of a pupil. The give-and-take and the friendly exchange of opinions on controversial issues arising in class discussion provide a basis for judgment regarding the degree of tolerance possessed by the individual and the group.

Finally, one may employ a paper-and-pencil test to measure thinking about tolerance. We suggest that you do the test that appears as an illustration on the following pages. We feel sure you will be interested in comparing your responses with those of your classmates.

A Sample of New Techniques in the Social Studies[1]

A large high school has a large number of foreign-born boys and girls among its students. One of these was Yuki, a well-dressed, gentle, and friendly Japanese girl. She spoke good English and made a wonderful record in scholarship during her high-school career. At the end, her grades were higher than those of any other student in her class. Since the best student usually becomes the valedictorian of the graduating class, the principal decided to make her the valedictorian. Immediately a storm of protest broke loose. Newspapers took it up; citizens called on

---

[1] This is a slightly modified form of "Test 1.4—Social Problems," in the *Evaluation of the Eight-year Study* of the Progressive Education Association.

the principal and threatened him; classmates announced they would not appear on the platform with a Japanese girl as their leader.

The principal's reply to these protests was that Yuki should lead the class or else there would be no valedictorian.

What do you think about the course of action?

DIRECTIONS: Choose the course (or courses) of action.

Courses of Action:

A. He was right in doing what he did.

B. He was right in his first decision but he should have given in when there was so much protest.

C. He should have let the faculty and the students participate in making the decision at the beginning.

D. He should not have allowed the girl to become valedictorian.

DIRECTIONS: Choose the reasons which you would use to support your course (or courses) of action.

Reasons:

1. An established tradition should be followed without regard for racial differences.

2. The principle of racial equality is all right in theory but it is impossible to act on it in all practical situations.

3. No matter how right, we should not push our ideas to the point of offending influential people.

4. It is more important for the principal of a school to keep the good will of the community than to fight for the principle of racial equality.

5. The students learn racial tolerance better by discussing the matter than by submitting to the principal's decision.

6. Race prejudice is inborn and nothing can be done about it.

7. In a democracy there should be no racial discrimination.

8. In cases such as this it is wise to try to reform the community before pressing the issue.

9. Democracy means that the will of the majority must be obeyed.

10. Americans would not like an alien to be put above their children.

11. In a democracy those affected by a decision should have part in making it.

12. Citizens who pay taxes have the right to determine what the school should or should not do.

13. Class honors should be given strictly on the basis of merit.

14. Race prejudice would probably be deepened if the principal did not yield to the community demand.

15. Other foreigners would be encouraged to insist on social equality.

16. Letting students discuss questions like this is a way of educating them to be democratic.

17. The newspapers had no right to fight against the principal's decision.

18. Had the principal yielded to community pressure he would have been supporting unreasonable race prejudice.

19. It is important to maintain the dignity of white people.

20. Schools are especially responsible for cultivating a democratic spirit.

21. The principal's first duty was to avoid any action that would stir up ill feeling.

22. Public schools are free to all children of school age.

23. The prejudices of a majority should not be allowed to deprive a person of an honor he has earned.

24. The best way to break down race prejudices is to deal with them firmly as the principal did.

DIRECTIONS: Select from the 24 statements above all those which you consider as important values or important facts which any reasonable person would seriously consider in coming to a decision about Yuki. You may or may not agree with the statements—but you recognize that they are *relevant* and *important* if all sides of the situation are to be considered.

Practice in New Appraisal Techniques. The teacher experimenting with the new techniques soon discovers that a number of broad concepts—*e.g.*, cooperation and social-mindedness—appear in many units of the different school subjects. Moreover, any single appraisal device is not likely to be limited to the measurement of merely one intangible outcome. Then, too, he will discover that the law of diminishing returns soon begins to operate because descriptions of behavior designed to identify several traits become strikingly similar.

However, it will be worth your while to apply the procedures suggested by the preceding illustrations. To that end we now direct your attention to a page from a Journal Record. In a school that does not keep a Journal Record you might yet find a page like the one shown here in the pupil's folder. Note that for each trait a few leads are given to help you get started. Your first job is to add one item under each trait in order to show the kind of evidence you would record, in case you observed it, to measure the presence or absence of the trait in question. Your second task is to extend the list of traits of this behavior pattern by adding three and providing two items for each.

A PAGE FROM THE BEHAVIOR JOURNAL OF ROBERT RALEIGH RICKARD

1. *Respect for Property:*
   a. Takes excellent care of books that are lent to him.
   b. Doesn't mark up school furniture.

2. *Respect for Law and Government:*
    a. Is concerned about disorder in the fire drill.
    b. Criticizes people who drive through a red light.
3. *Social-mindedness:*
    a. Argues for giving Christmas gifts indirectly to the family adopted by his home room.
    b. Gives generously through the Community Fund to an agency dealing with juvenile delinquency.
4. *Appreciation of the Home:*
    1. Enjoys being at home.
    2. Works all Saturday morning to make things easier for other members of the family.
5. *Cooperativeness:*
    a. Behaves himself in a group even when the chairman is a weak leader.
    b. Often volunteers to do the disagreeable part of a class project.
6. *Concentration:*
    a. Can sit down at a desk and shut out the rest of the world when working on a problem.
    b. Completes a task that is set for him even though there are recreational distractions.
7. *Open-mindedness:*
    a. Admits he is wrong when the facts are against him.
    b. Enjoys reading a newspaper article that reflects a point of view different from his own.
8. *Scientific-mindedness:*
    a. Traces a short circuit in his radio by Dewey's well-known formula for how to think.
    b. Prefers to read biographies of great men of science.
9. *Creativeness:*
    a. When ill in the hospital carved a statue of fine quality.
    b. Made a great many ingenious suggestions used in the staging of the Christmas play.
10. *Tolerance:*
    a. Is a bit prejudiced against Negroes but told the librarian he enjoyed a biography of George Washington Carver.
    b. Can sit down with a friend of opposite religious faith and have a good talk about religion.
11. *Loyalty:*
    a. Is convinced he is a pupil in a good high school.
    b. Though in high school, he went back to his elementary school and donated his time and energy on two Saturday afternoons helping to build a softball diamond.
12. *Appreciation of Fine Quality of Workmanship:*
    a. Revised a theme after the teacher had marked it *A*.
    b. Made the comment after an assembly talk, "That speech was really planned."

13. *Reverence:*
    a. Volunteered to lead in prayer at a Sunday morning assembly in a summer camp.
    b. In the pinewoods in the moonlight by the fireside said, "Ain't this swell!"

EVALUATION OF YOUR TEACHING

We should not conclude this chapter on appraisal without considering devices for evaluating the effectiveness of your own teaching. This section will provide you with a check list. You will profit by using it one or more times.

Evaluating Instructional Activities. The first illustration is a check list for instructional activities.[1] The use of a check list rather than a scale suggests that we do not have a yardstick for measuring the efficiency of a teacher; however, there are certain things that every teacher needs to learn to do well. The use of this check list has value not only for teachers in training but for experienced teachers who wish to improve their work. We suggest the following procedure:

1. Begin your work with the check list by reading carefully the standards proposed for each item.
2. If feasible, visit a teacher and check the work or prepare a report on a present instructor. Note carefully the directions for using the check list. You will probably profit most if two or more students use the check list on the same teacher independently and then compare judgments.
3. Having used the check list one or more times, write a brief paragraph indicating what you may have learned by using it.

CHECK LIST FOR INSTRUCTIONAL ACTIVITIES OF TEACHERS

Directions: In using this check list you are to draw a circle around the figure that most nearly expresses the quality of work as you see it. You will note that the scale provides for five levels of work in which "5" is defined as superior, "3" is average, and "1" is inferior.

    1. *Arranging the Classroom.* Making the classroom healthful, comfortable, and attractive, by proper adjustment of lighting, heating, ventilating, and seating; by neatness and order; by decorations. Letting pupils share in these responsibilities for their own development. Creating a suitable atmosphere for stimulating interest in the subject being taught, through display of exhibits, posters, models, etc.

| 1 | 2 | 3 | 4 | 5 |

[1] Many valuable contributions to this check list were made by J. Blair Buck of the state Department of Public Instruction, Richmond, Virginia.

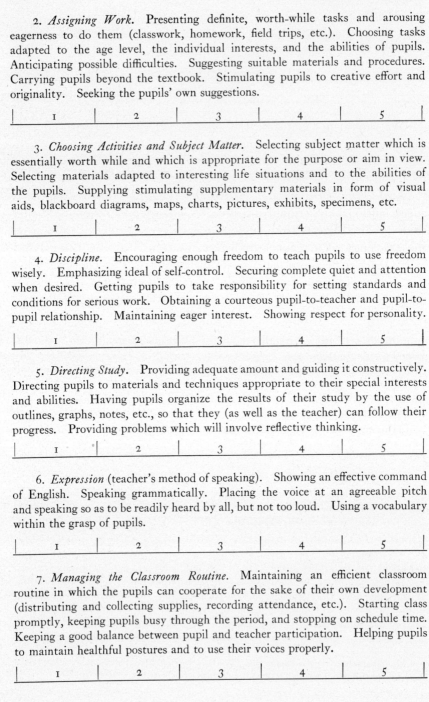

---

2. *Assigning Work.* Presenting definite, worth-while tasks and arousing eagerness to do them (classwork, homework, field trips, etc.). Choosing tasks adapted to the age level, the individual interests, and the abilities of pupils. Anticipating possible difficulties. Suggesting suitable materials and procedures. Carrying pupils beyond the textbook. Stimulating pupils to creative effort and originality. Seeking the pupils' own suggestions.

| | 1 | 2 | 3 | 4 | 5 | |

3. *Choosing Activities and Subject Matter.* Selecting subject matter which is essentially worth while and which is appropriate for the purpose or aim in view. Selecting materials adapted to interesting life situations and to the abilities of the pupils. Supplying stimulating supplementary materials in form of visual aids, blackboard diagrams, maps, charts, pictures, exhibits, specimens, etc.

| | 1 | 2 | 3 | 4 | 5 | |

4. *Discipline.* Encouraging enough freedom to teach pupils to use freedom wisely. Emphasizing ideal of self-control. Securing complete quiet and attention when desired. Getting pupils to take responsibility for setting standards and conditions for serious work. Obtaining a courteous pupil-to-teacher and pupil-to-pupil relationship. Maintaining eager interest. Showing respect for personality.

| | 1 | 2 | 3 | 4 | 5 | |

5. *Directing Study.* Providing adequate amount and guiding it constructively. Directing pupils to materials and techniques appropriate to their special interests and abilities. Having pupils organize the results of their study by the use of outlines, graphs, notes, etc., so that they (as well as the teacher) can follow their progress. Providing problems which will involve reflective thinking.

| | 1 | 2 | 3 | 4 | 5 | |

6. *Expression* (teacher's method of speaking). Showing an effective command of English. Speaking grammatically. Placing the voice at an agreeable pitch and speaking so as to be readily heard by all, but not too loud. Using a vocabulary within the grasp of pupils.

| | 1 | 2 | 3 | 4 | 5 | |

7. *Managing the Classroom Routine.* Maintaining an efficient classroom routine in which the pupils can cooperate for the sake of their own development (distributing and collecting supplies, recording attendance, etc.). Starting class promptly, keeping pupils busy through the period, and stopping on schedule time. Keeping a good balance between pupil and teacher participation. Helping pupils to maintain healthful postures and to use their voices properly.

| | 1 | 2 | 3 | 4 | 5 | |

8. *Organizing and Planning Instruction.* Planning units of instruction with pupils about life situations of interest to the pupils. Choosing an effective method or methods. Providing at suitable times an appropriate amount of review and enough drill for mastery of fundamentals. Providing for differences in the interests and abilities of pupils. Arranging appropriate sequence, and emphasizing the most significant points.

| 1 | 2 | 3 | 4 | 5 |

9. *Questioning.* Phrasing questions definitely and clearly to stimulate reflective thinking. Distributing questions well to attain wide participation when arriving at accurate and adequate answers.

| 1 | 2 | 3 | 4 | 5 |

10. *Evaluating* (regarded as part of instruction). Checking on pupil progress continuously, through questioning, formal examination, oral and written reports, standardized and informal tests, etc. Adapting testing procedures to purposes; *viz.*, diagnosis, evaluation, etc. Selecting testing devices appropriate for the outcomes to be measured; *viz.*, appreciations, understandings, skills, etc.; sensing individual pupil needs. Using test results as a basis for subsequent teaching.

| 1 | 2 | 3 | 4 | 5 |

SUMMARY OF RECENT DEVELOPMENTS IN EVALUATION

The preceding sections suggest, by implication at least, the following trends with respect to the new appraisal techniques:

1. *The Attempt to Measure the Most Important Objectives.* The emphasis is on the pupil's behavior and attitudes rather than on his ability to supply information in response to questions. We are more concerned with the change which an experience makes in a pupil than we are with the product of his efforts.

2. *The Development of Appraisal Techniques in Terms of Specific Pupil Goals That Stem from the Teacher's Philosophy of Education.* The first step is for the teacher to formulate his philosophy of education, the second step is to manage the environment of the individual pupil so that he will strive for desirable goals, and the third step is resourcefully to design ways of measuring goals.

3. *The Recognition That the Appraisal Procedures Employed to a Large Extent Determine the Curriculum.* If no measuring devices are employed nothing much of importance may happen to the pupil. If standardized tests measuring only skills are used, the emphasis is almost certain to be on drill. Therefore, in planning a unit of work

or an activity it is sensible to write the objectives first, next to construct the test, and finally to select the teaching experiences.

4. *The Effort to Develop Appraisal Techniques That Recognize the Essential Unity of the Pupil's Growth.* Traits tend to overlap and be related, and certainly they establish behavior patterns. We seek not only to measure attitudes but the relationships between traits by evaluating behavior responses.

5. *The Effort to Involve Both Pupils and Teachers in Evaluation.* Both should have a part in fixing the goals and in planning the program.

6. *The Appearance of New Areas for Measurement That Suggest the Concept of Subject Matter as a Means Rather Than as an End.* It is significant that we have in the testing literature new instruments that attempt to measure work habits, beliefs, interests, thinking, social adjustment, creativeness, and the like.

Finally, two notes of caution need to be expressed: (1) Any new movement is likely to stimulate a vast number of workers with inadequate ability and background to unusual activity. Witness the large number of crude and worthless tests that were constructed in the early days of the standardized-test movement. The same thing is happening now with respect to the new appraisal techniques. (2) Most of the new measuring instruments, if they are at all objective, are in the last analysis paper-and-pencil tests. As has been pointed out earlier, the pupil may provide you with all the right answers, and yet respond in a very different way when he faces the real situation. Any teacher of experience knows how glibly and vigorously a pupil who cheats on examinations may condemn the practice.

For Discussion

1. Sometime during your period of student teaching the class will probably take a standardized test, as for example, in reading. If this happens, prepare a 10-minute talk interpreting the results to the pupils concerned. In particular, tell what the results mean to the teacher, to the class as a unit, and to individual pupils.

2. Study the important tests in your major field of interest and inspect the accompanying manuals. Select two tests. Are you confident that you could administer them? Could you interpret the results?

3. If you are now teaching a unit, what specific method are you proposing to use in providing an opportunity for pupils to appraise their own progress?

4. What is your opinion with regard to the desirability of assigning marks to a class on a basis of the normal probability curve?

5. Report briefly on the marking system employed by some school.

6. If possible, visit a high school that does not employ a conventional marking system. How does the pupil measure progress? How does the school report to the parents?

7. If possible, study the effectiveness of a report card that meets desirable specifications.

8. Principal Hart sent a memorandum to his teachers on the topic of specific objectives. In it he said: "I am convinced that the specific goals for most of our subjects are exceedingly vague. A list of things which the pupil is expected to learn at a high level of mastery is of great value alike to pupil, parent, and teacher. Although it is not to be expected that such a list will completely solve the problem of low mastery, it nevertheless provides a much needed checking device which calls attention sharply to the prime essentials of the course. I therefore request that each teacher send to me before the end of the school year a list of specific things he is trying to achieve each semester for at least one subject he is teaching."

Consult the best and most recent book on the teaching of the subject in which you have a special interest. Try to find a list of specific objectives. Does the list fulfill the request in Principal Hart's memorandum?

Suggested Readings

Bulletin of the National Association of Secondary-school Principals: "Using Tests in Modern Secondary School," December, 1948.

Educational Temperatures. Washington: Cooperative Study of Secondary School Standards, 744 Jackson Place.

This monograph provides a graphic summary of the findings secured by application of the Evaluative Criteria to a school.

Evaluative Criteria. Washington: Cooperative Study of Secondary School Standards, 744 Jackson Place.

The chief instrument provided by the Cooperative Study for use in evaluation of schools. It comprises eleven sections dealing with the various phases of the school program. Each section includes a check list by which the school may judge the effectiveness of its work.

How to Evaluate a Secondary School. Washington: Cooperative Study of Secondary School Standards, 744 Jackson Place.

This monograph includes a brief history of the Coöperative Study, description of the steps in validation of the data secured, and complete directions for use of the materials by schools and by accrediting agencies.

Mursell, James: *Successful Teaching.* New York: McGraw-Hill Book Company, Inc., 1946. Pp. xi + 338.

The student teacher who has extra time for reading might well consult the Table of Contents and read the chapters that supplement the discussions in this book. The chapters are uneven—for example, the discussion of discipline is weak, whereas the four chapters dealing with evaluation and appraisal are strong.

Olson, Willard C.: *Child Development.* Boston: D. C. Heath and Company, 1949. Pp. xiv + 417.

This book has been called to your attention earlier. At this point it will be helpful for you to read Chap. 8 and the part in Chap. 11 entitled "Reporting the School Progress of a Child."

TYLER, RALPH W.: "Evaluation: A Challenge to Progressive Education," *Progressive Education*, XII (December, 1935), 552–556.

Points out the need for new techniques in appraisal and outlines a suggested program aimed to make evaluation more comprehensive.

WILLIAMS, L. A.: *Secondary Schools for American Youth.* New York: American Book Company, 1944. Pp. xii + 531.

You will probably want to delay reading the first part of this book until the day when you have taught several years or are taking a graduate course in secondary education. However, you will find brief chapters in the second part on specific topics that you can read with profit as a beginning teacher. This reference is listed here so as to direct your attention to Chap. 6, which is concerned with the nature and role of specific objectives; an adequate discussion of specific objectives is difficult to find in pedagogical literature.

WRIGHTSTONE, J. WAYNE: *Appraisal of Newer Practices in Selected Public Schools.* New York: Teachers College, Columbia University, 1935. Pp. viii + 117.

Chapters III and IV present an appraisal of practices in selected secondary schools. The book includes a summary and implications of newer practices.

WRIGHTSTONE, J. WAYNE: "Constructing an Observational Technique," *Teachers College Record*, XXXVII (October, 1935), 1–9.

Describes the use of controlled observation techniques in obtaining objective measures of pupils' behavior and conduct.

WRIGHTSTONE, J. WAYNE: "New Tests for New Needs," *Educational Method*, XV (May, 1936), 407–411.

A brief discussion of (1) traditional tests, (2) need for new tests, and (3) new appraisal techniques that are being devised.

Chapter XIV

Professional Growth and Personal Advancement

Since teaching is one of the two professions which have the principal responsibility for the preservation of democratic government, it is our sincere hope, as you [beginning teachers] go from here to take up your life work, that you will respect and practice the ideals of the service you are expected to give to your fellow men.

I give you this thought: He who governs well, leads the ignorant; he who teaches well, trains them to govern themselves in justice, mercy, and peace.

—ALEXANDER G. RUTHVEN

This final chapter will make practical suggestions on growth in service and on such details as the letter of application, the interview, the first day of school, and your emotional adjustment to the new environment. These items are far from trivial, and it is sensible for you to supplement your common sense by profiting from the experience of others. Let us leave for the last the matter of growth on the job and start with some things that are just ahead of you.

FINDING A POSITION

In addition to classroom teaching, schools now offer a great variety of positions at all levels. There are many special services, as for example, guidance personnel, curriculum workers, audio-visual specialists, that usually call for the master's degree or at least a fifth year of training and some experience. It is assumed that you are aiming to start as a classroom teacher. This is wise even if your ultimate goal is supervision, administration, or a special service.

In every field of education, and especially in classroom teaching, there has been at all times—even in the years of a depression—a tragic shortage of competent and well-trained workers. Moreover, we need at least twice as many teachers as we now have in our schools, and let us hope that the public will come to realize this fact before it is too late. In any event, if you are professionally minded, well trained, and competent, you will not stay on the shelf very long.

351

Many principals assign extracurricular duties according to special recreational interests of teachers. This teacher devotes many hours to the camera club but for him it is fun—not overtime work.(N)

LETTERS OF APPLICATION

Many letters of application[1] are promptly discarded because the writer does not show good judgment or uses poor English. It is no exaggeration to say that candidates applying for important positions have written letters in much worse English than a competent eighth grader would produce. In writing your letter of application, it may be helpful to observe the following guides:

1. Always address the person directly responsible for the nomination of teachers. As a rule, the superintendent of schools receives all applications for positions, as he usually has the responsibility of nominating all teachers. This is true, regardless of the size of the system, in both rural and city systems.

2. Avoid familiarity or lack of good form in the salutation. Address the superintendent simply as "Dear Sir," "My dear Mr. Smith," or "Dear Superintendent Smith." Do not be so familiar, even if he is a friend, or so careless as to say "Dear friend," "Dear John," "Dear Smith," or "Dear Supt. Smith."

3. Apply at a time when your application will be most likely to receive prompt consideration. The large city school systems and the better rural systems usually

---

[1] The practice of mailing multiple application forms or cards to school superintendents is considered by many teachers as harmful to the profession, presumably because it gives the employing officers the impression that there are several times as many applicants as there really are.

preserve applications and file them in the order of preference.   Inquiries addressed to them will receive attention almost immediately.   This does not mean that one will know at once whether he will be given a position, but merely that the application is a matter of record and will be considered in due season.   It is better in the small systems to make application two or three months before the close of the school term.

4. Answer promptly and positively the first offer that comes to you.   It is not unethical for a teacher to file applications in several places at the same time.   When this is done, the applicant must stand ready to give an immediate and positive reply to each offer.   To bargain for a position or to hold off a prospective employer while waiting for a better offer is considered unethical.

5. Withdraw all other applications upon accepting a position.   It is not fair to school superintendents to whom you have made application or to other teachers to keep applications out after you have accepted a position.

6. Use standard-size business stationery for all correspondence. Social correspondence paper is not suited to office files and is generally undesirable. Paper 8½ by 11 in. is standard.   Envelopes used for social correspondence are usually too small to carry return letters or forms.   Do not use them.

7. Enclose a self-addressed and stamped envelope for reply.   This is a business principle which teachers should observe.   It is quite expensive to reply to the hundreds of letters received annually by superintendents, making application for positions.

8. Return promptly, properly filled out, the forms which may be sent to you. These are used to assist superintendents in getting all data on applicants in some uniform manner.   Although you may have sent an application letter which gave full details, the form should be sent in, as requested.

9. Enclose a recent photograph of yourself in the first communication.   The photograph is almost universally required.   Size 2½ by 3 in. is sufficient.

10. Pay extreme care to the form and content of your letter.   Errors in spelling, sentence structure, paragraphing, and organization are likely to prove fatal.

11. Avoid flattery, self-praise, and family distinctions or connections.   The one considering your application for a position in a good school will be interested in your fitness for the position, not in these extraneous matters.

12. Confidential communications are much more effective than open letters of recommendation.   It is important, therefore, that you give as references only those persons who really know you and your qualifications.

13. Observe the ethics of the profession in making application.   Do not apply for the position of another teacher.   Apply only for positions that are known to be open.

14. Keep your letter brief, and organize all essential matter in a data sheet to be attached to your letter, or better still, state that your credentials have been forwarded by some occupational bureau.

THE DATA SHEET

In case you do not have the necessary information on file with some occupational bureau where it is readily accessible to employing officers, you may wish to include a data sheet with your brief letter of application.

This detailed information about your training, experience, and personal qualifications should be typewritten on a separate data sheet and be attached to the letter of application. Regarding this, the superintendent and the Board of Education will wish to know the following:

1. For what specific work you wish to apply.
2. Your specific and special training for this work.
3. Your experience in this and other work, including dates and places.
4. Your general training: high school, normal school, college or university, and the credits you have received.
5. Your specialties: the things you can do exceptionally well, either in the regular academic field or in extracurricular activities.
6. Your references: the people who can testify especially concerning your (a) skill in teaching, (b) ability to guide and control pupils, (c) moral character, (d) personality, (e) scholarship, and (f) cooperation and loyalty.
7. Your physical characteristics: age, height, weight, general health, and physical defects, if any.
8. Where a detailed record of your qualifications may be secured—such as the placement bureau of your college or some commercial agency.
9. Where you may be reached in case communication is desired by letter, telegram, or telephone.
10. Your church affiliation in some instances, and also the salary for which you are willing to serve. This is not essential for, if you are desired, an offer will be made to you in keeping with your qualifications and other salaries paid.

THE PERSONAL INTERVIEW

In many cases superintendents do not employ a teacher without an interview. Holding such an interview is an important step in securing a position and, if practicable, should be taken advantage of when the invitation is given.

Unless it is excessively costly in time and money, visit the school where you hope to be employed. This will give you an opportunity to get a picture of the school, its staff, and the community. If you have a choice, pick the school which provides *good leadership* and which is located in a community that is really concerned about the education and the welfare of its youth.

With regard to the interview, two series of suggestions follow, the first relating to your own attitude:

1. Be on time, alert, and attentive to the business before you.
2. Be courteous, tactful, frank, and truthful.

3. Be good-natured.

4. Present as good a personal appearance as possible.

5. See something of the community and the school before the conference if possible.

6. Think the job over beforehand.

7. Do not tell the superintendent how to run his school.

8. Do not boast about your "connections."

9. Do not make promises which you cannot fulfill.

10. Do not "talk" yourself out of a job.

The second list suggests the things that the superintendent will wish to know about you from the interview:

1. Is your appearance pleasing, sensible, and wholesome?

2. Are you freakish or queer in any way?

3. Are you evasive or open, frank, and sincere?

4. Are you forward or self-effacing? too retiring?

5. Do you have sympathy and love for children?

6. Do you have an interest in teaching and in the profession of teaching in general?

7. Do you express yourself well and unhesitatingly in the field of your preparation and on questions propounded to you?

8. Do you possess initiative to carry forward the work to be done?

9. Can you be relied upon to be discreet in the discussion of school matters and your fellows in general, or are you inclined to gossip?

10. Can you take criticism without offense?

11. Do you possess the strength and force of personality and character to manage boys and girls of high-school age so as to command their respect and admiration?

12. Will you reflect credit upon the faculty and the school by your life as a citizen of the community?

13. Are you a teacher by desire or by circumstance?

14. Do you have the "human touch" in dealing with children?

CONTRACTS

Although the laws governing the form of contract and the interpretation of contracts for teachers vary somewhat in different states, every teacher should certainly be familiar with (1) the statutes governing the contracts of teachers in the state in which he teaches and (2) the general character of contracts and the main agreements relating to the problem of ethics. The first item is obviously outside the scope of this chapter. As for the problem of ethics with respect to contracts, the main things to keep in mind are the following:

1. Making a formal contract is in reality a means of protecting the welfare and interests of both parties: the school, the community, and its pupils on the one hand, and the teacher on the other.

2. The general character of a contract implies the right of either party to sever its terms if the agreements listed or implied in it are not carried out by either one of the parties concerned.

3. The members of the Board of Education are the official representatives of the people in the community in all matters relating to the public schools.

4. The superintendent of schools is the chief executive officer and is appointed by the Board of Education to administer its policies. With regard to contracts,

One of the ways for a teacher to keep growing as a personality is to pursue a hobby. Fortunately there are a great many available for all kinds of people; as for example, weaving, music, play production, tennis, and gardening.[E]

the superintendent is usually asked to recommend the selection, contracting, retention, and dismissing of personnel in the system. In the large city school system these tasks may be delegated to an assistant superintendent or to the director of the personnel office.

5. Regarding the question of release from contract, it is not ethical for a teacher to break a present contract in order to accept another position unless the superintendent and the Board of Education indicate their willingness to release him, or unless the terms agreed upon have not been carried out by the Board of Education.

Though a contract is a formal agreement, in general teachers do not have much difficulty getting released from a contract when the reason is valid. Then, too, it is well to remember that the school administrator is also a professional person and may be expected to meet you more than half way on all matters that are vital to your future growth. In regard to the last item which relates to release of contract, there are very few superintendents who would stand in the way of a teacher who has an unusual opportunity for professional advancement. The term of contract gives security to the teacher and protects a community against the whims of one who may be tempted to change positions for some trivial reason, such as a paltry increase in salary.

Professional Ethics

From time to time, various professional organizations, such as the N.E.A., have attempted to formulate codes of ethics for teachers; but it must be admitted that there is no code in existence which all teachers accept without reservation. In the following code[1] the term "teacher" includes all persons directly engaged in educational work, whether in a teaching, an administrative, or a supervisory capacity.

1. The teacher should be courteous, just, and professional in all relationships.

2. Desirable ethical standards require cordial relations between teacher and pupil, home and school.

3. The conduct of the teacher should conform to the accepted patterns of behavior of the most wholesome members of the community.

4. The teacher should strive to improve educational practice through study, travel, and experimentation.

5. Unfavorable criticism of associates should be avoided except when made to proper officials.

6. Testimonials regarding the teacher should be truthful and confidential.

7. Membership and active participation in local, state, and national professional associations are expected.

8. The teacher should avoid indorsement of all educational materials for personal gain.

9. Great care should be taken by the teacher to avoid interference between other teachers and pupils.

10. Fair salary schedules should be sought and when established carefully upheld by all professionals.

11. No teacher should knowingly underbid a rival for a position.

12. No teacher should accept compensation for helping another teacher to get a position or a promotion.

---

[1] A condensed statement of the Code of the National Education Association. See Appendix D for a more nearly complete statement.

13. Honorable contracts when signed should be respected by both parties and dissolved only by mutual consent.

14. Official business should be transacted only through properly designated officials.

15. The responsibility for reporting all matters harmful to the welfare of the schools rests upon each teacher.

16. Professional growth should be stimulated through suitable recognition and promotion within the ranks.

17. Unethical practices should be reported to local, state, or national commissions on ethics.

The term "teacher" as used here includes all persons directly engaged in educational work.

For Discussion

Respond to each of the following questions by "No," "Yes," "Depends," or "No opinion." Is it ethical for a teacher:

(1) To apply for a position not known to be vacant?

(2) To apply for a position directly to a board instead of to the superintendent?

(3) To accept a position from which the immediately preceding occupant was dismissed unjustly?

(4) To fail to withdraw outstanding applications when a position has been accepted?

(5) To accept a position in a community where a relative is a member of the board or is superintendent of schools?

(6) To discuss deficiencies of pupils in such a way as would embarrass them or their parents?

(7) To teach one's religious, political, or other private beliefs to pupils?

(8) To accept pay for tutoring one's own pupils?

(9) To mark the work of a pupil in another teacher's class or to interfere in disciplinary or other problems?

(10) To fail to defend members of the profession when they are unjustly attacked?

(11) To censure and disclose unprofessional or immoral conduct, including inefficiency, within the profession?

(12) To fail to encourage the fit to enter, and to discourage the unfit from entering, the profession?

(13) To use the profession as a steppingstone to other professions or vocations?

(14) To go "over the heads" of one's superiors?

(15) To fail to support school policies until they are changed, even though one does not agree with them?

(16) To break a contract to accept another position?

It may be worth while for your class to appoint a committee and instruct it to summarize and interpret the responses given by all the members of your class to the preceding questions. For some of the items, the response, "Depends," will be high and you may wish to consult the Code of the National Education Association given in full in Appendix D, to see what it suggests on the issue.

Many of the causes of unusual success or unnecessary failure stem from what a teacher does in the early weeks.

ROOMING AND BOARDING

The problems of adjustment that frequently arise from the board-and-rooming place, combined with the strain of emotional adjustment to a new teaching situation, are likely to have a cumulative effect on mental health that may seriously limit your success. A little careful planning and the exercise of sound judgment may yield good returns. To the end that the new teacher may make a wise choice of living arrangement, we make the following suggestions: (1) Discuss the problem with your superintendent or principal, or some friend who knows the town, in the event that you are not already familiar with the community—particularly, with its social and religious structure and its economic problems. (2) Make a selection of living arrangements well in advance of the opening of school, or at least several days in advance. The housing situation, especially with regard to families, is tense in nearly every community in all sections of our country. You may safely assume that the school administration will be anxious to help you.

In general, the following factors should be considered in selecting a board-and-rooming place:

1. *Social Status of the Family.* While it is not to be expected that the mayor or the minister will open his home to roomers, the family with whom one resides should be held in high regard by the townspeople. Fortunately, people living in good homes who rent only one or two rooms are likely to favor teachers.

2. *Degree of Privacy and Freedom.* In general, it is not wise to be "one of the family." It is far easier to break down formality in the event that it seems to be desirable than it is to build up formality out of informality. While the degree of privacy and freedom is always a matter of chance when you have to make a decision, the factors which have a bearing on this status should be weighed carefully before choosing a rooming house; *i.e.*, the number and ages of children, the location of one's room in relation to the other rooms in the house, the attitude of the landlady, the number of other boarders, etc.

3. *Cost.* Since economic conditions vary so widely in different communities, it is desirable to discuss the question of what is usually charged for room and board with your superintendent or principal before making any decision.   In general, one may expect quality to be consistent with higher prices, and under some conditions a difference of $5 a month may pay handsome dividends in your mental and physical health.

4. *Meals.* While it is obviously impossible to determine the exact menu, the question of food should be discussed tactfully before one moves in.   Naturally, the times when meals are served may also influence your choice.

5. *Other Factors.* The selection of living quarters depends also upon the following: (*a*) distance from school; (*b*) comfort and appearance of room; and (*c*) heating and ventilation.

While the selection of a board-and-rooming place may, at first thought, seem to be a very trivial matter in relation to the total teaching and community situation, there is convincing evidence that the careful selection of these arrangements is one of the important contributing factors in a pleasant and successful year's work.   At any rate, this issue appears very often in letters from beginning teachers who seem to be making a bad start.   Consider the following letter, which is a composite of several such reports from distressed teachers:

> Middletown, Any State
> October 9, ——
>
> Dear Folks,
>
> Please overlook my silence during the course of the last few weeks. I have hesitated to write my impressions of the school and townspeople because I didn't want you to worry about me.   Nor did I want to appear prejudiced on the matter.   I've stood it though as long as I can, so "here goes" for the complete story of my troubles.
>
> Since my boarding and rooming place is uppermost in my mind at the present moment, I'm going to start with that topic.   As you know I had some difficulty in finding a place that was reasonable in price.   Finally, I did find one five blocks from school that to all appearances suited me.
>
> The landlady (Mrs. Henry) told me I would be treated "just like one of the family" and that sounded quite homelike.   But believe me, I didn't know "what a family" I was getting into.   The boys, age four and seven respectively (bless their hearts), fight continually.   The youngest one has taken a remarkable liking to me, and since I am "one of the family" he informally pops into my room at all hours.   There's no need for an alarm clock around here.   The oldest boy is a radio bug and keeps programs going full force from five o'clock

to six-thirty every evening listening to a conglomeration of everything from the "Box X Ghost Returns" to "Seven Buckets of Blood." From eight o'clock to eleven, Mr. Henry takes over the radio—and he's hard of hearing!

About the food?—Well frankly, I haven't seen enough to form a judgment. After a week or so of dieting, I started to keep fruit in my room, but Bobby (age 4) discovered that (probably he was as hungry as I) and told his mother. One of my fellow teachers quoted Mrs. Henry as saying to her neighbors that I was too particular about my eating. Mrs. Henry works in several clubs, and meals are served at any time convenient to her.

The school seems to be the big topic of conversation in this community, and since I am "one of the family" I go through a regular cross-examination at the dinner table, night after night. Mrs. Henry wants to know whose children are making low marks, why the principal doesn't keep stricter discipline, and why we don't "teach 'em facts." I already know why every teacher for the last fifteen years has been fired. According to Mrs. Henry, the whole town is "up in arms" because the teachers are showing marked favoritism to the trustees' children. It looks as though the whole faculty will be dismissed at the end of the year if half of what Mrs. Henry says is correct.

I dislike to move at this time. In fact, I'm actually afraid to move. You see, I am known by very few people and I'm certain Mrs. Henry would excuse my leaving by telling all her neighbors and friends that she couldn't stand me any longer. In fact, if you could hear her talk about others, you would certainly conclude that she would start in on me if I moved.

I am sorry I can't write you more cheerfully. Perhaps I'll do better in my next letter. And now to planning my work for tomorrow.

Love,
Ruth

Teaching in itself will involve many adjustments, and the prospect of a private comfortable room free from distracting influence, together with well-balanced nourishing meals, can do much to improve one's efficiency on the job.

THE FIRST FACULTY MEETING

A few schools—fortunately an increasing number—provide workshops of one or two weeks' duration for teachers (with compensation) prior to the opening of school. At any rate, it is common practice in good schools to hold general and departmental faculty meetings a day or two before the opening of school. The purposes of such meetings are:

1. To provide an opportunity for teachers informally to meet new and old members of the staff.
2. To acquaint everyone with policies relating to various phases of the school's program, such as guidance activities and extracurricular work.

3. To develop teamwork on the part of the staff.

4. To give teachers time to plan the early days of school so that these days may be devoted to purposeful activities.

5. To enable teachers to plan new curriculum units cooperatively.

In brief, school administrators realize that the spirit developed on the opening days of school has an important bearing on the degree of success to be achieved the rest of the year. In any case, these days should be devoted wholeheartedly to two purposes as far as the beginning teacher is concerned: (1) having a good time learning to know new people, (2) planning the details of the opening days.

THE FIRST DAY OF SCHOOL

If it is the policy of the school to start regular work on the first day, then make, for every period of the day, a plan that is complete, unique, interesting, and purposeful. More specifically, routine matters should be handled efficiently, if possible instructional materials should be on hand, and the work assigned to pupils should be definite and challenging. The preliminary planning by the teacher should ideally be carried to the point that an atmosphere permeates the classroom which to pupils seems to imply: "This is a work period, there is something for all to do, and it is interesting. Let's work together and get it done."

The preliminary planning of such a comprehensive nature will involve at least in part:

1. Making a tentative bibliography of reference materials in the central library that relates to your area; *e.g.*, books, magazines, pictures, etc.

2. Inventorying the school's supply of visual-aid equipment; *e.g.*, projectors, stereopticons, films, slides, pictures, etc.

3. Checking the laboratory equipment of the classroom; *e.g.*, maps, charts, globes, dictionary, volumes in the classroom library, etc.

4. Making the classroom attractive for the opening day; *e.g.*, giving it at least a touch to suggest the subject-matter area.

5. Evolving a plan of the instructional phases of the first day's work that will: (*a*) reduce routine matters to a minimum, (*b*) employ purposeful pupil activities, and (*c*) include a carefully estimated time budget.

When this has been accomplished, the teacher is well started on a program that ensures direction, aim, and continuity to classroom activities in daily plans and in the larger units. Moreover, careful planning in the early days of teaching will do much to alleviate the mental strain and worry.

HOME VISITING

How much home visiting you can do in the early months depends on your teaching load, on the attitude of the administration, and on the character of the community. For example, in some communities teachers never visit the homes. On the other hand, when a very large city was forced to delay the opening of school on account of an

The janitor is an important member of the school community. In a small school where the turnover is rapid, he may be the only one in the building who knows very much about the school. His full cooperation goes a long way toward giving the new teacher a good start.[D]

epidemic, thousands of teachers spent two solid weeks visiting homes and accomplished amazing results. Here we shall attempt no more than to convince you of the worth-whileness of home visiting and to suggest a few helpful procedures. We shall attempt to do this by inviting your attention to the following report of a committee on home visiting:

Each member of our committee has carried out a regular program of visiting homes during the past two years. We wish to make the following summarized report:

1. We believe that our relations with parents and pupils have been tremendously improved through home visiting.

2. In nearly every case we found that parents had fine human qualities, a fact that was sometimes difficult to believe before visiting.

3. Some parents seemed to be surprised to find that we were really human beings. In some of the poorer families, they were suspicious of us at first; some even tried to avoid seeing us. These same people were very grateful for our visit after learning of our friendly mission.

4. We find that we are able to work in a more intelligent and sympathetic manner with those pupils whose homes we have visited.

5. In light of our experience, we offer the following brief suggestions to those teachers who expect to enter upon a visiting program:

   a. Learn as much as possible from office records and other teachers about the child whom you are to visit.

   b. If the child has brothers or sisters in the same school, you are certain to be asked questions concerning them. It would be well, therefore, to inform yourself concerning them.

   c. You will be asked many questions of a general nature concerning the school, especially concerning administrative aspects. You should learn as much about your school as possible before visiting.

6. We should like to make the following suggestions for the consideration of the administration:

   a. A bulletin or handbook of general information about the school should be placed in the hands of every teacher, and a consistent effort should be made to keep teachers properly informed with respect to the schools.

   b. Since most of the dissatisfaction with our schools seems to be based on ignorance or false rumors, we suggest that the administration use every available medium for keeping the community properly informed concerning the various phases of our school life.

   c. Records of home visits might be filed and passed along with other personnel data as the child advances through school.

Emotional Adjustment

When the human being adjusts to a new situation he is likely to undergo strains and stresses. The emotional adjustment that a beginning teacher has to make when the picture is completely new is probably far greater than most people appreciate. In the early days you will have great difficulty remembering anything that you learned about pedagogy and you will go home terribly weary, believing that it is the work that makes you tired when actually it is the long period of unrecognized emotional strain. You make the adjustment by cutting down the number of little problems and by solving the big ones at least partially. To aid you in cutting down the little ones, we now call your attention to a statement in the form of a letter that contains many sensible suggestions.

BOARD OF EDUCATION

J. B. Johnstone, President

MIDDLETOWN, ANY STATE

June 1, ——

DEAR GEORGE AND NANCY:

Both of you are going to do your beginning teaching next year, and as I know something about the situations that you will have to face, I may be able to help you meet some of your problems. For twenty-three years I have been president of our school board and have seen many teachers come and go. Some were great successes and many were sad failures. Most of the failures had a good education and knew how to teach, but they didn't know how to get along with us. You've had good training in college for work in the classroom, but you need some advice from your old uncle on fitting in to a new community. So here's a summary of a whole course of lectures. Don't leave this stored away with your college notebooks. I'm just sure enough of its value to advise you to carry it along with your money and your toothbrush. Read it on the way down on the train, read it once a day for the first week, and read it whenever you need it later.

You are facing a situation in which you can learn more than you ever learned in a year of your life before. You will be under contract to teach, but your most important task is to learn. Even though you are thoroughly at home in the subjects you will teach and though you know how to teach them, your most important task is to learn to work with the most difficult material in the world—folks.

To deal wisely with boys and girls in the classroom, you must know the home and the neighborhood which are helping to make them what they are. Don't overestimate your share in their training. The home and the neighborhood are also on the job of changing children. You need to understand parents, "substantial citizens," and others who are factors in the life of the town because you have to live with these folks day in and day out as a teacher and as a member of the community. You cannot have much influence at school unless you are approved by the town. Their approval will depend on your character and common sense.

How can you win the town?

First, be professional. Put the rights of parents and children ahead of your personal interests. Give your best to your work. Think twice before you talk about the school or the teachers—many of its problems are not suitable for general discussion. If you feel you must let off steam or burst, keep a diary (under lock and key) or write to some discreet friend who lives 3,000 miles away.

Second, proceed as if you were going to spend the rest of your life in that town. Make its interests your interests. Don't criticize. Don't quote some other town where you have lived. Don't talk about college: College may still loom large to you, but it does not seem of great importance to the town, and folks may even think you are trying to show off.

Third, go slow, socially. Don't overdo the social side. Don't gossip. Don't make friends too rapidly. Take pains to make the right friends, avoiding those who are considered extreme. Be friendly, of course, and seize opportunities to become acquainted with the homes of your pupils. Don't "date" with high-school boys and girls. Many of them will be near enough your age so that you could enjoy "playing around" with them as you have done with your friends at college. But you can't afford to do it.

Fourth, accept the standards of conduct approved by the town, unless this would mean lowering your standards. We are all apt to feel that our standards are reasonable or necessary. You must expect to be the one to be tolerant, and to accept different ways; the town will not. Be alert to sense local points of view, and don't raise issues. It may be that visiting in cocktail bars, smoking, Sunday movies, and so forth are activities that you approve, but if they are not approved by the town, you can't afford to do them, or to discuss them.

Fifth, be appreciative. Say and do the courteous thing when an effort has been made to please you. It may be that the entertainment did not exactly meet your standards, but it was on a high level of giving if your hosts gave their best. Cultivate the understanding heart.

Do you know the "Wise Old Owl"?

> A wise old owl sat on an oak.
> The more he saw, the less he spoke.
> The less he spoke, the more he heard.
> Why aren't we like this wise old bird?

Since your most important task for the coming year is to learn in the school of life, you will find it profitable to imitate him.

Write me about you successes, and let me help you with your problems if I can.

Your affectionate
Uncle John

Your desirable adjustment can be furthered by liking the children, the town, and your work. We can hear you say "commonplace," and "try and do it." Our answer is that unless you like all kinds of youngsters from the first day you ought not to be teaching school; and as for liking the town, if you think of it as a sociological laboratory in which you can study and learn to understand all kinds of people and, further, if you will undertake a systematic study of one of the town's important problems, you will very quickly find it to be as fascinating a place as you will ever know. As for learning to like the people of the community, one may find in a small town or in a country community the most valued friends that life ever provides. Let no teacher coming from a college or a university imagine himself too good for any country community. It is possible that the man on the cracker barrel would have been president of your college if he had had your opportunity. Study him carefully and he may some day reveal to you a depth and range of interest that are truly cultural—indeed, his intelligence quotient may be higher than yours. Moreover, the radio and the daily papers keep him well informed. To be sure, his dress, manner, and habits may be very different from yours. Beneath his crust of self-consciousness, you may find a human spark responding to the warming rays of a confiding friendship. The idea is expressed in the following quotation:[1]

We have heard laments about the arid wildernesses in America where no library service is available. It is reported that approximately forty million people are without such contact. Accustomed as we are to associating popular educational service with print and other library accessories we are prone to forget that simplicity of surroundings, even hardships, have educational effects often enriched by the fact that these untaught people are masters of their own destiny, humble as it may be. With confusion and helplessness all about us we might be tempted to ask if standards of life—national or individual—and character-making are not realized in the quiet corners of our land where life is a little primitive quite as soundly as in the great centers of energy where life is a little hectic and under the whip of the sensational.

No doubt it has been within the experience of our field workers to meet and be honored with the confidence of the simple, kindly folk of rural habitation, where the friendly return of a greeting and many other expressions of good-will—with no thought of profit—are forthcoming quietly and in accordance with an ancient, unwritten code. These people know little of organized welfare work, but they have the ability to stand on their own feet—give a lift where it is needed, help their friends without imposing upon the self-respect of either.

Many of these folks of broken speech have their sanctuaries both within themselves and in the open where nature has revealed herself to their seeing eyes. Thither they wander in their hours of ease and commune with the mysterious truth of life, feeling its strength, as does the Arab kneeling on his prayer rug. Out of such golden threads are woven folk history, national culture, and deep attachments—the soil out of which national literature blossoms and comes to harvest. We might find that more human virtues and a deeper unselfish affection are born and kept

[1] ADAM STROHM. "Intellectual Freedom and Integrity," *School and Society*, XXXIV (July 18, 1931), 72.

alive in the "wee hoose in the heather" than in the Alpine country of American skyscrapers.

Poor emotional adjustment may take the form of your having more than your share of acute discipline problems. Hence we return once more to this topic. Read again, when you have taught several days, the chapter on discipline; for by that time you will have an experience basis to appreciate the suggestions.

When you are off by yourself, do not worry long without seeking help. If feasible, telephone, write to, or consult with your former supervising teacher. Or you may be able to find someone in a nearby institution for the education of teachers who will give you a opportunity to get your troubles "off your chest" and treat what you say in strict professional confidence.

On Dealing with Controversial Issues

Many a beginning teacher gets into difficulty by attempting to deal with issues that are too "hot" for him to handle. In far too many cases trouble could have been avoided if only the teacher had kept the problem and his own role clearly in mind.

Educators must establish emphatically and soak into the thinking and feelings of the people the right to know the truth. An unswerving allegiance to the facts of our modern economic and political society must become a passion of society. If the control of the government ultimately resides in the realm of the people, then the people must be constantly schooled in seeking the facts, must have access to the facts in every situation, and must learn to make important decisions with regard to public policy in the light of those facts. It is true that facts and statistics may be misleading, but the correction for this error comes not from subterfuge and concealment but through more facts and more inquiries. Nothing is too sacred to be dragged out into the open for discussion and examination when it touches the public welfare. The public welfare is too important to be determined by anything less than the tested truth. If we accept this thesis of democracy, then we need to examine the extent to which this practice is now true.

One tragic element about modern democracy is that important issues are not discussed openly and the spirit of scientific and democratic inquiry is not followed in making knowledge available to the masses. Impartial sources of information are difficult to secure.

Newspapers are for the most part notoriously colored in their services by the interests which support them. The research of the expert is stored away in some great library. The implication for education of this discussion is clear. *School and public libraries should subscribe to a variety of books and periodicals representing widely divergent viewpoints in order that pupils, teachers, and the general reader may be able to compare and contrast presentations.* No serious-minded reader can secure a complete view of international or domestic problems today when he is confined to the narrow range of reporting represented by the average periodical list offered by the average school and public library.

Furthermore, there should be free and unrestricted discussion of so-called controversial issues. Both sides of disputed points should be deliberately presented. Fair play should cover all parts of a controversy, even if it is offensive to the audience. If something we fear is the truth, our fear will never save us from the consequences of our ignorance. If something we fear or hate is wrong, then free inquiry and the illumination of examination will reveal the error and dissipate the fear. Democracy can never lose by loyalty to the scientific pursuit of truth, but democracy is in serious danger if that right is ever qualified. In this day of tyranny abroad and milder manifestations of tyranny in our own country, democracy must thoroughly establish the right to know the truth and insist that ways and means be constantly developed whereby that truth is open to the humblest citizen, uncolored by special interests or distorted by an alien spirit.

There are other important implications of this discussion for educational practice. *The entire curriculum, teaching procedure, and administrative practice should carry responsibility for inculcating the American spirit and method of democracy.* A school administration can be a dictatorship stifling student and teacher participation in cooperation and control, or it can be a creative democracy in which the superintendent shares his task of leadership with every person involved in the system. The teacher can be a tyrant, pounding his pupils into submission, or he can lead them into higher levels of richer individuality. The curriculum can be imposed by fiat with no other justification than the inertia of tradition, or it can be modified on the basis of the vital needs and purposes of the pupils. And an educational method can develop such dependence of the pupil on routine requirements handed down from above that he becomes servile in mind and supine in personality. Or it can inculcate the habit of taking responsibility for the setting of tasks and the outlining of plans for their accomplishment, thereby leading the pupil into independence in adjusting to the common good.

These few examples suffice to indicate that there is an autocratic and a democratic way to conduct our schools. The democratic way is the American way. And educators cannot avoid its fundamental challenge.

It is clear from the preceding discussion that the teacher's role with respect to controversial issues is one of fundamental importance. It yet remains true that in many instances a teacher has got into trouble either because he did not know enough about the issue or because of the way in which he dealt with it.

Respect for pupil personality requires that a teacher will refrain from presenting a single solution to a pupil as a sort of fixed pattern that a pupil must accept. The democratic and American way of solving a social problem demands that the greatest number possible of our future citizens shall be taught to consider fairly the arguments for each of a number of alternative solutions. Hence there can be no question as to the teacher's right to deal with controversial issues, if the continued improvement of our fundamental institutions is to be assured. But to be able to "get away with this" the teacher must have a very broad scholarship, the ability to deal with delicate matters in an impersonal, objective, and fair-minded way; the disposition to keep an argument free from emotion; and the habit of keeping his own views out of the picture until some pupil says, "Where do you stand?" then taking a definite position, but admitting that we all have our biases and prejudices and that at best his own opinion is merely one of alternative solutions.

Although the attitude of communities is changing very rapidly, there are still many parents who are skeptical when teachers undertake to deal with highly controversial issues. For practical purposes our parents can be classified into two groups—the stupid and the thoughtful. The stupid parent wants his children taught the same narrow views that he himself holds. The intelligent parent, recognizing the limitations in the scholarship of the typical teacher, has the "jitters" as he contemplates what is likely to happen to his children when this teacher, with deep emotionalized prejudices, proceeds in the name of academic freedom, to inculcate these narrow patterns of thought. The fundamental problem presented to the schools by both types of parents is not so much the preservation of academic freedom; it is rather the proper selection and the thorough education of teachers.

The preceding discussion throws considerable light on the much-debated issue, "Shall the schools be used to construct a new social order?" This question seems more pertinent: Who knows what is to be the new social order? If we have faith in the ideals of American democracy, we will allow no one, not even the teachers in our schools, to force a final solution or a fixed pattern upon the minds of our children. The votary of academic freedom too often emphasizes freedom to *teach* what he pleases and overlooks a far more important issue: freedom to *learn*, or the right to know the truth. Admitting that occasionally a teacher becomes an innocent victim of a powerful pressure group or of selfish persons with influence in a community, it is also true that the occasions when teachers get into difficulties will be sharply decreased when they learn to be broad-minded and tactful, and thus become capable of respecting the personality of the pupil. The teacher's real opportunity, namely, to develop the pupil's own capacity to think, will be greatly enhanced if he constantly guards against imposing his own viewpoint. We must have faith that the people will make wise choices when they have been taught how to gather all the available facts which are significant to an issue, and when they have discussed these facts adequately. To this end, a greater percentage of our people must be taught to think, and to think unselfishly from the social point of view. If this does not provide a way out, then there seems to be little hope for mankind to control his own destiny. The school faces two dangers: first, the adoption of a policy of drift and evasion which will allow it to be controlled by the dominating groups in the community; and second, the surrender of its democratic ideal to the forces that spread propaganda for any fixed solution.

DON'T LET IT HAPPEN TO YOU

We come now to the question: What can you do to keep growing as a personality and alive on the job as a professional worker? Few workers have better opportunities than teachers for continued growth, and yet the fact is that some teachers fail to take steps as insurance against certain hazards. High-school youngsters become aware of the situation in hours of deadly boredom. Age forty to fifty is a critical period! And yet this need not be. The fact is that many teachers plan their professional careers so as to stay young to an amazing age.

Among the steps that a teacher can take to increase his efficiency and to maintain his enthusiasm as the years roll by are:

1. *Travel.* Though there is no effort here to arrange the steps in order of importance, we would put travel highest on the list. Aside from the obvious advantages such as increased information and experiences, travel for a teacher, of the type that enables him "to get away from it all" and undertake something entirely new, is a matter of mental hygiene. Do not overlook the fact that you may be able to take an exciting trip on a freighter to the South Sea Islands or a thrilling trip to a foreign country at less than the cost of attending a single summer session. Few experiences build for greater culture than travel.

2. *Apply the exchange idea.* There comes a time in the experiences of most teachers when they simply go stale on the job. If a teacher has established a reputation, he may be able to arrange an exchange with a teacher of another school system rather easily. Then, too, one may confidently expect that in a shrinking world there will be many attractive opportunities to travel and to teach in foreign countries. It is admitted, of course, that this suggestion is difficult of execution for a teacher with dependents who cannot easily be moved.

3. *Continue as a student.* (*a*) Take advantage of summer sessions, extension classes, workshops, or part-time campus study to keep out of ruts. (*b*) Form the habit of singling out your difficulties and analyzing them for solution. (*c*) Experiment with appraisal techniques.

4. *Read the professional literature.* Obviously you will not have time for extensive reading, but there is no excuse for not reading at least several professional magazines dealing with the progress of general education and one or two magazines that deal with the specific problems of your teaching field. The teacher of English, for example, should read the *English Journal* regularly.

5. *Read widely books of general interest.* The main purpose no doubt should be sheer enjoyment and expanding interests, but there

is a very practical reason why a teacher should form the habit of reading one or two of the best newspapers and general magazines regularly. It is that the intelligent members of a community, granted that they may be few in number in a small town, will very promptly label a teacher who is the last one to read a popular biography, novel, or book on social trends as insufferably stupid.

6. *Cultivate a hobby.* In addition to being fun and expanding one's interests, a hobby for a teacher is a means of improving mental health that may be a good deal cheaper than travel, and more easily undertaken.

7. *Affiliate with professional organizations.* The teaching profession supports many voluntary organizations, the dues of which are very much less than is the case in other professions or in labor organizations. Of course, you are altogether within your legal rights if you do not belong, but you are undoubtedly gaining advantages for which some one else has paid in energy, time, and money; for the fact is that these professional organizations are improving the salaries and the conditions under which teachers work. The beginning teacher should give the matter of belonging to professional organizations a fair trial. The chances are that he will soon come to the point of looking forward to attending the local meeting regularly, the meetings of state organizations frequently, and a national meeting occasionally. The programs should, and probably do, provide valuable experiences for him. Furthermore, you may confidently look forward to these meetings as opportunities for renewing contacts with an increasing circle of friends in the profession.

GROWTH THROUGH EXPERIMENTATION

The individual teacher can often evade the limitations of a threatening pressure group and secure a large measure of academic freedom from excessively conservative school administrators and a critical public through careful experimentation and systematic investigation of a delimited problem. But there are two additional values that accrue to the teacher through experimentation: (1) it is the way to make significant changes in the curriculum and in method; and (2) it is the surest method by which the teacher can wake up and keep alive.

Let us consider these values in a greater detail. With regard to greater freedom, intelligent and resourceful teachers can often secure the needed permission (which otherwise might have been denied) to undertake some progressive innovation in method or curriculum when it is undertaken as a properly controlled study. In many communities it may be wise to avoid the word "experiment" when dealing with laymen, and to refer to it merely as a "study of what some teachers in good school systems believe to be a better plan." In

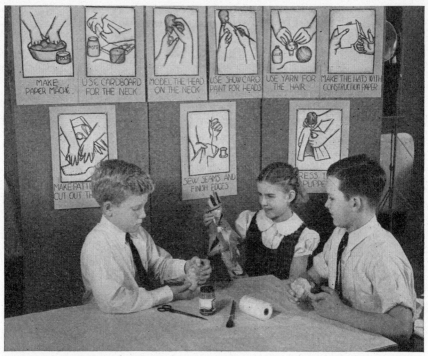

Probably one of the best ways for a teacher to keep alive and growing is to teach at least one unit each year in a different and better way. Note the splendid use of visual aids for showing steps in the construction under way.[D]

dealing with school people, you can get almost anything in the name of an experiment.

Our second thesis is that experimentation is the sound conservative policy for making changes in schools because it challenges the old and tests the new. A teacher who goes the experimental route is less likely to seize avidly a thing that is new merely because it is new. Proposals for reform in the curriculum are often written by laymen in such brilliant style that a wholly fallacious nostrum may seem plausible to the uninitiated and the uninformed. Then, too, the beginning teacher needs protection against the excessive and untested ideas of educationists. It is difficult indeed for the teacher, busy with many routine tasks, to winnow the grain from the mountain of chaff. The teacher's protection against the illusive snares of the educational propagandist on the one hand and the excessively conservative layman on the other is careful experimentation, by which we mean the systematic study of a well-defined problem. The teacher who grows as a classroom practitioner is one who is a student of method—one who is never satisfied with his teaching skill, and who will, from time to time, want to investigate whether a proposed method is better than the one he has been using. By carefully checking and studying the results of his own teaching, he is more likely to be stimulating and efficient in his classroom.

Teaching Is a Big Job

It is no overstatement when you are told that the immediate welfare of our people, the future destiny of our nation, and the ultimate existence of civilization rests on the shoulders of the schoolmaster. To function effectively you must ever keep in mind what the job is that schools are trying to do and how well equipped we are to do it. Moreover, you must ever be alert in incidental moments to seize every opportunity to drive the facts home to citizens. As the years go by, keep informed as to what the general picture is. One way to keep up to date is to watch the magazines and read articles by our educational leaders. The public press and the radio have in recent years become very active in advancing the cause of education. A teacher should do no less. The following quotation[1] is a sample of the kind of information that you should have:

Every winter weekday some 28,000,000 children dawdle through their dressing, gobble their breakfasts and head for school. One in twenty-five goes to a one-room schoolhouse where a young woman—who will probably soon give up teaching—is teacher, nurse, cook and janitor. Approximately one in fifteen goes to a school considered unsafe, or planned as a temporary structure. Approximately one in ten goes to a private school—probably a parochial school. More than half study under teachers paid less than many unskilled laborers receive for their efforts. And about one in ten of the grade-school children will drop out before the sixth grade.

[1] John W. Studebaker. "The ABC's of Public Education," *Ladies' Home Journal*, February, 1948, pp. 71, 98. Reprinted by special permission from the *Ladies' Home Journal*. Copyright 1948. The Curtis Publishing Company.

Three in ten will not complete high school. Only one in seven will go on to college.

These are a handful of America's educational averages.

Today's educational problems are the greatest our country has ever faced. Unless we solve them, it is a proved fact that we can expect our prosperity to decline, our crime rate to rise, and our proud democracy to tremble. It is easy to say that the war, the teacher shortage, the apathy of many communities, political chicanery or lack of money is to blame. But no one of these provides an answer; all in their own way are *results*—not causes.

Let us leave captious glibness to our foreign critics—like the Canadian who remarked that the United States is "substituting the *little read* schoolteacher for the little red schoolhouse." Let us dig in and find out how we who preen ourselves on our public education, our high standards of culture for all, our know-how, our democracy, have neglected education so much that headline writers dare say that our schools have rapidly deteriorated. Let us see, too, *why* we need public education, *what* our educational needs are, *how* our schools are set up and *wherein they are failing and succeeding* before we determine our manner of support.

Early in our history, when the newly established America was struggling to break away from European ideas of education and establish education for the people, by the people, Thaddeus Stevens, a Vermonter, was asked by an aristocrat who sent his children to private schools why one should be called upon to support public schools when he had no intention of using them. Mr. Stevens replied suavely, "I trust it is not your intention to use the public jails you support either?" With this thought—that the public schools are the concern not only of parents, but of all citizens of our society—let us first take up the question of *why* we need education.

A healthy public-school system means a healthy nation—and it also means a wealthy one.

Great resources avail us little if we are not educated to utilize them. Many studies, including the notable one by the United States Chamber of Commerce, entitled *Education, an Investment in People*, have made clear that some countries— and even some of our states—rich in fertile land and other resources but with low standards of education, have low per-capita assets. On the other hand, some countries, handicapped by relatively poor natural resources but with good systems of education, have known how to develop and conserve their resources and establish a relatively high standard of living.

It was no coincidence that the great growth of our country occurred during the same years that education saw its greatest period of growth. Just as from 1801 to 1931 the wages of American workingmen increased by over 1300 per cent, so, during the same years, did education increase from an average of 82 days of schooling per person to an average of over 1400 days—an increase of 1600 per cent. And it is important to note that the increase in education preceded the increase in prosperity; that the profits from wider educational facilities for more people were to be reaped only *after* the seeds of knowledge had been sown.

As I have indicated, what is true for countries is true, too, of our states.

Those states with the lowest teachers' salaries are also on the bottom of the list of per-capita income. One may twist this to say that because the state's income is low, the pay of the teachers is low—but it is certain fact that so long as state, or city, or county invests little in knowledge, it can expect little in prosperity.

Its citizens will desert it for better educational opportunities elsewhere; its electorate will be apathetic and willing victims to demagoguery; its native businesses will fail; its resources will lie only partially used—or will be exploited by others for others. This is the condition of some of the states already; others are heading in this direction. It behooves all of us to interest ourselves in the welfare of not only our own neighborhoods' education, but that of the nation as a whole, if we truly desire prosperity and security.

And what of the individual himself? How closely is his prosperity related to his education? The psychological assets of education are intangible, but the material assets are more easily assessed. A survey published in 1943 estimated that the average life earnings of a grammar-school graduate are $45,000; of a high-school graduate, $78,000; of a college graduate, $150,000.

Today, in terms of production and income in this period of educational decline, we are still reaping the profits of past education. While the average American today is likely to go to *better* schools for *longer* periods than his father did before him, the question of whether he can expect a greater success or more happiness in life is directly related to whether our present educational facilities meet the needs of our time.

No one will gainsay the fact that our civilization is now much more complex, its demands more specialized, its tempo faster than it was, say, fifty years ago. "No greater crisis," Dr. Raymond B. Fosdick, president of the Rockefeller Foundation, and a lifelong student of America's educational problems, declared recently, "was ever faced by any generation in history. . . . Whether the future is to be a nightmare without end depends on our ability to make some headway in finding the answers." Our two world wars, our discoveries of methods of wholesale destruction, violence and disruption are evils that must be conquered if we are to live in stability and harmony. It is a major part of our schools' responsibility to make our young people at home in the world, to give them a confident sense of mastery and competence with which to counteract the already too widespread sense of insecurity and frustration.

Yet it is a fact that after more than a century of increasingly better education we are now in danger of going backward—not forward. In 1946 we invested only 2.2 per cent of our national income in education, although in 1933 we invested 3.7 per cent! But as individuals we are paying 5.2 per cent of our earned income for alcohol.

What we sow, we reap. Unless we take up the challenge and invest in better education for all, we can rest assured that the harvest we can expect from our present investments will *not* be those things which, in the past, we have grown to believe are synonymous with the American way of living.

THE PRINCIPAL AND THE SUPERVISOR LOOK AT THE
BEGINNING TEACHER

Many a new teacher has wondered what the principal really expects of him. We turn now to the minutes of a panel discussion in which a number of people widely experienced in inducting new teachers into their problems have a part.

PANEL LEADER: The topic today is, What we as supervisors and principals expect of the beginning teacher. Mr. Kane, I know that you have long been especially interested in giving the right kind of help to new teachers. Will you open the discussion?

MR. KANE: In recommending a beginning teacher for a position in my building, I assume that he is not only willing, but is perfectly capable of handling the "little problems" that inevitably arise in the classroom. I certainly do not want the beginning teacher to assume that my office can be converted into a "dog pound," to which every disagreeable problem case can be sent. It isn't that I'm not anxious to help my teachers, particularly the new ones, but rather, by insisting that teachers handle their own disciplinary cases, I feel I really am giving them the most valuable help I can. There are two exceptions to this general statement. First, if a teacher has failed in his treatment of the case, I certainly expect him to come to me for suggestions. Finally, if the problem is of a very serious nature, I want it brought to my attention. In short, I expect my beginning teacher to handle his own "little problems" while we solve the larger ones together.

MR. BLAINE: I expect my beginning teachers to accept the constructive suggestions of supervisors. Far too many beginners create an imaginary barrier between the supervisor and themselves. They seem to have the feeling that supervision is a matter of espionage instead of a source of help and inspiration to better teaching. The load of the beginning teacher is lighter if he is wise enough to permit his supervisor to give him a helping hand.

MR. CARROLL: I want my new teacher to have a philosophy of education consistent with that held by the rest of the staff; for after all, if the school is to get anywhere on its program, each classroom activity must emerge from and be related to the larger aims of general education and the needs of the community. There is no place in our school for any "one-room schools" in which misguided teachers with rugged individualistic tendencies can shut themselves away from the rest of the program.

MR. BROWN: I agree that a new teacher should from the first day be "one of the group." By this I mean that I expect them to become enthused with the program of the school, help develop a good tone in the school, cooperate with all the staff, and contribute at least some one thing that is distinctly unique during the year.

MR. BYRN: I wonder if you will agree that one of the common mistakes of beginning teachers is their failure to make prompt and complete reports? I refer particularly to absence and tardy reports, summary of marks, and semester scholastic reports, although there are of course other periodic reporting forms that the office must have from time to time from classroom teachers. This is purely a matter of cooperation. Failure to make reports promptly to the office is often symptomatic of poor classroom management and planning.

MR. HARDIN: I would like to express the point of view of the principal in a smaller high school in a community of about 5,000 people. Here the successful beginning teacher is expected to help in interpreting the school to the community.

This matter of interpretation has both its positive and negative aspects. On the positive side it means visiting parents, taking advantage of opportunities to meet a number of people in the community and acquainting them with the constructive things the school has either done or is planning to do. Furthermore, we expect a new teacher to refrain from gossiping, criticizing the work of one's colleagues, and passing on information of a confidential nature about pupils and things that happen from time to time in the school.

Mr. Kane: Before we adjourn, I want to bear down on Mr. Hardin's suggestions which I think are important in any school, small or large. I expect my beginning teacher to realize that he is a very important part of our public-relations program. The school must have satisfied customers, and even the best school must make certain that the facts are made known to a goodly number of people in the community. Now the teacher has at least two important contacts in making clear to our public what the school is doing; the first of these contacts obviously is the children. On any school policy that is valid the teacher can set the stage so that pupils will aggressively enlist the active interests of parents. Often this procedure is not only valid, but a highly desirable part of the regular work of a class. The second opportunity for contacts that I have in mind is with the parents. Too often these contacts are negative in that a teacher does not see a parent unless something has gone wrong, as for example, failure in studies, discipline problem, etc. The chances of setting up a right relationship with parents when there is already something wrong in the picture are low, and the teacher should at least equalize these negative contacts by deliberately planning to establish friendly relationships.

Mr. Jones: The question brought up by Mr. Kane is of great importance in our school system as well, and I am reminded of two further good opportunities for contacts. One may be established through teacher participation in various social groups in the community. It is immaterial whether persons contacted in this manner are parents or not. The point is that all count as voters, and if they have valid criticisms we ought to know them; and if they are not valid, we should provide them with the facts. As an administrator, I readily admit that a teacher can on some problems be more helpful than we who are in the administration. The public has great faith in what a successful teacher says. Finally, the teacher can help us develop our public-relations program in participation in the various community organizations. The word of a teacher who is a constructive worker on some project in which the community is interested carries conviction.

Panel Leader: Since our time is up, we must now adjourn without attempting a summary.

The Road Ahead for the Teaching Profession

If you are convinced that education is crucial in the lives of people, then you have a supreme duty. You must seek as long as you live, as a professional worker or as a citizen, to place a good teacher in every classroom. We need about one million competent teachers. We will never get them, and certainly not hold them, under present conditions.   We must strive hard to improve the *status and the work-ing conditions* of teachers.   One difficulty, we believe, is that society has not generally recognized certain rights of teachers.   Presumably teachers themselves will, in the end, wish to formulate their own "bill of rights."   To speed the process we suggest that you read the follow-ing statement which has been widely discussed in the public press.

The ultimate goal of education is the making of good citizens.   Here the emphasis is not on academic subjects but rather on the child himself, with his complex urges for expression and need for development.   Your growth as a teacher will depend on the extent to which you help society achieve this goal.[D]

An Evolving Bill of Rights for Teachers[1]

In recent months newspapers, magazines, and government reports have printed convincing facts regarding the shortage of qualified teachers.   The prospects of getting enough good teachers in the next decade are poor.   The fact is that many

[1] This proposal by the author was published originally in the May, 1946, issue of the *University of Michigan School of Education Bulletin*.   It has been reprinted in more than forty magazines and newspapers and has been used in numerous editorials and articles in the public press, as for example, *Time*, *Ladies' Home Journal*, *Christian Science Monitor*, and *The New York Times*.

able young persons now in training, who under proper conditions would prefer to teach, are rejecting teaching as a career. Salary is an issue, but there are about a dozen additional reasons why young people turn away from teaching. Most of these relate to the *working conditions* of teachers.

These various reasons why teaching fails to attract as many able young people as the schools need are listed in the following pages in a Bill of Rights for Teachers. It is hoped that a valid bill of rights will emerge from study groups in order that the public may come to realize that we will never get enough good teachers, nor will the competent teachers now in service ever be able to do reasonably efficient work until certain working conditions are improved.

Inasmuch as every boy and girl of school age is entitled to good teachers, in a very real sense the proposal is a bill of rights for youth. However, a direct attack on the problem is forthright and presumably is more likely to be understood by the public.

THE RIGHTS OF A CLASSROOM TEACHER

1. *The right to teach classes that are not too large—in general, from ten to twenty pupils.*

The average class size in the schools of the armed forces for more than twelve million men and women was less than one-half of the actual class size of civilian schools in our metropolitan areas. Individual attention and proper guidance cannot be given by a teacher with oversized classes. Experts insist that crime and delinquency which now cost us, annually, at least six times what the nation pays for its schools, could be sharply reduced if teachers knew enough about their pupils and did the right things for them. A policy of small classes is economical in money and, above all, in human resources.

2. *The right to have time in the school day for planning.*

In general, the instructors in the schools of the armed forces had at least one hour to plan and to prepare for each hour of teaching. Teachers need to plan with their pupils, and with supervisors, parents, and other teachers. Planning is not possible if there is little or no time for planning, and if the people concerned cannot find the time to meet. It is not sensible for a teacher to operate hour after hour without a plan. Moreover, it is a waste of public funds. Wise observers of high-school instruction have stated time and again that more than half of the pupil's time is wasted. Surely the public will want to allow a teacher of 100 pupils three hours a day for planning if by so doing perhaps some 400 hours of his pupils' time can thereby be put to better use.

3. *The right of a 45-hour week.*

In general, the teacher's week should include (*a*) 15 hours of teaching, (*b*) 15 hours of planning and pupil guidance, and (*c*) 15 hours devoted to sponsoring extracurricular activities, participating in community activities, and grading pupils' written work. It is extremely important for teachers to supervise student activities and to engage in community projects, but it is impossible for a teacher to maintain a high level of efficiency in his classroom if at the same time he is expected to be a social worker, a director of activities, and a guidance official. A teacher's extra work—grading papers, planning, visits to homes, etc.—cannot be left on the desk at the end of the school day. No one knows the average number of hours per week for all teachers, but it is probably much closer to 60 hours a week than it is to 45 hours.

4. *The right to an adequate amount of helpful and constructive supervision.*

The valid purposes of the right kind of supervision are (1) to help the teacher plan, (2) to aid in providing good materials and effective methods, and (3) to insure that the teacher grows on the job. In many of the schools of the armed forces an instructor was supervised from 40 to 60 per cent of the time that he taught. It is uneconomical to operate schools without good supervision. An occasional brief visit, inspectional in character, is in many cases unfair to teachers. The teacher who, day after day, does a good job, finds it difficult to maintain morale and to avoid devastating frustration when no one ever comes to see his work or to discuss his plans with him. The right kind of supervision in adequate amounts is deeply appreciated by teachers.

5. *The right to adequate compensation for the full year of fifty-two weeks.*

The teaching profession includes an astonishing number per hundred who labor with high competence and missionary zeal regardless of compensation. For that we are grateful and proud, but a million persons do not, year after year, give themselves to any calling without appropriate salary. What really happens is that many of our best prospects for teaching are attracted by better-paid jobs in industry, in commerce, and in the other professions. Witness the fact that in the three years preceding the Second World War the University of Michigan, a school of more than 10,000 students, recommended for certification a total of only eight teachers in chemistry and two in physics, whereas many times this number went from this university into industrial research. Society is unwittingly paying a devastating penalty when it employs persons who never should teach children merely because they are cheaper than good teachers.

Teachers should be paid on a twelve-months basis with a month's vacation each year allowed with pay. The summer months can profitably be devoted to (1) participation in workshops where they might construct and revise units of instruction, (2) editing reports of in-service study groups, (3) studying the needs of their graduates in industry and business, (4) traveling in order to get new and better materials of instruction, and (5) attending colleges and universities to obtain broader and deeper preparation.

6. *The right to have good materials and enough of them.*

The disposition of society toward the cost of educating for living in a peaceful world presents a sharp contrast with the attitude toward the expense of training for combat. The Army and Navy operated schools at a cost per student several times as large as the average spent per pupil in civilian schools. Thousands of mechanics were trained at an annual cost per man greater than the annual salary of the industrial arts teacher in the home school.   Some of the schools of the armed forces had magnificent classrooms and laboratories such as teachers in civilian schools can scarcely imagine.   Too often a teacher is expected to perform miracles, without the materials needed for the tasks.   Such a teacher may have nothing in the classroom beyond a textbook—and that may be hopelessly out of date.   School boards and administrators should check each year to insure that teachers have at least the minimum materials needed for effective work.   Of especial importance are such audio-visual aids as are genuinely useful and readily available.

7. *The right to work in a room that, with the help of the students, can be made pleasant and appropriate to the tasks to be learned.*

Some industries have demonstrated that efficiency can be increased by the right working conditions.   Too many classrooms give the impression of being places of detention, with little to suggest what the group is trying to do.   The work of the teacher of English, mathematics, or Spanish will be easier and more effective if the atmosphere of his classroom contributes to the activities.   Whenever possible the teacher should have a workroom of his own where he can arrange the settings to make them appropriate to the units of instruction.   In the larger schools it is possible to avoid the wearying task of shifting disorganized materials from room to room throughout the school day.

8. *The right to the same personal liberties which other respectable citizens assume for themselves as a matter of course.*

Many of our best prospects for the teaching profession are rejecting teaching as a career because of the petty restrictions and prohibitions that many communities inflict on their teachers.   These trivial but annoying requirements in personal conduct vary from community to community.   Thus in one community the prohibition may be against teachers' playing cards; in another, dancing on school nights; and in still another, smoking.   Communities that object to a teacher's attending movies are rare, but they still exist.   However, the beginning teacher not uncommonly finds himself in a town in which the lawyer, doctor, business man, priest, and minister can drink any form of liquor any time anywhere and still be held in high regard, whereas a teacher may not have his contract renewed if he drinks a single glass of beer in public.   The truly professional teacher will, as a matter of course, respect the mores of his community and maintain at least as high standards as other respected citizens.   A teacher with high professional zeal probably would *want* to do very few forbidden things that other citizens can do without being censored, but he certainly should have the *right* to do them.   A community may well expect decency and idealism of its teachers, but it has no right to scrutinize every petty detail of their personal lives.   No group of intelligent citizens in other occupations and professions would want every detail of their personal lives supervised.   Teachers are only human beings and should be treated as such.   At any rate it is unwise for parents to annoy teachers with trivialities.   By doing so, they turn colorful, vigorous personalities away from the teaching profession and thus deprive their own children of teachers who might provide strong leadership for high ideals.

9. *The right to an externship.*

No institution of teacher education can turn out a finished product. Yet seldom is the beginning teacher given a light assignment and an adequate amount of supervision. Indeed he is lucky if he does not draw the heaviest load and the most disagreeable tasks.

The solution to the problem of the beginning teacher is the idea of externship. This idea, so vital in medical education, has long been advocated in teacher education and is generally approved, but seldom found in practice. The nature and character of the period of externship is suggested by the following provisions: (1) a light teaching load in the first year of teaching—perhaps half-time; (2) salary appropriate to the load, ideally a living wage for a single person; (3) experience in a great variety of tasks, as for example extracurricular, administrative, and teaching; (4) adequate and competent supervision; (5) an opportunity to study the school and community as a "whole" before being limited to the teaching of a single subject or grade; (6) an arrangement truly professional which guarantees that the externship concept will not be used as a means of hiring a cheap teacher to replace a more expensive but experienced teacher; and (7) the use of gifted teachers with special interest in professional problems to supervise beginning teachers, allowing them time in the school day to do the job and extra compensation for this valuable and technical service.

10. *The right to a realistic program of in-service education.*

By in-service education we mean training on the job. The experienced teacher from time to time needs to revise materials and methods. The in-service program should be geared to a competent department of research that will keep materials and techniques up to date without too much grief and waste of effort. Precious time and energy are now wasted by groups of tired teachers who, after school at the end of a long and weary day, are expected to revise the curriculum. Witness the fact that 85,000 courses of study, created largely by scissors and paste techniques, have been filed in the curriculum collection at Teachers College, Columbia University, and that only a few can be rated as helpful. Boards of education must come to realize that keeping the curriculum up to date is a difficult and technical task which, if attempted at all by teachers, must be done in the school hours of the work day and not in overtime periods without compensation.

11. *The right to participate in modifying the curriculum and methods and in formulating school policies.*

Sound administration of schools will utilize the constructive ideas of all teachers to make sure that the service of the school to its pupils may be made as good as possible, and to insure that a teacher will grow on the job.

12. *The right to keep from being lost in the profession.*

Many excellent teachers are lost in the vast numbers who, with relatively little ability, training, and experience, come and go. There is no systematic provision for continued recognition of growth in the service. All are teachers! There is little differentiation that recognizes competence or length of service except by meager annual increments in salary. To no small degree the gifted teacher is always in competition with all newcomers, however incompetent. Even the members of a strong school board may not be aware that they have especially fine teachers in their schools. Mere financial rewards are not sufficient to maintain morale. A good teacher has the right to be identified by professional recognition that will strengthen his hand in dealing with the public and the pupil. Such machinery for differentiation between the professional worker and the mere transient does not now exist. However, gifted teachers may reasonably look to their professional organizations for the design of a system of identification that is long overdue.

For Discussion

1. Principal Reed is very successful in dealing with parents. When asked for his formula, he responded, "When an annoyed parent appears at my office, I do just two things. First, I listen; second, I say something good about the child before I make any suggestions for improvement. If I can't think of something desirable, I have no business to have such an interview, for it means that I don't know enough about that pupil. The human being doesn't live for which something good can't be discovered."

Do you think that Principal Reed has a good plan for dealing with children and parents?

2. Mr. Smith, a teacher of science, is exceptionally popular with parents. His formula is: "I never criticize a pupil except in an interview with the parent. For example, I think it would be folly to telephone a father or mother to make a complaint. You simply do not know all that is annoying people at the other end, and the telephone is a futile instrument for adjusting differences. I want parents to sit and look me in the eye while they talk about their child. In that way they become convinced that while I am not so desperately concerned about Bill as they are, nevertheless I am very desirous to be of help.

"I always give notice of impending failure a long time in advance.

"I never send home a written report of the reason for failure. As I have said, I want to harness the human factor and make it work in my favor rather than against me over the telephone or on some printed and lifeless administrative form. We are at present unable to make exact statements to parents covering such items as (a) what the pupil has failed to do and (b) precisely what it is the pupil needs to do. Any effort, therefore, to make an exact diagnosis of the situation of the pupil is likely to meet with failure."

Why do you think Mr. Smith considers it so important to keep parents posted concerning impending failure?

3. An alert principal stated his formula for dealing with angry parents in the following words. "When a parent, who seems to be angry or quite annoyed about some school matter, appears at school and demands a conference with a particular teacher, as a general policy I try to have the parent relate his story at least once, and preferably twice, to sympathetic individuals, often the principal and the home-room teacher, before reaching the teacher he wishes to see. It is my belief

that such a procedure has a double effect: First, the problem dwindles in importance as it is retold; second, his bitterness becomes less intense as he discusses the
matter with sympathetic individuals who are not involved."

Does this practice seem to be based on sound psychology? How could you as a
teacher influence the adoption of such a policy?

4. A high-school principal suggests that, if a beginning teacher does not know
how to handle a particular problem in dealing with a parent, the teacher should say
as little as possible until she can confer with the principal. What argument can you
advance in favor of this policy?

5. Have you ever lived in a community where the chief topic of conversation
was "the faults of our schools"? Make a list of common complaints you have
heard about the teachers and schools of your home community. Which of these
might have been avoided?

6. Much has been said about the responsibilities of teachers for interesting a
community in its problems. This is a difficult undertaking because of certain
characteristics of communities, especially the small ones. The following summary
indicates some of these difficulties:

The typical small community is handicapped by:

a. Rivalry and marked lack of cooperation among the churches, clubs, and
other organizations.
b. The strife that arises from carrying partisan politics into local social-service
affairs.
c. The fact that a few individuals in it have met with marked success.
d. The lack of cooperative thinking.

The typical small community is inclined to ignore its own problems for the
following reasons:

a. The interest aroused by the daily paper in the affairs of a neighboring city.
b. The lack of aggressive leadership in its organized life.
c. The differences arising from religious, political, business, and social rivalries.
d. The self-satisfied spirit of many of the older families.
e. The failure to see that the world is changing and that other communities
have moved ahead.
f. The failure of many promising ventures by individuals, clubs, and churches.

Do you agree with these characterizations of the typical small community?

7. Principal Olson says, "I think I have a pretty good basis for predicting the
degree of success that a teacher new in our community will attain. I merely note
from whom she seeks advice and whom she cultivates as her special friends."

What do you think are some common and serious errors that Principal Olson
had in mind?

8. Other things being equal, would each of the following circumstances aid or
retard a beginning teacher's adjustment to a new school and community: camp
experiences, being an only child, coming from a cultured home, work experiences,
critical attitude toward the Sunday school, musical ability, travel experiences, and
having been reared in a community of a very different type?

9. Miss Chipman said, "I wish that all teachers might have more pride in their profession. There are so many fine things about it. Best of all is the daily association with hundreds of young people. The third year I taught I went to a new position in a college town. My mother and sister found that getting acquainted was a slow process, but in a month I knew half the children in the community and, through them, many of the grown-ups. A teacher has friends all over the town.

"A few weeks ago I went to a play. Next to me sat a nice-looking young woman. I couldn't refrain from speaking to her before the play began. I said, 'I'm sure you must be a teacher.' When she replied, 'Yes, I am, but how did you know?' I said, 'Well, I'm a teacher myself and I've been noticing that every child that didn't wave at me, waved at you.' And then we agreed that it is a fine thing to know so many delightful young people."

Do you agree that it may not be difficult for you as a teacher to win friends in a new community?

10. The program for one of the meetings of the parent-teacher organization of the Wilson Community School consisted of two parts: (*a*) a committee of parents reported on the topic, "What parents expect of teachers"; and (*b*) a committee of teachers reported on "What teachers expect of parents." The reports follow:[1]

Parents want teachers:

    (1) To treat them with courtesy and respect when they visit the school.
    (2) To be sufficiently interested in parents to want to talk with them about their children.
    (3) To know pupils well enough to appreciate their good points as well as to recognize their faults.
    (4) To give them a reasonable amount of warning concerning any expenditures for books, supplies, or social affairs.
    (5) To inform them about a problem situation before it gets serious.
    (6) To give special protection to the health of their students.
    (7) To emphasize the mastery of certain fundamental skills in reading and other subjects, and to teach children effective study habits.
    (8) To place emphasis on instruction in matters of honesty, clean speech, and other desirable character traits.
    (9) To be able to diagnose difficulties when students are not successful.
   (10) To develop a spirt of good will and success so that pupils will like to go to school.
   (11) To express a greater degree of confidence in the children than the parents themselves possess.
   (12) To assign homework in such a way that pupils know what to do.

Teachers expect parents:

    (1) To picture school as a good place to be in.
    (2) To make an effort to become acquainted with the teachers of their children.
    (3) To give prompt attention to requests of the school for information.

[1] Here the author is indebted for many suggestions to Dean J. B. Edmonson.

(4) To recognize that the education of children is a cooperative undertaking involving the home, the school, and other agencies.

(5) To acquaint the school with common criticisms of its work.

(6) To demand the facts from critics of the school.

(7) To recognize that the school has a very difficult task in educating all the children of all the people.

(8) To protest to the proper authorities the employment of unsatisfactory teachers.

(9) To expect efficient service in the teachers of their children.

(10) To assume that the teachers have made right decisions until they have themselves carefully investigated the situation.

(11) Not to permit trifles to interfere with punctuality and regular attendance.

(12) To praise and commend efficient teachers in conversation with their children and with other school patrons.

(13) To accept the methods of instruction used in the school and not attempt to substitute methods by which they were taught in an earlier day.

(14) To make every effort to provide their children with needed instructional materials.

(15) To respect the health regulations of the school.

(16) To provide satisfactory conditions for homework.

a. Which item in either list do you think is unreasonable or undesirable?

b. In the typical community each group is perhaps not aware of what the other expects. What steps do you think a teacher group could take to remedy such a state of affairs?

11. A group of superintendents and high-school principals contributed the following list of common mistakes of beginning high-school teachers:

(1) Talk too much in class.

(2) Do not make assignments clear.

(3) Expect too little or too much in the way of classroom work.

(4) Fail to evaluate carefully and to return written work.

(5) Attempt the ideal socialized recitation without sufficient classroom skill and experience.

(6) Try to win favor through leniency.

(7) Make a great many rules.

(8) Give too difficult or too easy tests.

(9) Try to get through the text too rapidly.

(10) Do not stress essential points and omit drill.

(11) Apt to talk too loudly, especially in reprimanding pupils.

(12) Lack of discipline.

(13) Lack of self-control.

(14) Tendency to mark very high or very low.

(15) Postpone the day of reckoning as to students' marks.

(16) Lack of organization of subject in the mind of teacher.

(17) Lack of self-confidence; timidity.

(18) Come into system without sufficient information as to textbooks, etc.

(19) Do not find out practices of school as to the manner in which to address pupils, and how to conduct classes.

(20) Inclined to carry out too literally rules and regulations from the principal's office.

(21) Show negligence in keeping up routine requirements—reports, etc.

(22) Talk too much about college life.

(23) Lack of specific daily preparation.

(24) Lack of knowledge of available reference material.

(25) Undue familiarity with the pupils.

(26) Do not want to take part in community work.

(27) Do not sense social conditions in the community.

(28) Take up too early with certain social groups or with individuals.

(29) Keep company with high-school pupils.

(30) Allow the classroom to become the center for a group trying to cultivate the teacher's good will.

(31) Try to use college methods in the classroom.

a. Which of the foregoing mistakes would you attribute to personality deficiencies? to lack of scholarship? to lack of adequate professional training?

b. (Optional.) Which of the mistakes are fairly common practices with your present instructors?

12. In seeking a position, should a candidate:

(1) Seek to verify the rumor of a vacancy before filing an application?

(2) Expect his friends to support his candidacy to the exclusion of the candidacies of others?

(3) Arrange, if possible, for a personal interview?

(4) Try to sell his services to an employer?

(5) Demand that employing officers state their reasons for failing to offer him a position?

13. Select some outstanding teacher whom you know, or of whom you have been told, and study that individual with reference to his activities and his attitudes. Is there any causal relationship between the two?

Concerning his activities:

a. Is he teaching this year's classes in the same way that he taught last year's?

b. Does his classroom presence in any way suggest rich and varied experiences in leisure and vacation time?

c. Is he serving on committees—local, state, or national—which are studying educational problems?

d. Does he have a part on the program of educational meetings?

e. Is he looked upon as a welcome companion by boys and girls?

Concerning his attitudes:

f. Is his spirit as gray as his hair?

g. Does he seem to find teaching monotonous?

h. Is life uninteresting to him?

14. Concerning the "Evolving Bill of Rights," discuss these questions:

a. Is there an item which you do not approve?

b. Is there a "right" that you would add?

SUGGESTED READINGS

BOSSING, NELSON L.: *Progressive Methods of Teaching in Secondary Schools*. Boston: Houghton Mifflin Company, 1942. Pp. xvii + 778.

As has been suggested earlier, this book is a good reference on many practical topics. Chapter 5 is concerned with management problems of the first day.

FUESS, CLAUDE M., and EMORY S. BASFORD: *Unseen Harvests*. New York: The Macmillan Company, 1947. Pp. xx + 678.

This is a book in which are brought together some of the many fine things that people of great distinction and achievement have said about school teachers. There are quotations from William James, Thomas Jefferson, Thomas Wolfe, Stephen Leacock, and many others. It is a very large volume and you probably can't read very much of it during student-teaching days. However, it is a good book for a professional library.

ROSS, LEONARD Q.: *The Education of H*Y*M*A*N K*A*P*L*A*N*. New York: Harcourt, Brace and Company, Inc. Pp. 176.

This is a book that you might well read when you are confined to a hospital, providing you are not recovering from an appendectomy. It is about the trials and tribulations of a teacher of a high school in an Americanization class. It is really very funny, but should be taken in small doses.

SIMON, HENRY W.: *Preface to Teaching*. New York: Oxford University Press, 1938. Pp. 98.

Often we are too close to our problems to see them in true perspective. So it happens that a visitor of a school, perhaps with little professional training and without broad experience, may time and again spot weaknesses.

The author of this volume is a discerning critic whose polished sentences sometimes hide half truths. Though a bit old, this book still has value for the supervising teacher. The beginner who desires to sample the book may wish to turn to the chapter dealing with some "do nots" when adjusting to the demands of a school and community.

The 1947 Report of the NEA Committee on Professional Ethics. Washington: National Education Association, 1947. Pp. 64.

Discusses professional ethics involved in: (1) employment, (2) tenure, and (3) social, political, and professional obligations and relations.

Growth and Development

Our knowledge of growth and development is accumulating. The following summary is one to which you may wish to refer from time to time. Of course the statements are only general guides in the sense that no one of them holds for *all* children at the age levels indicated. Nevertheless a teacher will find the summary useful, not only in studying the needs of her class, but also when planning to meet those needs. Perhaps you are asking, "Just how would a teacher use the summary?" Experienced teachers who developed the summary say, "By reading the section that most nearly coincides with her children's maturity level, and also studying the one preceding and the one following it, she will be able to recognize the spread of the group. Opportunities may then be provided to meet the needs of the group. The individual child may be helped through a study of the several maturation levels always found within an individual. A teacher may study the summary to see if children have progressed successfully through their earlier development and are progressing toward higher levels. Later, the summary may be used to reevaluate plans to see if they have met the needs of children in their various developments. In addition, the summary offers a starting point for planning from grade to grade, for home and school cooperation, and for the evaluation of community opportunities for children."[1]

---

[1] See *Organizing the Elementary School for Living and Learning*, p. 69. Association for Supervision and Curriculum Development, 1947 Yearbook. Washington: National Education Association, 1947.

Child Growth and Development, Characteristics, and Needs[1]

I. *Approaching Five Years*

  A. Physical Growth and Development

   1. Skeletal growth

      a. The rate of growth is slow compared to the first one and one-half years of life.

      b. Lateral-type (broad-built) children develop more rapidly than the linear-type (slender-built).

      c. The bones are not completely calcified. Their softness prevents breakage during the child's frequent falls.

   2. Dentition

      a. There is a full set of temporary teeth by three years.

      b. If deciduous teeth (baby teeth) decay, they should receive the same treatment as permanent teeth. Regular visits to the dentist should be initiated by three and one-half years.

   3. Muscular development

      a. Development is confined largely to the large muscles.

      b. Some skill is developing in the use of arms, legs, and trunk.

      c. The development of various motor skills is uneven. The child may lose interest and ability in one skill while acquiring another.

   4. Organic development

      a. The system is sufficiently mature so that desirable habits of eating, sleeping, and elimination are fairly well established.

      b. The child is interested in the genital organs and their function. Infantile masturbation is often an accompaniment of this interest.

      c. As the child increases his contacts outside the home, the probability of infectious diseases is increased for him.

  B. Characteristics

   1. The child approaching five years is very energetic and restless. He wishes constant activity. Fatigue may be indicated by a display of crossness.

   2. He is self-centered and has a growing desire to make his own decisions. Interference with his play or possessions is resented. There is a beginning sense of property rights. There is increased growth in social relationships with less grabbing, pushing, crying. He has learned to be verbally critical, but he now shares more.

   3. Cooperative play is much enjoyed. A child will play with the same age, younger, or older, but likes to be "bigger than." He shows off, but at times may be shy. He can recognize the skills of others. Boys' and girls'

[1] Public Schools of the District of Columbia, Washington, D.C. Curriculum Committee for Health, Physical Education, and Safety in the Elementary School, 1946.

interests are similar. They play together. Boys are more quarrelsome than girls.

4. Both locomotor and manipulative play are enjoyed. The use of imagination in play is seen.

5. Laughter is a frequent form of communication. Those who do not communicate readily through speech may be unable to achieve close relationships with other children.

6. Toilet habits, getting a drink, etc., are well established.

C. Needs

1. Security within the family is a primary need.

2. Companionship of other children is important. There is pleasure in initiating and playing simple games with several other children.

3. There must be a wide variety of activities to develop the muscles of arms and shoulders, the trunk, and the legs and feet. Climbing and hanging are essential. Kiddy cars, wagons, scooters, tricycles, and boats are enjoyed. Nail-pounding and block-building are desirable. Additional play may be with sand, toys, dolls, animals.

4. Adults should deal rationally with the child if he exhibits over-interest in the sex organs. Cleanliness, loose clothing, supervision of toilet habits, and substitution of other interests are needed.

5. The child should sleep eleven to twelve hours. Sleep is a prime essential in building sturdy health. Linear-type children need more sleep than laterals. An afternoon nap of one to two hours is needed.

6. Development of liking for all types of food is a necessity, but should be accomplished without stress and strain. Regularity of mealtime is important.

7. The child should have opportunities to do things for himself. He likes to "help." This takes longer for the adult, but is valuable for the child's development.

II. *Age Five, Six and Seven Years*

A. Physical Growth and Development

1. Skeletal growth

a. Growth is relatively slow during this period as compared to the early period.

b. An annual growth of two or three inches and a weight gain of three to six pounds is expected but there are wide variations, each with its own significance. Some change should be discernible within each three-month period.

c. At five years the legs are lengthening rapidly. The spine has adult curves. The six-year-old girl is as mature skeletally as the seven-year boy.

2. Dentition

a. The loss of deciduous teeth begins at five to six years. First permanent teeth to appear are the six-year molars, important as the keystone to hold the dental arch in place. Counting from the front, they are the sixth teeth. They are not replacements; their site is immediately beyond the baby teeth. The central incisors appear next.

b. The teeth help to affect the shape of the jaw.

3. Muscular development
   a. The large muscles of the arms and legs are more developed than the small muscles of the hands and fingers.
   b. Muscular development is uneven and incomplete but motor skills are developing.
   c. Some postural defects may have been established by the age of five years.
   d. At five, handedness and eyedness have been established and should not be changed. Ninety per cent are right-handed.
   e. Hand-eye coordinations are incomplete.

4. Organic development
   a. The lungs are relatively small.
   b. The heart is growing rapidly. It is easily changed by toxins and bacteria and must be protected against strain during convalescence from contagious diseases of childhood. Rheumatic fever, the disease most likely to cause death between five to fourteen years of age, can cause serious damage to the heart. It may be recurrent.
   c. Because of close contacts among children, the diseases of childhood may sweep through a group.
   d. These ages are highly susceptible to respiratory infections.
   e. The eyeballs are still increasing in size. Good habits of use, as in reading, writing, etc., are essential.
   f. If parents and teachers adopt a disturbed attitude toward masturbation, the habit may continue.

B. Characteristics

1. A healthy five-, six-, or seven-year-old has bright eyes, color in his face, straight legs, and great vitality.
2. Upon entering school there may be a resumption of certain earlier tensional behavior; thumb-sucking, nail-biting, knee-knocking, etc.
3. The child stands straight and sits well at his worktable without leaning or slumping. While at work he may rest by changing from sitting to standing.
4. He has urge to action and is still for only a short time. He is interested in the activity, not in the result. He has a sense of equilibrium. He can stand on one foot, hop and skip, keep time to music, and bounce and catch a ball. He likes to climb and jump from heights.
5. He is susceptible to fatigue and may withdraw from play when tired.
6. He is becoming self-dependent. He can brush his teeth, comb his hair, dress himself, and by the end of this period can tie his shoe laces if he takes

time. He can perform simple household tasks; empty baskets, sweep, clear table, wipe dishes, put out milk bottles, "mind" the baby, etc.

7. The child's questioning attitude extends to problems about sex differences. Knowledge is derived in the home.
8. Nutritional problems may arise when breakfast is hurried or there are frequent purchases of between-meal snacks.
9. The child can abide by certain safety precautions: cross streets on signals, keep toys from underfoot, avoid hot radiators, stoves, and food cooking. He can understand the necessity for remaining away from those who have contagious diseases.

C. Needs

1. Expression through movement and noise is necessary for growth. Vigorous exercise will increase the heart action and respiration, thus helping to build endurance. Active, boisterous games with unrestrained running and jumping are needed.
2. It is part of the child's development to play in mud, wade in puddles, fall in snow, walk in fallen leaves, and roll down hills. He may approximate rock-and-tree-climbing activities on playground climbing apparatus. Playing animals (walking on all fours) will develop muscles of the back and abdomen. Use of the walking board (balance beam) will help to correct pronation (flatfoot). Scooters and coaster wagons develop the leg muscles and fulfill a need for speed.
3. There must be opportunity to organize simple group play, to skip and dance in small groups. Half a dozen children are capable of playing together for a fifteen-minute period or longer. All demand attention from one another and demand their own "turns."
4. Dramatic activities and rhythmic activities are essential.
5. The withdrawn child must be encouraged gradually to find his own place in the group.
6. Since the attention span is short the periods should be short.
7. The child should sleep about eleven hours.
8. Although the child from time to time may reject certain foods because of texture or strong taste, variety in the menu will provide the full protective diet.
9. The child needs training both at home and in school in habits of personal hygiene: covering coughs and sneezes, using the handkerchief, keeping fingers away from mouth and nose, etc. He needs training in choice of clothing appropriate to weather.

III. *Age Eight, Nine, and Ten Years*

A. Physical Growth and Development

1. Skeletal growth
   a. Growth in height and weight are normally slow and steady at this age. There will be a lag just prior to pubescence.

    b. Girls have a spurt of growth at about ten years. They attain skeletal maturity before boys.

    c. Differences in individual ossification are very wide, as much as five or six years at a given age. Malnutrition or serious illness may delay ossification.

    d. Mental maturity and sexual adjustment have some correlation with skeletal maturity.

2. Dentition

    a. Permanent dentition continues. Incisors and lower bicuspids appear.

    b. This is often a period of dental neglect.

    c. Orthodontia (teeth-straightening) is necessary in some cases. The need may be apparent as early as nine years, but treatment may not be initiated until twelve years or later.

3. Muscular development

    a. The small muscles are developing. Manipulative skill is increasing.

    b. Muscular coordinations are good. The hand-eye coordinations are continuing to develop.

    c. Posture may be poor, not even as good as during the first year of school. The spindly type of body is most inclined to droop. In some cases, poor posture may be symptomatic. Its presence may indicate a condition needing attention: chronic infection, fatigue, orthopedic difficulties, emotional maladjustments, etc.

4. Organic development

    a. The heart develops in size less rapidly than the body. Its work is increased. Damage to the heart is prevented during play because the skeletal muscles fatigue first. Taxing the heart should be avoided by seeing that children do not compete with those who are stronger or more mature physically.

    b. The lungs are not fully developed.

    c. At the end of this period the eyes function as well as those of adults. Myopia (nearsightedness) may develop around the age of eight years. Many eye defects can be remedied by glasses.

    d. By the end of this period the child will have had many of the contagious diseases of childhood or will have built up immunity to them. The linear-type child is more susceptible to tuberculosis, a prevalent disease of childhood.

    e. Internal changes in glands and body structure are taking place. There is a wide range in the beginning of sexual maturity. The period of rapid growth comes earlier for girls than for boys. It lasts longer in boys.

    Boys: Beginning of puberty cycle: ten to thirteen years.

          End: fourteen to eighteen and one-half years.

    Girls: Appearance of menstruation: ten to sixteen years.

          Average: thirteen years.

B. Characteristics

1. The child of eight, nine, or ten years is sturdy though long-legged and rangy in appearance. His health is usually good and he has boundless energy. He seems hurried and untidy. He is prone to accidents.
2. He now has a wider range of interests and a longer attention span. His goals are immediate and consistency is demanded, as is individual justice.
3. He is learning to cooperate better. He plays in self-made groups over a longer period. He is beginning to be interested in teams and will abide by group decisions.
4. The child desires prestige and may seek it through size, boasting, and rivalry.
5. The rhythmic sense is much improved.
6. Sex antagonism may be acute. Sex interest is not detailed. Sexual "modesty" appears.
7. The appetite is good. The child is interested in eating. There now are fewer food preferences and refusals.
8. He is generally reliable about following instructions in household jobs. He can take care of his own room.
9. He can take responsibility for his own clothing. He is now more aware of his personal hygiene.

C. Needs

1. The child needs an assured position in a social group. Membership in a gang or a secret club fills this need. At this period children need a certain amount of freedom in setting up their own standards and rules, yet strongly desire understanding and sympathy from adults. Participation in family affairs is important.
2. There must be full opportunity to develop body control, strength, and endurance. The child of eight, nine, or ten years needs activities involving use of the whole body: stunts, throwing and catching, running, "it" games with their accompanying noise, etc. Seasonal play is important: kites, tops, marbles, etc.
3. He needs organized games for team play. He is willing to practice in order to become adequate in skills for games. He gains self-confidence by excelling in some one thing.
4. It is as important for children to learn good fellowship as it is for them to learn good leadership.
5. Encouragement to exercise creativity in rhythms should be given.
6. Activities such as playing in caves and brooks, gathering nuts, making campfires are needed. Bicycles and skates are enjoyed.
7. The child should sleep about ten hours. He usually does not get enough rest. A quiet period in the afternoon, not necessarily bed, may prevent over-fatigue.

8. The child's increased interest in foods provides a basis for better understanding of the seven basic foods in maintaining good health.

9. The teacher must see that pupils having visual or aural defects always maintain strategic positions in the class.

10. Close supervision is required to assure properly adjusted furniture and to prevent slumping over desks. Creation of an awareness that good posture is comfortable posture is important.

IV. Age Eleven, Twelve, and Thirteen Years

  A. Physical Growth and Development

    1. Skeletal growth

      a. This is a transitional period.

      b. During the "pubescent spurt" the rate of growth is very rapid. The lateral-type matures earlier than the linear-type.

      c. At eleven years, girls are usually taller and heavier than boys. Boys' hands and feet appear to be oversized.

    2. Dentition

      a. Permanent dentition of twenty-eight teeth is completed by thirteen or fourteen years.

      b. For those who need it, orthodontia will improve the appearance and prevent dental decay. The child needs guidance about accepting embarrassment and discomfort in order to achieve permanent correction.

    3. Muscular development

      a. Muscular growth is very rapid. Restlessness may be a concomitant.

      b. Poor control will ensue if the body framework and muscular development are out of proportion in their rate of growth.

      c. Posture may be slovenly. Awkwardness is prevalent.

    4. Organic development

      a. The heart is not growing as rapidly as the body.

      b. The blood pressure may fall. The fatigue point in competitive games should be anticipated. More rest is needed.

      c. There are many minor illnesses of short duration.

      d. The puberty cycle is in progress. The reproductive organs are maturing rapidly. Secondary sex characteristics appear. Many girls are embarrassed by the development of breasts and hips. The period of changing voice and initial hair growth on the face is equally embarrassing to boys.

  B. Characteristics

    1. Children of eleven, twelve, or thirteen years are strongly individual. They differ widely in physical maturity and in temperament.

    2. The lateral-type child may display overweight, slow movements, and placidity. The linear-type child may display drooping posture, fatigue, alternating alertness and irritability.

3. The increase in size and strength of muscles leads to greater interest in outdoor activities.

4. Competition is keen. There is respect for good sportsmanship. More highly organized team games are desired. There is a willingness to submerge personal ego for the good of the team or group. The unskilled child is self-conscious about undertaking new activities.

5. Some children may initiate too many activities and go beyond the fatigue point. Resultant chronic tension may cause strained relationships. Girls tire more readily than boys.

6. There is a shift to own-age codes. Prestige is more important than adult approval. The gang interest is changing to interest in one or two "best" friends.

7. Interest in money-making activities may lead some to work during afterschool playtime.

8. There is a strong interest in sex. These children may be emotional about bodily changes. Sex consciousness may cause self-consciousness and shyness with the opposite sex. Teasing may denote sex attraction.

9. A ravenous but capricious appetite may be noted.

10. The child may be overanxious about his own health. He appreciates first aid and can give it. To a certain extent he can appreciate group health problems.

C. Needs

1. There must be careful supervision in order that children of these ages may choose games proportionate to their strength and appropriate for their development needs.

2. Skill is essential for successful group participation. The child is willing to practice skills in order to gain proficiency, but needs informed guidance.

3. Games of increased organization such as softball, kickball, modified soccer, etc., are needed. The sedentary or self-protective child may need encouragement to play out of doors. Differentiation of activities for boys and girls may begin at these ages.

4. Special provision must be made for the child who is reaching his literate capacity and may be able to gain his chief satisfactions from muscular activities.

5. It is as important for children to develop good spectatorship as it is for them to develop good sportsmanship.

6. More mature interests must be met by more mature programs. There must be opportunity for many types of social contacts. Club programs, church groups, Boy and Girl Scouts, Y.M.C.A., Campfire Girls, and camping, etc., fill the need for guidance.

7. Provision must be made for a growing interest in social dancing.

8. The rest needs are about eight to nine hours or longer.

9. The child's increasing desire to improve his personal appearance provides excellent opportunity to remedy habitual postural defects and to establish a balanced diet.

V. *Age Fourteen, Fifteen, and Sixteen Years*

  A. Physical Growth and Development

    1. Skeletal growth

      a. The girls are about two years ahead of boys at this age.

      b. The lateral-type girl usually reaches adult height at about the age of fourteen years. Linear-type girls continue to grow for several years. The lateral-type boy attains adult height at about the age of sixteen years. Growth of linear-type boys continues to the age of twenty or later.

      c. Bone growth is completed with sexual maturity.

      d. The face and body are now attaining adult contours.

    2. Dentition

      a. A few children cut third molars (wisdom teeth) at the end of this period, but this is usually deferred for a number of years.

      b. Dental correction continues to be one of the greatest needs of childhood.

    3. Muscular development

      a. The awkward age is ending. There is improvement in coordination.

      b. The muscles of boys become hard and firm. The muscles of girls remain softer.

      c. Posture is improving. Control and grace are displayed, especially by those who have participated in rhythmic activities such as dancing, swimming, and sports.

    4. Organic development

      a. The heart increases greatly in size. Boys and girls should avoid strenuous competitive sports since the heart and arteries may be out of proportion.

      b. The puberty cycle is completed in the majority of cases.

      c. There may be a period of glandular instability with fluctuations in energy level. Ailments of this age may include headache, nosebleed, "nervousness," palpitation, and acne.

      d. The prevalence of active tuberculosis increases in the teen-ages.

  B. Characteristics

    1. The child of fourteen, fifteen, or sixteen may have reached physiological adulthood, but lacks its experiences. He may exhibit a "know-it-all" attitude. He is intensely emotional. He is seeking his own place in the life around him. There may be emotional instability while striving to understand social relationships.

    2. The desire to conform to standards of the age group is stronger than the response to adult guidance. Many respond more readily to the influence of the teacher than of the parent.

    3. During adolescence there may be close attachment to and almost unlimited admiration of some adult whom he considers to be outstanding.

    4. All can compete in games requiring higher skills. Groups evolve according to physical maturation and interests.

5. Boys like to be thought big, strong, and healthy. Girls desire prettiness. In both sexes there is interest in and emphasis on physical attractiveness and good grooming. However, because of a strong desire for uniformity, studied oddities in dress may be followed by all for some time.

6. Wage earning is desired by many.

7. Sexual manifestations may cause self-consciousness. Because of differences in maturity of the sexes at this level, girls are more interested in boys than boys are in girls. Many lack adequate sex information and guidance. Sexual delinquency may be caused by a feeling of nonbelonging in the home and the desire for other ties.

8. The appetite is enormous at this age, yet there is a tendency toward an inadequate breakfast or none at all. Overdeveloped girls may become intrigued by "reducing" diets.

9. The child may become overconfident about assuming personal responsibility for maintaining good health. He has an understanding of the nature of disease. He readily uses first aid. He is interested in community health problems.

C. Needs

1. Children of fourteen, fifteen, or sixteen need unobtrusive adult guidance that does not impinge upon their own feeling of being adults. A balance between security and freedom is needed.

2. Family solidarity as a retreat from the confusion of widened horizons and more complex experiences is important.

3. Children of this age need worthy causes in the promulgation of which they may utilize their excess emotions and energy.

4. Separate physical education programs for boys and girls should be planned since the difference in strength, maturity, and interests makes it difficult to organize activities beneficial to both. Boys follow youth sports. In addition to group games, girls like smaller group activities, to be carried on by two or more people.

5. Special provision must be made for the child who is reaching his literate capacity and may be able to gain his chief satisfaction from muscular activities.

6. Social dancing is a "must" at this level.

7. Rest needs are about the same as for adults, eight hours or longer.

8. School and community must unite to plan with and for these young people a worth-while afterschool program. The place and the activities must be agreeable to them. Provision must be made for the child who desires creative, manipulative, or contemplative activities, as well as for those who wish more active recreation.

Appraising Your Teacher Personality

The unique characteristic of the check list that is shown on the following pages is that it represents an effort to appraise teacher personality by noting its effect on others. It is also simple.

We suggest the following procedure:

1. If feasible, visit two teachers who differ widely in personality and use the check list in judging each. You will probably find your work more interesting if two or more students rate the same teacher independently and then compare results.

2. Principal Ames said, "Many kinds of people, very different in type, turn out to be good teachers. However, I believe that a check list such as the following suggests minima which should exclude applicants from the teaching profession." Is there any trait in this check list so important that a candidate for the teaching profession who made a very low score on it should be excluded? Is there any other personality trait of a teacher that you consider of sufficient importance to be added to this list?

CHECK LIST OF TEACHER PERSONALITY

Directions: You will note that there are five possible judgments for each trait. In using the check list draw a small circle around the figure in the description which is most characteristic of the teacher.

I. How does his general appearance impress you and others?

1	2	3	4	5	No Basis for Judgment
Is slovenly in appearance and unpleasant to look upon.	Is less attractive in appearance than teachers usually are.	General appearance makes a satisfactory impression.	Is more attractive in appearance than the majority of teachers.	Is unusually attractive in appearance. Provokes admiration.	☐

II. How are you and others impressed with his voice?

1	2	3	4	5	No Basis for Judgment
Voice is consistently difficult to hear and unpleasant. It does not command attention.	Voice has unnatural tone (*e.g.,* "stage voice"), or poor quality. It is somewhat indistinct.	Voice may be heard. Tone is natural, but lacks "color."	Voice is agreeable and may be heard distinctly.	Voice is highly pleasing in quality and pitch. It arrests favorable attention.	☐

III. Does he conduct his work in a manner to create a classroom atmosphere of "warmth," fellowship, and good cheer?

1	2	3	4	5	No Basis for Judgment
Conducts work in a dull, prosaic, wearying manner. Creates depressing atmosphere in the classroom.	Is a little reserved and matter-of-fact in conducting work. Classroom atmosphere is a bit strained.	Classroom atmosphere is neither especially dull nor lively. However, one does feel "at home."	Creates noticeably comfortable and pleasant classroom atmosphere. Wisely capitalizes playful spirit of pupils.	Enlivens classroom atmosphere with sparkling wit. Enjoys a good joke even at his own expense.	☐

Check List of Teacher Personality (*Continued*)

IV. Is he attentive to and considerate of the feelings of others?

1	2	3	4	5	No Basis for Judgment
Frequently antagonizes others by prejudices. Ridicules pupils' immature judgment. Makes unreasonable demands of pupils.	Tends to be insensitive to feelings of others. Occasionally "rubs the wrong way." Probably seeks to be just.	Treats others with ordinary civility and respect. Usually "gets along" with people. Is apparently accepted as fair.	Noticeably impartial in dealing with pupils. Does not embarrass pupils needlessly and has a good sense of justice.	Is wisely responsive to feelings of others. Offers suggestions and criticisms tactfully. Is highly and universally respected as fair and impartial.	☐

V. How do pupils respond to his leadership?

1	2	3	4	5	No Basis for Judgment
Pupils ignore his suggestions and show disrespect.	Pupils tend not to respond readily. They seem not to take him seriously.	Pupils are ordinarily responsive to his suggestions.	Pupils respond readily and do what he suggests.	Pupils seem very eager to follow his suggestions and directions.	☐

VI. How does he control emergencies or unexpected situations?

1	2	3	4	5	No Basis for Judgment
Is baffled and helpless in emergencies. Makes blunders and bad decisions.	Decides slowly on what to do in emergencies. Is uncertain of his decisions.	Copes fairly adequately with emergencies.	"Rises to the occasion" very well when faced with emergencies.	Calmly controls emergencies with marked skill and ingenuity. Quickly forms an effective plan.	☐

VII. How does he carry out responsibilities he has agreed to assume? — No Basis for Judgment ☐

1	2	3	4	5
Seldom does what he agrees to do. Habitually makes excuses.	Is somewhat inclined to slight his responsibilities. Tends to procrastinate.	Carries out responsibilities reasonably well.	Is noticeably attentive to responsibilities. Seldom fails to meet obligations on time.	Is markedly consistent and prompt in discharging all obligations.

VIII: Does he reach his conclusions after reflective analysis of valid and sufficient evidence? — No Basis for Judgment ☐

1	2	3	4	5
Hardly ever makes adequate analysis of even simple situations. Habitually jumps at conclusions.	Tends to be somewhat uncritical of conclusions. Seldom approaches problems reflectively.	Reasons with moderate care and precision, especially if he has some guidance.	Usually attacks problems reflectively. Seldom errs in judgment.	Consistently analyzes problems carefully, thinking them through to valid conclusions.

IX. Does he exercise creativeness and imagination in the performance of tasks? — No Basis for Judgment ☐

1	2	3	4	5
Gives no evidence of creativeness or originality in imagination or action.	Makes little creative contribution himself, but shows sufficient imagination to use creations of others.	Shows tendency to approach tasks creatively, but has made no very significant contribution so far.	Makes distinctly original contributions in one or more types of undertakings.	Attacks many tasks with creative imagination. Usually contributes something that is his own.

X. Does he maintain for himself high standards of accomplishment? — No Basis for Judgment ☐

1	2	3	4	5
Consistently performs on a low level, no matter how strong the incentive.	Accomplishment as a rule is only "fair" for his abilities. Is but little motivated by high ideals of attainment.	Shows tendency to perform on a high plane if sufficiently motivated by promise of reward or recognition.	Gives evidence of intention to do his best in most undertakings. Is not entirely consistent in performance.	Does his best in whatever he undertakes. Is motivated chiefly by satisfaction of superior achievement.

Appendix C

Questionnaire on Interests and Needs of Pupils in Junior and Senior High Schools

Directions: In order to be of more help to boys and girls, we are trying to find out some of the things that interest them, some of the things that trouble them, and some of the things that they want to know more about.

Will you assist us by thinking very seriously about a few questions and by answering them carefully?

You need not sign your name, so do not be afraid to write whatever is in your mind.

Part I

School.................. Grade.......... Age............ Sex.............

Senior-high-school course...

1. What are some of the things that you like about school? (Underline the one thing that you like best.)
2. What are some of the things that you dislike about school? (Underline the one thing that you dislike most.)
3. Which subjects in school do you think will do you the most good?
4. Which subjects do you think will do you the least good?
5. What would you like to have taught in your grade (or school) that is not taught now?
6. What other help or information which you are not now receiving would you like to receive in school?
7. In what ways do you think that your classwork could be made more interesting?
8. How much time do you spend in study each day outside of school?
9. To what clubs or organizations do you now belong? in school? outside of school?
10. Do you attend church? Sunday school?
11. What club, social, or leisure-time activities do you wish your school would provide?
12. What social activities do you wish the community would provide?

406

Part II

(Give Part I and Part II on different days.)

School................. Grade............ Age.............. Sex.........

Senior-high-school course..

1. In what particular thing are you most interested?
2. What things do you most enjoy doing during your spare time?
3. What magazines do you read?
4. What kinds of books do you like best?
5. What kinds of news do you read in the daily newspaper?
6. How often do you attend movies?
7. What is your favorite radio program?
8. What means of recreation do you have: at home? in your neighborhood?
9. Write down some of the things that trouble and worry you:
    a. About school?
    b. About home?
    c. About your health and appearance?
    d. About personal habits, traits, and feelings?
    e. About boy-and-girl relationships?
    f. About getting along with others?
    g. About your vocation (your future work)?
    h. About money matters?
    i. About religion, death?
    j. About other things?
    (Go back and underline the one thing that worries you *most*.)
10. Do you have a regular allowance?   What kinds of things do you buy with it?
11. When you have a personal problem, to whom do you go most often?
12. What do you consider your strong points to be?
13. What do you consider your weak points to be?
14. Are you having an opportunity to develop your talents?   (If not, why are you not?)
15. What work besides schoolwork do you do outside of school?

Appendix D

Ethics for Teachers[1]

ARTICLE I
RELATIONS TO PUPILS AND THE HOME

Section 1. It is the duty of the teacher to be just, courteous, and professional in all his relations with pupils. He should consider their individual differences, needs, interests, temperaments, aptitudes, and environments.

Section 2. He should refrain from tutoring pupils of his classes for pay, and from referring such pupils to any member of his immediate family for tutoring.

Section 3. The professional relations of a teacher with his pupils demand the same scrupulous care that is required in the confidential relations of one teacher with another. A teacher, therefore, should not disclose any information obtained confidentially from his pupils, unless it is for the best interest of the child and the public.

Section 4. A teacher should seek to establish friendly and intelligent cooperation between home and school, ever keeping in mind the dignity of his profession and the welfare of the pupils. He should do or say nothing that would undermine the confidence and respect of his pupils for their parents. He should inform the pupils and parents regarding the importance, purposes, accomplishments, and needs of the schools.

ARTICLE II
RELATIONS TO CIVIC AFFAIRS

Section 1. It is the obligation of every teacher to inculcate in his pupils an appreciation of the principles of democracy. He should direct full and free discussion of appropriate controversial issues with the expectation that comparisons, contrasts, and interpretations will lead to an understanding, appreciation, acceptance, and practice of the principles of democracy. A teacher should refrain from using his classroom privileges and prestige to promote partisan politics, sectarian religious views, or selfish propaganda of any kind.

Section 2. A teacher should recognize and perform all the duties of citizenship. He should subordinate his personal desires to the best interests of public good. He should be loyal to the school system, the state, and the nation, but should exercise his rights to give constructive criticisms.

Section 3. A teacher's life should show that education makes people better citizens and better neighbors. His personal conduct should not needlessly offend the accepted pattern of behavior of the community in which he serves.

[1] See 1947 Report of the Professional Ethics Committee of the National Education Association, Washington, D.C.

ARTICLE III
RELATIONS TO THE PROFESSION

Section 1.   Each member of the teaching profession should dignify his calling on all occasions and should uphold the importance of his services to society.   On the other hand he should not indulge in personal exploitation.

Section 2.   A teacher should encourage able and sincere individuals to enter the teaching profession and discourage those who plan to use this profession merely as a steppingstone to some other vocation.

Section 3.   It is the duty of the teacher to maintain his own efficiency by study, by travel, and by other means which keep him abreast of the trends in education and the world in which he lives.

Section 4.   Every teacher should have membership in his local, state, and national professional organizations, and should participate actively and unselfishly in them.   Professional growth and personality development are the natural product of such professional activity.   Teachers should avoid the promotion of organization rivalry and divisive competition which weaken the cause of education.

Section 5.   While not limiting their services by reason of small salary, teachers should insist upon a salary scale commensurate with the social demands laid upon them by society.   They should not knowingly underbid a rival or agree to accept a salary lower than that provided by a recognized schedule.   They should not apply for positions for the sole purpose of forcing an increase in salary in their present positions; correspondingly, school officials should not refuse to give deserved salary increases to efficient employees until offers from other school authorities have forced them so to do.

Section 6.   A teacher should not apply for a specific position currently held by another teacher.   Unless the rules of a school system otherwise prescribe, he should file his application with the chief executive officer.

Section 7.   Since qualification should be the sole determining factor in appointment and promotion, the use of pressure on school officials to secure a position or to obtain other favors is unethical.

Section 8.   Testimonials regarding teachers should be truthful and confidential, and should be treated as confidential information by school authorities receiving them.

Section 9.   A contract, once signed, should be faithfully adhered to until it is dissolved by mutual consent.   Ample notification should be given both by school officials and teachers in case a change in position is to be made.

Section 10.   Democratic procedures should be practiced by members of the teaching profession.   Cooperation should be predicated upon the recognition of the worth and the dignity of individual personality.   All teachers should observe the professional courtesy of transacting official business with the properly designated authority.

Section 11.   School officials should encourage and nurture the professional growth of all teachers by promotion or by other appropriate methods of recognition. School officials who fail to recommend a worthy teacher for a better position outside their school system because they do not desire to lose his services are acting unethically.

Section 12.   A teacher should avoid unfavorable criticism of other teachers except that formally presented to a school official for the welfare of the school.   It is unethical to fail to report to the duly constituted authority any matters which are detrimental to the welfare of the school.

Section 13.   Except when called upon for counsel or other assistance, a teacher should not interfere in any matter between another teacher and a pupil.

Section 14.   A teacher should not act as an agent, or accept a commission, royalty, or other compensation, for endorsing books or other school materials in the selection or purchase of which he can exert influence, or concerning which he can exercise the right of decision; nor should he accept a commission or other compensation for helping another teacher to secure a position.

Index

A

Activities illustrating supervised study, 180–184

Activity movement, 168, 188

Activity sponsor and extracurricular program, 297–298

Advancement, personal (*see* Personal advancement)

Aims of student teacher, 9–10

Application for position, 352–355

Appraisal, broader concept of, 315
  by marks and report cards, 323–335
  and measurement of intangible outcomes, 338–340
    of growth in tolerance, 340–341
    of scientific-mindedness, 340
  new techniques of, practice in, 343–345
    recent developments in, 347–348
    in social studies, 341–343
  observational techniques in, 336–338
  self-appraisal by pupil, 319
  of teaching effectiveness, 345, 402–405
    check list for, 345–347
  testing program in, guides for, 335–336

Arithmetic, measurement of ability in, 36

Assignment, student teacher's first, 24–26

Attention, study of, 207–208

Audio-visual aids, 269–283
  basic guides for use of, 279
  phony ideas concerning, 273–276
  practical suggestions for use of, 280–282
  standing committee on, 277
  systematic use of, 282–283
  (*See also* Graphic aids)

B

Bacon, Francis L., 113, 244

Barr, A. S., 189

Basford, Emory S., 390

Behavior, teacher's attitude toward, 75–82

Behavior Journal, 337

Bell, Howard M., 313

Benjamin, Harold, 226

Bill of Rights for Teachers, 380–385

Bode, Boyd H., quoted, 188

Borden Barbara, 288

Borgeson, F. C., 314

Bossing, Nelson L., 133, 244, 390

Briggs, Thomas H., quoted, 63

Broady, Knute O., 84

Brueckner, Leo J., 189

Burt, Cyril, 268

Burton, William H., 189

C

Carroll, Herbert A., 268

Case study, 43–51
  diagnosis of, 47–48
  diagnostic approach to, 45
  remedial program in, 48–51
  through visits to homes, 45–46, 363–364

Cassidy, Rosalind, 84

Chapman, J. Crosby, and Counts, quoted, 315

Chisholm, Leslie L., 84

Citizenship, 304
  good, analysis of, 305
    requirements for, 305–306

Classroom, personality of, 127–131

Classroom management, 115–133
  avoiding drudgery in, 121–122
  and correcting papers, 123–124
  principles of routine in, 115–119
    check list on, 118
  time savers in, 119–121

Clubs, criteria for judging, 303

Collins and Charlton, 314

Comenius, Johann Amos, quoted, 272

Community school, 211–220
  and community surveys, illustrations of, 215–220
  teacher's part in, 212–215
  using community resources in, 211–212

411